POLITICAL STUDIES
Nr. 12

Honoré M. Catudal
The Diplomacy of the Quadripartite Agreement on Berlin

ISBN 3-87061-138-3

Honoré M. Catudal, Jr.

The Diplomacy of the Quadripartite Agreement on Berlin

A New Era in East-West Politics

Foreword by
Ambassador Kenneth Rush

Berlin  Verlag

CIP-Kurztitelaufnahme der Deutschen Bibliothek

Catudal, Honoré M.

The diplomacy of the Quadripartite Agreement
on Berlin: a new era in East - West politics. –
1. Aufl. — Berlin: Berlin-Verlag, 1977
   ([Politologische Studien] Political Studies; 12)
   ISBN 3-87061-138-3

© 1978
BERLIN VERLAG * Pacelli Allee 5, 1 Berlin 33
ISBN 3-87061-138-3
Einbandentwurf: Arnold Harttung

CONTENTS

APPENDICES:

LIST OF ILLUSTRATIONS
(Courtesy of Landesbildstelle Berlin)

A popular Government, without popular information, or the means of acquiring it, is but the Prologue to a Farce or a Tragedy; or, perhaps both. Knowledge will forever govern ignorance: And a people who mean to be their own Governors, must arm themselves with the power which knowledge gives.

James Madison

PREFACE

This study attempts to put the many changes that have accrued in Berlin and beyond in the perspective of the diplomatic history of the Four-Power negotiations and the final settlement. In a soon to be published second volume, I attempt to evaluate the Quadripartite Agreement after five years of implementation.

In preparing this book, I faced a number of thorny problems, a brief mention of which should be included here. The first major difficulty I encountered concerned the method of investigation I should adopt. My intention was to provide a scholarly but readable account of the diplomacy of the Four-Power talks as they developed within the broader context of East-West relations. Yet the official diplomatic record of the negotiations was — and is — still classified and would not be available for many years. And what was available in the public domain about many of the behind-the-scenes maneuvers and "trade-offs," however useful, was very incomplete. Also, it was highly speculative, frequently even misleading and biased.

After giving the matter a great deal of thought, I developed the following approach. Since I could not afford to ignore the public record, I would put it to good use. In schematic form, this meant first compiling a "first draft," based on readily available public sources and then presenting it for comment to key participants and other Allied and German officials who possess first-hand knowledge of events. My hope was that these "insiders" although they could not show me classified documents, would be willing, for the sake of historical accuracy, to point out mistakes and distortions in my collation of the public record.

This approach proved successful. So much so that many (but, of course, not all) of my official contacts eventually came to confide in me, perhaps realizing the usefulness of having on record a comprehensive and convenient account of the Four-Power talks. As one authority who came on the scene after 1971 said to me: "We are expected to apply the Quadripartite Agreement, yet we do not know enough of its background. Perhaps, with the freedom you enjoy, you can pull it all togethe: for us."

To be sure, there are some not insignificant pitfalls in using this kind of "oral history" to supplement the written public record. For one thing, memories in the words of *Dean Rusk,* who talked with me at length about Berlin after he left his post as Secretary of State in 1969, "are hardly faultless." For another, each participant and/or observer sees things differently and, of course, has an inherent bias. (No one official is privy to the whole web of transactions, only part of which are acted out locally.)

Thus, in the interest of obtaining as accurate a body of information as possible, I adopted early the following "rule of thumb" with regard to handling confidential revelations. Before I would consider incorporating them in my study, two normally reliable and independent authorities would first have to confirm their veracity. When this was not possible, I so qualified my reporting and analysis (or used detailed supplementary footnotes) to indicate the possibility of error.

Even though I found myself in the extraordinary position of gaining the confidence and trust of many knowledgeable officials, they recognized for the most part my responsibility to describe and analyze events as I saw them after the necessary reflection and balancing of views. In fact, the picture which emerges from my research differs considerably from official representations repeated for public consumption. For example, while I do agree that the Quadripartite Agreement is basically a good accord, it is not as onesidedly beneficent as officials — taking advantage of the general public's ignorance of the actual "horse trades" — portray it.

Rather, the QA is a masterpiece of diplomatic writing, embodying delicately balanced language to describe compromises reluctantly made by the parties. Both sides chalked up "victories" and "defeats" because they, for admittedly different reasons, didn't want the negotiations to fail. On balance, Ambassador *Rush,* an unconventional diplomat if there ever was one, and his colleagues demonstrated remarkable skill in arriving at considerable practical improvements for local inhabitants even if in the process of bargaining they, realizing it was futile to get bogged down in interminable discussions of irreconcilable legal views about the status of Berlin, decided to concentrate their efforts on one part of the city.

The second major difficulty and, at the same time, one of the most difficult personal problems I had to resolve in this study concerned how I should treat the two so-called "gentleman's agreements" or "understandings" which I discovered in my investigation supplemented the written, published Quadripartite Agreement on Berlin. In the one case,[1] where the "understanding" of the Four Powers was a matter of public record (although little known), the decision was clear. In the other,[2] where the "gentleman's agreement" was still a closely held secret, it was not.

While I have great admiration and respect for the American Ambassador, without whose personal diplomacy (however controversial) I am convinced there would not have been such a good agreement if indeed any at all, and while I am very grateful for the great pains Ambassador *Rush* took in drafting his detailed foreword to this book, my obligations as a scholar to provide as complete and objective a picture of events as possible were decisive. Consequently, I chose in the end not to suppress this important finding but to include in this book a discussion of what I have learned about the two "gentleman's agreements." Although it by no means represents the last word on the subject, it should shed new light on the overall Berlin settlement.

I realize that publication of the contents of the secret "understanding" is bound to **make** the Western Three the subject of no little criticism. And, no doubt, some of this criticism will be justified. For even the most pro-Western observer must feel that

1 See p. 242.
2 See pp. 240-42.

the Allies acted shortsightedly in this matter. Not only was it a tactical mistake to think that the confidential "gentleman's agreement" could remain secret indefinitely. But as the contents of this informal accord make clear, the Four Powers, in their haste to wrap up negotiations in the end, showed a woeful lack of appreciation for constitutional processes and democratic norms.

But whatever people may feel about the conclusion of this secret agreement, I hope that they — in the public debate which may ensue – will not lose sight of the very positive aspects of the Quadripartite Agreement and what Ambassador *Rush* and his colleagues, bargaining under a great deal of pressure, have accomplished for Berlin and détente. For despite its obvious weaknesses, the QA has worked much better than many people originally expected both inside and outside government.

Acknowledgements

Many people have helped me with this book. I am especially grateful to the numerous Allied, West Berlin and West German officials who provided me on a not-for-attribution basis with inside information, thus permitting me to fill out the public record in many places. *(Pyotr A. Abrasimov,* the Soviet Ambassador to the GDR and one of the negotiators of the 1971 Berlin agreement, declined to talk with me or allow any members of his staff to be interviewed.)

Those individuals to whom I owe a special debt and who may be named include the following:

The members of the *Luftbrückendank-Stiftung,* who awarded me a grant and gave generous support to the writing of this book;

President *Michael Blecker* of St. John's University, Vice President *Gunther Rolfson* and my other friends and colleagues who gave me a year's administrative leave to conduct research in Berlin;

Professor *Joe Farry,* my departmental chairman, colleague and good friend, whose repeated kindness and advice have been a source of inspiration;

Ambassador *Kenneth Rush,* for talking at length with me, reviewing initial chapters on the negotiations and, above all, contributing a detailed foreword;

Martin J. Hillenbrand, formerly U.S. Ambassador to the Federal Republic of Germany, for his critical comments on draft chapters;

Hans-Peter Weber, Head of the Department for Youth and Education in the SPD Executive Committee, who opened many doors for me in my research;

Scott George, American Minister in Berlin, for his criticism of parts of the uncompleted manuscript;

Peter Lorenz, President of the Berlin House of Representatives, for his friendly help;

Dennis L. Bark, Assistant to the Director of the Hoover Institute, whose pioneering study of the Berlin negotiations laid the groundwork for this book and made my research considerably easier;

Hartmut Jäckel, Vice President of the Free University, and Professor *Karl Lenz* of the John F. Kennedy Institute, who supervised my work;

Frau Hildebrandt, Chief Librarian of the U.S. Mission in Berlin, who brought much important research material to my attention;

Norbert Böttcher, who assisted me in numerous ways;

Frau *Johanna Neumaier,* for monitoring the West Berlin press and bringing much valuable information to my notice;

My students *Randy Krzmarzick* and *Jim Zitzmann,* who helped me with the bibliography;

Arno Spitz, my publisher, who in the process of speedily and carefully steering this book through the complex stages of production, became cherished for his sound political advice and perceptive editorial suggestions;

Frau *Spitz,* Messieurs *Hecht* and *Oestreich* of Berlin Verlag and other staff, for their expert technical assistance and meticulous attention to detail;

My mother-in-law, *Käte Goerz,* who unconditionally opened her apartment to me and my rambunctious brood for fifteen months and provided a creative environment for the writing of this book;

Finally, my loving Berliner wife, *Renate,* for her continued demonstrations of flexibility and unflagging support through all the pains of authorship.

12

FOREWORD

Since shortly after the end of World War II until the Quadripartite Agreement on Berlin was signed on September 3, 1971, Berlin had occupied the unique and unenviable position of being a barometer of relations between the East and West – especially between the United States and the Soviet Union. It had been the focal point of confrontation, the perennial crisis area which at times had brought the parties near the brink of nuclear war and which had severely tested their political will and determination.

The critical issue had been access to West Berlin, and the principal cause for disruption of access in recent years had been the objections of the Soviet Union and East Germany (the German Democratic Republic) to the legal, political, economic, financial and cultural ties between West Berlin and West Germany (the Federal Republic of Germany). These ties are the life-blood of the city and their strength and adequacy determine its viability.

When President *Nixon* went to Europe in February 1969, shortly after his inauguration, he stressed the paramount interest of the United States in Europe, the need for a unified Western Europe, and a desire to commence negotiations for a normalization of relations with the Soviet Union and its Eastern European allies. Berlin was a key element in his discussions. He clearly saw that if no progress could be made in improving the situation in this critical area, further initiatives toward détente with the Soviet Union would be futile.

Accordingly, in his visit to West Berlin on February 27, at a time when the G.D.R. was harassing traffic between the F.R.G. and West Berlin in protest against the F.R.G. holding its forthcoming meeting of the Bundesversammlung in the city for election of a President, President *Nixon,* among other remarks calling for a settlement of the "Berlin problem," said:

"When we say that we reject any unilateral alteration of the status quo in Berlin, we do not mean that we consider the status quo to be satisfactory. Nobody benefits from a stalemate, least of all the people of Berlin.

"Let us set behind us the stereotype of Berlin as a 'provocation.' Let us, all of us, view the situation in Berlin as an invocation, a call to end the tension of the past age here and everywhere."

These remarks, endorsed by the F.R.G., were a signal to the Soviets which did not go unnoticed, and, as Mr. *Catudal* outlines, led, after protracted probing, to the initiation of the Four-Power Talks between the Ambassadors of the Allies to the F.R.G. *(Jean Sauvagnargues* of France, *Roger Jackling* of the United Kingdom, and me) and the Ambassador of the Soviet Union to the G.D.R. *(Pyotr A. Abrasimov).* These Ambassadors also, *ex officio,* have residual powers as the High Commissioners for Germany as a whole.

There was justifiable widespread suspicion among the Western Powers of the motives of the Soviets in agreeing to the talks and skepticism that any worthwhile results could be achieved in the negotiations. The legal positions of the two sides as to the legal status of Berlin were so fundamentally contradictory as to appear to be irreconcilable and to bar hope of any agreement granting substantial improvement in the situation of West Berlin. A very brief overview of these legal positions at the time of the negotiations is as follows:

The Soviet Position: Berlin was the capital of the "sovereign" German Democratic Republic. West Berlin itself was an independent political entity in the middle of the G.D.R. and located on the territory of the G.D.R. Since the G.D.R. had sovereignty over its own territory, it also had complete control over access to West Berlin, and all rights of this nature once held by the Soviets had been transferred to the G.D.R. There was no question of the right of the Allies to be in West Berlin; however, any presence of the Federal Republic in West Berlin without the consent of the G.D.R. was "illegal," a violation of the sovereignty of the G.D.R. over its territory. The Allies themselves had declared that West Berlin was not a "Land" of the F.R.G., and the Allies had no right to establish legal or political ties between West Berlin and the F.R.G. The Soviets intimated, however, that limited economic and cultural ties between West Berlin and the F.R.G. might be permissible.

14

The Allies' Position: All of Berlin was under quadripartite control by right of military victory in World War II, reinforced by agreements between the parties, particularly the Wartime Agreements of September 12 and November 14, 1944. By uncontested international law, unimpeded access to West Berlin was thus a matter of this original right, and insuring such access was the responsibility of the Soviet Union, over which Zone of Germany such traffic passed. The G.D.R. was not a sovereign state but was only the Soviet Zone of Germany as a whole, which in turn was subject to quadripartite rights and responsibilities. The G.D.R. had no rights whatever with regard to Berlin or its territory. Furthermore, each of the Occupying Powers of Berlin had the full right to establish any political or other ties it saw fit between its own Sector of Berlin and the F.R.G.

From the beginning of the negotiations, each side repeatedly emphasized its legal position and adamantly refused to modify it. At the same time, each side realized it was futile to attempt to impose its concept or legal position on the other. Practical improvements were the objective. And, as finally agreed upon, the Quadripartite Agreement itself expressly states that it is "without prejudice to their legal positions." In fact, however, the language of the Agreement on which accord was finally reached is in favor of the legal position of the Allies, and the vital concessions made and responsibilities assumed by the Soviet Union under the Agreement go well beyond its legal position. I will refer briefly to the most important ones:

1. Berlin and Quadripartite Rights

Until the final stages of the negotiations, the Soviet Union insisted that the Agreement must refer only to "West Berlin" or, at most, "Berlin(West)". References to "Berlin" or to the "Western Sectors of Berlin" were completely unacceptable to the Soviets because they contended that use of such terms would constitute acceptance of the Allied position that all of the city remained under Four-Power control, that East Berlin was not a part of the G.D.R., and that West Berlin was not an independent political entity.

The compromise in the Agreement, however, does refer in the Preamble to "the American Sector of Berlin" and contains references throughout the Agreement to "the Western Sectors of Berlin." These references imply that there must be one or more other Sectors of Berlin. Further, the Preamble expressly states that the parties are "acting on the basis of their quadripartite rights and responsibilities." A major objective of the Allies in the negotiations was a reaffirmation by the Soviet Union of these very rights and responsibilities. In fact, the entire construction of the Agreement, in which the Preamble and Part I of a general nature refer to the "relevant area" while Part II refers specifically to "the Western Sectors of Berlin," strongly evidences that the Preamble and Part I of the Agreement do refer to Berlin as a whole and that there are continuing quadripartite rights and responsibilities over the area and over Germany as a whole.

2. Access

Despite the Soviet Union's legal position that the G.D.R. had exclusive control of traffic over its territory between the F.R.G. and West Berlin and that the Soviets would under no circumstances assume any responsibility for such access, we were able to secure in the Agreement (Part II A) the unqualified statement by the Soviet Union that

"transit traffic by road, rail and waterways through the territory of the German Democratic Republic of civilian persons and goods between the Western Sectors of Berlin and the Federal Republic of Germany will be unimpeded; that such traffic will be facilitated so as to take place in the most simple and expeditious manner; and that it will receive preferential treatment."

This is a firm, unrestricted commitment by the Soviet Union on its own account and is supplemented in the Annexes by detailed provisions reinforcing this commitment. The fact that reference is made to "through the territory of the G.D.R." strengthens the Allied position that the Soviet Union has responsibility for traffic through the G.D.R. between the F.R.G. and West Berlin.

3. Ties

In keeping with its legal position, the Soviet Union emphatically demanded that the Agreement should forbid any official presence of the F.R.G. in West Berlin, and that it be expressly stated that West Berlin was not a "part" of the F.R.G. Included in its more extreme demands were that the then some 22,000 employees of the F.R.G. in West Berlin should be removed and the offices closed, that there should be no official meetings of Governmental bodies or political parties of the F.R.G. in West Berlin, and that the President, the Chancellor, and other officials of the F.R.G. must not make official visits or speeches in West Berlin.

The Agreement as finally reached, however, expressly provides that

"the ties between the Western Sectors of Berlin and the Federal Republic of Germany will be *maintained and developed,* taking into account that these Sectors *continue* not to be a constituent part of the Federal Republic of Germany and not to be governed by it." (Italics mine.)

Thus, the Agreement puts the maintenance and development of the ties into a positive formulation. The words "maintain" and "continue" make unmistakably clear that there is no change in the previous relationship as approved by the Allies. The term "developed" makes clear that future changes can be made to expand and strengthen these ties. Whether the flexibility obtained under this general language, giving an opportunity for a changing relationship rather than one that is frozen, is preferable to specificity is debatable but academic. No specific language acceptable to the Allies was negotiable. However, detailed supplementary provisions are set forth in the Annexes and other documents forming part of the Agreement.

The "taking into account" phrase must be interpreted in the light of background and history. In approving the Basic Law of the F.R.G. and the Constitution of Berlin, the Allies had expressly suspended those parts which stated that Berlin was a "Land" of the F.R.G. The phrase that West Berlin continues not to be "a constituent part" of the F.R.G. was not a new term but had for many years been used in official Allied and F.R.G. correspondence to describe the status of Berlin as established by the Allies. Similarly, the Allies had consistently established that West Berlin was not "governed" by the F.R.G. but by the Allies. Otherwise the legal basis for the Allies to be in West Berlin would be undermined. Accordingly, no change in the existing ties between the F.R.G. and West Berlin can be inferred from the language of the Agreement.

4. Other Provisions

The Agreement contains other vital improvements with regard to freedom of movement of West Berliners and other communications between West Berlin on the one hand and East Berlin and the G.D.R. on the other, representation abroad of West Berlin's interests, and the elimination of the small enclaves. The right for the Soviet Union to establish a Consulate General in West Berlin, with strict limitation as to size and operations, is also provided. Annexes and other documents, along with the agreement of the G.D.R. and the F.R.G. with regard to the details of access, fill out the Agreement, and all is then brought together in the Final Quadripartite Protocol.

For the most part, the Berlin Agreement has thus far worked satisfactorily. It must be recognized, however, that the actual practical effects of the Agreement will be directly dependent on the over-all status of East-West relations, primarily American-Soviet relations, at any given time. No agreement covering one segment of this relationship can contain sufficient intrinsic protection and assurance to continue unaffected in the event of a general worsening of the over-all relationship. However, the Berlin Agreement should go far in effectively insulating the area which it covers from a possible worsening of relations. Flagrant disregard of the protection accorded to West Berlin by the Agreement would have grave consequences.

I have mentioned the skepticism with which each side entered into the negotiations. In fact, against the background of the Cold War, which had had its practical manifestation in the Berlin problem, the entire negotiations were for a long time characterized by acute distrust on both sides. The Soviet leadership, and Ambassador *Abrasimov* himself, products of a political system which engenders distrust, were continually subjected to doubts about the feasibility of their own Western policy, which itself had been under attack by still more skeptical Soviet leaders. They had acute doubts as to whether the Allies, particularly the United States, actually wanted to conclude a Berlin Agreement or, in fact, wanted to use the negotiations to sabotage *Brandt's Ostpolitik* and the easing of East-West relations. These nagging doubts were evidenced by *Abrasimov's* continually questioning me as to whether the American Government really wanted an agreement. There was no doubt that the Soviets had concluded that the door to détente between the United States and the Soviet Union could be opened only by an acceptable agreement on Berlin, and, of course, Chancellor *Brandt* had expressly made his *Ostpolitik* conditional upon a Berlin Agreement. Similarly, the Western Powers had made the holding of a Conference on European Security, a long-time Russian proposal, conditional upon a Berlin Agreement. The latter was, however, in my opinion, of secondary interest to the Soviet Union. Its primary interest had shifted to *Brandt's Ostpolitik* and détente with the United States as a primary means of achieving its objectives, particularly Western recognition of the Soviet concept of territorial "status quo" in Europe.

President *Nixon* and *Dr. Kissinger* were, of course, fully aware of this problem, and in the early part of 1971 President *Nixon* instructed me to conduct closely guarded discussions with Ambassador *Abrasimov* and with Soviet Ambassador *Falin* in Bonn. These intensive discussions continued for several months and were very successful in dispelling suspicion, narrowing differences, and otherwise laying the groundwork for the ultimate Agreement. Such progress had been made by July that, in my opinion, the institution of continuing, marathon sessions by the Ambassadors finally to resolve all issues was justified. Such sessions were subsequently agreed upon by all parties.

At the same time, the atmosphere of the Four-Power Ambassadorial talks themselves had, in parallel, been gradually improving and progress was being made in non-substantive matters such as agreeing on a three-part structure for the Agreement; that is, it would take the form of (1) the Quadripartite Agreement itself, with its attached Annexes and Supplements; (2) the inner-German agreement on details with regard to access; and (3) the Final

Quadripartite Protocol, bringing all parts together into one legal package. Progress was also being made in finding acceptable language to be employed in a possible agreement, with blanks remaining to be filled in on the substantive issues. All aspects of the substantive issues also continued to be explored by the Four Powers.

However, at the time of the beginning of the marathon talks on August 10, not a single important substantive issue between the parties had been finally resolved in the Ambassadorial sessions. The task facing the Ambassadors, therefore, was formidable. However, because of the careful preparatory background which had been established, progress was rapid and, with some interruptions, the daily sessions were concluded on August 18. On that day, in a final 14-hour session, the remaining outstanding issues and details concerning wording were wrapped up and an agreement was virtually in hand. A few items remained, but these were cleaned up at a luncheon meeting in my residence on August 23. Holding this final meeting at my residence, rather than at the former Allied Control Authority building, was at the suggestion of Ambassador *Abrasimov* and was a generous gesture on his part. He and I had established a good relationship of mutual respect and trust in the course of our many meetings, a friendly relationship which still continues.

After some serious intervening difficulties with regard to a common, although unofficial, German translation were satisfactorily resolved, the Quadripartite Agreement was signed on September 3, 1971.

Considerable time was necessary for completion of the inner-German agreement on details of transit. The Soviets subsequently, however, established a reverse Junktim (link) and let it be known that the Final Quadripartite Protocol could not be signed until the Moscow Agreement had been ratified by the Bundestag and Bundesrat. After great difficulty, Chancellor *Brandt* was able to secure such ratification of this keystone of his *Ostpolitik* in May 1972. Thereupon the Four Powers signed the Final Quadripartite Protocol on June 3, 1972, and the Berlin Agreement came into full effect.

As I have frequently done in the past, I should like at this point again to pay high tribute to the close cooperation of my able colleagues, Ambassadors *Jackling* and *Sauvagnargues,* and to the invaluable support of our excellent staffs, particularly the Political

Counsellors, of our Governments and of the Government of the F.R.G. The close and understanding working relationship between us represents, in my opinion, an almost unequalled example of international effectiveness.

Post-war Berlin offers one of the most fascinating stories of the struggle among nations. In this foreword, I have attempted to put in perspective the high points of the Four-Power negotiations and Agreement. Although these are also the focal themes of his book, Mr. *Catudal* fits them into the framework of a wellrounded, detailed picture of the story of Berlin since the construction of the Berlin Wall in 1961, including the events leading up to the negotiations, the negotiations themselves and the personalities involved in them, an excellent analysis of the various elements of the Agreement, and how the Agreement has worked. Mr. *Catudal* deserves much credit for the painstaking, exhaustive, and skillful manner in which he has approached his work in this area. He has compiled a deeply researched, scholarly, and very readable account of an important chapter in post-World War II history.

My strong recommendation of Mr. *Catudal's* work, however, should not be interpreted as a blanket endorsement of the accuracy of all of his facts or the correctness of all of his interpretations and conclusions. In my opinion he has done remarkably well with the material available. However, most of the official record of the negotiations, particularly of my private talks with Ambassadors *Abrasimov* and *Falin* and other Soviet representatives, remains highly classified and has not been accessible to him. In turn, we who do know all or part of the record have, of course, been restricted in what we could disclose to him. Mr. *Catudal* of necessity, therefore, has had to rely primarily on other sources, such as press accounts, oral interviews, and the like. In doing so, he has inevitably received some misinformation, particularly in press accounts which were sometimes based on a degree of conjecture. In a research project of this magnitude, also, he has at times had to sort out and choose between conflicting accounts without being able to check them against the record. All this of necessity leads to a degree of error and omission. I should also point out that this, of course, is Mr. *Catudal's* own account and that naturally he has occasionally reached some conclusions in which I do not concur.

These comments, however, should not be considered to be in derogation of Mr. *Catudal's* essentially sound and authoritative work. As it now stands, his book, in my opinion, will take its place as one of the truly valuable studies of the events of the post-war period. However, I hope that when the full record is released and available to him he will devote his considerable abilities and profound knowledge of the subject to revising his work and giving us his views in the light of the new evidence thereby made available. Meanwhile, his book is indispensable reading material for anyone wishing to know the vital part played by post-war Berlin in man's continuing struggle for freedom.

October 26, 1976   *Kenneth Rush*

Before I built a wall I'd ask to know
What I was walling in or walling out
And to whom I was like to give offense,
Something there is that doesn't love a wall,
That wants it down.

Robert Frost, Mending Wall

Chapter I
THE BERLIN WALL CRISIS

It was a hot summer night in Berlin when the blow fell. Shortly after midnight, Sunday, August 13, 1961, large numbers of heavily-armed East German police and troop units, under the cover of heavy tanks, were deployed along the twenty-eight mile long intra-city boundary. While some took up battle positions, others brought up pneumatic drills, shovels, crowbars and rolls of barbed wire. Systematically, they began to tear up the streets at Friedrichstraße and at each of the other eighty crossing points (which now were reduced to thirteen). Double strands of barbed wire and other light obstacles were firmly emplaced. Approximately two and one-quarter hours later, the border closure was a fait accompli.

Although no Soviet soldiers participated in the actual sealing-off of the border, the East German action was supported by extensive Soviet troop movements throughout the country. Units of the Soviet armed forces in East Germany, headed by Marshal *Koniev,* former Commander of Warsaw Pact forces and an ex-Deputy Minister of Defense, moved out of their barracks and took up tactical positions around the city. The visibility of Soviet and East German military might in the countryside had the desired effect: There was no popular uprising.

In a bulletin which was flashed to the world that morning, the border closure was stoutly defended by the East German régime. It was specifically noted that this measure had been requested by the Warsaw Pact countries in a declaration adopted at a meeting in Moscow ten days earlier. According to this statement, the German Democratic Republic (GDR — East Germany) was authorized to put "an end to the hostile activities of the revanchist and militarist forces of Western Germany and West Berlin." This was to be accomplished by introducing controls "on the border of the German Democratic Republic, including the border with the Western sectors of Greater Berlin, which are usually introduced along the borders of every sovereign state." As a degree of reassurance to the Western powers, it was added that "these measures must not affect existing provisions for traffic and control on communication routes between West Berlin and West Germany."[1]

In the closing of the East Berlin border, *Khrushchev* and *Ulbricht* achieved complete tactical surprise. It was a weekend — a Sunday morning — and most people in Berlin were sleeping in their beds. Outside of Berlin, many Western leaders were caught far away from their capitals and communications centers. The Mayor of West Berlin, *Willy Brandt*, was in the Federal Republic electioneering; President *Kennedy* was sailing at Hyannis Port; Prime Minister *Macmillan* was in Scotland; and President *de Gaulle* was on vacation at his estate in Colombey. The only Western leader at his post was Chancellor *Adenauer*.

In West Berlin, the American Minister, *E. Allan Lightner,* was sleeping soundly when he was suddenly roused by a phone call at about six o'clock in the morning. As he recounted later: "I got out of bed and went down to take a look at what had been going on in the French Sector." But all "I saw was some building material . . ." At first, "it looked like barriers were being built to keep refugees in rather than to keep us out."[2] Not knowing quite what to make of the situation, he then went to the U.S. Mission where he dispatched a .report to the Embassy in Bonn and the Department of State in Washington.

---

1 East German decree, quoted in The New York Times, August 14, 1961.
2 Interview with E. Allan Lightner, February 7, 1967, Washington, D.C.

The man responsible for the German Desk in the State Department during this week-end was *John C. Ausland*. And it was he, alerted by the duty officer, who was one of the first individuals in the Office of German Affairs to report in early Sunday morning. Soon he was joined by *Frank Cash*, and *Karl* and *Martha Mautner*, all experienced officials. Together with other officers from the European Bureau they began in the newly-established Operations Center to consult with each other and pore over the few cables that had come in since Lightner's first message.

The most important issue on their minds, and the one on which elaborate contingency plans had been based, concerned the maintenance of Allied access to Berlin. Thus, during the early morning hours, August 13, they tended to view the crisis from this perspective.[3]

Hardly had State Department officials met to review cables before a German journalist, *Lothar Loewe*, appeared on the seventh floor. *Loewe* had heard the news over his car radio and had immediately rushed over to the Department to ask friends for details. He was informed that information was meager, conflicting and hard to interpret. When he inquired if anyone had telephoned Berlin, he was told there were no secure telephone lines through East Germany, and they were not authorized to call.

Loewe then went out to telephone Berlin himself. He put through a call to a friend of his working with USIA in the city. By then, it was almost noon in Germany. From his friend, he received an accurate and first-hand picture of events: The city was now divided by barbed wire, communist troops and tanks — but not yet by concrete. Returning to "foggy bottom", *Loewe* informed officials in the Operations Center of what he had learned.

There was a clearer picture of events by the time the Assistant Secretary of State for European Affairs and Director of the Berlin Task Force, *Foy D. Kohler*, came into the Department between eight and nine in the morning. Contingency plans had been reviewed, but unfortunately none of them covered the actual division of the city by barriers. (To the people who had been

3 It is worth noting here that contingency plans regarding the possibility of a border closure did exist. However, as one high-level U.S. intelligence officer who lived through the crisis told this writer, "these focused on a closure of Berlin borders with East Germany — and not on sector borders within Berlin."

entrusted with drawing them up, it had appeared logical that the border between East Germany and East Berlin would be closed.) There was some relief that Allied access to Berlin had not been affected. From all accounts, the measures seemed aimed at halting the refugee flow rather than at challenging the Western position in the city.

One hour later, Secretary of State *Dean Rusk* was in his office hard at work. *Rusk* knew Berlin well from his student days there in the early 1930s — just before the Nazis took over. He had thus taken a personal interest in the Berlin crisis ever since the *Kennedy* Administration inherited it in early 1961.

After discussing the details of the border closure with *Kohler* and members of his staff, *Rusk* was little inclined to take any precipitate action. As he told this writer later, any attempt to interfere physically with the barriers "might have resulted in war." For *Rusk*, the fact that "we didn't have the force in Berlin to knock down" the barriers was the crucial factor.[4]

Having made up his mind, he put through a call shortly before noon to the President who was vacationing with his family at Hyannis Port. *Kennedy* had already heard about the border closure on the radio but reports inevitably were conflicting. *Rusk* rounded out the President's first impressions with the necessary details.

The President agreed with his Secretary of State that the barricading steps taken thus far did not appear to be aimed at the Western position in Berlin. In view of this, he acknowledged that Western options were extremely limited. He decided to adopt a "wait and see" stance. Consequently, he instructed *Rusk* to pass the word along to do nothing to aggravate the situation further. "Go to the ball game as you had planned," he is reported to have told *Rusk*. "I am going sailing."[5]

Background

The Berlin crisis of 1961 represented one of President *Kennedy's* greatest trials in office. Only two years earlier, he had predicted as

4 Interview with Dean Rusk, August 14, 1969, Washington, D.C.
5 Eleanor Lansing Dulles, The Wall: A Tragedy in Three Acts (Columbia, S. C.: University of South Carolina, Press, 1972), p. 48.

much when he said in an interview that the Berlin question in time was certain to be a harsh "test of nerve and will."[6]

John F. Kennedy arrived in office half expecting, but hoping to avoid a crisis over the city. It was against this background that the new President, shortly after the debacle at the Bay of Pigs, dispatched a personal note to *Khrushchev* calling for a meeting of the two Chiefs of State. Even though both the President and Secretary of State had earlier expressed a marked distaste for "summit diplomacy,"[7] it apparently was now felt that a face-to-face encounter would serve to reduce the chances of Russian miscalculation of American intent and pave the way for the resumption of normal U.S. — U.S.S.R. relations. The Soviet leader, anxious to size up the young President personally, concurred with his proposal, and so the talks were held June 3-4, 1961, in Vienna.

The most important topic on the agenda was Germany and Berlin. And it was precisely on this subject that *Khrushchev* was toughest. The German situation, he argued, was intolerable. Here it was, sixteen years after the end of the war, and there was still no peace settlement. Moreover, now a rearmed West Germany had become dominant in NATO, threatening another world war, to alleviate this dangerous situation the Soviet Party Chairman reiterated his demand for a peace treaty. If the West balked, then he was determined to carry out his threat of a separate peace treaty with the German Democratic Republic and all that it entailed. *Khrushchev* handed the President an aide-mémoire and gave him six months to make up his mind.[8]

There has been some debate regarding *Kennedy's* reaction to *Khrushchev's* blustering performance. *George F. Kennan,* former Ambassador to the Soviet Union, later characterized the President at Vienna as a "tongue-tied young man, not forceful, with no idea of his own."[9] *James Reston,* The New York Times columnist who

6 Theodore C. Sorensen, Kennedy (New York: Bantom Books, Inc., 1966), p. 657.

7 Secretary Rusk effectively argued this case in an article entitled "The President," which appeared in the Spring 1960 issue of Foreign Affairs. It is reported that the President was quite taken with this piece, and that it had a great deal to do with Kennedy's decision to appoint Rusk as his Secretary of State.

8 For the text of the Soviet note see Department of State Bulletin, August 7, 1961, p. 231.

9 Quoted in The Washington Post, April 11, 1971.

saw him soon after he emerged from the conference room, described him as "shaken and angry."[10] But *Theodore Sorensen,* then Special Counsel to the President, insists that these accounts are an exaggeration. Whatever the case, President *Kennedy* was deeply impressed, so much so that afterwards he asked veteran diplomat *Llewellyn Thompson,* then Ambassador to Moscow, whether it was "always like this". The Ambassador replied: "Par for the course."[11]

As became obvious later, the Soviet leader had used the Vienna Conference to renew his assault on West Berlin. Following up his initiative, the Soviet news agency Tass published on June 10 the text of the aide-mémoire which had been presented to the President at Vienna. Then, five days later *Khrushchev* in an unprecedented television report to the Soviet people declared that the "conclusion of a peace treaty cannot be postponed any longer; a peaceful settlement in Europe must be attained this year . . . ."[12] In response to the growing crisis the *Kennedy* administration was compelled to give careful consideration to what strategy it would adopt.

Policy Formulation

A review of Berlin policy had begun well before President *Kennedy* went to Vienna in June. In fact, in the middle of February he had invited former Secretary of State *Dean Acheson* to undertake a special study of the problem in the context of NATO and Germany. The President chose *Acheson* for the job because he considered him one of the most intelligent and experienced men around and wanted to avail himself of his "hardline" views before making up his own mind.[13]

Prior to a visit in April by Prime Minister *Macmillan,* the former Secretary of State was asked to outline his views to the President.

10 Quoted in John C. Ausland, Kennedy, Khrushchev and Berlin: The 1961-1964 Berlin Crisis (unpublished manuscript, 1967), p. 7.

11 Quoted in Arthur M. Schlesinger, Jr., A Thousand Days (Greenwich, Conn.: Fawcett Publications, Inc., 1967), p. 341.

12 For the text of the speech as translated by Tass see The New York Times, June 16, 1961.

13 Arthur M. Schlesinger, Jr., opus cit., p. 353.

Acheson's thesis boiled down to this: *Khrushchev* was using Berlin not to rectify a local situation but to test American will to resist generally. If we backed down during this test, our power and influence throughout the world would be seriously undermined. Since the basic issue concerned a test of wills, any willingness to negotiate would be taken in Moscow as evidence of weakness. His solution to the problem involved taking strong action that would convince the Soviet leader that the United States intended to back up its commitment to defend Berlin — even to the extent of using nuclear weapons.[14]

When *Acheson* delivered his final report to the President, just three weeks after the Vienna meeting, its policy implications caused great debate in the State Department. Secretary *Rusk* preferred negotiations to *Acheson's* military alternatives.[15] But *Foy Kohler* was a firm supporter of *Acheson*. His view, as related to this writer, was that "The Soviets would back down to over-whelming force."[16] Standing in between were *George McGhee*, Director of the Policy and Planning Council, *Abram Chayes*, State Department Legal Adviser, and *Llewellyn Thompson*, U.S. Ambassador to Moscow. They insisted that plans for negotiations as well as for military action should be prepared.[17]

Following a discussion of *Acheson's* report to the National Security Council on June 29, the President was still not satisfied that he had all the information he needed. Consequently, he made two decisions to rectify the situation. His first and most basic action was to direct the Secretaries of State and Defense to study the matter further and to prepare their recommendations. His second was to ask *Acheson* to look into the other alternative — negotiations.[18]

Under the direction of *Rusk* and *McNamara*, work on the State-Defense study was conducted by an experienced team of officers. *Kohler* headed the State Department group. At his side was *Martin Hillenbrand*, who had headed the German Desk since 1958 (later U.S. Ambassador to the Federal Republic). Assistant Secretary for

14 Arthur M. Schlesinger, Jr., opus cit., pp. 353-356.
15 Interview with Dean Rusk, August 14, 1969.
16 Interview with Foy D. Kohler, December 20, 1966, Washington, D.C.
17 Arthur M. Schlesinger, Jr., opus cit., p. 357.
18 Ibid.

International Security Affairs *Paul Nitze* headed the Defense contingent. The Joint Chiefs of Staff were represented by Major General *David Gray.* And General *Maxwell D. Taylor,* Special Assistant to the President for Military Affairs, served in the capacity of White House observer. Working far into the night and often around the clock for three straight weeks, they prepared two basic reports.[19]

President *Kennedy's* second decision was to involve himself in the contingency planning on Berlin. Basically, this unusual step by a President stemmed from his well-known wish to be his own Secretary of State. As *Theodore Sorensen* points out in his monograph *Decision-Making in the White House,* the President liked to select key issues like Berlin in which to interest himself, and then saturated himself in the problem.[20]

Another motive was undoubtedly *Kennedy's* deep suspicion of contingency plans. According to Emery Smith, a member of the Berlin Task Force in the mid-1960s, *"Kennedy* was very much impressed with *Barbara Tuchman's* book *The Guns of August,* which showed so well how planning could have a snowball effect and get completely out of hand."[21] The President saw his job as preventing this from happening.

Having decided to take charge personally of Berlin contingency planning, the President began an intensive review of existing plans prepared by NATO and the Joint Chiefs of Staff. He was immediately dismayed at what he found. While there had been considerable Allied planning after 1958, most of these plans were addressed to the problems of access. And they left the United States in an entirely unfavorable position. In the event of communist aggression, the U.S., lacking the capability to wage a conventional war on the ground, had little alternative but to rely on atomic weapons — or do nothing.[22]

Faced with this dismal situation, the President decided to heed the advice of Generals *Maxwell Taylor* and *James Gavin,* both of

19 John C. Ausland, opus cit., p. 9.

20 Theodore C. Sorensen, Decision-Making in the White House (New York: Columbia University Press, 1963), p. 17.

21 Interview with Emery Smith, January 4, 1966, Washington, D.C.

22 Theodore C. Sorensen, Kennedy (New York: Bantam Books, Inc., 1966), p. 662.

whom had resigned in protest in the mid-1950s because of American reliance on nuclear weapons. He decided to fill the gap with a rapid build-up of combat troops in Central Europe. As General *Gavin* later told this writer, "When I suggested to President *Kennedy* in 1961 that he send troops to Europe to re-inforce our position there, it was because if we were going to have war it would be better to have it on equal terms."[23]

Having decided on a rapid build-up in conventional strength in Europe, the President was next faced with the question of whether or not he should declare a "national emergency". Such a declaration would certainly enable him to call up one million men, extend terms of service, bring back dependents from Europe and impress America's allies, its citizens and most importantly, *Khrushchev*. But in shoring up Western confidence in his leadership after the Bay of Pigs fiasco he could not afford to over-react. The fact that *Khrushchev* could turn the pressure on and off in Berlin put the President in a difficult position.

What decided him in the end was the advice he received from the American Embassy in Moscow. The Embassy insisted that the Soviets were more likely to be impressed by substantial but unsensational steps that did not panic America's friends. Dramatic gestures were less impressive to Moscow, it was argued, than a long-term build up. As *Sorensen* reports: "This was in keeping with Kennedy's own philosophy: a decision to go all the way can afford to be low-key because it is genuine, while those who flail about are less likely to frighten anyone."[24]

By July 19, two days after the long-awaited American reply to *Khrushchev's* aide-mémoire, the President had put the finishing touches on his policy. Essentially, it represented a compromise between the "hawks" and the "doves" within the administration. Specifically, it called for additional military budget requests totaling $ 3.2 billion. The Congress was to be asked to provide stand-by authority for the call up of the reserves. Draft calls were to be tripled. West Berlin was to be readied with additional stockpiles of supplies and airlift preparations. Allied concurrence

23 Interview with General Gavin, February 6, 1967, Cambridge, Massachusetts.
24 Theodore C. Sorensen, Kennedy (New York: Bantam Books, Inc., 1966), p. 664.

was to be sought on economic sanctions to be applied against East Germany in case of serious provocation. A temporary tax increase was to be requested (later this decision was reversed). However, no declaration of "national emergency" was to be proclaimed.[25]

In addition to the above specific measures, the President also decided to launch a diplomatic offensive. It was his firm belief that the United States could not "leave it to others to choose and monopolize the forum and the framework of discussion."[26]

One week later, on July 25, the President went on nation-wide television to inform the world of his course of action. It was a strong speech and clearly reflected American determination to remain in Berlin. Generally, it was well received. But it was especially encouraging to Major General *Albert Watson* II, U.S. Commandant in Berlin. He thought it "was the strongest speech he had heard on Berlin."[27]

Soon after this speech was given, an American delegation of experts, headed by *Foy Kohler,* was dispatched to Paris. While their general aim was to lay the groundwork for the forthcoming conference of Foreign Ministers, their specific goals included the ironing out of last-minute disagreements with the British, French and Germans over the formulation of detailed Allied contingency plans about Berlin.

Unfortunately for the Americans, the threat to Berlin did not unite the Western Allies as much as they had hoped. No doubt, one of the greatest sources of divergence came over U.S. emphasis on negotiations. While the French were against all negotiations with the Soviets, the British were opposed to risking war without first attempting to negotiate. The Germans, for their part, were seriously split on the issue as Federal elections were just around the corner.[28]

The focus of the inter-Allied debate was over the use of force by NATO. Earlier, the Allies had interpreted the President's call for a massive build-up of conventional strength in Central Europe as a sign of American reluctance to use nuclear weapons to defend

25 Theodore C. Sorensen, Kennedy (New York: Bantam Books, Inc., 1966), p. 665.

26 Ibid.

27 Interview with General Albert Watson, January 3, 1967, Washington, D.C.

28 John C. Ausland, opus cit., p. 17.

East German soldiers close Brandenburg Gate, August 14, 1961.

American tanks face Soviet armor
on Friedrichstraße (Checkpoint Charlie),
October 27, 1961

Berlin. The truth was, however, that although *Kennedy* was prepared to go to war over the city, he was convinced that *Khrushchev* would act in such a way as to minimize his risks. Therefore, he concluded, NATO should adopt a more flexible response, i.e., it should have a full range of options in its defensive strategy, from a limited probe all the way up to nuclear war. But the Allies were averse to planning on this basis; they only agreed to do so if the point at which nuclear weapons would be used were left undefined.[29]

Between August 5 and 7 Secretary *Rusk* conferred in Paris with his British, French and German counterparts. The results of these meetings were mixed and details have yet to be published. However, according to *E. Allan Lightner,* the U.S. Minister in Berlin, who accompanied the Ambassador to West Germany *Walter Dowling* to Paris, the Foreign Ministers agreed that "we had three vital interests in Berlin which we would protect even to the point of going to war if necessary . . ."[30] Called "the three essentials," they were

(1) the freedom of West Berliners to choose their own form of government;
(2) the maintenance of Allied presence and garrisons in West Berlin; and
(3) free access to the city for both Allies and West Germans.[31]

Unfortunately, according to *Lightner,* "freedom of movement through the whole city was not mentioned". At the time, both *Lightner* and *Dowling* "were disappointed at this omission". By failing to consider Western rights in East Berlin "a vital interest", the Western powers were effectively writing off the Soviet Sector altogether. However, *Lightner* now feels "the Russians were determined to take drastic steps to stop the flow of refugees, regardless of what we said."[32]

The importance of the Paris conference cannot be overestimated. For what was spelled out there (and what was omitted!) was to serve as the guide to Allied, and particularly to American,

29 John C. Ausland, opus cit., p. 16.

30 Interview with E. Allan Lightner, February 7, 1967, Washington, D.C.

31 These three essentials were formulated for the first time by the State Department following Khrushchev's ultimatum. They were subsequently incorporated in Acheson's position paper and adopted by Kennedy.

32 Interview with Lightner.

response on August 13. Nothing was said there that might have given support to a prompt local reaction to the closing of the border. The Ministers departed from Paris with no agreement on a move to counter *Khrushchev's* threat to sign a peace treaty by the end of the year.[33]

The Refugee Deluge

During the second week of August 1961, an atmosphere of anxiety and expectation hung over Berlin. The flow of refugees from East Germany, increasing steadily since the Vienna Conference in June, was now reaching monumental proportions. A sense of imminent disaster, what the Germans call Torschlußpanik, had clearly set in.

Washington, at this time, was becoming increasingly worried about the growing flood of refugees. For in the words of Secretary of State *Rusk*: "East Germany was hemorrhaging to death."[34] Between 1945 and 1960 an estimated 3,300,000 Germans had fled the German Democratic Republic — about one-fifth of its population. Of these, more than 2,600,000 had left since records began to be kept in the Federal Republic in 1949. During the first six months of 1961 alone, about 150,000 persons fled East Germany.[35]

The drain on the East German economy represented by this mass exodus was so severe that the *Ulbricht* government obviously could not long endure it. While most of the refugees consisted of workers fleeing "the worker's paradise," a high percentage were professionals, e.g., managers, physicians, teachers, engineers and skilled artisans. Significantly also, a majority were young people — approximately fifty percent under the age of twenty-five. All were desperately needed and could not easily be replaced.

To stem this tide of refugees, the GDR régime had sharply restricted travel for East Germans and had sealed the border between East Germany and the Federal Republic. From 1953 on,

33 John C. Ausland, opus cit., p. 19.

34 Interview with Dean Rusk, August 14, 1969, Washington, D.C.

35 Statistical information is taken from German Information Center, Berlin: Crisis and Challenge (New York, 1963), pp. 27 - 30.

the dividing line was guarded by barbed wire, watch towers, sharpshooters and a "death strip" of mine fields.

However, until mid-August 1961, a refugee who reached East Berlin could still cross to West Berlin. Usually, border crossers made their escape on foot without any tell-tale luggage. But as communist guards, stationed at the inter-city boundary, became increasingly more watchful, most attempts were made in ways harder to control — by subway (U-Bahn) or the elevated line (S-Bahn).

Once in the West of Berlin, refugees were processed at a special center set up in Berlin-Marienfelde. Those who chose to remain in West Berlin could and were helped by the government to start a new life. Others — and these were the majority — were transported by air to West Germany, where arrangements were made for their housing and employment.

During July 1961, the refugee flow hit a new high, when more than 30,000 Germans (nearly double the previous year's monthly average) took refuge in the West. All flights of the regular civil airlines — Pan Am, BEA and Air France — left Berlin packed with passengers. As Allied officials speculated whether a military airlift would be necessary, additional civilian aircraft were thrown into the breach.

GDR officials reacted to this new deluge by redoubling their efforts. On July 6, *Ulbricht* launched a campaign against the "border crossers" (Grenzgänger). These were some 60,000 Germans who enjoyed the best of both worlds — living in East Berlin where rents were low, but working in West Berlin where they were paid in a currency three to four times the value of the East Mark. On July 22, rigorous curbs were put on passenger rail traffic into East Berlin from East Germany. On July 26, the *Ulbricht* régime demanded that "all means" be taken to halt the refugee flow. From now on anyone detected trying to flee the GDR would be subject to two years' imprisonment.[36]

Commentators have remarked how surprising it is that no action was taken at this time by Western officials in response to these restrictions, since the right to circulate freely in the city had long been recognized as inherent in the Four-Power status of Berlin. It

36 Jean Edward Smith, The Defense of Berlin (Baltimore: The Johns Hopkins Press, 1963), p. 258.

has been pointed out that when the GDR took similar measures the previous autumn, the Allied threat of economic sanctions had brought the East German government around.[37] However, the American, British and French Commandants did protest these restrictions on August 3, after conferring with Mayor *Willy Brandt.* But by this time, *Ulbricht* and *Khrushchev* were already plotting in Moscow, with representatives of the Warsaw Pact, their next and boldest stroke.

The erection of the Berlin Wall might have been forestalled if the Western Allies had learned in time of the Warsaw Pact decision of August 3-4; or at least this is the assumption of those who place great importance on the failure of Allied intelligence to detect communist intentions beforehand.[38] As one noted authority has argued: "The days of opportunity to deter this action were almost certainly in July, and the period of acute danger was in August." But only a "reliable intelligence report quickly transmitted and correctly evaluated to indicate a complete closing of the border could have brought the Allies together in time for convincing and concerted action."[39]

In retrospect, it seems clear that Allied intelligence left much to be desired. Contrary to what one sometimes hears or reads now, the Western intelligence establishments were caught by surprise on August 13. As *Allen Dulles,* former Director of the CIA, told this writer in a telephone interview: "From the evidence we had at the time, we had anticipated that the East Germans were going to take

37 Ibid., p. 259.

38 Previous knowledge of the East German intention to build the Wall probably would not have done any good even if conveyed to the Western Allies in time. Consider the case of the Czechoslovakian invasion in August 1968. According to Andrew Tully in The Super Spies (New York: Pocket Books, 1970), pp. 60 - 73, the Central Intelligence Agency had obtained detailed plans of the invasion well in advance through an agent in East Germany. But allegedly "The war in Vietnam . . . had so complicated the international situation that the United States could not afford to engage in a brinksmanship (sic) contest with the Soviet Union." Purportedly this information was kept secret and when the invasion did come the U.S. reacted as if it had been taken by surprise. (One American intelligence official, for whom this writer has high regard, totally discounts this "story, which floated around Germany at the time." In this view, it "probably originated as a Soviet disinformation effort.")

39 Eleanor Lansing Dulles, Berlin: The Wall is not Forever (Chapel Hill: University of North Carolina Press, 1967), p. 49.

certain restrictive measures, nothing like the Wall, of course."[40]
Later President *Kennedy* gave General *Maxwell D. Taylor* the job of reviewing the intelligence "to see if anything had been overlooked which should have warned us." According to his account: "There were fragmentary reports of the movement of engineer materials near Berlin, but nothing that suggested the construction of a wall in the city."[41]

The American Minister in Berlin on August 13, *E. Allan Lightner,* contends that "It was impossible for our G-2 (Military Intelligence) patrols in East Berlin or our Potsdam Mission to be all that well informed." For they "had no knowledge of what was being transported on the Autobahn from Leipzig to East Berlin." And this was the critical factor because "the barbed wire and materials needed for the building of the Wall, like the East German troops, were brought in from East Germany by a well-executed, surprise move during the night of August 12/13."[42]

There can be little doubt that the Western intelligence failure was affected by British and French intelligence scandals which took place in Berlin earlier. *Geoffrey McDermott,* British Minister in the city when the Wall went up, explains in his personal account of the period what happened to Allied intelligence because of the activities of *George Blake,* a Soviet double agent employed by MI 6 in Berlin from 1955-59. Allied intelligence, which a few years back had greatly flourished in the city, had taken a "hard knock" as a result of Blake's double dealing and treachery. It was a blow from which it took the Western intelligence community in Berlin a long time to recover.[43]

As *McDermott* points out, what is more surprising is that the West Berlin government's own information was not more complete. With relatives of inhabitants in the other part of the city, and more than the usual supply of agents and informers in Berlin, one might have expected the Senat to have gotten wind of the impending East German move. But it did not.

40 Interview with Allen Dulles, December 29, 1966, Washington, D.C.

41 Interview with General Maxwell Taylor, June 18, 1966, Washington, D.C.

42 Interview with E. Allan Lightner, February 7, 1967, Washington, D.C.

43 Geoffrey McDermott, Berlin: Success of a Mission? (New York: Harper & Row, 1963), p. 31. (One U.S. intelligence official with first-hand knowledge of the period has this to say: "If Blake caused the 'intelligence community' trouble, it was only the British community; no one else."

Nor did the West German press have any inkling of the imminent closing down of the border. In retrospect, the signs appear conclusive, but they were not seen as such at the time. As *Kurt L. Shell* writes in his comprehensive study of the crisis: "In no West Berlin newspaper was the possibility of a total control ... seriously discussed ... No one believed that the régime would go as far as to take the measures for a complete sealing off (of the Western Sectors)."[44] It was presumedly thought that *Ulbricht* would "recognize the significance of a channel which served to lessen the danger of a serious uprising as the more rebellious of his people fled to the West."[45] Then there was the credibility of the Allied guarantees that had to be considered, and it was assumed to be the desire of the communists to want to avoid any action which might be considered provocative.

Passing reference should be made to *Ulbricht's* often-quoted statement of June 15 about "a wall", some two months before the actual Wall went up. At that time, in response to a reporter's question about the refugee situation, he inadvertently spoke of a wall, although denying that he intended to build one.[46] Why wasn't his statement picked up? According to *John Ausland,* the man responsible for the Berlin Desk in the State Department during the week of August 12/13: "Officials were simply drowned by words and his response was lost in the background noise."[47]

Finally, there is the statement by *Oleg Penkovskiy,* the late Soviet defector, who maintained that he "learned about the Berlin closing (of the border) four days before the Soviet government actually closed it off."[48] If *Penkovskiy* knew of the prospective border closure on August 9 or 10, then — as one authority has observed — one might have expected the normally alert Allied intelligence agencies to have had "similar information somewhere

44 Kurt L. Shell, Bedrohung und Bewährung (Köln and Opladen: Westdeutscher Verlag, 1965), p. 30.

45 Eleanor L. Dulles, The Wall: A Tragedy in Three Acts (Columbia, S.C.: University of South Carolina Press, 1972), p. 59.

46 Pierre Galante, The Berlin Wall (Garden City, N.Y.: Doubleday, 1965), p. 9.

47 John Ausland, opus cit., p. 30.

48 Oleg Penkovskiy, The Penkovskiy Papers (New York: Avon Books, 1966), p. 242.

between the 10th and the 13th (of August)."[49] But the fact remains that while they expected the East Germans would take some step at the time to control the refugee flow, they did not know exactly what it would be. "No one," in the words of the American Commandant in Berlin, "expected a wall."[50]

It is easy to see why the myth persists that President *Kennedy* had been informed of communist intentions to close the East Berlin border and had agreed not to interfere. Otherwise, why would he have been so far away from Washington at such an obviously important time? And why would he have gone sailing immediately after being told of developments by his Secretary of State? There are answers to these questions: They have to do with miscalculation and lack of information. But it is unlikely that those who criticize the failure of the United States to act will ever be convinced. Nevertheless, the record is clear on this point for those who care to examine it closely: In the words of Secretary *Rusk,* the Western Allies were simply caught "by surprise" on August 13, 1961.[51]

Alternatives

The sealing of the East-West border in Berlin and the erection of the Wall were obviously difficult decisions for the Soviet leaders to make. It was an open admission of the bankruptcy of the East German régime. The flow of East German refugees had gone beyond the point of sheer embarrassment to the Soviets. If the serious loss of technical and professional manpower had continued much longer, it would have spelled economic and political disaster for the communist government.

In response to the East Berlin border closure, what could or should have been done? The most often discussed alternative after the Wall went up was the calling out of the Western garrisons to "knock down" the hastily built communist barriers.[52] As Minister

49 Eleanor L. Dulles, The Wall: A Tragedy in Three Acts (Columbia, S.C.: U. of South Carolina Press, 1972), p. 59.

50 Interview with General Watson, January 3, 1967, Washington, D.C.

51 Interview with Dean Rusk, August 14, 1969, Washington, D.C.

52 Former President Eisenhower was probably the most outspoken about this. As he told this writer in an interview on September 13, 1966 at

Lightner said later: "On August 13 the border construction could have been knocked down by jeeps or trucks."[53]

In the view of General *Lucius D. Clay,* hero of the Berlin "airlift" and President *Kennedy's* personal representative in the city following the erection of the Wall: "If the Allies had acted swiftly and authoritatively, ... the Russians would have backed down." But because "there was no immediate response from us, it became a fait accompli." Had General *Clay* been in the city at the time, he doubts the Wall would have gone up. For he "would have had our tanks driven back and forth in the city."[54]

But active Allied resistance involved serious risks. It was the evaluation of the Western Allied governments that the Soviet Union was determined to halt the flow of refugees, and that any attempt to use force to prevent the construction of the Wall "would have involved serious risk of war." Accordingly, it "was concluded that such a risk was unjustified."[55]

Subsequently, it has been suggested that had the Allies interfered with the border closure, barriers would merely have been placed a block or two inside East Berlin. And then had the West moved into the Soviet Sector, it would have been charged with an invasion. Since the Soviets could not possibly have allowed their Sector to be occupied, it is argued, they would have swung into action. And in all likelihood, there would have ensued a battle in which the Western forces, which were hopelessly outnumbered in Berlin, were bound to be defeated and forced to retreat to their Sector. At worst, there would have been a war.[56]

Despite the superiority of Soviet military strength, there was the consideration, taken seriously — perhaps too seriously — by

Gettysburg, Pennsylvania, the United States should have "knocked down" the barriers "to begin with" because "Berlin is technically a four-power controlled city with freedom of travel written into the agreements." (According to one knowledgeable U.S. official, who served under Eisenhower and Kennedy, this statement "does not fit with Ike's modus operandi, nor his behavior on Berlin while in office. He always avoided action.")

53 Interview with E. Allan Lightner, February 7, 1967, Washington, D.C.

54 Interview with General Lucius Clay, December 20, 1965, New York City.

55 Undated State Department paper entitled "United States Attitude on Closure of Berlin Border."

56 Geoffrey McDermott, opus cit., p. 34.

Western planners at the time, that an East German uprising such as had occurred on June 17, 1953, might take place. As *Lightner* has pointed out, it was thought at the time that any "signs of a Western military move might be misunderstood as a step to liberate the East Zone, which could instigate an uprising, which could end disastrously for the populace."[57]

Moreover, there was the question whether the United States could have persuaded the British and French to go along had it decided to intervene. According to Secretary *Rusk*: "It is doubtful whether the British and French would have gone along."[58] And since only seven miles of the twenty-eight-mile-long border in the city is tangent to the U.S. Sector, it would have been "inadvisable" for the Americans to go it alone.

No doubt one of the most important considerations for the lack of response on August 13 were previous precedents of American inaction. Although the U.S. had watched with pain as the Soviets crushed the spontaneous revolt in East Germany in June 1953 and again in Hungary in October 1956, it had not moved to intervene.

Western Reaction

During the early morning hours of August 13, the border closure was carried out swiftly and efficiently by East German police and troop units. By about 2 : 30 a.m., the entire East Berlin boundary had been sealed. The significance of the East German action was not immediately apparent to Western military headquarters in West Berlin. But the mere presence of so much communist power in and around Berlin led the Allied commanders to think in terms of tactical preparedness and the security of the Western Sectors. Accordingly, the three Allied garrisons were put on full combat alert and confined to their barracks. After all troops were told to stand by, the Commandants met with their staffs at ten o'clock at the Allied Kommandatura to discuss the explosive military situation. Since it was the American turn to be "in the chair" that month, Major General *Albert Watson*, II presided over the meeting.

57 Letter to the writer, March 13, 1970.
58 Interview with Dean Rusk, August 14, 1969, Washington, D.C.

One of the better accounts of this gathering is given by *Geoffrey McDermott,* British Minister and Deputy Commandant in Berlin at the time.[59] His report has been confirmed by the American Minister, *E. Allan Lightner.*[60] Talk ranged around the border activities along each of the three Sectors of West Berlin. Possible countermeasures, both local and further afield, were discussed in detail. But nothing conclusive was decided upon.

After about an hour had elapsed, Mayor *Brandt,* accompanied by his deputy, *Franz Amrehn,* was invited to join the Allied deliberations. As *McDermott* vividly recounts, *Brandt* "was grave but statesmanlike." And, contrary to some later accounts,[61] "never demanded any rash action from the protecting powers" nor reproached them "for lack of firmness."

The Commandants remained in the Kommandatura for the rest of the day, watching and waiting. Towards the late afternoon, it was agreed that they would make an official protest to the Soviet Commandant in East Berlin and recommend that the three Western governments do the same on a higher level. Telegrams asking for instructions were dispatched. Finally, a "resounding tripartite press release" was readied for public consumption. But at the last minute, the Commandants were informed by their governments not to release it.[62]

Shortly after 5 p.m. in Berlin (twelve noon in Washington), Secretary of State *Rusk* finally broke the silence which had enshrouded the nation's capital. The East German action, *Rusk* said, was a violation of the Four-Power status of Berlin and would be "the subject of vigorous protest through appropriate channels." But "available information," he said, "indicates that measures taken thus far are aimed at residents of East Berlin and East Germany, and not at the Allied position in West Berlin or access thereto."[63] By this statement *Rusk* indicated that there was no threat of Western counteraction nor any planned attempt by the United States to intervene.

59 Geoffrey McDermott, opus cit., pp. 32 - 33.

60 Interview with E. Allan Lightner, February 7, 1967, Washington, D.C.

61 See Jean Edward Smith, opus cit., pp. 273 - 274.

62 Letter to the writer from E. Allan Lightner, March 13, 1970.

63 U.S. Department of State, Berlin-1961 (Washington, D.C.: Government Printing Office, 1961), pp. 41 - 42.

The hours following the closing of the border were full of confusion and shock. No one knew whether or not this was the first step in a new Soviet offensive designed to remove the long-standing "bone in the throat" that the Soviets considered West Berlin to be. Since for a long time the West had expected much worse, a deep sigh of relief was made when it became evident that the East Germans did not intend (immediately) to infringe upon the vital Allied interests in West Berlin.

But from this point on, the situation grew progressively worse. Encouraged by the lack of Western response, the East Germans expanded their level of activity. Beginning at four a.m. Monday morning, all telephone and postal service with West Germany was severed. Later in the day, East German soldiers proceeded to close the Brandenburg Gate. The number of crossing points between East and West Berlin, which had been narrowed from eighty-one to thirteen the night before, was now reduced to twelve. And even at these entry and exit points, obstacles had been put into place to impede traffic.[64]

The next day, August 15, East German authorities went one step further. At one o'clock Tuesday morning it was announced that West Berlin vehicles would no longer be allowed to enter East Berlin without a special permit. This move was particularly significant, since it was a direct attack on Western rights. The original measures taken to seal the border had meticulously avoided any interference with traffic flowing from West to East.[65]

Later in the day, the formal Allied protest against the border closure on August 13 was finally delivered to the Soviet Commandant in East Berlin. On the following day, the Allied governments protested in Moscow. Given the considerable problems of inter-governmental co-ordination, this — in the view of one State Department official — was "a back-breaking performance."[66] But it was still much too slow.

64 Jean Edward Smith, opus cit., p. 279.
65 Ibid.
66 John C. Ausland, opus cit., p. 33.

As it became clear to Berliners that their "protecting powers" did not intend to actively resist the East German action, a feeling of betrayal set in. And morale plummeted. Dozens of posters appeared in Berlin protesting Allied inaction. The American President was singled out and condemned. A group of university students in Bonn sent him a black umbrella, reminiscent of *Neville Chamberlain* whose policy of appeasement had sold out Czechoslovakia in 1938. But Washington only slowly perceived the consequences of its policy.

As the week wore on, the shortcomings of Western policy became increasingly evident. By mid-week it was realized that August 13 had been a traumatic experience for Berliners. To counter the loss of confidence in the Western powers something had to be done. But what?

According to *John Ausland's* inside account: "The official position before August 13 was that the Allies would counter the division of the city with restrictions on travel by East Germans to NATO countries." Consideration would also be given to "restrictions on trade." But while the United States, Great Britain and France "were fairly united on travel restrictions, it took time to work out the details." And since restrictions on trade "would have been just as painful for the Allies as the East Germans," they were never agreed to.[67]

The turning point of the crisis for Washington came on Thursday, August 17, when *Edward R. Murrow,* the new Director of the U.S. Information Agency, visited the divided city on a world tour and took note of the deteriorating situation. A close friend of Kennedy, he cabled Washington that morale was "going to pot" in Berlin and predicted the total failure of administration policy unless rigorous action was taken.[68]

Also by this time a personal letter from Mayor *Brandt* had been received by *Kennedy*. In this highly unusual communication, the Mayor of West Berlin recommended a number of important steps the President should take to restore morale. Among other things,

---

67 John C. Ausland, opus cit., p. 31.
68 Jean Edward Smith, opus cit., p. 285.

he requested *Kennedy* to send a high-level official to Berlin as his representative and reinforce American troop strength in Berlin.[69]

Although *Kennedy* thought *Brandt* was "playing election politics" (the West German parliamentary election was just weeks away), he could not overlook the *Murrow* report. For it represented the first high-level account he had received from what could be considered an outside and objective source. Up to this time, communications from the Berlin Mission predicting dire consequences of the failure of administrative policy had been taken lightly, as coming from people "too closely involved to have a proper perspective."[70]

In response to the "crisis of confidence" in which he suddenly found himself, the President decided to approve two of *Brandt's* requests. First, as evidence of the seriousness with which he regarded the American commitment to Berlin, he decided to dispatch Vice President *Johnson* to the beleaguered city. Second, to bolster the faltering morale of local citizens he named General *Clay* — hero of the Berlin "airlift" — to accompany the Vice President. Finally, *Kennedy* directed Secretary *McNamara* to reinforce the Berlin garrison in an ultimate test of *Khrushchev's* intentions.

Troops to Berlin

The President's decision to send 1,500 additional troops to Berlin was not made easily. This contingency had been discussed earlier. But *Kennedy,* not wanting to provoke *Khrushchev* unnecessarily, was reluctant to approve this action. It was only at the urging of his advisers that he gave in.[71]

The generals maintained that access to the city had not yet been interfered with, and that we were well within our legal rights to send a convoy overland through the East German hinterland. The

69 The full text of Brandt's letter is published in Eleanor L. Dulles, The Wall: A Tragedy in Three Acts (Columbia, S.C.: University of South Carolina Press, 1972), Appendix II.

70 Hermann Zolling and Uwe Bahnsen, Kalter Winter im August (Oldenburg: Gerhard Stalling Verlag, 1967), p. 142.

71 Jean Edward Smith, opus cit., p. 287.

advantages of such a military move were twofold: Not only would the arrival of additional troops in Berlin go far to soothe the shattered nerves of the local population, but it would also be a way of testing communist intentions. If our men were halted or interfered with to any great extent, this would surely demonstrate that our right of free access was being tampered with, and we would then know exactly where we stood.

The President agreed that access had not yet been curtailed, but he had serious doubts about going too far. Therefore, before he decided, he carefully reviewed the possibility of airlifting American troops to Berlin. At the last moment, however, he desisted from this course of action and announced the movement of troops along the Helmstedt Autobahn in armored trucks. Apparently, with word already leaked out of an impending convoy movement, an "airlift" might seem like the United States was backing down.[72]

Never sure what to expect from the Russians who manned the Autobahn checkpoints and handled Allied movements, the President reviewed the military plan in great detail. Because army commanders did not want to withdraw troops from the West German border facing Warsaw Pact forces, the 1st Battle Group, 18th Infantry was chosen. Although these soldiers were stationed in Mannheim, nearly four hundred miles away from the East German entry point at Helmstedt, they were on the Autobahn and could proceed almost at once.

The route of march was to take the battle group from Mannheim to Frankfurt and Kassel by way of the West German Autobahn, and then past the Harz Mountains to Braunschweig. Its orders were to bivouac in Braunschweig for the night, and early on Sunday morning, August 20, to enter East Germany. Upon entering the German Democratic Republic, the trucks were to go in serials; this would enable them to move more easily and avoid the "accordion" action that could snarl a long line of vehicles. Also, if trouble developed, not all of them would be caught inside communist territory.

It was vital that the convoy arrive in West Berlin shortly after noon, Sunday, August 20. For at that time Vice President *Johnson*

72 Hugh Sidey, John F. Kennedy, President (New York: Crest Books, 1964), p. 222.

and General *Clay* were to be on hand to greet it. To boost the morale of the Berliners, the day was to be turned into a spectacle of American force and determination.

As the troop "train" crossed into East Germany as planned, the United States government was on an hair-trigger alert. Unlike the previous weekend, *Kennedy* decided to forego the pleasures of sun and water on Cape Cod and remained at his post. Perhaps reminded that General *Marshall* had a hard time explaining where he was on Pearl Harbor Day, he did not want to seek a declaration of war from Hyannis Port. As one White House staff member later recalled: "It was a much greater crisis than people know."[73]

But as the President's military advisers had predicted, the troop movement passed across East Germany unharmed. And shortly after one p.m., the leading elements of the 18th Infantry roared into West Berlin as expected. Vice President *Johnson,* General *Clay* and Mayor *Brandt,* as well as thousands upon thousands of enthusiastic Berliners, were there to greet them. And they stayed until the last vehicle had safely cleared the Soviet checkpoint just outside Berlin.

It was near 8 p.m. in Washington when the final group of soldiers went by the checkpoint. And great sighs of relief went up in the White House. The situation now seemed under control and the threat to West Berlin contained. But though the President had redeemed himself, his gesture did not end the continuing Berlin crisis.

73 Hugh Sidey, opus cit., p. 225.

Chapter II

A NEW ERA IN EAST-WEST RELATIONS

The erection of the Berlin Wall represented a decisive turning point in East-West German relations as well as between those of the Soviet Union and the Western Allies. For the West German government, the existence of the "Wall" meant the abandonment of the idea of solving the German problem through the collapse of communist rule in East Germany and the reconstitution of some form of a united German state. Priority was now given to the policy of establishing contacts, negotiations and attempts on a wide front to re-open interaction between the two German social systems and diminish tensions between them. As *Egon Bahr,* the "chief architect" of *Willy Brandt's* Ostpolitik,[1] explained some nine years later:

(On August 13, 1961) it became clear in the most brutal way, where the border lies between east and west, and that no one could reach beyond the wall. ...the question was: if you cannot do away with the wall... then one must make an attempt despite the wall so that the people on one side could visit again their relatives on the other side. In a nutshell, the attempt was to come to terms with the realities despite the realities.[2]

This rethinking of West Germany's Deutschlandpolitik, which began in 1961, culminated in major policy changes under the "grand coalition" government of Christian and Social Democrats headed by *Kurt-Georg Kiesinger,* 1966 - 69. But it received its greatest impetus under the SPD—FDP régime of Chancellor *Willy*

---

1 For an excellent analysis of Bahr's contribution to Ostpolitik see Walter F. Hahn, "West Germany's Ostpolitik: The Grand Design of Egon Bahr," Orbis, Vol. 16, No. 4 (Winter, 1973), pp. 859-880.

2 Statement recorded in a TV interview on August 3, 1970. See Kommentarübersicht (Bonn: Federal Press and Information Office, August 4, 1970).

U.S. Military Police escort American diplomatic vehicle
returning from East Berlin, October 27. 1961.

Egon Bahr (FRG) greets his GDR negotiating partner Michael Kohl at Schönefeld Airport after arriving in East Berlin on West German airplane, December 21, 1972.

Brandt (1969-74), which also set about to improve relations with the Soviet Union and the countries of Eastern Europe.[3]

It is perhaps ironic that the prerequisite for East German success remains its worst humiliation. But it cannot be disputed that the Wall — generally regarded as an admission of failure in the West — created the essential conditions for economic and political stability in the former Soviet Occupation Zone. Most importantly, it closed the last escape hatch, thus effectively damming a ruinous human hemmorhage.

But if the construction of a state frontier between East and West Berlin stabilized the work force of the German Democratic Republic, it also served to bolster a tottering regime, which could now bring dissident elements within its territory under effective control. Moreover, it could now concentrate on building an economy rivaling in some ways that of West Germany. Thus, in less than ten years, the East German government could boast that the GDR had become the world's tenth most important industrial country.[4] (This achievement is even more impressive when it is realized that it was accomplished without a Marshall Plan while at the same time the GDR suffered from "disguised reparations" in the form of an adverse trade relationship with the Soviet Union!)

As far as the East German attitude towards West Berlin is concerned, the building of the Wall had important policy ramifications. Essentially, it led the German Democratic Republic to regard the existence of a Western outpost in its territory as no longer posing a direct threat to its rule. However, if the GDR — with the passing of time — outwardly seemed to accept the fact of West Berlin's existence, this did not mean of course that it was satisfied with the status quo.

After the 1961-62 phase of the Berlin crisis, communist pressure on the isolated city was largely of East German design and aimed at Bonn. Unlike earlier Soviet attempts, which for the most part represented unilateral efforts to alter the legal basis for Western rights in the divided city, East German demonstrations of

3 For an informative and thorough study of the evolution of West Germany's relations with the GDR in the post-Wall period see Peter C. Ludz et al, Deutschlands Doppelte Zukunft: Bundesrepublik und die DDR in der Welt von Morgen (Munich: R. Oldenbourg Verlag, 1974).

4 For details see Welles Hangen, "New Perspectives Behind the Wall," Foreign Affairs, Vol. 45, No. 1 (October, 1966), pp. 135-147.

West Berlin's vulnerability after 1963 appear directed at undermining public morale, eroding the Federal Republic's ties with the divided city and gaining de facto recognition of the GDR's claim to administer certain West Berlin functions. In this way, the GDR tried to shift confrontation from the arena of Soviet-Allied relations to that of Soviet-East German and Soviet-West German relations.[5]

For the Western powers — particularly the United States, — the erection of the Wall signified the need to attempt to establish a new relationship with the USSR. This was done by singling out areas of common concern where both sides could cooperate in the interest of world stability. First pressed by President *Kennedy* in the context of a "strategy for peace," this policy of "change through rapprochement" was carried further by President *Johnson* under the rubric of "bridge building" and "peaceful engagement" (until it was abruptly sidetracked by the Soviet invasion of Czechoslovakia in August 1968) and received its decisive impetus with President *Nixon* who, after taking office in January 1969, issued his famous call for the beginning of an "era of negotiation."

The American Initiative

In assessing the world scene in early 1969, the President — with the support of his influential Special Assistant for International Security Affairs (and later Secretary of State) *Henry Kissinger* — concluded that the key to peace and stability continued to lie in Europe and that the cornerstone of peace there would have to be laid in Berlin. Consequently, some five weeks after his inauguration, he decided to back up his words with a trip to Western Europe and a demonstrative visit to the isolated city on his first trip abroad as President.

Nixon went to Berlin with the expressed purpose of showing as concretely as possible the firmness of the American commitment to that troubled city. But he also assigned another equally important task to his first official visit to Berlin. Namely, that as

5 See Lawrence L. Whetten, "The Role of East Germany in West German-Soviet Relations," The World Today, Vol. 25, No. 12 (December, 1969), p. 515.

far as Europe was concerned, the transformation of an "era of confrontation" to an "era of negotiation" could only start there. For no matter how successful a dialogue in other areas might prove to be, talks could have no real result until the nagging tensions surrounding the divided city were somehow eased.[6]

Flying into Berlin on February 27, the President was enthusiastically greeted by hundreds of thousands of West Berliners. They hurled flowers and chanted "Ha-Ho-Hey — Nixon ist O.K." Although *Nixon's* visit had been threatened with obstructions, they never materialized. (Massive police forces were needed, however, to shield the presidential cavalcade from demonstrators around the city.)

It was perhaps inevitable that President *Nixon's* trip to Berlin would be compared and contrasted with that made by *John F. Kennedy* approximately six years earlier. Like President *Kennedy, Nixon* solemnly reaffirmed American pledges of support to an ever jittery population. And similar to the "new frontiersman" who declared "Ich bin ein Berliner" in 1963, he said "All the people of the world are truly Berliners" in the sense they are striving for freedom and peace. However, unlike *Kennedy,* who was moved to comment that Berlin showed it was impossible to "work with the Communists" (a statement he later came to regret), *Nixon* carefully balanced his statements of support with a plea for negotiations to reduce tensions in Germany and elsewhere. At the same time, he never mentioned communism or communists and even deleted a prepared reference to "adversaries" from one speech.[7]

"No one should doubt the determination of the United States to live up to its obligations," President *Nixon* said shortly after peering across the Wall. But he quickly added: "The question before the world is not whether we shall rise to the challenge of defending Berlin — we have already demonstrated that we shall. The question now is how best to end the challenge and clear the way for a peaceful solution to the problem of a divided Germany."[8]

6 For more detailed analysis see Kenneth Rush, "The Berlin Agreement: An Assessment," The Atlantic Community Quarterly, Vol. 10, No. 1 (1972), pp. 55-57.

7 The New York Times, February 28, 1969.

8 Speech before workers at the Siemens plant in West Berlin, February 27, 1969.

A Crisis over Berlin

President *Nixon's* visit to Berlin coincided with the election (actually one week later) of the West German Bundespräsident in the city and a major crisis.[9] Only two weeks earlier, the USSR and the GDR had charged that the meeting was "illegal" and a "deliberate provocation."[10] Subsequently, they proceeded to show their displeasure with the event by launching a carefully calibrated "war of nerves" over the city.

In the main, the communist protest took the form of a propaganda campaign against West German activities in Berlin, backed up by a series of measures designed to impede overland travel.[11] Beginning on February 15, the East Germans and Russians instituted a travel ban on select groups of individuals using the access lanes (e.g., delegates to the Federal electoral body and off-duty West German army personnel). At the same time, they increased the time required for processing ordinary civilian traffic and made unusually thorough checks of all trucks carrying shipments from West Berlin to West Germany. Several times the communists rejected various types of merchandise, including some alleged war materials.[12] And on at least one occasion they temporarily closed

9 In West Germany, the Federal President is elected by a joint parliamentary body called the Federal Assembly. This body is specially convened for the occasion and consists of all the members of the Bundestag, the lower house of parliament, and an equal number of members chosen by the state diets in accordance with the proportional strength of their political parties.

10 See The New York Times, February 13, 1969. It should be pointed out here that the election in 1969 of the West German President in West Berlin was not without precedent. In fact, with the exception of the first time, such elections always took place there every five years without prompting any major communist reprisals against Bonn's use of the city as a symbolic capital: in 1954, 1959 and 1964. Interestingly, although the GDR initially welcomed the decision to hold the presidential election in Berlin in 1954, East Germany and the USSR now claimed the meeting violated the quadripartite status of the city.

11 Ostensibly, this step was taken to demonstrate that Berlin's vital traffic links with the West exist only with GDR and Russian consent. On this point refer to Neues Deutschland, February 16, 1969.

12 As one of the pretexts for interfering with traffic on the Autobahn, the Soviets and East Germans charged that Western vehicles were being used to transport illegally war materials from factories in West Berlin. (Under Berlin's demilitarized status, the production, storage and delivery of

down the Berlin-Helmstedt Autobahn, the main highway linking the city with the West.[13]

In the view of one knowledgeable student of Soviet and East German behavior, "the distinguishing characteristics" of this crisis over Berlin were "Moscow's timidity, Pankow's assertiveness and Bonn's self-confidence."[14] On the one hand, it appeared as if the Kremlin really wanted to avoid a confrontation over Berlin at this time. On the other, it seemed equally clear that East Germany's communist party leader *Walter Ulbricht,* who a decade earlier said it was worth "risking a conflict" to grab West Berlin, and in 1968 was one of the chief architects of the anti-Czechoslovakian coalition, was determined to force Moscow's hand by increasing its propaganda attack on West German activities in Berlin.

As early as January, Soviet diplomats had informed their Western counterparts that the Kremlin did not desire a confrontation in Berlin and that the presidential election there was not a significant matter. Evidently, the Russians adopted this unusual stance so as not to jeopardize the highlevel SALT talks which were just beginning to take shape.[15] In any case, the USSR was careful

military goods and armaments is forbidden.) These measures restricting access, then, were taken to "effectively counter" this alleged traffic. Although there is little doubt that the communist charge was in the main unfounded, it is noteworthy that following the crisis the business manager of a major West Berlin firm resigned in face of a government investigation of the allegation. For details see The New York Times, March 13, 1969.

13 U.S. Mission (Berlin), Berlin Accessways, Transportation, Communications and Utilities (Berlin: Economic Section, 1970), p. 11.

14 Lawrence L. Whetten, op. cit., p. 515. One Soviet expert has this to add: "In the context of this episode, you should point out to your readers that at the end of January 1969, the GDR and the USSR signed an agreement on military coordination which was never published but which led to General Hoffmann going to Moscow the end of February and remaining there for a full month together with the Bulgarien Defense Minister. The Defense Minister's departure in the midst of the crisis was obviously a signal that the worst wasn't expected. At the same time, it implied that the Soviets had agreed to back GDR protests on the Federal elections in return for GDR cooperation in a Warsaw Pact military integration move."

15 On the day of Nixon's inauguration (January 20, 1969), the Soviet Union offered to renew discussions with the U.S. on the limitation of strategic arms. In that this proposal came less than six months after the Russian invasion of Czechoslovakia, it was important and represented one of the major preliminary steps in the effort to transform confrontation into co-operation.

throughout the crisis to limit the arena of conflict while it kept up a barrage of signals indicating it wanted to avoid a military showdown.

A few days before the West German presidential election was held in Berlin, the Soviets made a last-minute bid to head off the steadily mounting crisis. They offered to mediate a major concession from the GDR in exchange for a shift in the election away from the isolated city.[16] Essentially, the Russian quid pro quo involved obtaining passes from East German authorities allowing West Berliners to visit relatives in East Berlin for the first time in three years.[17]

This proposal was conveyed by Moscow Ambassador in Bonn, *Semyon K. Tsarapkin,* who flew to Stuttgart on February 23 to confer with Chancellor *Kiesinger* near his weekend retreat. Unfortunately, nothing ever came of the Soviet initiative because the USSR and East Germany were not prepared to extend any pass arrangement beyond the immediate Easter period. And this concession was not enough for the West German side to agree to an eleventh-hour change of the election site.[18]

President *Nixon's* visit to Berlin on the eve of the last major crisis over the city (and his speeches there) represented the first significant move toward discussions with the Soviets on improving conditions in and around Berlin. But at the time he was not at all convinced his initiative would pay off.

16 According to an East European source, this apparent shift in Russian tactics reflected a division in the 11-man Politbüro, the ruling body of the Soviet communist party. The source, who claimed he was quoting an official of the Soviet party Secretariat who recently visited his capital, said it was significant that Russian leaders who had supported a conciliatory policy on Berlin in Presidium meetings were the same ones who pleaded against the invasion of Czechoslovakia. The source named Premier Aleksei N. Kosygin and Aleksandr N. Shelepin as "doves" on Czechoslovakia and now on Berlin. Mikhail A. Suslov, ideological specialist in the Politbüro, was said to have abstained on both occasions. The New York Times, March 4, 1969.

17 During the 1960s four pass agreements (in 1963, 1964, 1965 and 1966) were concluded between the West Berlin Senat and GDR officials enabling West Berliners to visit relatives in East Berlin for short periods. Altogether, about 5.5 million people took advantage of these arrangements. But due to the problems of protocol and "unacceptable demands" no further pass agreements could be reached after June 1966.

18 The New York Times, February 25, 1969.

Generally, he believed — as he later told Chancellor *Kiesinger* in Bonn during a talk designed to sort out their long-term objectives in Europe — that Moscow's desire for agreement on the projected SALT talks would enable him to extract concessions in the Middle East and Vietnam. But whether the Russians were ready to talk productively about the thorny Berlin problem was another matter. The city involved serious questions that heretofore had defied all attempts at solving. Nevertheless, the West German leader encouraged *Nixon* to include Berlin on his agenda for negotiations with the USSR while informing him that the Federal Republic would undertake its own initiatives to improve relations with Eastern Europe.[19]

Sino-Soviet Conflict on the Ussuri

But not all momentum for improving East-West relations was provided by the decisive efforts of President *Nixon* and Chancellor *Kiesinger*. Worsening relations between the Soviet Union and China also played a crucial role.

Beginning in March 1969, the first reports of armed clashes between Soviet and Chinese troops along the disputed Ussuri River boundary received headline attention in the Western press.[20] Unlike previous occurrences of this kind, which were never published by either side, this time both Russia and China embarked on a highly publicized propaganda campaign.[21] This unprecedented move indicated a serious deterioration in Sino-Soviet relations, just as the People's Republic was emerging from the excesses of the "Cultural Revolution". And it caused nervous observers in the U.S. and Europe to fear a Soviet invasion of China or a nuclear attack against it.

19 Die Welt, February 27, 1969.

20 As far as is known in the West, these incidents involved two brief but serious battles on Damansky (Chenpao in Chinese) Island in the Ussuri River. One of the best short treatments of the border dispute can be found in Thomas W. Robinson, "The Sino-Soviet Border Dispute: Background, Development, and the March 1969 Clashes," American Political Science Review, Vol. 66 (1972), pp. 1175-1202. See also Tai Sung An, The Sino-Soviet Territorial Dispute (Philadelphia: Westminster Press, 1973).

21 The major documents on the border dispute can be found in Studies in Comparative Communism, Vol. II (1969), pp. 149-382.

Following the American initiative on Berlin and Russian border clashes with China, the Kremlin embarked on an "agonized appraisal" of its European policy. There are several reasons for this. First, Moscow appears to have been impressed by *Nixon's* unwillingness (unlike the *Johnson* administration) to draw a line between the debate on disarmament and discussion with the Soviet government of general East-West problems. And since Russian leaders were extremely interested in cooperation with the United States on matters of armaments' controls, they apparently felt bound to meet the American President half-way.[22]

Second, the *Brezhnev-Kosygin* régime was probably fearful of a two-front confrontation in both Asia and Europe.[23] The clashes with China on its Far Eastern boundary had made the Soviet leadership acutely aware of its vulnerability in that part of the world. And until differences with the People's Republic were successfully resolved, the USSR may have wanted to secure its Western flank in case of real trouble in the East with the People's Republic. It should be recalled that at the time of the *Molotov-Ribbentrop* Pact in August 1939 the Soviet Union faced a similar threat from Japan along its Eastern border.

Lastly, Moscow was in dire need of Western technology.[24] Although this factor is frequently exaggerated in influencing the Kremlin to change its policy, there is little doubt that it was a consideration. Ever since the early 1960s, the USSR (and for that matter its East European allies as well) had been suffering major economic problems. This perplexing situation led Soviet leaders to experiment with various types of economic reform. But as things turned out, these initiatives were not enough to overcome poor harvests, the declining rate of Soviet industrial growth and other internal domestic difficulties.

As more than one Kremlinologist has pointed out, it is fortunate from Moscow's point of view that its "agonized reappraisal" of foreign policy coincided with that in the West. Thus, its need to lower the level of tensions in the world was no

22 For one of the best studies on the SALT and Kiesinger's linkage theory see John Newhouse, Cold Dawn (New York: Holt, Rinehart and Winston, 1973).

23 Refer to Roger E. Kanet, "The Soviet Union and China: Is War Inevitable?," Current History, Vol. 65, No. 386 (October, 1973), p. 148.

24 See Adam B. Ulam, op. cit., p. 728.

greater than that felt in Washington and some of the other European capitals.

In any case, it is apparent that the aforementioned considerations led the Kremlin to become more tractable and to seek a temporary accommodation with the United States and Western Europe in early 1969. Specifically, it was led to

(1) call for a European security conference;

(2) modify its attitude towards the Federal Republic; and

(3) agree to talks about the prickly Berlin issue.

All three of these elements became key aspects of Moscow's new "peace offensive."

Proposal for a European Security Conference

The Soviets broached their proposal for a conference on European security at a meeting of the Political Consultative Committee of the Warsaw Treaty Organization held in Budapest on March 17, 1969.[25] Although this was not the first time Moscow had called for such a convocation,[26] the context was new and the priority it was given seemed fresh. In the beginning, the Kremlin made no effort to go into details. But in the so-called Budapest Appeal three "basic prerequisites" of European security were listed. These were:

25 For details and analysis see Department of State, "Conference on Security and Cooperation in Europe," Current Foreign Policy (Washington, D.C.: U.S. Government Printing Office, 1972).

26 At various times previous to 1969 the idea of an all-European security system had been specially stressed by Soviet leaders only to retreat into the background of fast-moving international events. Following World War II, the first major enthusiasm for holding a European security conference came in February 1954. At that time, the idea to set up an all-European system of collective security was introduced by Vyacheslav M. Molotov at the conference of the Big Four Foreign Ministers. Later, the proposal was expanded to include U.S. participation. Nothing ever came of this trial balloon, however, because Western statesmen — particularly American — viewed it as another attempt to block West German participation in NATO via the West European Union (WEU), then still in the early stages of discussion. — For an excellent brief analysis of the history of Soviet proposals in this regard see Boris Meissner, "The Soviet Union and Collective Security," Aussenpolitik, English ed., Vol. 21 (Summer, 1970), pp. 272-284.

the inviolability of the existing boundaries in Europe, including the "Oder-Neisse boundary and the border between the German Democratic Republic" and the Federal Republic;

"recognition of the existence of the German Democratic Republic and the Federal Republic"; and

renunciation by Bonn of the possession of nuclear weapons in any form.

Fulfillment of these basic conditions was said to permit all-European cooperation "in great projects" on economic and environmental matters.[27]

In the main, the Warsaw Pact statement was conciliatory in tone. And, of particular importance, it omitted the anti-German polemics that had characterized earlier pronouncements on this subject. Nevertheless, it did not mention U.S. participation in the negotiations and thus seriously alienated the American government.

Washington's initial reaction (and some of its Allies) was to treat the Warsaw Pact communiqué with great coolness. For the most part, these quarters suspected that the idea of a European security conference was merely a Soviet ploy to effect the ratification of a permanent division of Europe and/or gain Western acquiescence in the *Brezhnev* Doctrine of limited state sovereignty for socialist states.[28]

That American reluctance to respond favorably to the Warsaw Pact offer was eventually overcome was due in no small part to the lobbying efforts of *Willy Brandt,* then Foreign Minister in West Germany's "Grand Coalition" government. During the twentieth anniversary meeting of NATO in April 1969 he pointed out it had long been realized within the Atlantic Alliance that its military task of protecting members from aggression should be coupled with equally important active endeavors to reduce tension. Furthermore, he argued, it would be a mistake for the West to pursue détente on a selective basis while the USSR was trying to dispel

---

27 For the text of the Warsaw Pact communiqué see Europa-Archiv, Vol. 24, Documents (1969), pp. 151-153.

28 As late as December 1969, Secretary of State William P. Rogers denigrated the idea of a European security conference and Soviet motives. Before the Belgo-American Association in Brussels, he said the proposal was based on a "nebulous and imprecise agenda" and that it failed to deal with fundamental political questions. See The Washington Post, December 7, 1969.

unpleasant memories of the Czechoslovakian invasion by conciliatory gestures towards Western Europe.[29]

In a communiqué released upon the termination of the NATO meeting, Western Ministers offered to explore with the Soviet Union and other East European states those "concrete issues" which best lent themselves to fruitful negotiation. But they insisted that the United States and Canada, as well as the European states, should take part in any discussions. Thus, in this way, there began a kind of dialogue of communiqués between NATO and the Warsaw Pact on the timing and content of the European security conference.

Soviet Agreement to Talk on Berlin

If President *Nixon's* speeches in Berlin in February 1969 may be taken as a desire of the United States to end tensions in Berlin and open a dialogue with the Kremlin on resolving some of the problems of the isolated city, then the speech by Soviet Foreign Minister *Andrei Gromyko* before the Supreme Soviet five months later represents Moscow's response.[30] This speech is important because as well as indicating the first real sign of Soviet willingness to negotiate on Berlin it presented the first concrete evidence of the stern position the USSR would take later in the quadripartite talks. In general, *Gromyko's* speech of July 10 reflected a favorable reaction on the part of the Kremlin to the President's initiative but gave it a new twist.

Gromyko suggested "an exchange of opinions" with the three Western powers on "how to prevent complications on West Berlin now and in the future." But he quickly added that "their approach to this question" must "take into account the interest of European security." The Soviet Foreign Minister went on to say that any such talks, as far as Moscow was concerned, would not "allow anything to impinge" on its own interests or "the legitimate interests" of the GDR or to "violate the special status of West Berlin."

Gromyko's speech was greeted with mixed emotions in the East as well as in the West. For their part, the Chinese saw it as another Soviet attempt to secure its Western flank so as to be free to move

29 Die Welt, April 11, 1969.
30 For the text see Pravda, July 11, 1969.

against the People's Republic in the East. In a scathing attack in The Peking Review,[31] the Chinese charged that "the Soviet revisionist chieftains" are up to "more dirty deals" with the United States against China. Moreover, it lambasted the USSR for being "ready to further sacrifice the interests" of East Germany and to "make a deal" on West Berlin "or even on the question of Germany as a whole."

In the West, a much less negative attitude prevailed. For the most part, Western public opinion warmly welcomed Soviet willingness to discuss the Berlin problem. But this enthusiasm was not at all shared by officials in Washington, Paris and London. For the most part, they were sceptical of the proposed talks. This point is worth stressing here in view of the general state of euphoria which existed in Western and Eastern Europe following the successful outcome of the Berlin negotiations.

Many of the "old German hands" — like those in the Departments of State and Defense and CIA had survived one or more Berlin crises and the frantic attempts of the Western Three to negotiate their way out of them. And it was these officials, in particular, who mostly had negative things to say about the chances of opening a constructive dialogue with Moscow. To them, *Gromyko's* speech merely reflected the old Soviet desire to discuss only West Berlin. Nothing was said about Four-Power responsibility for all of the city. "What's mine is mine, what's yours is negotiable" is the way they characterized this bargaining tactic.[32]

Not atypical in this respect was the attitude held by former Secretary of State *Dean Rusk. Rusk,* as it may be recalled, although considered a "hawk" on Vietnam, took a much less hard line in the *Kennedy* administration when it came to the divided city. Moreover, he possessed a great deal of personal negotiating experience with the Russians on Berlin, having participated in two years of long, drawn-out bargaining sessions with them during the 1961-62 phase of the Berlin crisis. Perhaps influenced by this unpleasant memory, *Rusk* warned this writer in a personal interview on August 13, 1969 that the forthcoming Four-Power negotiations could serve no useful purpose because the Soviets were not about to agree on a solution of the Berlin problem.

31 September 1969 edition.
32 This is a reference to President Kennedy's speech of July 25, 1961.

60

The Western powers responded to *Gromyko's* trial balloon in early August, shortly after President *Nixon's* dramatic visit to Rumania. Although highly sceptical of Soviet intentions, they agreed among themselves to first explore Russian flexibility before proposing formal negotiations. Consequently, in identical notes, they suggested on August 6-7, 1969 a more detailed exchange of opinions on the Berlin question.

The Western notes, like subsequent correspondence from the Soviet Union, have not been made public. Nevertheless, the general thrust of their contents in known. In the main, at this early stage, the Allies were concerned with the resolution of the long-standing problem of access — particularly the lack of written guarantees regarding surface transit. And they set about to feel out the USSR on this crucial issue. Other matters for discussion reportedly concerned methods by which future crises over the city could be avoided and the initiation of talks between representatives of the two Germanies on matters of mutual interest — specifically transit and postal questions. In regard to this last point, the Western Three were said to have expressed the view that Moscow should encourage its East German ally to sit down at the table with the Federal Republic but that these inner-German negotiations should take place within the framework of Four-Power responsibility for Germany and Berlin.[33]

The Soviet Union answered the West in a note, dated September 12, 1969. Generally, its contents paralleled the ambiguous statement about Berlin made by *Gromyko* on July 10 before the Soviet "parliament." In this note, Moscow reiterated its familiar preconditions for relaxing tensions in Central Europe. Briefly, these required the West to take into account "the facts" of European reality. According to the Kremlin, these were the inviolability of existing boundaries, the legitimate interests of the German Democratic Republic and the special status of West Berlin as a Four-Power responsibility.[34] Although a close scrutiny of the Russian note reveals it offered little that was new, its tone nevertheless was encouraging. For the first time since 1955, the Soviets were willing to discuss Berlin in a peaceful atmosphere.

33 Die Welt, August 8, 1969.

34 Lawrence L. Whetten, "The Role of East Germany in West German-Soviet relations," The World Today, Vol. 25, No. 12 (December, 1969), p. 517.

A Change of Government in Bonn

While Britain, France and the United States proceeded to formulate their response to the Soviet note on Berlin, crucial parliamentary elections were held in September in West Germany. The result marked something of a watershed in postwar German history. For the elections finally retired the Christian Democratic Union/Christian Social Union (CDU/CSU) as a governing party of twenty years standing.[35]

In this unprecedented electoral upset, the CDU/CSU bloc won a plurality but not a majority of the seats in the Bundestag, the important lower house of parliament. (The Christian Democrats obtained 46.1 per cent of the popular vote, followed by the Social Democrats with 42.7 per cent and the Free Democrats with 5.8 per cent.) This surprising development enabled the Social Democratic (SPD) and the Free Democratic Party (FDP) — both of which received fewer seats than the Christian Democratic and Christian Social Union parties — to form a coalition giving them a narrow, twelve-seat majority.

Both in West Germany and abroad, the SPD/FDP victory was viewed as a popular mandate for German Ostpolitik initiatives. Since December 1966, the Social Democrats had served as the junior partner in a government coalition dominated by the CDU/CSU bloc. Although this alliance had taken a number of important steps to improve relations with the countries of East Europe and the Soviet Union, Chancellor *Kiesinger* (CDU) and *Franz-Josef Strauss* (CSU) were strongly opposed to recognition of the German Democratic Republic and acceptance of the Oder-Neisse-line and the inviolability of European boundaries. As a consequence, the 1969 election campaign — fought between members of a coalition whose cooperation hardly concealed deep differences of

35 It was, of course, not the destribution of votes that was responsible for bringing Brandt to power but the decision of the FDP, under the leadership of Walter Scheel, to form for the first time a governing coalition with the SPD.

Technically, of course, the CDU and the CSU represent two entirely different parties. In order to maximize their numerical strength, however, the CDU and its Bavarian affiliate the CSU have constituted a single caucus in the Bundestag since 1949. This strategy has made the coalition the largest parliamentary party in the lower house with the right, or at least the votes, to propose the president of the chamber until 1972.

opinion — was more bitterly contested than any before in the history of the FRG.

Major credit for developing Bonn's "policy towards the East" during the years of the "Grand Coalition," of course, goes to *Willy Brandt*.[36] Between 1966 and 1969, he served as Foreign Minister and Vice Chancellor in *Kiesinger's* government. Before that the enterprising leader of the Social Democrats had been Governing Mayor of West Berlin (1957-66). Upon assuming the Chancellorship of a new coalition (SPD/FDP) government in the fall of 1969, *Brandt* immediately tackled the objectives of his Ostpolitik with a dispatch borne of years of observing the ups and downs of East-West relations.

An East German fait accompli

During the hard-fought West German election campaign in September the GDR régime agreed to talk with Federal authorities about long-standing postal, telecommunications' and railway problems. This decision, which was seen as part of the communist response to Allied notes of August 6 and 7, was warmly greeted in Bonn. But it was soon followed up by an East German fait accompli.

Coincidental with the staging of parliamentary elections in the FRG, the East German government chose to accord full voting rights to East Berlin deputies in the Volkskammer, the GDR's "parliament." (The communist action, however, did not eliminate the special status of East Berlin delegates, who are not elected directly — but are appointed by the local "parliament.") Ostensibly, this very provocative move was taken to provide ratification by all East German representatives of the nuclear non-proliferation treaty. But in fact, it presented the occupying powers in West Berlin with an accomplished fact that increased East Berlin's identification with the GDR. Heretofore, neither East nor

36 Later former Chancellor Kiesinger claimed in a personal interview with this writer on June 26, 1975 major credit for the formulation and implementation of West·Germany's Ostpolitik. Although he regrets he didn't make this clearer at the time, Kiesinger insists that Brandt and he "were united on all aspects of policy. We were so close in fact," he says "that not once during those years did Brandt disagree in public." Had Brandt disagreed "that would have led to a serious row in the Cabinet." See Honoré M. Catudal, "Kiesinger Recalls his Coalition's Successes, Failures," St. John's Magazine, Vol. 14, No. 1 (Summer, 1974), p. 11.

West Berlin delegates possessed such rights in their respective parliaments.[37]

Speculation immediately focused on the possible motive behind the GDR's dramatic gesture. Some West German editorials argued that the move was probably inspired by Moscow. According to this view, the Kremlin sought to provide the SPD with an addition to its slim parliamentary majority in Bonn.

If indeed this was the reason for the East German maneuver,[38] it did not work. True, the Mayor of West Berlin immediately petitioned the Allies for similar rights for the twenty-two West Berlin deputies in the Bundestag (thereby gaining thirteen additional votes in the lower house for the SPD.) But this was rejected by the Allies on the grounds it would complicate settlement of Berlin's status. Legal considerations aside, the Western Three were also apprehensive about appearing to favor one German political party over another in a crucial election year.

The Way is Cleared for Talks on Berlin

One month following the election outcome in West Germany, considerable diplomatic movement began to take place between East and West. Bonn was the first to lead off. On November 11, the Federal Republic's newly appointed Foreign Minister *Walter Scheel* (now Bundespräsident) announced his government would shortly initiate talks with the USSR concerning an agreement on the mutual renunciation of force. This statement was followed five days later (on November 16) by a formal proposal to the Soviet

37 This unusual situation arose out of the legal tangle concerning Berlin's Four-Power status. Because the Western powers do not consider West Berlin to be legally part of West Germany, they have not permitted the city's twenty-two members of the Bundestag (indirectly elected by the Berlin assembly rather than directly by the people as is common elsewhere in the FRG) to exercise full voting rights in the lower house of parliament. Almost as anxious at times as the West to observe the formalities of Berlin's Four-Power status, the Soviet Union until 1969 did not allow East Berlin members of the Volkskammer to possess full voting rights.

38 Others saw the East German move as an attempt by the GDR to achieve a major démarche against the Kremlin. See Frankfurter Allgemeine Zeitung and Neue Rhein Zeitung, October 7, 1969; Handelsblatt and Stuttgarter Zeitung, October 1, 1969; and Die Zeit, October 10, 1969.

régime. At that time, the West German leadership declared its hope that negotiations with Moscow would coincide with the holding of Four-Power discussions on Berlin. For its part, Washington announced on November 17, 1969 the start of the long-delayed SALT talks with the Soviet Union in Helsinki.

The following month, consultations among the Allies and West Germany now complete, the Western governments delivered their answer to the Soviet aide-mémoire of September 12, 1969. In their note, dated December 16, the Allies outlined a detailed proposal for specific negotiations with the Kremlin on Berlin. Discussions on the basis of inter-Allied agreements on the whole of "Greater Berlin" were requested "with the aim of improving the situation with regard to Berlin and free access to the city."[39] It was suggested that these talks could be held alternately between the two parts of Berlin. However, the Western Three stressed that they should take place "at an early date."

Details of the Allied note still remain secret. But on the same day the note was handed over to Soviet officials, American spokesmen in Washington let it be known that the Western proposal made clear that the West was not prepared to negotiate over the status of Berlin. (This was a rebuff to Soviet demands that negotiations take place over West Berlin.) These officials said only "practical" matters were involved.[40]

Altogether, five points for discussion were suggested. These specific topics dealt with such problems as
(1) the lack of an access guarantee for non-Allied surface traffic,
(2) the need for regular simplified crossing of the Berlin Wall,
(3) the restoration of telephone service between East and West Berlin, the easing of postal and transportation restrictions and
(4) the removal of discriminatory treatment of the economy of the Western Sectors by the Soviet Union, the GDR and certain East European nations.[41]
Improvements in these areas, it was said, would increase the probability of the convening of a conference on European security.

The detailed Allied proposal was followed in December by an important NATO meeting in Brussels. Here the fifteen members of

39 The Washington Post, February 11, 1970.
40 The Washington Post, December 17, 1969.
41 Ibid.

the Atlantic Alliance agreed to back up the Western Three in exploiting the linkage between Soviet cooperation on Berlin and the holding of a European security conference. For the first time, they made their approval of such a meeting dependent on progress in the West German-Soviet negotiations, talks with the Russians on a balanced reduction of troop strength in Europe and Soviet diplomatic movement on the Berlin question.[42]

Less than two months later, Britain, France and the United States had the Soviet reply in hand. While a careful reading of the Russian aide-mémoire of February 10, 1970 revealed no major change in Kremlin policy, its form clearly paved the way for the opening of specific conversations on Berlin. According to a U.S. State Department spokesman, the Soviet note "in substance" followed "closely the remarks made by Foreign Minister *Gromyko*" the previous July. And to the disappointment of the Western powers, it "did not respond to specific points" mentioned in the earlier Allied communication. The USSR merely stated its willingness to talk about Berlin "for the purpose of improving the situation in West Berlin and eliminating frictions in this region."[43]

In its diplomatic note, Moscow specifically expressed the desire to discuss certain "activities," which it maintained "were not in conformity with the status of West Berlin." Above all, the Kremlin was concerned about efforts of West German authorities to treat the city as a constituent part of the Federal Republic by regularly staging national political events there. To off-set this situation, the USSR called for recognition of the German Democratic Republic as a sovereign state and acceptance of its contention that West Berlin as a "special political entity" was not tied to West Germany.

The Russians suggested that talks be held in the Western Sectors, although no specific date for their start was given. The defunct Allied Control Council building was their choice for the actual site of the negotiations. This building, the seat of the inter-Allied governing body for all of Germany after 1945, was now deserted except for the Berlin Air Safety Center, which the Four Powers used to control air traffic into the city.

This portion of the Soviet proposal represented a rejection of the Western suggestion that discussions on Berlin take place

42 The Washington Post, February 11, 1970.
43 Ibid.

alternately in both parts of the divided city. Moreover, it reinforced Allied suspicions that Moscow only intended to establish its share of Four-Power responsibility for West Berlin, leaving the Soviet Sector completely out of any conversations.[44]

Although this and other points in the Russian note left a lot to be desired, Western diplomats decided to view the Soviet reply in its most favorable light. Therefore, its receipt was interpreted as a sign by Moscow that it was ready to allow discussion of the vital issue of access and consider improvements in the life of West Berliners.

The Allies, after extensive consultations among themselves, responded to the Soviet aide-mémoire on February 27. In their answer, they agreed to confer with the USSR in the Allied Control Council building in West Berlin. But to underscore Four-Power authority for "Greater Berlin" they proposed that negotiations be conducted at the ambassadorial level by representatives of the Western Three in Bonn and the Soviet envoy in East Berlin, who exercise residual powers as High Commissioners.[45]

Admittedly, Western agreement to conduct talks in the Allied Control Council building represented a modest concession by the Allies. However, here again they tried to put the best face on their decision. Thus, the Western view of the site for negotiations, rather than suggesting that only matters concerning West Berlin would be discussed — as the Russians would have it, — symbolized Four-Power authority over the entire city.[46]

With the transmission of the Western reply, the groundwork was now laid for the opening of the Four-Power talks on Berlin. This announcement was subsequently made public one month later, on March 20, 1970. And negotiations began in earnest six days thereafter — with no agenda and neither side knowing how long discussions would be dragged out.

---

44 U.S. Mission (Berlin), Post-War Berlin — An Unofficial Chronology (Berlin: USIA, April 1970), p. 2.

45 Refer to the Tripartite Agreement on the Exercise of Retained Rights in Germany, signed on October 23, 1954 in Wolfgang Heidelmeyer et al (eds.), Documents on Berlin, 1943-1963 (Munich: R. Oldenbourg Verlag, 1963), pp. 145-146.

46 See Dieter Mahncke, "In Search of a modus vivendi for Berlin: Prospects for Four-Power talks," The World Today, Vol. 26, No. 4 (April, 1970), p. 138.

Conclusions

The year 1969 represents a watershed in East-West relations. As fate or circumstances would have it, the interests of the two superpowers — the United States and the Soviet Union — and the dominant economic power in Western Europe — West Germany — in reducing tensions and engaging in productive dialogue all converged with a timeliness and sense of urgency that was unprecedented.

Looking back on this period, there is an unfortunate tendency in the West to ascribe the new diplomatic activity in Europe to *Willy Brandt's* statesmanship and Moscow's attempted exploitation of it. However attractive this view may be to the Western publics, it puts too great a burden on one man. A careful review of events at the time shows the actual picture is much more complex.

For its part, a new administration in Washington demonstrated it was ready to re-evaluate its relationship with the USSR and other communist countries. Unlike in the past, ideological differences between the two superpowers would no longer be allowed to prevent close cooperation on matters of mutual concern. Times and the priorities of the United States and the Soviet Union had changed. And it was this recognition that led President *Nixon* to issue his famous call for an end to the "era of confrontation" and the beginning of an "era of negotiation."

In contrast to the American effort, the Soviet "peace offensive" was not the product of new insights into international politics (or any basic change in philosophic attitudes). Rather it received its impetus from concrete domestic and foreign considerations. Most important here seems to be the growing intensity of the Sino-Soviet rift and the increased threat to Moscow of a nuclear-armed China.

The motivation behind West Germany's rapprochement with the USSR, the countries of East Europe and the GDR can be explained by a growing frustration over the European status quo and the inflexible and outdated "policy of strength," pursued by Bonn in the 1950s and 60s. This policy was based largely on a subservient relationship with the West — particularly the United States — and saw the solution to the reunification question in terms of a strong, Western oriented nation-state. So long as the "cold war" threat could be cited, the leadership in Bonn was under little pressure to cut its umbilical cord with the West and embark on a more creative albeit risky course. Gradually, however, as the "cold war" waned, the "political midget" become "economic giant" began to alter its attitude toward the East. This push for change reached its climax in the election of *Willy Brandt* as Chancellor of the Federal Republic.

The Berlin question became involved in this intricate matrix of interwoven national interests because of the Western desire to make it a "test of détente." Basically, this decision was in line with *Henry Kissinger's* theory of linkage in international relations, i.e., that cooperation with the Soviet Union in one area of détente cannot be divorced from progress in others.

The major problem with this conceptional innovation is that it tended to downplay — or even ignore — the complexity of local issues, which heretofore had defied every attempt at resolution. Besides the general complexity of matters, which led President *Eisenhower* once to refer to Berlin as a "jungle of technicalities," the interests of too many governments were at stake in the isolated city. This greatly complicated the situation and made the task of arriving at key compromises doubly difficult.

If the selection of Berlin as a "test case" was fraught with risks, the Western side possessed one major bargaining advantage. This was the obvious wish of Moscow to gain Western approval for the holding of a conference on European security. Presumably, such a convocation would permit the Kremlin to ratify the fruits of World War II and contribute to the removal of Western Europe as a threat to Soviet interests. As a result (if this theory is correct), the USSR would then be able to devote its energies more fully to unsettled problems with China and pressing domestic issues.

As far as Western goals at the beginning of the talks are concerned, they were fairly clearcut. In general, the Allies wanted
(1) to confirm the Four-Power status of Berlin;
(2) to secure assurances of unimpeded access to the city;
(3) to obtain entry for West Berliners to East Berlin and East Germany on the same basis as accorded West German visitors;[47]
(4) to improve communications among West Berlin, the GDR and East Berlin;

47 Following the closure of the East Berlin Sector border in August 1961, West Germans — but not West Berliners — could still visit the Soviet Sector.

(5) to end discrimination against West Berlin in the East, particularly with regard to economic matters; and

(6) to gain acknowledgment by the Soviet Union and the GDR of West Berlin's social, economic, cultural and political ties with the Federal Republic.

For Soviet concessions in these areas, the Western Three were prepared to urge Bonn to cut back on its presence in West Berlin.

Soviet objectives and the readiness of Moscow to make specific concessions were less clear. But they appeared to include the following points:

(1) eliminating or seriously undermining the Four-Power status of Berlin;

(2) gaining recognition of West Berlin as an "independent political entity" under Four-Power control;

(3) winning Allied diplomatic recognition of the German Democratic Republic;

(4) securing the withdrawal of all West German authorities in West Berlin; and

(5) obtaining Western guarantees that Bonn would stop treating the Western Sectors as a constituent part of the Federal Republic.

To realize these aims, the USSR seemed prepared to offer limited assurances regarding access to Berlin and to agree to a few practical improvements in the daily lives of West Berlin citizens.

As the two sides made ready to begin serious negotiations, prospects were not very encouraging. For one thing, the desire of each party to make the necessary substantial concessions was subject to serious question. For another, the matters to be discussed were far from settled. In the West, for instance, a major search was underway to determine which elements were essential for the survival of West Berlin — and hence "non-negotiable" — and which had more of a symbolic than a practical significance. Still the local scene had to be put in the international context, and there signs were good.

*As somebody once said, the Federal Republic ought
to recognize itself — and that is precisely a part of
the foreign policy which we are striving to develop
at present.*

Willy Brandt

Chapter III
THE ROAD TO ERFURT

The opening of diplomatic conversations in Berlin toward the
end of March 1970 took place against the background of East-
West German reconciliation. Decisive impetus to it had been given
by *Willy Brandt,* shortly after becoming West Germany's Chancellor in the fall of the previous year. In his inaugural address, delivered
before the Bundestag on October 28, 1969, the Social Democratic
leader first enunciated the doctrine of "two states in one German
nation" and his aim of instituting a "special relationship" with the
German Democratic Republic.[1] While stopping short of full international recognition of the GDR, *Brandt* by implication abandoned
reunification as a viable option in the foreseeable future.

Brandt's Regierungserklärung represented a radical departure
from the past, in that it was the first not to explicitly use the term
reunification. Although this fact did not mean that the new
Chancellor was uninterested in German unity, it represented a
recognition that Bonn's traditional Deutschlandpolitik — based as
it was on the primacy of reunification — had resulted in the
atrophying of contacts between the GDR and the FRG by
encouraging East Berlin to maintain its defensive posture. Public
acceptance of the impracticability of reunification would, it was
felt, enable the East German leadership to feel secure enough to
agree to liberalize contacts between the two states and thus
strengthen the sense of Zusammengehörigkeitsgefühl (feeling of
belonging together).[2]

1 For the English text see The Bulletin, November 4, 1969. This publication
  is circulated in the United States by the West German Information Center
  in New York.
2 W.E. Paterson, "Foreign Policy and Stability in West Germany," International Affairs, Vol. 49, No. 3 (July, 1973), p. 424.

While openly challenging the SED to open the way to a peaceful contest of systems and normal relations, *Brandt* said he would not negotiate an agreement with the GDR incorporating the same conditions as those contained in the proposed treaties with the USSR and Poland. In them, confirmation of the status quo would lead to normal relations. But the converse was true for the GDR. Appealing to the "unity of the nation," he demanded reciprocal services before formally confirming the status quo in Germany. By this tactic, the Chancellor neatly put the onus for contributing to Entspannung on the East Berlin régime.[3]

While a public survey revealed that 74 % of the population of the Federal Republic supported *Brandt's* efforts to open a dialogue with the GDR,[4] the leadership in East Germany apparently felt greatly threatened by such a move. Thus, *Walter Ulbricht* flatly rejected in December 1969 the concept of "special intra-German relations," declaring the GDR to be a foreign country to Bonn. The reluctance of the First Secretary to engage in dynamic bilateral negotiations with the FRG at this time, however, was cleverly camouflaged by exorbitant demands on West Germany. These included the end to alleged "juridical aggression" and a reduction in Bonn's arms expenditures by fifty per cent.[5] Moreover, in the attempt to do *Brandt* one better, recognition was set as the precondition for talks on normalizing relations.

Ulbricht's Sudden Turnaround

Ulbricht's attempt to swim against the tide of Entspannung was seriously undermined by Warsaw Pact members in December 1969. Meeting on the 3rd and 4th of that month in Moscow, the Warsaw Pact Political Consultative Committee formally abandoned the so-called "*Ulbricht* Doctrine." In conformity with it, previous Warsaw

3 See Robert Bleimann, "Ostpolitik and the GDR," Survey, Vol. 18, No. 3 (Summer, 1972), p. 36.

4 The results of this poll, taken by the Institute for Applied Sociology in Bonn, were published in Die Süddeutsche Zeitung, November 18, 1969. The survey also showed that more than half the citizens of West Germany (fifty-two per cent) expected positive results from the Eastern policy pursued by the SPD-FDP government coalition.

5 See Neues Deutschland, December 14, 1969.

Pact summits had put forward the demand — at East German insistence — that East Berlin must be recognized by Bonn as a precondition to bilateral discussions between any of the East European states and the Federal Republic. Now they merely affirmed in a joint communiqué that they would encourage bilateral relations with Bonn on the following principles: "equality of rights, non-interference in internal affairs and recognition of the sovereignty, territorial integrity and inviolability of existing boundaries."[6]

The impact of this change in Warsaw Pact policy on East-West German relations became immediately apparent as *Walter Ulbricht*, seizing the initiative in the middle of December, responded directly to *Brandt's* eastward diplomatic drive by sending a personal letter by special emissary to West German President *Gustav Heinemann*. The contents of this letter, dated December 18 and written by *Ulbricht* as head of state rather than party leader, were not immediately made public. But the fact that the note was written and received was almost unprecedented in the relations between the two states.[7]

The letter, which also included a treaty proposal,[8] contained the following key points:

(1) the recognition of all postwar European boundaries, particularly the border between the GDR and the FRG and the one between the German Democratic Republic and Poland;

(2) the exchange of ambassadors by Bonn and East Berlin; and

(3) the recognition of West Berlin as an "independent political entity" with appropriate separate relations between the city and West Germany.[9]

6 Neues Deutschland, December 5, 1969.

7 The last correspondence, between Premier Willi Stoph and then Chancellor Kurt-Georg Kiesinger, was broken off in late 1967 when the GDR régime demanded a state treaty granting it sovereign recognition as a prelude for talks. For details see Hartmut Jäckel, "Kontakte ohne Anerkennung? Der Briefwechsel Kiesinger-Stoph," Der Monat, No. 235 (1968).

8 The treaty was essentially the same as one proposed by the East Germans in 1967 and rejected by the West Germans over the question of GDR sovereignty. The text is contained in Bundesminister für innerdeutsche Beziehungen, Die Entwicklung der Beziehungen zwischen der Bundesrepublik Deutschland und der Deutschen Demokratischen Republik (Melsungen: Verlagsbuchdruckerei A. Bernecker, 1973), pp. 49-51.

9 Ibid.

Ulbricht's communication was answered promptly several days later by President *Heinemann*. Although he did not mention the draft treaty, he said he welcomed the First Secretary's offer of negotiations.[10]

Bonn Responds to Ulbricht's Initiative

But it wasn't until January 14, 1970, in a major address to the Bundestag, that *Brandt* gave a substantive reply to *Ulbricht's* initiative.[11] In his "report on the state of the nation" the German Chancellor said he did not regard the East German treaty draft as a useful basis for negotiations. Consequently, he proceeded to set forth six principles of his own which were to guide talks with the GDR.

Generally, these points reflected the position of the Western Three in their negotiations with the USSR on Berlin. According to them, both sides should respect

(1) the obligation to preserve the unity of the German nation;
(2) the application of generally recognized principles of international law;
(3) the understanding not to seek to change the social structure in the territory of the other;
(4) mutual efforts aimed at neighborly cooperation;
(5) the rights and responsibilities of the Four Powers regarding Berlin and Germany as a whole; and
(6) attempts by the Four Powers to bring about improvements in the situation in and around Berlin.

Taken together, these principles were concrete evidence of *Brandt's* wish to begin negotiations with the GDR on the basis of "equality and nondiscrimination."

Subsequently, *Egon Franke,* Minister for Inner-German Affairs, outlined the various improvements to be discussed within the framework described by *Brandt.* In the first place, an attempt would be made to obtain practical improvements in the lives of those people most directly affected by the division of Germany. In

10 The Heinemann letter was published in Neues Deutschland, December 21, 1969.

11 For the English text see supplement to The Bulletin, January 20, 1970.

this connection, concrete proposals leading to increased contacts between relatives, friends and neighbors on both sides of the border would be tabled. He singled out the reunification of families cruelly separated by the partition as being of particular importance. In addition, contacts between East and West German youth groups would be stressed. Another objective concerned the promotion of cultural relations between the two parts of Germany. Lastly, Bonn would seek to facilitate inner-German trade, improve postal and telephone communications and obtain a relaxation of travel restrictions. In thus describing the kinds of agreements the Federal Republic hoped to conclude with the GDR, *Franke* took pains to discourage undue optimism by pointing out that the talks would be extremely difficult and would probably take a long time.[12]

Jockeying for Position

Just five days after Chancellor *Brandt's* speech of January 14, *Walter Ulbricht* gave the East German response. At his first open press conference since the Berlin border was sealed in 1961, the 76-year-old communist leader announced that his government was prepared to begin "negotiations on fundamental problems, to which questions of renunciation of force naturally belong." Presumably under pressure from the Soviet Union and other communist allies to make a conciliatory gesture to Bonn in the wake of its month-old dialogue with the USSR on renunciation of force, the First Secretary — in what marked a dramatic departure from past demands of diplomatic recognition — added: "We have no preconditions."[13]

In connection with prospective Four-Power negotiations on Berlin, *Ulbricht* went out of his way to spell out the East German position on the status of the city and the existence of "a West Berlin problem." Looking dapper in an excellently tailored navy blue suit and gold-rimmed glasses, he reiterated the communist claim that Berlin, as "the capital city of the German Democratic Republic," is "not subject to Four-Power control." Replying to a

12 See K.W. Beer, "Acht Verhandlungspunkte," Deutsche Korrespondenz, Vol. 20, No. 4 (January, 1970), pp. 2-5.

13 The New York Times, January 20, 1970.

question submitted in writing, he said the Wall would not be "an object of discussion" in the quadripartite talks. But "West Berlin is another question." He added: "I would not like to interfere in that occupation régime."[14]

Bonn's reaction to *Ulbricht's* sudden turnaround on preconditions for inner-German talks was soon forthcoming; it took the form of a specific offer to begin negotiations, transmitted by personal letter from Chancellor *Brandt* to Premier *Stoph* on January 22, 1970. In general, this proposal followed the set of guidelines outlined in *Brandt's* "state of the nation address." It offered "a wideranging exchange of views on the settlement of all issues outstanding between our two states, including those relating to ties on the basis of complete equality."[15]

Stoph responded to the Chancellor's initiative with a letter of his own on February 11.[16] In this correspondence, the East German head of government invited *Brandt* to meet with him in East Berlin for talks. The third most powerful man in the GDR wrote: "I believe it is necessary in the interest of peaceful coexistence and the regulation of (our) relationship by treaty and on the basis of generally recognized norms of sovereignty that we meet for direct negotiations." It was suggested that conversations take place on either February 19 or 26 in the Council of Ministers' building, one of the GDR's proudest symbols of statehood. As a way of underlining the separate nature of the two states, *Stoph* named Foreign Minister *Otto Winzer* as his negotiating partner.

To go to East Berlin or Not

The East German offer to meet *Brandt* at an unprecedented summit conference came as a bombshell dropped on Bonn. No one seemed to be able to explain satisfactorily why the SED wanted to stage such high-level talks. One view held that *Ulbricht* believed

14 Neues Deutschland, January 20, 1970.

15 For the text see Bundesminister für innerdeutsche Beziehungen, Die Entwicklung der Beziehungen zwischen der Bundesrepublik Deutschland und der Deutschen Demokratischen Republik: Bericht und Dokumentation (Melsungen: Verlagsbuchdruckerei A. Bernecker, 1973), p. 52.

16 For the text see ibid., pp. 52-53.

such a meeting would enhance the international status of the GDR. While another asserted that East Berlin hoped the Federal Republic would reject its proposal thus enabling the GDR to emphasize West Germany's intransigence and show its true aims to those Eastern countries eager to normalize relations.

For *Brandt* personally, the proposed summit in East Berlin brought forth vivid memories of the times, when as Mayor of West Berlin and later Foreign Minister he had made trips to the Soviet Sector to talk with the Russian Ambassador. Although these visits across the Wall were criticized at the time for implying recognition of the communist régime, *Brandt* never had official contacts with members of the GDR leadership. In July 1966, after the collapse of the plan for an exchange of prominent speakers between the two Germanies, in which he was to participate, the then Mayor delivered in West Berlin the speech he had originally intended to give on East German territory.

In his reply, sent by teleprinter to the GDR capital on February 18, the Chancellor expressed his willingness to meet with Premier *Stoph* in East Berlin.[17] But *Brandt* said he would not be able to come on either of the two suggested days because of an obligation to take part in parliamentary debate on the Federal budget. Instead he declared that officials of his government would be available starting the following week to work out technical details for a meeting during the second or third week of March, with the expectation that the second round of talks would take place in Bonn.

By agreeing to visit *Stoph* in East Berlin, *Brandt* had to weigh the risk of failure in the proposed summit against the value of his presence in the communist capital as a sign that he was willing to try to move the dialogue along. Nevertheless, he seized on the idea as a way of clearly surmounting the legalism of both sides and dramatically demonstrating his desire to establish a practical relationship with the GDR leadership based on the reality of a divided Germany.

17 For the text see Bundesminister für innerdeutsche Beziehungen, Die Entwicklung der Beziehungen zwischen der Bundesrepublik Deutschland und der Deutschen Demokratischen Republik (Melsungen: Verlagsbuchdrukkerei A. Bernecker, 1973), pp. 53-54.

As events were to show, *Brandt's* Government underestimated the difficulty of negotiating technical and protocol preparations for the summit. One of the main stumbling blocks was East German opposition to the Chancellor's expressed wish to stop off in West Berlin on his way to and from East Berlin. Keenly aware that such a stopover would only emphasize West Germany's claim to West Berlin, the SED leadership threatened to call the whole thing off.

To avoid embarrassment to his country, the GDR negotiator Dr. *Gerhard Schüssler,* Deputy Chief of the Council of Ministers Office, proposed that *Brandt* travel to the meeting in East Berlin by plane, arriving at Schönefeld Airport and thus avoiding the Western Sectors entirely. But this plan was unacceptable to Bonn. Although the West Germans were prepared to back down cheerfully on many points of protocol, they could not afford to overlook the symbolic value of a stopover in that part of the city where the Chancellor had built much of his early political career as the tough Mayor of a beleaguered West Berlin. To do otherwise would put the former Mayor in a particularly embarrassing position. Moreover, it would appear to reinforce communist claims that West Berlin is a separate entity with no ties to the FRG. It was clear that the SPD-FDP coalition, with only a slim, twelve-vote majority in the Bundestag, could ill afford at this time to provide ammunition to the Christian Democratic opposition in parliament. Its leader, *Rainer Barzel,* already had made a big issue out of the matter. And he was now warning that any attempt to skip around the Western Sectors would be a "death blow against the affiliation of West Berlin with the Federal Republic."[18] Thus, by the middle of March, officials in Bonn were no longer excluding the possibility that the talks with *Stoph* might fall through. "The trend of things," conceded government spokesman *Conrad Ahlers,* "must be assessed rather sceptically."[19]

With deliberations on the technical arrangements of the historic visit now deadlocked, *Brandt* instructed the West German negotiator to offer an alternative site for the summit. At first, it was not known whether the East Germans would accept another

18 The Washington Post, March 6, 1970.
19 Newsweek, March 16, 1970.

place for the meeting, anxious as they were to stage it in the capital of the GDR — thereby reaffirming the alienation of East Berlin from any Four-Power status. But the Chancellor, determined not to allow technical details to sidetrack his campaign to improve relations with the Soviet Union and its communist allies, made the gesture to test the seriousness of SED intentions to hold the conference.

Brandt's gambit proved successful. After weeks of sensitive negotiations, both sides agreed to hold their first highlevel meeting in the Thuringian Forest city of Erfurt, located forty-four miles from the West German border. As part of a predicted ongoing series of such summits, the two parties also consented to stage later in the year a second round of talks involving both heads of government. For this purpose, Bonn was to be considered seriously as a possible summit site.[20]

Ulrich Sahm, Departmental Chief for Foreign Political Affairs in the Federal Chancellery, who after *Brandt* had become Chancellor had been plucked out of the Foreign Office, was responsible for negotiating arrangements for the meeting with *Jürgen Weichert,* a high official in the Federal Ministry for Inner-German Affairs. And he credited *Stoph* with finding Erfurt as an acceptable compromise site. *Sahm* (later Ambassador to Moscow) said GDR officials had reversed their earlier demands and now promised to keep ceremonies to a minimum — thus avoiding *Brandt* the domestic political embarrassment of seeing the trappings of East German sovereignty. Consequently, there would be no review of communist troops and no playing of national hymns. Although East Berlin pledged its "best efforts" to assist the hords of Western journalists expected to cover the unprecedented meeting, it would not allow direct television broadcasts to the West.

According to East-West German agreement, the conference was scheduled to take place on March 19, lasting only a day. *Brandt* would cross the most heavily guarded frontier in Europe in a special train which was to be freed of the usual stringent border formalities. At the demarcation line, the West German locomotive and crew would be replaced by East German ones.

20 The Washington Post, March 10, 1970.

An Exchange of Views

Despite fears that the SED would cancel the summit at the last minute just as it had backed out of the speakers' exchange four years earlier, the *Stoph-Brandt* meeting took place as scheduled in a setting fraught with nostalgia and symbolic meanings for both sides. (In 1850, Erfurt was briefly the scene of an unsuccessful attempt at forging a unified Germany, fostered by princely notables from Prussia, Hannover and Saxony. Later, in 1891, it was the site of a merger convention of the radical Social Democratic Worker Party and the reformist-minded Universal German Worker Association. Out of this historic conclave came the new name Social Democratic Party and the so-called Erfurt Program.)

In anticipation of the impending summit, the citizens of this grimy rail junction (pop.: 200,000) in the forests of East Germany could hardly recognize their surroundings. Hundreds of local police, road crews and soldiers launched a kind of "operation face lift." Facades along the main thoroughfares received long-overdue coats of paint. Potholes in roads were filled. And scarce imported items suddenly turned up in food stores.

At the same time, the GDR régime sought to camouflage the feelings of their people. To avoid an overly warm welcome for the first West German Chancellor to set foot in East Germany, communist officials instructed workers to remain at their jobs and students to stay in class. Furthermore, to discourage an influx of visitors, Erfurt-bound trains were cancelled and roadblocks were set up on all roads leading to the city.

Despite these measures, the public welcome given *Brandt* was extraordinary. A huge outpouring of emotion ensued as the Chancellor, accompanied by Premier *Willi Stoph,* walked across a square to the Hotel Erfurter Hof, a good fifty meters from the yellow-brick railroad terminal where the two had met and shaken hands for the first time a few minutes before, at 9:30 a.m. on the station platform. Thousands of East Germans scaled rooftops to wave a welcome and burst through police lines chanting "Willy, Willy!" Soon realizing there were two Willies present, they switched to "Willy, Willy Brandt!"[21]

21 For an authoritative and detailed account of the Brandt-Stoph meeting in Erfurt see David Binder, The Other German: Willy Brandt's Life and Times (Washington, D.C.: The New Republic Book Co., 1975), Chapter I.

GDR Communist Party leader Walter Ulbricht
discusses relations with the Federal Republic, January 1, 1970.

Soviet Ambassador Pyotr Abrasimov enters Allied Control Council Building for Four-Power talks on Berlin, August 16, 1971.

The two Germans, middle-aged, well dressed and looking fairly handsome, presented a sharp physical contrast. On the one hand, there was *Willy Brandt*, who was nearly a head taller and had on a colorful tie, which just peeked out of the vest of his dark blue overcoat. On the other, there was *Willi Stoph*, who had his neck securely wrapped in a red muffler to ward off the blustering March winds and carried a felt hat in his hand. Looking somewhat stiff and awkward, the two of them walked abreast, almost in cadence to their destination with history.

Once inside the hotel, *Brandt* began to freshen up after his trip when his preparations were suddenly interrupted by shouts from outside. A tumultuous crowd of some two thousand persons had gathered outside the Erfurter Hof and were shouting wildly for him to come to the window. After some hesitation, the Chancellor responded. He put in a brief appearance at a third-floor window and gazed down at the masses waving and shouting below. Although he was plainly moved by the demonstration, his face was expressionless. And the mouth of the man, whose oratory and take-charge manner back in 1956 had been responsible for almost singlehandedly turning back an angry West Berlin mob from marching on the Brandenburg Gate in the Soviet Sector — thereby narrowly averting an ugly international incident — remained gravely silent. As *Brandt* recalled later, I realized that "hopes could be stirred which could not be fulfilled. That shouldn't be. So I exercised the necessary caution."[22]

About ten o'clock, the two German heads of government accompanied by a flurry of advisers took seats at a rectangular table covered with green baize in the Erfurter Hof. Next to and behind the Chancellor sat Minister *Egon Franke*, FDP representative *Wolfram Dorn*, *Conrad Ahlers*, *Ulrich Sahm* and *Jürgen Weichert*. Surrounding *Stoph* were *Otto Winzer*, his subordinate in the Foreign Ministry *Günter Kohrt*, *Dr. Michael Kohl* (Later plenipotentiary in Bonn) and *Dr. Gerhard Schüssler*. The East German Foreign Minister was clearly present to personify *Ulbricht's* argument that the Federal Republic remained "foreign" to the German Democratic Republic, and one participant recalls the diminutive *Winzer* "hopping up every few minutes to telephone

22 Quoted from Brandt's memoirs of the period as serialized in Der Spiegel, May 17, 1976. (Author's translation.)

his superior in East Berlin."[23] Similarily, the West German Minister for Inner-German Affairs, *Egon Franke,* was there with *Brandt* to underscore the position of Bonn that relations between the two Germanies had a "special" character.

There was no fixed agenda, although each side had taken considerable pains to prepare declamations of some five thousand words in length. *Stoph* led off with a detailed and onesided rehearsal of events leading up to the division of Germany.[24] In his hour-long speech, the former bricklayer, who ran East Germany's brutal secret police after the war and served as GDR Defense Minister, repeated the long-standing demand that Bonn formally recognize the GDR as an independent nation. Speaking with quiet courtesy, the head of the East German government since 1964 tacked on several other claims, including the payment of one hundred billion marks in "reparations" for "economic damages" stemming from the pre-1961 loss of East German refugees and "economic discrimination" suffered at the hands of the FRG. When his turn came, *Brandt* ignored the economic demands of his "discussion" partner while rejecting outright the recognition ploy. He reminded *Stoph* that the constitutions of both countries envisioned a reunified Germany. However, he hinted that some degree of "semi-recognition" might be worked out to satisfy communist desires. It is a "matter of course," he said that any eventual accords with the GDR would have the same standing as those with other states.

As might be expected, the two leaders could not help but discuss Berlin once they got down to serious bargaining. It had been a central issue in the difficult preparatory negotiations and now played a key role in the summit talks. For his part, the Chancellor declared that agreements between the two Germanies could not affect or replace the Four-Power accords concerning Germany and Berlin, nor could they be affected by agreements between the Federal Republic and its allies or between the GDR and the USSR. "We do not want to change the status of Berlin," *Brandt* said, "as long as the German question has not been resolved."[25] The Chancellor put special emphasis on the links between West Berlin and West Germany. After pointing out the

23 David Binder, opus cit., p. 7.

24 The text is reprinted in Erfurt March 19, 1970: A Documentation (Bonn: Federal Press.and Information Office, 1970).

25 Die Frankfurter Allgemeine Zeitung, March 20, 1970.

82

necessity of these ties, he went on to say that "neither the three Western powers, nor the FRG nor the directly affected Berliners would agree to any change in Berlin's status, as laid down by the Four Powers, that would lead to a change in these links." For his part, Premier *Stoph* denied any claim of "Four-Power responsibility for the German Democratic Republic and its capital of Berlin." And he reiterated the demand that the two states establish formal diplomatic relations.

Despite their glaring albeit expected differences, some agreement was discovered by the two sides. For example, *Brandt* agreed to accept recognition of the GDR by third parties (no big concession), and he held out the prospect that Bonn might under certain circumstances try to help East Berlin into international organizations from which it was barred. Moreover, the Chancellor promised to drop West Germany's claim to represent all Germans (Alleinvertretung). Both parties consented to sign a renunciation of force pact (eventually) and to apply individually for membership in the United Nations. Finally, before the meeting drew to a close, *Stoph* said he was ready to return *Brandt's* visit, possibly on May 21 in the North Hessen town of Kassel, situated twenty miles from the East German border.[26]

As *Brandt* recounts in his memoirs of the period, he and *Stoph* were able to break away twice from their delegations for private talks. *Stoph*: "We can both speak German" (this means, we can be frank because no one else is present). The Chancellor had been led to expect that the GDR leader would be "rigid," and he was prepared to be inundated with polemics. Instead, he was pleasantly surprised to find his host a modest, comfortable man, who was able to convey nuances in conversation. During their private talks, *Brandt* reportedly told *Stoph* to forget about his demand for repayment of a hundred billion marks or anything else which stemmed from East Germany's unfriendly politics.

Conclusions

The meeting between the heads of government of East and West Germany was truly an historic occasion. Not only because it took

26 The Washington Post, March 20, 1970.

place at all but because it confirmed a new stage in East-West relations. To be sure, *Willy Brandt* and *Willi Stoph* went to Erfurt for very different purposes. But therein lay the certainty that there would be no quick or sure progress arising from it.

By crossing Europe's greatest political divide and entering the German Democratic Republic, the Chancellor hoped generally to emphasize — at the most sensitive point — his continuing effort to normalize Bonn's relations with the Eastern countries. As far as his Deutschlandpolitik was concerned, he sought not to end the division of Germany — that just would have frightened people in the East as well as West. Rather he aimed at making that division more tolerable and human. Hence, the first agreement he attempted to reach with the GDR pertained to the restoration of human contacts. "Germans must be able to talk with one another" is the way *Brandt* characterized this approach.[27]

The Social Democratic leader, of course, was aware that his attempt to close the gap between the two halves of the divided nation was a calculated gamble and one bound to disturb East Berlin. The GDR leadership had always been reluctant to permit this. In the main, it feared that if West Germans were free to come in they would bring with them the spirit of freedom, and if East Germans went out they would not return home. These were not idle fears. But as the moving reception which the East German populace gave *Brandt* at Erfurt showed once again, they were grounded in experience.

Because of East Berlin's reluctance to engage Bonn in productive dialogue, *Brandt* was convinced that the key to his Deutschlandpolitik and his drive for reconciliation with the nations of Eastern Europe lay in Moscow. Thus, he saw the fate of the German minisummit closely linked to *Egon Bahr's* talks with Soviet Foreign Minister *Andrei Gromyko* in Moscow. Ostensibly, these discussions centered on a "renunciation-of-force" accord between the two parties. But in general they amounted to a "test flight" for *Brandt's* Eastern initiatives.

Although *Bahr* had been dispatched once more to the Kremlin in mid-March for crucial talks with Soviet leaders, many issues

27 For an excellent analysis of the GDR to the challenge of Ostpolitik, see David Childs, "The Ostpolitik and Domestic Politics in East Germany," in Roger Tilford (ed.), The Ostpolitik and Political Change in Germany (Farnborough, England: Saxon House, 1975), pp. 59-75.

still divided Bonn and Moscow. Among them was Russia's insistence that any treaty renouncing the use of force should include a pledge against changing boundaries. In other words, the FRG might have to oppose the reunification of Germany — even if it became feasible one day. This situation was wholly unacceptable to *Brandt's* government which teetered on a razor-slim majority in parliament.

Throughout the talks in East Berlin aimed at hammering out technical and protocol details of the proposed summit, Bonn realized that prospects for a meeting between *Brandt* and *Stoph* — and the future of the Chancellor's Eastern policy — depended on how far the Soviets were willing to go. If they were genuinely interested in reducing European tensions, then they could choose, at the very least, to string the Chancellor along. At best, they might well be persuaded to make some solid diplomatic gestures in the hope of elicitating concessions from Bonn in return. In any case, the final outcome in Erfurt was viewed as evidence of the ability of Moscow to influence critical policy decisions in the GDR.

All animals are equal, but some animals are more equal than others.

George Orwell

Chapter IV
THE TALKS ON BERLIN BEGIN

From the outset of the quadripartite talks, which began with a great deal of fanfare and publicity on March 26, 1970, the two sides were under no illusions about the difficulty of concluding a mutually satisfactory agreement on the divided city. Too often in the past, hopes had been raised by the start of negotiations on Berlin only to come crashing down because of irreconcilable differences.[1] If the Soviets saw in the beginning of discussions a hope that starting from an understanding of the status quo in Europe as a whole — and acceptance of it — it might be possible to reach an accord that would prevent a further build-up of tension in and around Berlin, the Allies believed the talks represented a test case regarding the seriousness of Soviet interest both in détente and

1 The first important post-war negotiations on Berlin took place in Paris at the Foreign Ministers level in 1949. These diplomatic conversations, along with the key Jessup-Malik talks at the United Nations in New York, resulted in the lifting of the Berlin Blockade and the restoration of the status quo ante. In 1955, a "Big Four" summit conference was held at Geneva, but it failed to reach any agreement on "the German question." Thereupon, the Soviet Union signed a treaty with the GDR, affirming its sovereignty and giving the East Germans the power to control all traffic to and from Berlin — except for that of Allied forces, which the Russians continued to monitor. Four years later (May 1959), a conference of Foreign Ministers of the Four Powers (with the East and West Germans present as "observers") convened in Geneva. Although it had been called in response to Khrushchev's "ultimatum" on Berlin (November 1958), this meeting adjourned after three months without reaching any agreement on Germany or Berlin. Finally, between 1962 and 1963, Secretary of State Dean Rusk — at the direction of the American President — conducted a series of unsuccessful negotiations on Berlin with Soviet Foreign Minister Andrei Gromyko. For details see Wolfgang Heidelmeyer et al (eds.), Documents on Berlin 1943-1963 (Munich: R. Oldenbourg Verlag, 1963).

long-term European cooperation. In the end, after almost a year and a half of difficult and complicated negotiations in a long series of meetings, the Four Powers reached an agreement far better than Western Foreign Offices dared hope when talks began.[2]

The process of reaching overall agreement on Berlin went through three distinct phases. During the first and most difficult stage, representatives of the United States, Great Britain, France and the Soviet Union worked out a general accord of principles, initialled on September 3, 1971. This agreement was the product of "intensive consultation between the Soviets and the GDR on the one side, and between the three Western powers and the FRG on the other — so that the main elements and essential framework for the negotiations which took place in the second stage were fairly well pre-ordained." Since basic responsibility for Berlin lies with the Four Powers, the Allies insisted (the Soviets at first strongly disagreed) that any agreement on the city first be reached by them.

In the second stage of obtaining agreement, negotiations took place on two separate levels — between representatives of the German Democratic Republic and the Federal Republic of Germany, on the one hand, and between East German and West Berlin government officials on the other. These authorities hammered out the details of the quadripartite "umbrella" accord in two supplementary agreements, concluded just three months later in December 1971. Finally, during the third stage, approvement of the inner-German agreements was obtained from the Four Powers. These went into effect simultaneously with the Quadripartite Agreement on June 3, 1972.

The Actors

In Berlin, the actual negotiations among the Four Powers were conducted by British, French and American Ambassadors accredited in Bonn and the Soviet envoy posted to East Berlin. For it is they who still hold some residual powers as High Commissioners for Ger-

2 See for instance Robert G. Livingston, "East Germany between Moscow and Bonn," Foreign Affairs, Vol. 50, No. 2 (January, 1972), p. 299. The author headed the Eastern Affairs Section of the U.S. Mission in Berlin during the middle and late sixties.

many. The Ambassadors were, in turn, supported by a complex bureaucratic structure. On the Western side, this involved a great deal of preparatory staff work and included several inter-agency and inter-Allied consultation bodies in Washington and Bonn.

The basic American position in the negotiations was developed in Washington. There a number of agencies — particularly the State Department, Pentagon and CIA — were drawn together at various levels to consider U.S. objectives and plan strategy.

Of no small importance in this regard was the Berlin Task Force. This body, which consisted of a number of personnel drawn informally from various parts of the State Department had been initially established to deal with the Berlin crises of the late fifties and early sixties. Under the direction of the Assistant Secretary of State for European Affairs, it was now utilized to formulate State's recommendations for the negotiations.[3]

The initial position papers drafted by the Berlin Task Force were forwarded after careful consideration for review by the European Inter-Departmental Group. Chaired by the Assistant Secretary of State for European Affairs, this body met as a sub-committee of the National Security Council and included representatives from the various governmental agencies and a White House NSC staff representative. Since the subject at hand was a political-diplomatic negotiation in the first instance (no one was proposing the removal of U.S. troops from Berlin), the State Department had the strongest hand in interagency discussions at this level.

After a basic American position for the negotiations had been agreed upon by the European Inter-Departmental Group, this position was then reported to a higher-level sub-committee of the National Security Council. This was the Senior Review Group, which was chaired by *Dr. Kissinger,* then serving as Special Assistant to the President for National Security Affairs. This key committee acted as a clearing house for all position papers submitted for Presidential approval. (It should be noted, however, lest a false impression be given, that "numerous" position papers were not cleared by the Senior Review Group and then submitted for

3 Department of State, United States Foreign Policy 1971: A Report of the Secretary of State (Washington, D.C.: US Government Printing Office, 1972), p. 44.

Presidential approval. As Ambassador (then Assistant Secretary of State for European Affairs and Chairman of the European Inter-Departmental Group) *Martin J. Hillenbrand* writes: "One of the interesting facts about the handling of the Berlin negotiations was that, once initial Presidential approval had been obtained for U.S. participation in the negotiations and the broad outlines of the U.S. position to be followed, there was for a year practically no White House involvement in the actual formulation of positions. The basic instructions for the American negotiating team were developed in the Inter-Departmental Group, and very frequently solely in the Bureau of European Affairs of the Department of State, with no further onward reference. It was only at a later stage that the White House role became somewhat more pronounced.")[4]

Major position papers only twice during the course of negotiations were channeled through this complex machinery for consideration of the President — and they were issued more than six months apart. These were National Security Staff Memorandum (NSSM) 111, issued December 29, 1970, and NSSM 136, dated July 30, 1971. Whereas the former represented the American draft of an Allied proposal for a Berlin agreement, tabled with modifications on February 8, 1971, the latter consisted of specific trade-offs which might be made to the Soviet Union to obtain its agreement on critical issues such as access, visits across the Wall by Berliners and recognition of Bonn's ties to West Berlin.[5]

Once the basic American position (or a change in it) had been formulated and approved in Washington, it was then sent out as guidance to the U.S. Ambassador in Bonn. There coordination among the Western Three was centered in the so-called "Bonn Group." Originally, a tripartite body, this inter-Allied consultation agency had been expanded in 1961 to accommodate West German participation.

The "Bonn Group" was composed for the most part of heads of political sections in the British, French and American Embassies together with the chief of the German Section of the West-German Foreign Ministry. These individuals were delegated the

4 Letter from Ambassador (to Bonn) Martin J. Hillenbrand to author, dated June 7, 1976.
5 Wilfred L. Kohl, "The Nixon-Kissinger Foreign Policy System and U.S.-European Relations: Patterns of Policy Making," World Politics, Vol. 28, No. 1 (October, 1975), p. 26.

ticklish task of reconciling often widely divergent points of view and developing a common Allied position in the talks. Generally, the wording of texts tabled by the Western side was drafted by this body.[6] Thus, throughout the negotiations, initial positions were formulated on the Western side in capitals — but developed and coordinated by American, British, French and German officials meeting almost without interruption in Bonn.

If the bureaucracy in Washington was at first sceptical of negotiating prospects, the attitude of members of the "Bonn Group" was not much different. A number of British and French representatives believed it was a mistake for the West even to seek agreement with the Soviet Union since the present situation seemed to guarantee essential Western interests more effectively than any likely accord would do.[7] This rigidity in their position (which was also shared by some Soviets who were under strong pressure from the East Germans not to agree to strengthening West Berlin's ties with the Federal Republic) led sometimes in the beginning to heated exchanges among the Western Three. Gradually, however, as time passed and people became better acquainted, the process of arriving at a consensus was smoothed out, and the "Bonn Group" did a great deal of valuable work. On those rare occasions, however, when particularly difficult problems arose and all attempts to build a consensus on a lower level failed, the three Ambassadors would meet to iron out differences. Thus, the Western envoys, always kept well informed of the process of Allied coordination and having on occasion directly participated in Allied

---

6 Department of State, United States Foreign Policy 1971: A Report of the Secretary of State (Washington, D.C.: U.S. Government Printing Office, 1972), p. 44.

7 This view reflected a "normal" bureaucratic attitude whereby "the bureaucracy prefers the known dangers of an existing course to the uncertain costs and gains of change." See Francis E. Rourke. Bureaucracy and Foreign Policy (1972), p. 60.

Ambassador Hillenbrand strongly disagrees. As he says: "My own view would be that the caution displayed on the Washington side had very little to do with what you call "a normal bureaucratic attitude," but rather was a realistic appraisal of the situation itself. The entire framework for the negotiations, as well as most of the contents, were actually developed in the bureaucracy and reflected, as I think the record when it is available will show, a considerable degree of initiative and imagination." Letter from Hillenbrand to author, June 7, 1976.

discussions in Bonn, were able in the Berlin meetings to function as a team in dealing with their Soviet colleague.[8]

The Role of Personalities

In analyzing the development of the Four-Power talks, one should not overlook the bureaucratic complex and the route of the paper flow in the decision-making process; nor can one ignore the key role played by certain personalities:

Of special importance on the American side were the personal interest shown by President *Nixon,* his close relations with the U.S. Ambassador in Bonn *Kenneth Rush,* the "riding herd" efforts in the "Bonn Group" of his able political adviser *Jonathan Dean,* the "donkeywork" of some "old German hands" in the State

8 Ambassador Rush has these remarks to make about the "Bonn Group": It "is a very useful and constructive meeting of Political Counselors, but it is not a decision-making group. It is a group designed to formulate various positions, discuss the various issues involved, and prepare and submit those issues to the Ambassadors for decision. While it is primarily concerned with Berlin problems, it also discusses other issues with which the three Powers are jointly concerned. The Ambassadors, of course, consult with the Political Counselors both before and after meetings of the Bonn Group, and the Bonn Group meetings have as one of their principal purposes the clarification of issues to be considered at regular meetings of the three Ambassadors and the Senior State Secretary for Foreign Affairs of the Federal Republic of Germany. These meetings consist of at least one lunch each month, with rotating hosts, and also ad hoc meetings as the need arises. This concept has been in effect for many years and, I understand, still continues.

This organizational form continued after the Berlin negotiations began. However, there were much more frequent meetings of the Bonn Group and of the three Ambassadors, usually accompanied by their Political Counselors and usually without the presence of the State Secretary for Foreign Affairs. These meetings of the Ambassadors became increasingly frequent as time passed, sometimes occurring almost daily as the negotiations approached and reached their climax. At all times I maintained close contact with Foreign Minister Scheel, Chancellor Brandt, and State Secretary Egon Bahr. Contrary to the impression you received that the meetings of the Ambassadors were 'rare' and only for discussing important issues, in fact, meetings were frequent, every issue of consequence was discussed by the Ambassadors, and decisions with regard to these issues were made by them." Letter from Ambassador Rush to author, dated May 6, 1976.

Department in Washington — particularly *Martin Hillenbrand* in the European Office, *James Sutterlin* in the German Bureau, *Nelson Ledsky* on the Berlin Desk, *Helmut Sonnenfeldt* and *John Hyland* on the staff of the National Security Council in the White House and, of course, the personal interventions of *Dr. Kissinger.*

On the British and French side, there were the important roles played by Ambassador *Rush's* counterparts: *Roger Jackling* and *Jean Sauvagnargues* respectively. Together these men faced the ever resolute Soviet "pro-consul" *Pyotr A. Abrasimov.*

Lastly, because of the problem of coordinating the Allied position with the West German government — and the impact of Ostpolitik on the negotiations, one cannot overlook the input of *Willy Brandt,* his Foreign Minister *Walter Scheel* and the controversial *Egon Bahr.*

Rush and Dean

When *Nixon* suddenly plucked the former president of New York's Union Carbide Corporation from the corporate boardroom in July 1969 and dispatched him to Bonn as the American envoy, European observers were notably unimpressed. For the most part, they were quick to point out his lack of previous diplomatic experience. The early betting was that the rookie Ambassador would be "eaten alive" by such old diplomatic pros as the Soviet Union's *Pyotr Abrasimov, Rush's* adversary in the difficult quadripartite talks.

It was not by accident, of course, that President *Nixon* chose *Rush* to represent American interests in the sensitive Berlin negotiations. He was impressed by the quiet competence of the man. They had first met back in 1936 when *Rush* was an assistant professor of law at Duke University. At that time, the President was a young law student and happened to enroll in one of *Rush's* courses. As *Rush* recalls: (At Duke) *"Nixon* and I became friends, although we were never very close. We later played golf occasionally together and saw each other off and on."

If the Europeans were at first dismayed by the absence of *Rush's* diplomatic credentials in the sensitive Berlin negotiations, the former corporate executive was seemingly unperturbed. Shortly after taking up residence in Bonn, he responded to one reporter's challenge with a confident chuckle, adding that he had become president of Union Carbide even though "I hadn't studied any chemistry, either." Recalling his legal background, the former law professor emphasized he had been "negotiating all my life. A lawyer is always forced to acquire instant expertise."[9]

As soon became evident in preparation for the quadripartite talks, the new Ambassador was not a man who is afraid to delegate responsibility. Thus, he immediately took advantage of the services of *Jonathan Dean,* an energetic and exceptionally skillful foreign service officer. The 47-year-old *Dean* enjoyed the complete confidence of *Rush* and represented him in the "Bonn Group" and was often at his side during the formal negotiations with the Soviets. *"Jock" Dean's* "contribution was invaluable to me," *Rush* says in retrospect. As one Western diplomat who participated in the talks graciously acknowledged later: *"Rush* and *Dean* really pulled this off. They carried the ball."

Old German Hands

The highly publicized activities of *Rush* and *Dean* in Bonn and Berlin were backed up by the quiet and little-known efforts of several "old German hands" in the Department of State in Washington. Especially important here were the coordinating measures taken by Assistant Secretary of State for European Affairs *Martin Hillenbrand.* As Chairman of the NSC European Inter-Departmental Group, he reported directly to the Senior Review Group in the White House and *Dr. Kissinger.* Having served as Director of the Office of German Affairs during the 1958-62 Berlin crisis and for a year as head of the Berlin Task Force, *Hillenbrand* was a man of considerable experience. He was also well-liked by subordinates, who appreciated his "low-key" manner and modest personality.

If *Rush* and *Dean* were the "ball carriers" in the Four-Power negotiations, *James S. Sutterlin,* Director of the Bureau of German Affairs, and *Nelson C. Ledsky,* who was in charge of the Berlin Desk at the time, were the "back stoppers" in the U.S. Department of State. As their boss, *Martin Hillenbrand,* has pointed out: "the main burden" of analyzing developments in the negotiations, formulating the department's position and dispatching instructions to American officials in the field fell on them.[10]

9 Newsweek, September 6, 1971.
10 Letter from Ambassador Hillenbrand to author, dated June 7, 1976.

According to former underlings, "one couldn't imagine two more different personality types." *Sutterlin,* a "flinty, no-nonsense fellow," is "a man of few words," one official remembers. But he "has a mind like a steel trap." Another not unadmiring friend recalls him as being a "very demanding but capable individual." Although *"Jimmy" Sutterlin* was responsible for "overseeing" the American effort in the German Bureau, the real "detail work" was done by *Nelson Ledsky.* "He was the driving force," one former colleague says. As this person describes him, *"Ledsky* is a very energetic, bright and very tough negotiator." He has "the ability to focus immediately on a problem, analyze all its ramifications very quickly and come up with the ideal solution, which takes into account the interests of the other side." During the Berlin deliberations, this source recounts, *Ledsky* "was as tenacious as a bulldog."

Strangely enough, despite the fact that *Sutterlin* and *Ledsky* possessed very different personalities, they apparently worked well together. According to one insider, they got to know each other during the "cold war" period, when the two of them were stationed together in Bonn. There they became "fast friends." It "was a good thing *Rush* and *Dean* had them in the Bureau backing them up," says an experienced official. "Otherwise, the outcome in the talks could have been disastrous."

In addition to the "nuts and bolts" work performed by *Sutterlin* and *Ledsky* in the German Bureau, there was the "brainstorming" effort conducted by *Eleanor L. Dulles.* Sister of the former Secretary of State, she has been described as an "indefatigable woman," who years earlier won her position as "Berlin Desk Officer" out of sheer ability rather than any help from her brother. She had made her mark on the divided city by organizing relief packages for East Germany after the June 17, 1953 uprising, raising funds for a Free University dormitory and huge medical center (Klinikum) — "part of an economic answer to *Khrushchev's* 1958 ultimatum" — as well as for the Berlin Congress Hall (affectionately dubbed "Mrs. *Dulles'* Hat" by thankful Berliners). During the *Kennedy* administration, she retired from formal State Department work, only to return in 1969 as a "Special-Consultant" to the German Bureau at State. Already over seventy at the time, she is credited with developing several important Allied initiatives regarding practical improvements in the Berlin situation.

94

There is no question that *Rush's* personality was a distinct asset in dealing with the Soviets. For all his inner drive, he projected a disarmingly mild character. Then sixty, bespectacled and white-haired, he was almost always soft-spoken, invariably courteous and difficult to provoke. These qualities, as one colleague recalls, made the Ambassador "terrifically effective in dealing with the Soviets." He could be tough and at the same time polite, thus avoiding offending their sensibilities.

No doubt *Rush* enjoyed personal attributes which enhanced the effectiveness of the Western negotiating position. But he also possessed another important asset that may well have been more useful in bringing the Soviets around: he had direct access to both President *Nixon* and his National Security Adviser, *Henry Kissinger.* This personal relationship with the President paid off at several critical junctures in the talks. During these times, when the negotiations threatened to become deadlocked, the President and/or *Kissinger* were in direct contact with *Rush.* They gave him instructions, frequently catching the Department of State off-guard. Later the Ambassador described *Nixon's* crucial role in the deliberations in this way: "During the talks I was in touch with him frequently and received from him direct and frequent guidance." According to *Rush,* the President intervened "personally with Soviet officials to overcome difficulties which arose during the course of the negotiations." In sum, *Nixon's* help "was inestimable in bringing the negotiations to fruitation."[11]

As *Wilfred Kohl* reveals in his incisive analysis of the *Nixon-Kissinger* foreign policy system: "A further element in the back-channel network was *Henry Kissinger's* discussion of Berlin issues with Soviet Ambassador *Anatoly F. Dobrynin* at several points."[12] *Dr. Kissinger,* of course, relied heavily on the analysis of his own National Security Council staff. Critical here was the role played by *Helmut Sonnenfeldt,* a former Soviet specialist in the Department of State's Bureau of Intelligence and Research, and his associates. These individuals were very concerned that the bureau-

11 See "The Berlin Agreement: An Assessment," address by Kenneth Rush before the Berlin Chamber of Commerce and Industry, September 22, 1971, in Department of State Bulletin, Vol. 65, November 1, 1971, p. 493.

12 Wilfred Kohl, opus cit., p. 27.

cracy not rush prematurely into agreement with the Soviets. (*Dr. Kissinger,* himself, was opposed to the talks "from the very beginning," according to a well-informed inside source.)

Jackling and Sauvagnargues

It was a very real (though certainly not very pleasant) fact of life for *Rush's* British and French counterparts that the American envoy, because of the power position of the United States and his personal contact with the President, would play the dominant role among the Allies in the Four-Power negotiations. Thus, from the very beginning, there was bound to be certain friction and resentment towards "the American upstart." If *Rush* at the onset, however, could not impress his British and French colleagues with extensive diplomatic experience, he was able eventually to win their respect by his action and initiative.

Of his two counterparts, Sir *Roger William Jackling* (three years *Rush's* junior) had been Ambassador to the Federal Republic the longest; he had presented his diplomatic credentials on May 17, 1968. Like the American representative, *Jackling* was a lawyer by training (in British terms, a solicitor). He began his diplomatic career in 1939 as a Vice Consul in the British Consulate General in New York. During the war, he served a brief stint as a junior official attached to the Embassy of the United Kingdom in Washington. In 1957, after a four-year tour in Germany where he served as economic adviser to the British High Commissioner, he returned to the American capital – this time with the rank of Minister. He left the United States two years later with a promotion and began work in the British Foreign Office as Assistant Undersecretary of State; his efforts over the next four years were closely connected with the first negotiations for British membership in the Common Market. Between 1963 and 1967, he was posted to the United Nations in New York, where he served with distinction as the British Deputy Permanent Representative. His last post, before his appointment as Ambassador to Bonn, was Deputy Undersecretary of State in the Foreign Office in charge of economic affairs.

When asked in November 1971 about the role he played in the Berlin negotiations, Ambassador *Jackling* replied in the following manner:[13]

13 Interview with the Süddeutsche Zeitung, November 10, 1971.

"Successive British Governments had given consistent support to the objectives of the Federal Government's Ostpolitik and to the achievement of a Berlin agreement in that context. We appreciated the need for the Western side to present a solid front against the Soviet Union and the GDR in order to derive maximum benefit from the negotiations.

I would regard our major contribution as helping to provide a consistent thread to the Western position throughout the negotiations, so that the Russians were never able to take advantage of any disunity or contractions in the Western position."

Like his British colleague, *Jean Sauvagnargues,* age 55, was a man of considerable diplomatic experience in general and, in particular, had first-hand knowledge of the German scene. Shortly after the Berlin negotiations began, he officially replaced *Francois Seydoux de Clausonne* (on April 4, 1970) as French Ambassador to Bonn. A graduate of the prestigeous Ecole normale supérieure, *Sauvagnargues* entered the French diplomatic service in 1941. Several years later, he joined forces with *de Gaulle's* "Free French" movement, taking part in the invasion of Normandy and the liberation of his country as an officer of the famous Second Tank Division. During the early post-war period, he served in several high governmental positions dealing with German affairs. Between 1949 and 1955, he was chief of the Bureau of German-Austrian Affairs in the French Foreign Ministry. Then, he was made adviser for German and European affairs in the Office of the Foreign Minister. One of the highlights of his diplomatic service came subsequently when he was appointed head of the French delegation — at the experts level — in negotiations with the FRG over the disputed Saar territory. In the period 1956-1970, before he was dispatched to Bonn, he worked almost exclusively on African problems, serving first as Ambassador to Ethiopia (1956-60), then as Director of the Office of African and Near East Affairs in the Quai d'Orsay (1961-62) and finally as Ambassador in Tunis (1962-70).

During the Berlin talks there were serious differences of opinions among the Allied governments, and this was reflected in the interaction of *Rush, Jackling* and *Sauvagnargues* in the "Bonn Group." As one U.S. official recounts: At that time "relations between the French and Soviet governments were good." And it "was the policy of Paris to move closer to Moscow." This governmental position was not unlike that taken by Washington, but the Americans felt that the French were "moving too fast" and not exercising "enough caution." In any case, the cleavage between Washington and Paris on the matter of rapprochement with the Soviet Union "was reflected in the ambassadorial exchanges" and not infrequently was the "cause of considerable headache" to the U.S. negotiating team. Fortunately, for *Rush* and *Dean,* however, *"Sauvagnargues"* took a more independent line" than the French Foreign Ministry. But not always. "Sometimes," one American participant remembers, "after agreeing on a joint Western position, we would walk into a meeting with the Soviets, and the French Ambassador would proceed to side with or show sympathy for the Soviet position."

If there were some not inconsequential difficulties in American dealings with *Sauvagnargues* or other French officials during the talks, this reportedly was not the case as far as *Jackling* and the British were concerned. "The British usually gave us strong support," a delegate recalls. To no small degree, the closeness of the *Rush-Jackling* relationship stemmed from the fact that relations between the United Kingdom and the Soviet Union "weren't good." A "great breach between these two states had been created in 1971" after the Tory government of *Edward Heath* expelled a large number of Soviet personnel from Britain as spies. And this deterioration in relations hung over the last part of the Four-Power negotiations "poisoning" *Abrasimov's* dealings with *Jackling.*

Bahr and Scheel

During the Berlin deliberations, the Allies maintained close liaison with the West German government. As *Rush* said later, "Throughout the negotiations we received the fullest support from political leadership in the Federal Republic . . ."[14] On occasion, the Western Three dealt personally with Chancellor *Willy Brandt* himself (on a one-to-one basis). But most of the time their "contact man" was either *Egon Bahr,* State Secretary (Staatssekretär) in the Chancellor's Office during the first *Brandt* government (1969-72) or Foreign Minister *Walter Scheel* (later Federal President). The dapper *Scheel* unquestionably carried more weight. He was more than simply Foreign Minister in *Brandt's* Cabinet as he was also

14 Quoted from Rush's speech of September 22, 1971.

head of the Free Democratic Party, continued coalition with which remained essential to the survival of the Chancellor's government. Yet, as far as relative influence upon *Brandt* in "broad policy conception" is concerned, there is stronger evidence of the power of *Bahr's* influence.[15]

Probably better known outside Germany for his contribution to Ostpolitik, *Bahr* was instrumental during the early 1960s in helping give precision to *Brandt's* ideas in the area of all-German policy (Deutschlandpolitik). One of the most important was Wandel durch Annäherung (change through approach). This in reality described a way — not of overcoming the division of Germany[16] — but of easing conditions caused by the split. The second was the "policy of small steps" (kleine Schritte). *Bahr* and *Brandt* came to the conclusion in the early post-Wall period that the only way to prevent a further widening of the German division was to initiate a program of increasing contacts.

Bahr's role in the Four-Power negotiations is the subject of great controversy. Although *Rush* maintains in retrospect that "I personally liked Bahr and got along well with him," it is no secret that the State Secretary's relations with the governments of the Western Three were strained. In large part, this was due to the fact that the Allied bureaucracy did not trust him. As one high-level American official with extensive dealings with *Bahr* says: "The people in the State Department were against him because they thought he was too shifty in his dealings with the Soviet Union. They thought he gave in too much, that his policy was creating an ambivalent Germany and making her less of a staunch NATO ally."

Abrasimov

In *Pyotr A. Abrasimov,* 58 of age, the Western Three were up against "a very tough, hard bargainer," who was intimately familiar with that "jungle of technicalities" known as the Berlin problem.

15 See for instance Walter F. Hahn, "West Germany's Ostpolitik: The Grand Design of Egon Bahr," Orbis, Vol. 16, No. 4 (Winter, 1973), pp.860-861.

16 Interestingly enough, and hard for some outsiders to comprehend, Bahr has maintained throughout that he continues to see Ostpolitik in terms of eventual German re-unification. The ambiguity in the policy of successive West German governments has prompted one serious student of German politics (Peter Bender) to remark that the "only way to introduce a new policy in the Federal Republic is to guarantee that it is merely a continuation of an old one."

Titled the "proconsul" by the Allies because of the "iron hand" he allegedly held over the East German leadership,[17] the Soviet Ambassador had been stationed in Germany longer than *Rush, Jackling* and *Sauvagnargues* together. He was first dispatched to the Soviet Embassy in East Berlin in 1962. By the time the Four-Power talks began, he had already spent eight years in the divided city.

Not much is known publicly about the Soviet representative; his biography in Allied hands remains highly classified. A Byelorussian, *Abrasimov* was born on May 16, 1912 in what is now Vitebsk Oblast. He pursued a technical career until mid-1930, when he suddenly switched to the cultural field, becoming representative to a local Philharmonic society and art director. During the first year of the war he was wounded twice. Subsequently, in 1942, he transferred to the Byelorussian party Central Committee and began work for a local partisan movement against the Germans in occupied Byelorussian territory. At the end of the war, *Abrasimov* emerged as a major figure in the Byelorussian communist party and government. From 1948 to 1957, he served alternately as First Deputy Chairman of the republic's Council of Ministers and a Chairman of the Byelorussian party Central Committee. In 1957, he was unaccountably transferred to the Soviet Foreign Ministry and posted to Moscow's Embassy in Peking as Deputy Chief of Mission. Nine months later, he was named Ambassador to Warsaw, a post he held for the next four years. In 1961, he resumed his party career for a brief period, winning election as First Secretary of Smolensk Oblast (RSFSR region bordering on Byelorussia) and as a voting member of the Central Committee of the communist party. A year

17 Allied officials maintain that this relationship remains more or less the same today. After departing Berlin in 1971 shortly after the conclusion of the Berlin talks to take up the position of Soviet Ambassador to France, Abrasimov returned to the GDR in March 1975 for a second tour as Ambassador to East Germany. At that time, there was speculation that his presence signalled either that Moscow would now take a harder line on Berlin or that the Kremlin, concerned about the opening up of the GDR to the West, would try to clamp down on these contacts. This latter theory seems to have been realized. Abrasimov, for instance, informed his American counterpart that he (Cooper) should go through the Soviet representative (Abrasimov) if he needed anything from the East German leadership. At the time of this writing (1977), U.S. Embassy officials in East Berlin were limited to three official contacts with the GDR régime.

later, in November, he returned to the Soviet foreign service and was immediately ordered to East Berlin to take over as Soviet Ambassador to the GDR.

During the Berlin negotiations, the Western Three got to know *Abrasimov* — the party man, the diplomat — quite well. A participant describes the relationship *Rush, Jackling* and *Sauvagnargues* had with the Soviet "proconsul": "Our relationship had all the elements of a classic love/hate relationship. At times, it was full of spite; at other times it was open and warm." *Abrasimov* was "a very difficult, volatile, emotional man. He was very ideological." As a negotiator, the Soviet representative "thought he could wear us down to a point where we would be grateful for anything he was willing to give us."

Working Methods

Crucial in appreciating the success of the Four-Power talks is an understanding of the working methods of the parties. That the Ambassadors spent over 152 long and tedious hours in formal conference is well known. However, the most constructive dialogue frequently did not take place there. Rather it occurred over lunch afterwards in a greatly relaxed atmosphere or in private (secret) sessions, conducted on a one-to-one basis.

Formally, the negotiations took place at two distinct levels. On the one hand, there were the face-to-face plenary sessions of the four Ambassadors meeting with their delegations. On the other, there were the so-called meetings of the "experts," when the Political Counselors of the four would sit down to "tidy up" the details. In their plenary sessions, the envoys were accompanied by a small staff of about five, including an interpreter. (This was to keep things "functional.") Each of these rounds had a chairman, and the chairmanship was rotated among the powers. For the most part, as one member of the U.S. delegation recounts, "these meetings started off with a formal statement, drafted by each side, and then we went from there."

The sessions of the experts were greatly overshadowed by these ambassadorial meetings and consequently received little attention in the press. But they played a major role in the negotiations. The four chief participants here were *Jonathan Dean* (USA), *René*

Lustig (France), *Christopher Audland* (UK) and *Julij Kwizinsky* USSR).

Initially, there was some controversy among the political advisers over the language to be used in their discussions. Although each party was equipped with its own interpreter, the American side preferred to work in English and the Soviet side in Russian. Both sides were wary of the pitfalls of trying to operate in the native tongue of the adversary. Eventually, this hurdle was overcome, however, and German was agreed upon informally as the common working language. (In the exchanges among the Ambassadors, *Rush* used English; and *Abrasimov* Russian; *Sauvagnargues* would usually wave the use of French since he was fluent in English.)

This decision by the experts was made in the spirit of compromise, but apparently its implications were not fully appreciated at the time. In any case, it put the American side at a distinct psychological and working disadvantage. For *"Jock" Dean's* notetaker — although he spoke fluent French — was in the process of coming to grips with what *Mark Twain* called the "awful German language". This situation later led to no small confusion — even though participants now tend to play down its importance, arguing that "this was hardly a significant U.S. disadvantage since the first sessions were pro forma rounds."

In the beginning, the political advisers did not meet at all on the "experts" level. It was only in October, 1970 (as it became clear that the Soviets were really prepared to negotiate an agreement the West could accept) that they began serious work. At that time, they were put to work drafting the first common "talking paper." All ambassadorial exchanges were subsequently preceded by the extensive preparations of these men. Later, in May 1971, they set about formulating the first common quadripartite draft text. Then, in June and July 1971, as the envoys began to rush toward agreement, they were called into almost continuous session to firm up the details and, at the last minute, to supervise the drafting of an unofficial German translation.

If much of the written detail work took place in formal conference at both the ambassadorial and expert levels, this was greatly facilitated by the informal, off-the-record talks held by the Big Four in private. Especially important in this regard were the free-wheeling discussions, held by the Ambassadors over lunch after the regular Four-Power exchanges had concluded, and the many long hours spent by *Rush* in private conversation with *Abrasimov* (and *Falin*, the Soviet envoy stationed in Bonn).

The lunches were *Rush's* idea. As he recollects: "After the first (conference) meeting, I invited all the Ambassadors over to my house for lunch. They liked the procedure so well that they just followed up on it." Present at these meals, which often would continue "into the late afternoon," were only the four envoys and their interpreters. The political advisers and other staff members were deliberately excluded from these affairs, which so often turned into "informal bargaining" rounds.

From the onset, Ambassador *Rush* was determined to develop good personal relations with his Soviet counterpart. "Somehow we had to overcome Soviet suspicions and demonstrate to them that we were serious about détente," he confided later. In the beginning, this meant having *Abrasimov* and his family over for small "get togethers." But later, as the two men got to know each other better, they spent long hours together in private but "very productive" conversation.

Looking back on these private sessions, *Rush* feels that they were of great importance in smoothing the way for Four-Power agreement. Often during these times, *Abrasimov* would outline some of his problems in the negotiations on a certain issue. Grasping the opportunity, the American representative would then tell him: "Well, if that is your problem, why don't we just settle matters this way." *Rush* would then proceed to outline a "face-saving" solution, which would adequately take both Soviet and Allied interests into account. "If I hadn't done that," he insists, "we wouldn't have had any Berlin agreement." What "some people fail to understand today," *Rush* says, "is that in negotiations you can't force the other side to agree to something. You have to take its interests into consideration."

Because of the "negative attitude" of the bureaucracy, *Rush* kept these private meetings with *Abrasimov* confidential. "If the bureaucracy had known about them," he explains, "it would have tried to sabotage them. I would have been told I was exceeding my authority." In these private dealings with *Abrasimov*, the American Ambassador says he received President *Nixon's* full support. "He told me to keep in close contact with him through *Dr. Kissinger* and *Al Haig*" (at the White House), but otherwise "I was free — even encouraged — to bypass the bureaucracy."

The First Meetings

When the victorious powers of World War II gathered in Berlin on March 26, 1970 to discuss the problems of the divided city for the first time in eleven years, the scene was reminiscent of the early occupation period in Germany: The baroque council chamber in which the American, British and French Ambassadors to Bonn sat down with the Soviet envoy to East Berlin was the same room from which Allied governors had tried briefly to rule a defeated Germany after the war.

The Opening Session

The first meeting of the Big Four was the subject of a great deal of international attention. The much heralded event was covered extensively in the press and on television, yet it produced little in the way of concrete results. In fact, it first appeared as if the warnings of sceptics had been realized as the two sides could not even agree on the subject matter to be discussed.

The first round of negotiations lasted just two and a half hours. But such was the secrecy shrouding this session that outsiders for a long time were kept in the dark about the basic irreconcilability of the two initial bargaining positions. It was only learned much later that the March 26th meeting had witnessed a sharp clash of legal views, which threatened to make impossible desired practical improvements in the Berlin situation. The Soviet emissary, apparently on strict orders from the Kremlin to press for Allied acceptance of the Soviet right to have a say in affairs regarding West Berlin, insisted that only the Western half of the city be open to discussion. "It is well known," *Abrasimov* argued, that East Berlin had long ago become irrevocably integrated with the German Democratic Republic. Therefore, the Russian Ambassador said, it could not possibly be a matter of concern here.[18]

Rush, acting as the spokesman for the Western powers, countered the Soviet assertion by recalling the historical basis for the quadripartite position in "Greater Berlin," which also included its Eastern Sector. The special status of Berlin, he stressed, had been determined by those agreements which were drafted by the European Advisory Commission in London during 1944 and

18 See Der Spiegel, April 6, 1970.

1945.[19] Essentially, these accords fixed the post-war Occupation Zones in Germany and provided for the joint occupation and administration of the former Reichshauptstadt. Accordingly, the victorious Allies never intended the "Greater Berlin" area to be either a "part" of or "on" the territory to be occupied by any of the Four Powers.[20]

In retrospect, the adamant stand taken by the two sides in regard to their respective legal positions appears to have reflected a basic initial unwillingess to seem "soft" on specific issues. Thus, the West rejected as "extreme" Soviet demands concerning the removal of a West German political presence in West Berlin.[21] And the

19 The European Advisory Commission (EAC), consisting of American, British and Soviet representatives, was established in 1943 to consider the problems of conquered enemy countries in detail. In all, the EAC held some twenty formal and ninety-seven informal meetings and was finally dissolved by the Potsdam Conference in 1945. Altogether, it concluded twelve tripartite accords, dealing with the surrender and peace settlements in Austria, Bulgaria and Germany. France, under German occupation at the time, was not a member of the EAC. For details see Philip Mosley, "The Occupation of Germany," Foreign Affairs, Vol. 28, No. 4 (July, 1950), pp. 580-604.

20 In total, there were three agreements on Germany and Berlin hammered out by American, British and Soviet representatives on the EAC. The first was signed on September 12, 1944 and was responsible for dividing Berlin and Germany into three Sectors and Zones respectively. The second was an amendment signed on November 14, 1944; it allocated the northwest parts of Berlin and Germany to the United Kingdom, established the Bremen territory for the United States and assigned the southwest parts of Berlin and Germany to the United States. The third and final accord was also an amendment signed on July 26, 1945. It provided for the French occupation of part of Berlin and Germany in accordance with the Yalta Agreement. For the texts see Wolfgang Heidelmeyer et al (eds.), Documents on Berlin 1943-1963 (Munich: R. Oldenbourg Verlag, 1963).

21 Soon after the creation of the West German Federal Republic thoughts were already being given in Bonn to the opening of Federal offices in West Berlin. This move was conceived to underscore Bonn's status in the German Constitution (Basic Law) as a provisional capital and the West German claim that Berlin is the real capital of Germany (a point of view taken by the Bundestag in a formal declaration on February 6, 1957). Consequently, on October 29, 1949, the FRG decided to establish in West Berlin offices representing the various West German ministries. The one exception was the Defense Ministry, which was forbidden by the Western Three to operate in the city out of respect for the demilitarization provisions in the Potsdam Agreement. For details see Walter Krumholz et al,

USSR declared as "non-negotiable" the Western proposal regarding freedom of movement for *all* Berliners, relaxation in communications, trade, access and West German representation abroad of the Western Sectors. All in all, it was a most disappointing — but understandable — beginning for the quadripartite talks.

At the end of the first session, the four diplomats issued a terse, 18-line communiqué. But instead of providing any inside information as to what problems had been discussed, this joint statement merely underscored by its silence the frustration of the conference. According to it, the three Western Ambassadors had limited themselves merely to "an exchange of views" with their Soviet colleague. The communiqué noted that another gathering would be held in late April.[22]

The Four-Power communiqué was unique in that it made no mention of the word "Berlin." Although the reason for its absence was not made public at the time, it reflected general disagreement over the proper term to be used. The Soviets wanted to insert the word "West Berlin" to support their view that only the Western Sectors were the subject of discussion. Whereas the United States, Great Britain and France insisted on the term "Berlin," which represented their position that all of the city was the focus of negotiation.[23]

Suspension of Allied Travel Office

The only major development to arise from the March 26th meeting concerned the decision by the Western Three after the opening session to suspend indefinitely the activities of the Allied Travel Office (ATO) in West Berlin. Initially, this announcement touched off a flurry of speculation that the move was tantamount to recognizing East German passports or that the West was

Berlin-ABC, rev. ed. (Berlin: Press and Information Office, 1968), pp. 298-299. At the present time, there are more than fifty Federal bodies and agencies based in Berlin, employing some 23,000 people. These include the Bundespräsident's Office, located at Schloss Bellevue, and the agencies of the various Bonn ministries, housed in Berlin's Bundeshaus.

22 For the text see Archiv der Gegenwart, April 1, 1970.

23 Der Spiegel, April 6, 1970.

moving toward recognition of the German Democratic Republic. But Allied officials denied this.[24]

Previously, they said an East German had to go to West Berlin and obtain a special travel document from ATO before applying for travel in thirteen of fifteen NATO countries. Effective March 27, however, individual members of the alliance would have the sole responsibility for issuing documents to East German nationals wishing to visit them. Western authorities were quick to point out, however, that the abolition by the Allies of one of their few remaining levers in dealing with East Germany did not imply even de facto recognition of the GDR. For NATO members had agreed among themselves not to stamp visas directly in East German passports but to affix them to a separate piece of paper.[25]

Western sources explained that the Allies were taking this step because the old system had been bitterly denounced by the GDR as degrading to its citizens and often cited as one reason why it did not give East Germans the right to travel freely in the West. These sources said they hoped the long-planned gesture would be reciprocated by progress in the negotiations on access and visits by West Berliners across the Wall.[26]

What officials failed to point out to the press, however, was that the Western Three had initially attempted to obtain Soviet approval of this "concession" and have it recorded in the official minutes of the meeting. But *Abrasimov* balked, refusing to accept the Western wording which spoke only of "East Germans" and not "citizens of the GDR."[27]

If the relaxing of travel restrictions on East Germans represented a gesture of good will to the GDR on the part of the Western powers, it also served to remove a source of disharmony in NATO. During the "cold war" individual members of the alliance had stood firmly behind the Allied policy of issuing Temporary Travel Documents ("TTD") to East Germans travelling to NATO countries. But in the new era of détente this unity began to crack. First, Italy and Canada, believing the preservation of the old

24 See U.S. Mission (Berlin), Berlin 1970 — An Unofficial Chronology (43) (Berlin: USIS, April 1970), p. 4.

25 Die Welt, March 31, 1970.

26 The Washington Post, March 27, 1970.

27 Der Spiegel, April 6, 1970.

system no longer to be worth the trouble, began to disregard the Allied device. Then Denmark and Norway started pressing for suspension of the "TTD." With NATO support of the Allied procedure thus dwindling, the opening of the Four-Power talks was opportunely seized upon as the ideal moment to suspend the controversial activities of ATO while at the same time scoring a propaganda advantage.[28]

The Second Meeting

The pace of the quadripartite negotiations between March and July 1970 was in the words of U.S. Ambassador *Kenneth Rush* "extremely difficult."[29] During the six sessions held at this time

28 The Allied Travel Office (ATO) has an interesting history. Originally, it had been set up at the end of 1945 as an organ of the Allied Control Council. At that time, it was known as the "Entry and Exits Branch" and operated on a quadripartite basis. Its purpose was to issue "a Temporary Travel Document" to all German citizens desiring to travel outside Berlin and the four Occupation Zones. Subsequently, in 1947, the three Western powers decided to replace the Four-Power Entry and Exits Branch with the Tripartite Combined Travel Board. This agency became defunct two years later (1949) except for one remaining office which continued to operate in West Berlin. In 1951, this office — under its new name (ATO) — was transferred from its residence at the American Headquarters to the building in the U.S. Sector which housed the former Allied Control Council. One year later, American, British and French officials empowered the West German government with the authority to issue its own passports. Thereafter, the Allied Travel Office was responsible only for issuing Temporary Travel Documents ("TTD") to citizens of East Berlin and East Germany who wished to visit countries (primarily Western) which did not recognize the GDR passport as a valid travel document. They were required to have a "TTD" in their possession before they could obtain a visa from the Western state they wished to visit. The GDR protested this procedure, claiming it violated its sovereignty and that of the host country. But to no avail. In retaliation for the closing of the East Berlin border in 1961, ATO refused to issue travel documents to East Germans except under unusual circumstances. This meant that GDR nationals who wished to travel to the West under government auspices were generally barred from doing so. This policy of restricting the travel of East Germans in the West remained in effect through the late sixties when the Allies — under mounting pressure — decided to relax controls. For details see The Allied Travel Office (ATO) in West Berlin: Illegal Obstruction on the Road to the Guarantee of European Security (Dresden: Verlag Zeit im Bild, 1970).

29 Kenneth Rush, "The Berlin Agreement: An Assessment," The Atlantic Community Quarterly, Vol. 10, No. 1 (1972), p. 57.

the Soviets reiterated their well-known position that they had transferred full control of East Berlin and the access routes to the GDR. The British, French and Americans countered by repeating their public position that the Four-Power status of Berlin encompassed both parts of the city and that there were quadripartite rights of access — civilian as well as military.

The second meeting of the four Ambassadors took place without ceremony on April 28, barely four weeks after the opening session. But if the Western powers had hoped that their announcement of the easing of restrictions on travel of East Germans to NATO countries at the end of the first gathering would lead the Soviets to reciprocate by at least persuading the GDR régime to allow some resumption of telephone service between the two parts of the city, they were bound to be disappointed. For this did not happen.

Rather, the GDR chose on the day of this second meeting to take the provocative step of announcing a 20-30 percent increase in the tolls it charged on truck and barge traffic entering West Berlin from the Federal Republic. This measure was designed to affect about eleven million tons of goods transported annually and was expected to cost West German shippers an estimated three million dollars more in toll charges. The timing of this announcement indicated that the East German régime was still a long way from being in an accomodating frame of mind on Berlin.[30]

That provocation on the access lanes was matched by Soviet intransigence in the two-hour round of ambassadorial talks held the same day. The Russians claimed that they could not interfere in the affairs of a sovereign country such as the German Democratic Republic and could not recommend restoration of the customary transit regulations until the desire of the GDR for full international recognition had been met. The Allies, who continued to hold the Soviet Union responsible for East German actions on the accessways, rejected this argument. And so the second meeting came to a speedy conclusion without the two sides even starting to negotiate on specifics.[31]

30 The Washington Post, April 29, 1970.
31 Christ und Welt, July 3, 1970.

West German Moves

In view of the slow and laborious pace of the Berlin talks, public attention returned in May 1970 to the intra-German discussion and Soviet-West German negotiations. Of immediate importance here was the return meeting in Kassel by the two German heads of government. It was scheduled to take place one week after the third round of ambassadorial deliberations.

The Second Brandt-Stoph Summit

To smoothe the way for this second summit, the two German governments had undertaken in the months following the historic Erfurt meeting in March a series of smaller steps to improve the general climate of their relations. Negotiations held in Bonn between the Federal Ministry of Posts and the East German Ministry for Posts and Telecommunications resulted on April 29, 1970 in a partial agreement on postal traffic. According to it, the West German government undertook, retroactive to 1967 and until 1973, to pay East Germany 30 million marks as an annual lump sum compensation for the costs of inter-German postal communications as well as those from the FRG through the GDR to other East European countries. At the same time, the two German states agreed to increase the number of telephone lines between them, from 34 to 74 and of telex lines from 19 to 35.

This accord was followed a day later by the West German decision to take several unilateral tax measures vis-à-vis the GDR. On the one hand, it moved to make sales to East Germany less profitable; on the other, it proceeded to make purchases of industrial goods from the GDR cheaper. These measures were taken to reduce the large West German surplus in trade with East Germany. Finally, Bonn moved in the Bundestag to repeal the Act of 1966, granting safe-conduct in the FRG to certain representatives of the East German SED (Socialist Unity Party) who might have been previously connected with the prevention of escapes of Germans from the GDR to the West (a punishable offense under Federal law). This legislation had been passed in the context of the abortive proposal that SPD leaders should address an SED meeting in Karl-Marx-Stadt and East German communist party leaders an

SPD meeting in Hannover. And it had aroused strong hostility on the part of the GDR and Soviet governments.[32]

Chancellor *Brandt* and Premier *Stoph* met on May 21 in Kassel, the economic capital of the West German state of Hessen. As the train bearing *Willi Stoph* rolled across the border, the East German Premier had reason to believe that his own reception in the Bundesrepublik would be at least as tumultuous as the greeting his citizens gave *Brandt* in Erfurt. For in preparation for his visit, almost every member and sympathizer of the small but newly licensed West German communist party (DKP)[33] had been encouraged to flock to the conference site to root and demonstrate for their man. As things turned out, the communist turnout was considerable. Cheered by a delegation of supporters in Kassel, *Stoph* confidently announced to newsmen that he "noticed everywhere how friendly the welcome was."[34] But he had spoken too soon. To the embarrassment of the West German host, the dramatic return engagement threatened to turn into a fiasco before it even got underway and deal a stunning blow to *Brandt's* Deutschlandpolitik.

Stoph and *Brandt* had scarcely shaken hands before the trouble began. The black, red and gold East German flag was hauled down and torn to pieces by three right-wing teen-agers with forged press passes which enabled them to get close to official activities.

The most serious confrontation, however, occurred at a monu-

32 See Keesing's Contemporary Archives, August 29 - September 5, 1970, p. 24158.

33 According to the West German Constitution, political parties are considered official organs, and as such they have particular responsibilities. Perhaps one of the most important is upholding the democratic order. Given the "anti-democratic" political aims of the German Communist Party (KPD), the Federal Constitutional Court suppressed it in 1956. However, since the KPD was such a negligible political force in the Federal Republic, the political efficacy of this decision was hotly disputed at the time. As some liberals did not hesitate to point out, the court, by declaring the KPD illegal, actually helped to camouflage the electoral weakness of the party. This attitude largely explains why no legal action was taken against the communists in 1968, when their party reemerged under a new name (DKP). As anticipated, the reestablished party won only 114,000 votes or 0.3 percent of the total cast in the parliamentary elections of 1972. For details see Heino Kaack, Geschichte und Struktur des deutschen Parteisystems (Cologne: Westdeutscher Verlag, 1971).

34 Newsweek, June 1, 1970.

ment dedicated to the victims of fascism. There *Stoph* was scheduled to lay a wreath. But the wreath-laying ceremony had to be postponed after an attempt was made to stop the limousine in which the two were riding.

About this time thousands of demonstrators of right and left-wing persuasions clashed with each other in bloody street riots. During the turbulent street clashes, the local police were rather ineffectual and the official SED newspaper Neues Deutschland complained of "unheard of provocations."[35]

With the summit visit thus turning into an embarrassing public brawl, there was mounting speculation that *Stoph* would stage a dramatic walkout. At the morning session, the East German leader strongly protested the desecration of his country's flag and extracted an apology from the nervous *Brandt*. Following this session, *Stoph* made a mile-long trip back to his private train, from which a private telephone call could be made to *Walter Ulbricht* in East Berlin. Although the communist party leader had never been enthusiastic about the Chancellor's initiatives in the first place, *Ulbricht* had just returned from Moscow where interest in improving relations with Bonn was still high. In the end, the summit was salvaged, and after a tense twenty-six minute delay the afternoon conference session began.[36]

During his talks with *Stoph,* the Chancellor discussed Berlin and its role in the efforts of his government to improve East-West relations. But more importantly, *Brandt* set forth a bold program of twenty points, in which he offered the GDR important accommodations in many fields. In the main, his detailed plan expanded on those points the Chancellor had already presented to the Bundestag in his address of January 14 and had repeated at Erfurt. While supporting an expansion of trade between the two countries, *Brandt* proposed greater cooperation in the areas of transportation and traffic, postal communications and telecommunications, science, education, culture, environmental problems and sports. Last but not least, the Chancellor — although he was not prepared to grant the GDR the desired full diplomatic recognition — was prepared to "respect the independence and autonomy of each of the two states in affairs affecting their internal sovereign authority." As evidence of his good will, *Brandt* announced his readiness —

35 Neues Deutschland, May 22, 1970.
36 Newsweek, June 1, 1970.

after practical improvements in inner-German relations had been obtained — to conclude a treaty with the GDR formally regulating their relations.[37]

Premier *Stoph* responded to *Brandt's* sweeping proposals with a 22-page riposte. It ripped apart the underlying assumption of the Chancellor's Deutschlandpolitik — that small steps in minor matters could ultimately lead to a rapprochement. He derided *Brandt's* "arrogant demands" and declared that Bonn first recognize the GDR as a sovereign state. Likewise, he rejected out of hand his counterpart's thesis that the two German states could exist within a single German nation.[38]

As far as Berlin was concerned, the East German leader dismissed bluntly "all attempts" by the West German government "to interfere" in West Berlin affairs. Claiming that "the independent political entity" was situated "in the middle of the German Democratic Republic," he continued to insist that the Federal Republic possessed "no rights or competencies whatever in and for West Berlin." Lastly, *Stoph* denied that a settlement of the "problem of West Berlin" was connected with the issue of the establishment of relations between the FRG and the GDR.[39]

The two heads of government left Kassel without having come any closer to agreement. And no date was set for another summit. In his press conference following the meeting, the Chancellor hinted that contacts would continue on a technical level. But as far as the big political issues separating the two states were concerned, *Brandt* let it be known that he and his guest had decided to institute a Denkpause (thinking pause) for the time being. Obviously, this formula had been devised to hide the evident lack of concrete results of the talks.

The Bonn-Moscow Treaty

As the two German governments took time during June and July to reconsider their positions, the quadripartite discussions dragged

---

37 A copy of Chancellor Brandt's remarks is contained in Kassel, May 21, 1970: A Documentation (Bonn: Press and Information Office, 1970).

38 For the full text of Stoph's remarks see ibid.

39 See Kassel, May 21, 1970: A Documentation (Bonn: Federal Press and Information Office, 1970).

on without notable progress. The third, fourth, fifth and sixth sessions continued to focus on the Soviet view of the status of West Berlin and so-called "illegal" West German political activities in the city that must be suspended. The Soviet Ambassador rejected all political and legal claims by West Germany on West Berlin and insisted that the Western powers had no authority to delegate any rights in the city to the Bonn government. He reiterated that the Western Three were carrying out only administrative functions in Berlin and could not make any decisions affecting Four-Power agreements or permit in the Western Sectors actions by third states without exceeding their authority. If *Abrasimov* took a "hard line" with regard to West Berlin's legal and political links with the Bundesrepublik, he nevertheless indicated that the Soviet Union might be willing to accept economic and cultural ties between the two.[40]

The Western Three replied that they were prepared to make a number of adjustments in exchange for adequate reciprocity. Thus, after conferring with Bonn, they supported the possibility of a substantial reduction in the demonstrative Federal presence and constitutional transactions in the Western Sectors. In return for normalization of the access routes, they advanced the possibility that the Bundespräsident would refrain from conducting official actions in West Berlin and the Bundestag from holding sessions. But the Allies refused to accept the Soviet demand that the Federal agencies already situated in Berlin should be dismantled and their 23,000 employees discharged.[41]

With public interest in the Berlin negotiations flagging, *Brandt's* Ostpolitik became the center of attention once more. For the most part, the flurry of diplomatic activity focused on Moscow, but a platoon of diplomatic emissaries from Bonn also descended on Warsaw, Prague, Budapest and Bucharest. They offered favorable credit and commercial arrangements as well as assurances about the peaceful aims of the Federal Republic. Generally, they were favorably, if cautiously, received.

Brandt singled out the Soviet Union for special treatment because he felt the key to diminished tension between East and West Europe lay in Moscow. His efforts in this regard had begun already in September 1969, when as Foreign Minister he made

40 Christ und Welt, July 3, 1970.

41 Lawrence L. Whetten, "The Problem of Berlin," The World Today, Vol. 27, No. 5 (May, 1971), pp. 224-225.

public a Soviet note proposing talks on a nonaggression pact.[42] Although the Russians offered negotiations in Moscow, the proposal was caught up in election politics and so a positive response was not immediately forthcoming. Once he became Chancellor, however, the Social Democrat gave reconciliation with the Kremlin top priority.

After a mere five weeks in office, the new Chancellor put an end to West Germany's 18-month reluctance to sign the Nuclear Nonproliferation Treaty and attached the signature of the FRG. This step went a long way to assuage Russian fears that Bonn sought nuclear weapons. And it was followed in early 1970 by a huge pipe deal. Under it, a consortium of West German banks put together an enormous credit to finance the Soviet purchase of 1.2 million tons of West German-made large diameter steel pipes. The pipes were to extend Soviet gas lines from Siberia. As part of the total deal, which is valued at about one billion dollars, the Russians agreed to supply a tenth of the natural gas requirements of the FRG from 1973 to 1993.[43]

Arrangements for the pipe deal provided the background against which extensive exploratory talks began with the Kremlin regarding an agreement on the mutual renunciation of force. These negotiations were conducted in Moscow by *Brandt's* diplomatic trouble-shooter and chief foreign policy adviser State Secretary *Egon Bahr*. There he met with Foreign Minister *Andrei Gromyko* about forty times during the early spring and summer of 1970. For the most part, these discussions were hard going, but in the end they produced a draft treaty — the so-called *"Bahr* text." Among other things, this very controversial paper contained a number of important accommodations by Bonn including a call for West Germany and the Soviet Union to "respect" the territorial integrity of all states within their existing borders.

The practical effect of this draft seemed to take Bonn a big step down the road toward irrevocable recognition of the GDR and the Oder-Neisse line. Consequently, it came under heavy fire from the Christian Democrats who assailed the text as a "sellout," in which Bonn made all the concessions while obtaining nothing in return. In particular, the opposition trained its attack on the failure of

42 The Washington Post, September 17, 1969.
43 The Washington Post, September 19, 1971.

Bahr to obtain mention either of West Germany's ties to West Berlin or affirmation of Germany's right to eventual reunification. Apparently, in the effort to arouse popular opposition to the *Bahr* text, an enemy of *Brandt* high in the government leaked excerpts from the paper to Hamburg's very popular newspaper Bild-Zeitung.

With public pressure thus mounting, *Brandt* was eventually persuaded to send Foreign Minister *Scheel* to Moscow to renegotiate the terms of the draft treaty. *Scheel* arrived in the Soviet capital on July 27 without a single member of the opposition Christian Democratic Union in his entourage. (The CDU/CSU chose to break a West German tradition by refusing bipartisan participation in the delegation.) Direct talks between the informal *Scheel* and the austere *Gromyko* began on the same day.

Scheel set about his task with an astuteness that surprised his critics at home. No doubt, the fact that the Kremlin was open to changes in the *Bahr* text was greatly encouraging to *Scheel* and reinforced his conviction that the Russians were serious about wanting to improve relations with Bonn. Skirting pitfalls with the adroitness of a professional diplomat, the former Luftwaffe pilot wrapped up negotiations in record time.[44]

Just before *Scheel* was to depart Moscow after eleven days of hard bargaining, *Gromyko* disappeared into the depths of the Kremlin. There the Soviet Foreign Minister conferred with Russian leaders. And at a special session of the Politbüro the new draft was approved. The next day it was initialled by the two diplomats.

The signing of the Bonn-Moscow Treaty five days later (August 12, 1970) was an historic event.[45] For it represented the first major breakthrough for *Brandt's* policy of reconciliation with the communist nations of Eastern Europe. To underscore this point, the Chancellor personally travelled to the Soviet capital to attach his signature to this important document.

The document signed by *Brandt* was noteworthy for its brevity. Moreover, it was considerably changed from the working draft.

44 As one critic has pointed out: "Scheel did a nice job, but the treaty remained essentially the first four points of the text Bahr negotiated. Basic changes were not made; it was more a matter of finding means to take care of what the FRG needed for domestic political purposes."

45 For the text of this treaty see The Treaty of August 12, 1970 between the Federal Republic of Germany and the Union of Soviet Socialist Republics (Bonn: Press and Information Office, 1970).

116

Six of the original ten articles were dropped altogether; this represented no great loss to either side since they were merely designed to spell out "intent" anyway.[46] In total, the final version consisted of a preamble and five articles. The last one was tacked on at the last minute and outlined procedures for promulgating the treaty.

The key points of the agreement, whose contents were highly publicized, are articles two and three. These provisions pledge both governments to a mutual renunciation of force as a means of settling disputes and to respect the "inviolability" of all European nations within their existing frontiers. The latter point was a matter of great controversy within the Federal Republic because it amounted to de facto recognition by Bonn of the division of Germany as well as the loss of former German territory east of the Oder-Neisse line.

Recognizing this, and with an eye to easing the passage of the pact through a sceptical West German parliament, the Soviets agreed to accept two auxiliaries to the treaty. The first involved a written safeguard of the German right to unity. And it took the form of a letter from *Brandt* (a device known as "the German option"), stating his understanding that German aspirations towards eventual reunification through peaceful means are not contradictory to the spirit or intent of the new treaty. A German spokesman said this communication had been handed over formally to the Soviet Foreign Ministry half an hour before the signing ceremony. Consequently, Soviet acceptance of the letter without comment meant under international law that it became a valid part of the agreement.

Another "separate instrument" to the treaty consisted of an exchange of notes between the Federal Republic and the three Western powers. In general, it reaffirmed that the pact in no way substitutes for a peace treaty ending World War II, and hence it does not infringe on Allied rights in Germany, including Berlin. Like the *Brandt* letter, the exchange of notes was not formally part of the treaty text but was deposited with the treaty package and is viewed as legally binding.

---

46 Despite the fact that the six articles were not in the treaty text, they remained on the negotiating record; and they have proved highly useful in subsequent Soviet-West German dealings in clarifying intent.

The Junktim

During the bargaining over the Bonn-Moscow Treaty it became clear that a favorable outcome would depend on progress made on the Berlin issue. Thus, when West German Foreign Minister *Walter Scheel* arrived in the Kremlin to renegotiate the *Bahr* text, he stressed that Soviet concessions on the divided city were essential to any agreement. His remarks so annoyed the Soviet Foreign Minister that at one point *Gromyko* snapped at *Scheel:* "Berlin is not your concern." Later the Soviet diplomat mellowed and promised *Scheel* privately that, once the renunciation-of-force treaty was signed, the USSR would cooperate with the West to improve the position of West Berlin. The German diplomat subsequently proceeded with the initialing of the treaty, but insisted that the West German government would not submit the document to the Bundestag for final ratification until progress on the Berlin question had taken place. This connection between the isolated city and the West German-Soviet treaty was dubbed "the Junktim" by the West German press.[47]

During his short trip to Moscow for the official signing ceremony, Chancellor *Brandt* sought at every opportunity to engage Soviet leaders on the subject of Berlin and press home his view that ratification of the pact by parliament was linked to a successful outcome of the Four-Power talks. At his final meeting with the Soviets, Premier *Kosygin* begged off by saying that the Russians, after all, had only a fourth of the responsibility for the discussions on the divided city. In reply, the Chancellor quoted *George Orwell's* famous aphorism: "All animals are equal, but some animals are more equal than others." Premier *Kosygin* was forced to allow that *Orwell* was "undoubtedly right."[48]

In an interview with Newsweek in August 1970, Chancellor *Brandt* spelled out his government's view of the link between a "satisfactory" settlement of the Berlin problem and West German ratification of the treaty. We "can only ratify (the) treaty," *Brandt* said, "if by then progress, considerable progress, has been made toward stabilizing the status of West Berlin." We "are not thinking of security solely in the military sense of the word," he

47 See Dennis Bark, Agreement on Berlin (Washington, D.C.: American Enterprise Institute, 1974), p. 57.

48 Time, August 24, 1970.

continued, "but security also in terms of viability, including both a firm Western presence and also an acceptance by the other side of the fact that Berlin, for all practical purposes, belongs together with West Germany, and that free access to Berlin is necessary if Berlin is going to have a reasonable future."[49]

The initial reaction of the Western powers to this *Junktim* was passing resentment. They objected to being saddled in this way for the success or failure of *Brandt's* Ostpolitik. Nevertheless, they, too, regarded the Berlin issue as a test case of the genuineness of Soviet intentions in détente. As a consequence, they soon formulated a second link: The convening of a European security conference, long desired by Moscow, was now made conditional on the successful conclusion of the Berlin negotiations. Thus, the quadripartite talks were slotted into the overall framework of efforts as a relaxation of tensions in Europe.

Conclusions

As the foregoing analysis shows, American (and Western) policy on the Berlin discussions was the result of a number of complicated factors. It developed from suggestions made by the bureaucracy, particularly the Department of State in Washington with input from the staff of the U.S. Embassy in Bonn, led by *Jonathan Dean* working in the "Bonn Group." It was tempered – and at times even redirected by "back channel" interventions with Ambassador *Rush* and the Soviets – by *Dr. Kissinger* and President *Nixon*. Although *Rush* played a key role in the talks, there were times when even he – despite close personal ties to *Nixon* – was unaware of what was transpiring between Washington and Moscow.

As expected, the negotiations on Berlin progressed slowly. The main sticking point in the first two discussions concerned the deadlock over opposing legal views. For their part, the Western Three could not allow the absolute rights which they claim to have in the entire city, stemming from the right of conquest and the

49 Newsweek, August 10, 1970. The CSCE link, of course, was advanced by Brandt and his advisers long before this.

assumption of supreme authority in Germany in 1945, to be called into question.

For their part, the Russians — known as hard and untiring bargainers — were reluctant to abandon their long-held view that there was only a "West Berlin problem." They claimed that East Berlin was the capital of the GDR and hence not subject to negotiation. (In the Russian view, the Allied presence in Berlin could no longer be justified on the grounds of military victory, but only on the sufferance of the Soviet Union.) But West German ties to West Berlin were an entirely different matter. Although Moscow seemed willing to accept some formula recognizing economic, cultural and financial links between the Federal Republic and the city, it was adamantly opposed to allowing any political links, which were described as "provocative" and "illegal."

If the pace of the "Big Four" discussions on Berlin was sluggish, this was not true of Bonn's rapprochement with East Berlin. Following their unprecedented summit in the GDR during March 1970, the two German heads of government met for a return engagement on West German soil just two months later. However, unlike the first meeting at Erfurt, which was dominated by the common sense of its being historic simply because it had taken place, at Kassel the fundamental issue was joined. There Chancellor *Brandt* put forth a bold program conceding East Germany's "inner sovereignty" (one word away from formal diplomatic recognition), offered to exchange "plenipotentiaries" (Ambassadors in all but name) and proposed a wide-ranging number of concrete steps leading to the normalization and humanization of daily relations between the two Germanies. These were to culminate in a treaty that would regulate their relations "on the basis of human rights, equality, peaceful coexistence and non-discrimination."

Brandt's proposals were made against a background of local violence, leading to fears that Stoph might stage a walkout. Although the meeting was salvaged, little concrete progress was forthcoming. The East German leader merely responded to *Brandt's* creative initiatives with a blunt demand that Bonn first recognize the GDR as a fully sovereign state. There the German dialogue, at least in its summit aspect, was temporarily laid to rest.

That it was for a time put to rest, however, did not mean it was of no avail. The dialogue served to clear the air: Bonn, having laid its cards on the table, now was free to proceed with its diplomatic initiatives in Moscow and the capitals of Eastern Europe, free of reproach that it was sacrificing concern for fellow Germans to ambitions of its own international role.

Bonn's rapprochement with Moscow was eminently successful; for it resulted not only in the placing of the capstone on *Brandt's* controversial Ostpolitik, but it led to the opening of a new era in relations between the Federal Republic and the Soviet Union, which in turn would encourage its allies to increase their contacts with Bonn. The GDR, in particular, would no longer be able to hide behind the example of Soviet intransigence in its dealings with West Germany.

To be sure, the Bonn-Moscow Treaty — although it was of great symbolic significance — contained little in substance. In the main, it was built around mutual declarations renouncing the use of force. This was something previous German governments had offered the Russians without getting a positive response. For various reasons (not the least of which was to keep *Brandt* in power), Moscow very quickly showed considerable interest when *Willy Brandt* as the first socialist West German Chancellor renewed the proposal. Thus, even before negotiations began, Soviet leaders backed off from their long-standing insistence that Bonn first recognize the German Democratic Republic (a move that reportedly infuriated *Walter Ulbricht*).

In its treaty with the USSR, the Federal Republic recognized all European boundaries as "inviolable" (though, as the West Germans were quick to point out, not as "immutable"). That is to say, the borders could be changed by mutual consent — and most importantly Germany could one day be reunited. These boundaries included the disputed Oder-Neisse line and the frontier separating the FRG and the GDR.

If the Bonn-Moscow treaty represented a major breakthrough for *Brandt's* Ostpolitik, it was still open to criticism. For one thing, the apparent haste with which the treaty was negotiated by *Scheel* and *Gromyko* was hard to justify. And the vagueness was open to criticism. For example there is no date affixing the point in time when the Oder-Neisse line became the legal Western frontier of Poland. The reader of the text is left merely to surmise whether the signatories intended the end of the war (1945), the date of a Polish-East German accord (1950) or the signing of the Moscow Treaty itself (1970).

But it is not true, as some in the Christian Democratic opposition charged, that all the concessions were on Bonn's part. In the official West German view, the treaty was an unavoidable consequence of World War II. According to this interpretation, the pact offered the Federal Republic an important psychological opportunity — the chance to wipe clean the slate left over from the war. As *Willy Brandt* so poignantly told his countrymen in a television broadcast from Moscow on August 12, 1970: "Nothing is lost with the treaty that was not gambled away long ago."[50]

The treaty does not mention Berlin specifically. But the link between the accord and progress in the quadripartite talks was made abundantly clear by Foreign Minister *Walter Scheel* and Chancellor *Brandt*. Both tied the granting of Soviet concessions on the divided city to the ratification of the treaty by the West German Bundestag. Granted Russian leaders were at first perturbed with Bonn's proposed linkage (and subsequently the tieing by the Allies of a successful outcome in the Berlin negotiations to the holding of a European security conference). However, if they publicly denounced such an effort as "unrealistic" and even "wrong,"[51] they soon adapted to it in practice.

50 See The Bulletin, No. 109, August 17, 1970.
51 See Pravda, January 17, 1971.

Chapter V
NEGOTIATING UNDER PRESSURE

The completion of the Soviet-West German Treaty opened the door to progress in the heretofore dilatory Berlin discussions. It appears as if the Soviet leadership had come to the conclusion — despite what was said publicly — that the Western Three would not agree to any Berlin arrangement without some Russian acquiescence on their standpoint of Four-Power responsibility. Furthermore, it seems the Kremlin began to realize that the failure of an attempt to reach a settlement on Berlin would in the long run block its Western policy initiative, in particular as it affected the convening of a European security conference.[1] Apparently for these reasons then, the Soviet side started to take a more flexible stand at the ambassadorial negotiations.

1 Ambassador Rush downplays the importance of holding the European security conference as an incentive to the Soviets in their talks on Berlin. As he wrote this author on March 24, 1976 from his post in Paris: "hope of promoting the convening of a European Security Conference, in my opinion, was at most a very minor item in influencing the decision of the Soviets . . . A desire to advance the Ost-Politik (sic) of Chancellor Brandt looking for improvement of relations between Germany and Russia and Germany and the other Warsaw Pact countries, was one of the two major considerations. I think that a further major one was the hope of pushing forward to an easing of tensions with the U.S. Of course, in fact the achievement of these objectives might lead in time to a European Security Conference."
A distinguished colleague of Ambassador Rush with the same rank does not want to be cited by name as "taking issue" with him but writes: "I think that historical accuracy does require that you at least make mention of the fact that there is a considerable body of opinion which holds, on the basis of good evidence, that the Conference on Security and Co-operation was an important Soviet objective and that the NATO linkage had significant causal effect."

The Quadripartite Talks Gain Momentum

The Berlin talks were in recess during the period in which the Bonn-Moscow Treaty was wrapped up. But after a ten-week break, the Four Powers returned to the bargaining table in September 1970. At first, the West German government wanted the Allies to settle down to more or less continuous session with the USSR. Bonn was "in a hurry" because it desired to bring up the agreement with Moscow for ratification as soon as possible. But the Western Three, who looked askance at the Chancellor's rush, favored a slower and more deliberate pace. Consequently, quadripartite meetings during the next four months took place only every third or fourth week.

At the seventh session on September 30, the two sides exchanged "talking papers" for the first time. In the main, the "working concept" tabled by the Western powers focused on the priority issue — the Berlin access routes. It was designed to reduce delays and unwarranted interference, while at the same time it sought to provide East German authorities with adequate assurance against the smuggling of refugees by sealing all freight shipments crossing the territory of the GDR.[2] Importantly, all Autobahn visas and tolls would be paid in one lump sum by the West German government rather than individually. And an international authority, including both East German and Soviet officials, would be established to mediate grievances and complaints. Lastly, the so-called "Berlin clause," incorporating West Berlin into the Federal Republic for commercial reasons, would be automatically accepted by the Soviet Union and its Eastern European allies in all transactions with Bonn. Thus, in this draft, the Western Three outlined their broad position and presented their initial proposal for meeting their respective expectations.

Although the Soviet "talking paper" was encouraging, Western officials described it as "short" and "not very precise." Generally, it appeared to fit the promise Soviet Communist Party leader *Brezhnev* gave *Brandt* in Moscow. Namely, that the Kremlin was

2 Certain Federal officials in Bonn maintain that the idea of sealing vehicles in transit through East Germany originally came from the FRG. It was drawn from the praxis between the wars when railroad cars in the Polish corridor were sealed on the way to and from East Prussia.

indeed serious about trying to reach agreement on Berlin. And the Western negotiators promised to give it careful study.[3]

The Soviet proposal sparked optimism initially for two reasons. First, it contained a reference to "uninhibited access." And second, it did nothing to contradict previous Soviet hints that Moscow was willing to recognize ties between West Berlin and the Federal Republic in economic, cultural and social matters. In regard to the access question — a priority item for the West, — the Soviets no longer rejected from the outset the Western demand for a package deal for civilian transit to West Berlin, which could then be followed up by detailed arrangements between the two German states and subsequent sanctioning of the overall agreement by the "Big Four." Up to then, a procedure of this kind had been refused out of deference to the exclusive sovereignty rights of the German Democratic Republic with respect to the issue of access.[4]

While the Russian Ambassador did hint at possible concessions on the crucial matter of access and Bonn's economic, social and cultural ties to West Berlin, these points were embraced in a larger formula that envisioned a separate status for West Berlin. And this special status for the Western Sectors precluded political and legal ties with West Germany. The Soviet negotiator also continued to contend that Allied jurisdiction applied only to West Berlin. Soviet intransigence on these issues was backed up by demands that the United States close down its radio station in West Berlin (RIAS) and that the Western Three cease all intelligence-gathering operations in the city.[5]

In the aftermath of the September meeting, Western officials began for the first time to openly speculate on the possibility that any agreement on Berlin might increase "Soviet responsibility" in the Western Sectors. This discussion encouraged rumors that following an accord the USSR would reoccupy the building it owned on Lietzenburger Strasse in the U.K. Sector in order to establish a trade mission. Because of previous assertions by Moscow and East Berlin that West Berlin was "an independent political entity" existing under Four-Power status, a considerable body of West

3 The Washington Post, October 1, 1970.
4 See Gerhard Wettig, "East Berlin and the Moscow Treaty," Außenpolitik, English ed., Vol. 22 (1971), p. 266.
5 Time, October 12, 1970.

German public opinion became seriously disturbed about communist encroachments in the Western half of the city.[6]

Reportedly, this controversy was touched off by Russian willingness to discuss representation by Bonn of West Berlin abroad. Up to now, this had been a sore point in West German — communist bloc relations. Although representation of the city abroad was provided for in the West by Embassies and Consulates of the Federal government, this was not the case in the Soviet Union or Eastern Europe, where Bonn's political and legal ties to West Berlin were not recognized. Apparently, the Soviets were at long last prepared to acknowledge de facto representation of the Western Sectors abroad by West Germany in exchange for increased influence in West Berlin.[7]

If Soviet movement in the Berlin talks was encouraging, it took place against a puzzling and initially unpublicized incident involving the air corridors leading to West Berlin.[8] One day before negotiations were to resume (on September 30), Russian technicians at the Berlin air traffic control center announced to their Western colleagues that it would be unsafe to fly at certain altitudes. Western officials ignored the statement, however, and there was no interruption of traffic.[9] While some Allied authorities thought the Soviets were underscoring West Berlin's vulnerability to Soviet pressure, others saw the threat as a repetition of the familiar Russian bargaining tactic of demanding the maximum before settling for something less.

A Flurry of Diplomatic Activity

During the month of October the talks entered a new phase as it became clear the Soviets were taking the secret discussions

6 See Frankfurter Allgemeine Zeitung, October 2, 1970.

7 See Der Spiegel, October 5, 1970.

8 Under Four-Power agreement (November 30, 1945) aircraft of the British, French, Russian and American governments are authorized to be operated in the Berlin Control Zone (BCZ). The BCZ is defined as the air space between ground· level and 10,000 feet (3,000 meters) within a radius of twenty miles (thirty-two kilometers) from the Allied Control Authority Building situated in the U.S. Sector, in which the Berlin Air Safety Center is established. For details see Wolfgang Heidelmeyer et al (eds.), Documents on Berlin 1943-1963 (Munich: R. Oldenbourg Verlag, 1963), pp. 31-51.

9 The Washington Post, October 1, 1970.

seriously. For the first time, the political advisers of the four Ambassadors met on October 7. These so-called "experts" proceeded at once to draft the first common "talking paper." This informal text consisted in the main of a list of points which both sides wanted to see incorporated in a final settlement.

The eighth round of negotiations was originally scheduled to be held at the end of the month. But it was suddenly moved up to October 9, when it was learned that Ambassador *Abrasimov* and Soviet Foreign Minister *Andrei Gromyko* would be in New York later as members of their country's delegation to the opening session of the United Nations. At the eighth meeting the Russian representative took the opportunity to "clarify" the Soviet proposal made the week before. But although he revealed another instance of Moscow's new willingness to talk seriously, his statement fell far short of offering the kind of concessions the Western powers deemed necessary for an agreement.[10]

With the Berlin negotiations in recess, the next three weeks saw a flurry of informal consultations between the various governments directly or indirectly involved in the Four-Power talks. First, Chancellor *Brandt* and Foreign Minister *Scheel* met separately with Ambassador *Rush* on October 12 to inform themselves about the deliberations. Then, on October 20, Soviet Foreign Minister *Gromyko* conferred with Secretary of State *William Rogers* at the United Nations in New York on the state of the negotiations and other matters of mutual concern. While in New York, *Gromyko* received an invitation to meet privately with President *Nixon* in the White House. On the same day, October 22, that the Soviet Foreign Minister was talking with the President, Ambassador *Abrasimov* sat down for an extraordinary five-and-a-half-hour talk with Assistant Secretary of State *Martin Hillenbrand* in Washington. Of all these conferences, the *Nixon-Gromyko* session proved the most decisive as far as Berlin was concerned.

Nixon's session with *Gromyko* was the result of an initiative taken by Ambassador *Rush*. He had previously informed the President that the quadripartite negotiations were getting nowhere because of *Abrasimov's* refusal to discuss the crucial access issue and his attempt to shirk Soviet responsibilities for certain matters by injecting the competence of East German authorities. In an

10 The Washington Post, October 10, 1970.

effort to overcome this deadlock in the talks, *Nixon* agreed to pursue the matter on a higher level.[11]

The Soviet Foreign Minister conferred with the President for two and one-half hours. It was the longest conversation *Nixon* had held with a foreign statesman since taking office ten months earlier. During parts of it, he was accompanied by Secretary *Rogers* and *Henry Kissinger,* the President's Special Assistant for National Security Affairs. Although *Nixon* and *Gromyko* covered a wide range of topics in their talk, including European security issues, the Middle East, reports of Soviet submarine base construction work in Cuba and the general state of Soviet-American relations, Berlin was singled out for special attention.

According to later accounts of the meeting, the President protested Soviet interference in the air corridors to Berlin and pressed for Russian concessions on the city. The Soviet diplomat is said to have told *Nixon* that the attempt to close down the air corridors on September 29 was the fault of a lower-ranking Soviet officer in the Air Safety Center and should not be construed as a deliberate communist provocation. Most importantly, *Gromyko* informed the President that East-West differences over the legal status of Berlin need no longer serve as an obstacle to agreement on the isolated city.[12] On this positive note, the conference broke up.

Upon leaving the United States, *Gromyko* travelled to Great Britain, West Germany and the GDR before finally heading home to report on his meetings with Western leaders. His stop over in the Federal Republic was unprecedented and received the greatest public attention. For although the two countries had established diplomatic relations fifteen years earlier, *Gromyko's* visit was the first by a Soviet Foreign Minister. Apparently, his brief stop over represented a bid to speed up ratification of the Soviet-West German nonaggression treaty. *Walter Scheel,* who met with the Soviet diplomat near Frankfurt, later told newsmen that *Gromyko* had told him the difficulties marking the early stages of the quadripartite talks were put out of the way by his trips to Washington, London and through contacts between the USSR and France (between Ocotober 6 and 13 President *Georges Pompidou*

11 See The Los Angeles Times, August 30, 1971.
12 Der Spiegel, November 9, 1970.

was a guest in the Soviet Union). The German Foreign Minister said his conversation with *Gromyko* also indicated that the time had come to "move the Four-Power Berlin talks toward the written-agreement stage."

The Ninth Round of Talks

At the first plenary session (the ninth since the quadripartite talks began) following *Gromyko's* visit to the United States, the "Big Four" reported important movement on the part of the Soviet Union. At the insistance of the Russian representative, the Ambassadors stated in a communiqué issued on November 4 that real "progress" had been made. Their joint announcement was significant because it was the first to say more than just that the talks had taken place and would be continued.[13]

The Allies had reason to be optimistic because Ambassador *Abrasimov* spoke of the willingness of his government to improve access to and from West Berlin. Previously, the Soviet negotiator had rejected several Western proposals on the access issue. He argued that transit was a matter to be settled not with the USSR but with the German Democratic Republic. Now the Russians appeared to take a more flexible position.

If the initiative for using such an unexpected word like "progress" to characterize the ninth session came from the Soviet side, Western officials were quick to point out exactly what the term meant. In the main, it consisted in the establishment of techniques for reaching a possible agreement — not movement toward an accord itself. As they were careful to explain, the Soviets merely agreed to the Western contention that the outcome must be a package deal. And that while each part should be separately discussed, there would be no agreement on any part until there was unity on all parts of the package.

As the Western Three saw it, the Four Powers should construct a general "umbrella" agreement for Berlin. This accord would consist of a number of clearly stated principles and guidelines leading to improvements in and around the city -- particularly regarding access. Under it, officials of the FRG and GDR would

13 See Dennis L. Bark, Agreement on Berlin: A Study of the 1970-72 Quadripartite Negotiations (Washington, D.C.: American Enterprise Institute, 1974), p. 59.

129

bear the responsibility of working out the details, which would subsequently be reviewed by the Ambassadors.[14]

But if the Russians were ready to discuss specific improvements in the Berlin situation, they were not yet ready to authorize the East and West Germans to hammer out all the details. The reason why was made clear in an editorial in the official GDR newspaper Neues Deutschland on November 5. Coming a week after East Germany suddenly offered to resume talks with the Federal Republic, it carried special weight. As the communist paper authoritatively reported, "no agreement can be made between the GDR and the Federal Republic that affects the individual and freight traffic of West Berlin. Such questions only can be regulated between the GDR and the West Berlin city government." In other words, the Russians and East Germans wanted to treat West Berlin as a separate entity thereby breaking its political ties with West Germany.

Several days later, East German leader *Walter Ulbricht,* in a rare television appearance, laid down his conditions for the resumption of GDR-FRG talks. He said East Berlin was prepared to negotiate with Bonn over questions of mutual civil and freight transit "provided that other states stop all activity in West Berlin . . ." Western officials interpreted the reference "other states" to mean chiefly West Germany.[15]

Incident at the Soviet War Memorial

A little over a week before the four Ambassadors were scheduled to resume talks, the hard-won conciliatory atmosphere was suddenly shattered by sniper fire. On November 7, the fifty-third anniversary of the Russian October Revolution, a 21-year-old right-wing hospital attendant *Ekkehard Weil* seriously wounded a Soviet sentry guarding the Russian war memorial in the British Sector.[16] Although his precise motive was not at first apparent, the sniper left behind handbills charging *Brandt* with abandoning West

14 The Washington Post, November 9, 1970.

15 Ibid.

16 This memorial, located near the Brandenburg Gate, was erected in 1945 in the form of a gate of honor and crowned with the bronze figure of a Soviet soldier. Although the war memorial is situated on West Berlin territory, it is guarded around the clock by Soviet soldiers. The Allies

Berlin. Later, under interrogation by the police, *Weil* admitted he had fired at the Soviet sentry because he wanted to prevent ratification of the Bonn-Moscow Treaty.[17]

When the quadripartite talks resumed on November 16, the Soviets, as expected, took a very hard line. Out of the six hours of talks at the tenth session Ambassador *Abrasimov* was reported to have devoted three full hours alone to the shooting incident. Only when the British representative assured the Soviet diplomat that the sniper would be brought to trial before a military court could other matters be discussed.

Whereas at the previous meeting *Abrasimov* spoke of Soviet willingness to improve access to Berlin, he now reversed the Russian position. He insisted the Allies recognize GDR sovereignty over the transit routes and proposed that the Four-Power talks on access be replaced by discussions on an intra-German level. Moreover, he demanded that the Federal Republic should end its political presence in West Berlin. Taken aback by this turn of events — and ever wary of Soviet motives, — the Western powers reiterated their view that FRG-GDR technical agreement on transit be subordinate to a general accord asserting quadripartite responsibility for access.[18] On this note, the two sides broke off their conversations.

Three days later *Ekkehard Weil* was back in the news again. On November 19, he was reported to have escaped as he was being taken from his prison cell to police headquarters for questioning. His alleged escape immediately evoked strong criticism by Berlin leaders, the public and the communist side. A massive search by police, however, led a day later to the discovery that Weil had merely hidden from authorities in the cell of a fellow inmate.[19] (He was subsequently sentenced by a special British military court to serve six years in prison.)

regard this situation as somewhat anomalous, but it is tolerated because of custom. The Russians support their right to guard the site with the argument that the memorial stands atop a World-War-II Soviet burial plot. In the past, the memorial has been the scene of frequent anti-Soviet demonstrations. Following the construction of the Wall through Berlin in 1961, British soldiers fenced it off as a retaliatory measure.

17 U.S. Mission (Berlin), Berlin 1970 — An Unofficial Chronology (45) (Berlin: USIA, January, 1971), p. 3.

18 The New York Times, November 17, 1970.

19 Der Spiegel, November 23, 1970.

Resumption of the Dialogue between the FRG and the GDR

The search for agreement on Berlin continued through November and the beginning of December with conference sources reporting an atmosphere of "no progress." Meetings eleven (November 23) and twelve (December 10) ended with both sides still extremely far apart on the crucial issue of access. Thus, in the wake of this critical impasse, the four Ambassadors decided to take a six-week recess, while instructing lower-ranking officials to fill this pause with periodic technical discussions on the expert, working level.

But if progress in the secret talks with the Soviets came to a startling halt in November, this was not true of the dialogue between the two Germanies. Dormant for the previous five months, it resumed on November 27, 1970. At that time, *Egon Bahr,* principal diplomatic adviser to *Willy Brandt,* and *Michael Kohl,* an undersecretary to *Willi Stoph,* met in East Berlin for the first of fifteen intra-German sessions.

When the Western Three learned of West German plans to resume talks with the GDR, they were reported to be decidedly unhappy with Bonn. In general, the Allies were afraid that the intra-German dialogue could not but intrude on the Four-Power negotiations. Previously, the Federal Republic, in order to protect the Western position that the GDR was not a sovereign state and that the Soviet Union together with the Western Three was responsible for access, had declined to begin serious discussions with East Berlin until the Four Powers instructed it to do so.[20] Apparently, *Brandt's* change of mind was due to his eagerness to speed up things and clear the way for ratification of the Bonn-Moscow Treaty, on whose fate his government now seemed to hang. Until recently, the expectation had been that the West German government would not put forward the pact for Bundestag approval until an access agreement had been reached by the "Big Four." But now Bonn wanted to go ahead with the ratification process as soon as possible. Its target date was early 1971, before the expected meeting in March of the Soviet communist party congress.[21]

During the first meeting between *Bahr* and *Kohl,* which lasted

20 The Washington Post, November 15, 1970.
21 Ibid.

four hours and twenty minutes, the East German representative insisted that talks focus on "mutual transit problems". By making this proposal, *Kohl* hoped to gain recognition by Bonn of GDR sovereign rights over the transit routes between Berlin and the Federal Republic. Recognizing the implications of this move, and under clear instructions from his government not to discuss issues which were the subject of quadripartite negotiation, *Bahr* limited his discussion with *Kohl* to general questions of East-West relations.[22]

Soviet-East German Differences

The GDR régime dramatized its ability to arbitrarily manipulate the access question by instituting slow-downs in late November (for four days) and again in mid-December (for three days) at the control points on the transit routes leading to Berlin through its territory. Ostensibly, traffic harassment was directed in the first instance against a parliamentary meeting in West Berlin of the Christian Democratic Union, West Germany's opposition political party, and in the second against a similar convocation of the Social Democrats. But the Western powers interpreted East German interference as an attempt by *Walter Ulbricht* to interject a note of bellicosity into the tangled Berlin negotiations.[23]

On the surface, the USSR appeared to support the East German denunciation of the West German political meetings in West Berlin as unwarranted and "illegal" attempts by Bonn to strengthen its political links with the city. Thus, Moscow delivered formal protests to the Western Three for sharing jurisdiction over the Western Sectors. But since East German leaders and newspapers were known to be taking a much harder line than the Soviets on West Germany and West Berlin, the extent of Russian support was uncertain. Generally, Western sources tended to emphasize Soviet reluctance to take measures that would jeopardize their conversations with the Allies.[24]

If the degree of Soviet approval for this particular display of GDR sovereignty was uncertain, there was no doubt about the

22 Der Spiegel, November 23, 1970.
23 The Washington Post, November 29, 1970.
24 The Washington Post, November 29, 1970.

growing rift between Moscow and East Berlin (and between the GDR and the rest of Eastern Europe). The *Ulbricht* régime had stood out in the communist world against a trend set by the Kremlin ever since the USSR had embarked on its rapprochement with Bonn in the fall of 1969. To the dismay of East Berlin, normalization of relations between Moscow and Bonn had led to similar movement by Poland and other East European states. In the main, the SED leadership was perturbed because its allies were not sticking to the previously agreed communist position that full recognition of the GDR must precede reconciliation with the Federal Republic.

Ulbricht chose to demonstrate his displeasure with this turn of events in two ways. On the one hand, he began to openly complain in his speeches of the lack of coordination by East Germany's allies. This was almost an unprecedented act for a communist political leader to make in a camp whose complaints are rarely aired publicly. On the other, he started to boycott high-level communist meetings. Throughout all this, *Ulbricht* kept up a steady attack against West Berlin, whose continued existence as a foreign body in the GDR seemed to cast doubt on the stability of the communist régime.[25]

The Soviets, having already made the basic decision to seek détente with the West and reach agreement on Berlin, were put in the rather difficult position of bringing the SED leadership around to acceptance of their point of view. Nevertheless, they reacted to this unexpected independence on the part of the GDR by a combination of private cajoling and public support. First, Soviet Foreign Minister *Gromyko* was dispatched to East Berlin on November 25 to put pressure on the staunch 77-year-old East German leader. When *Gromyko* failed to iron out the snarls in Soviet

[25] One expert on Soviet-East German affairs in the U.S. State Department disagrees with this analysis: "Your account of GDR reactions has plausibility but I doubt if it's the real story. There was considerable churning within the SED at the time — that's when the 'Abgrenzung' doctrine first surfaced — but I suspect Ulbricht's fate was already sealed by then (actually a case can be made that the shift to replace him dates back to mid-1969) and the problems of timing plus coping with the negotiations were causing domestic problems. I doubt if Ulbricht really boycotted meetings — he may not have been invited. In any event, the screws were put on finally at the Berlin session. (Gomulka's speech to the Polish miners after that meeting hints that Ulbricht was being pushed.)"

and East German approaches to the Berlin problem, and *Ulbricht* insisted on boycotting the gathering of Warsaw Pact leaders in Budapest in late November, they hurried to East Berlin on December 2 in what was described as a "showdown" with the stubborn old man.

The details of this one-day, seven-power confrontation never surfaced. But it is known that *Ulbricht's* allies impressed upon the aged East German leader the importance of unity in the Warsaw Pact. In particular, the Soviet delegation, headed by Communist Party Chairman *Leonid Brezhnev,* Premier *Aleksei Kosygin,* Foreign Minister *Andrei Gromyko* and Defense Minister *Andrei Grechko,* was reported to have put pressure on *Ulbricht* not to block its efforts at détente with West Germany. The Soviets were also said to have tried to persuade the SED Chairman that his best chance for prestige and recognition lay in the context of a European thaw.

If the Kremlin sought privately to bring pressure on the recalcitrant East German leader to knuckle under, it also went out of its way publicly to demonstrate its solidarity with GDR interests. Therefore, in a speech on November 30 at Erivan, celebrating the fiftieth anniversary of the Armenian republic, *Brezhnev* plainly indicated the limits of Soviet readiness to compromise resulting from consideration for East Germany. There he spoke of the possibility of quadripartite decisions on Berlin "which accorded with the wishes of West Berliners" but also took into account "the legitimate interests and sovereign rights of the GDR."[26]

More importantly from the Western viewpoint, the Soviet party leader acknowledged the linkage between improvement in the Berlin situation and West German ratification of the Bonn-Moscow Treaty. Up to this time, various statements by top Soviet officials had shown that the Kremlin was fully aware of this linkage. But such a reference in one of *Brezhnev's* speeches, which rarely dealt with the Four-Power talks, left no doubt that Moscow had formally accepted its responsibility for getting the Berlin negotiations moving again.

26 Pravda, December 1, 1970. One Soviet expert has this to say: "Brezhnev always took account of GDR interests, but by acknowledging only legitimate ones he was actually restricting them — and that is underscored by his deference to the wishes of the West Berliners, which were pretty extensive."

With the Berlin talks again deadlocked, public attention in December 1970 shifted to the dramatic efforts by *Brandt* at reconciliation with Poland. Flying into Warsaw on December 6, the West German Chancellor prepared to put the finishing touches on the second of two outstanding milestones produced thus far by his Ostpolitik. Specifically, this last breakthrough involved the signing of a treaty the next day aimed at erasing the bitter memories of World War II and beginning a new era of friendship between the German and Polish peoples.

It may be recalled that *Brandt's* attempt to reach an accomodation with the *Gomulka* régime had begun already in March 1968, when the then Foreign Minister had called for respect and recognition of the existing boundaries of Europe — especially the Oder-Neisse line — until such time that they could be finally settled by peace treaty. This statement, known as the "Nuremberg formula," was enthusiastically received by Warsaw. But the ensuing domestic controversy, in which the Christian Democrats warned that the Poles would not settle for anything less than a complete sellout of German interests in the East, made it impossible for *Brandt* to pursue the matter further until after Federal elections in the fall of 1969.

Upon assuming the Chancellorship, the Social Democratic leader let it be known that his government was determined to try for a permanent reconciliation with Poland based on full diplomatic relations. The first step he took in this connection was in November 1969 to upgrade the status of the West German representative in Warsaw. That same month *Brandt* offered "comprehensive negotiations" with the Polish government.[27] The vehicle the new Chancellor chose to use for laying the groundwork for normalizing relations with Poland was the same as that offered to the other states of Eastern Europe — the conclusion of a nonaggression pact. The Poles responded favorably to this initiative, and treaty negotiations were begun in February 1970. (These political conversations ran parallel to high-level economic talks, which were already underway.)

In some respects, these deliberations were more difficult for the

27 The Washington Post, November 26, 1969.

Federal Republic than its dealings with Moscow. For one thing, Bonn had to overcome the keen resentment against Germany felt by the Poles, who held bitter memories of the attack without warning by *Hitler's* forces in 1939. Aside from the murder of millions of Polish citizens, the destruction of major cities by the Nazis left scars that were impossible to forget. Understandably, then, the Poles, who had suffered so much from *Hitler's* aggression, were not easily persuaded by the West German negotiators.

For another, Bonn had to come to grips with the territorial status quo in Poland. The major sticking point here was Warsaw's claim to forty thousand square miles of formerly German territories in Silesia, Pomerania and Prussia. These areas lie East of the Oder-Neisse line, which the World-War-II victors set as Poland's "temporary" Western boundary. The final border was to be settled by a peace conference which was never held. Taking the position that it could not recognize the Polish-(East) German boundary unilaterally, no West German government up to now had ever formally renounced these old territories. Although public acceptance in the FRG of some sort of recognition was growing in 1969, there were still some formidable legal problems to be considered such as the rights of Germans living in the old areas. *Brandt's* major task then was to somehow devise a formula which, while safeguarding German interests, would also protect Allied rights regarding a final peace settlement.

In the end, Polish memories of wartime atrocities and German concern for legal questions were overcome and a treaty between the two countries could be signed on December 7, 1970. Like its predecessor with the Soviet Union, the Bonn-Warsaw pact was an act of reconciliation and was warmly welcomed as such throughout Eastern and Western Europe. With the August 1968 occupation of Czechoslovakia in mind, Bonn waited until the treaty with Moscow was signed before completing the terms of its agreement with Warsaw.

Like the Moscow accord, the Warsaw Treaty is a brief but weighty document.[28] No doubt, Article I, which accepts the Oder-Neisse boundary as it was laid down at the Potsdam Conference in July-August 1945, is the most important provision of the

28 For the text of this agreement see The Treaty between the Federal Republic of Germany and the People's Republic of Poland (Bonn: Federal Press and Information Office, 1971), pp. 7-9.

agreement. Both signatories affirm the inviolability of their existing frontiers and state that they have no territorial claims against each other. At the same time, they declare their intent to settle all their differences peacefully. Further they pledge themselves to take additional steps toward "full normalization and comprehensive development of their mutual relations." Of great importance to Bonn but not included in the text was the Polish promise to repatriate "some ten thousands" of its citizens of ethnic German origin on the humanitarian grounds of bringing families back together again. This last statement represented a major concession by Warsaw, and within a month after the signing the processing of more than fifty thousand people permitted to leave Poland began.[29]

One day after the accord with Warsaw was signed, the first West German head of government to set foot on Polish soil since that country was liberated from German occupation in 1945 spoke to his countrymen over radio and television. He told them that the treaty would close a dark chapter on European history and would create a "bridge between both states and both peoples."[30] But he was not satisfied with mere words. While visiting a granite sculpture in commemoration of the thousands of Jews who perished during World War II in the Warsaw ghetto, *Brandt* suddenly sank to his

29 The promise of the Polish régime to repatriate its citizens of ethnic German origin became a major source of controversy in the Federal Republic during the ratification debate in the spring of 1976 of two additional treaties and an ancillary protocol. These agreements, which were opposed by the Christian Democrats until a last-minute change of wording in the texts was made by Poland, foresaw the resettlement of an estimated 125,000 ethnic Germans over the next four years in exchange for 2.3 billion Deutsche Marks (about $ 1 billion) in low-interest, long-term credits and payments to Poland. Opponents of these accords charged that this was too much money, and that Warsaw was holding back an additional 160,000 Germans who wanted to leave the country. Part of the difficulty in 1975 and 1976 stemmed from disagreement over the number of Germans left in Poland. Warsaw put the number at about 70,000 and Bonn at a quarter million. (There are no official public figures because the Polish census does not identify members of ethnic minorities.) The figure of 125,000 ethnic Germans represented a compromise number. For details see The New York Times, August 3, 1975. The texts of the Bonn-Warsaw accords are published in Der Tagesspiegel, October 10, 1975.

30 Texte zur Deutschlandpolitik, Vol. 6 (Bonn: Ministry for Intra-German Relations, 1971), p. 263.

knees, his lips twitching with emotion and tears forming in his eyes. Many cynics and ardent nationalists subsequently criticized this spontaneous gesture, but somehow it suited the occasion more than all the formal champagne toasts that followed in the old Radziwill Palace.

American-German Differences

If most of the world was favorably impressed with the Chancellor's noble gesture in Warsaw, the refusal of his government to link directly a solution of the Berlin problem with ratification by the Bundestag of the Polish Treaty was somewhat disturbing to the United States. On the eve of the signing ceremony, the chief spokesman for the West German government *Conrad Ahlers* told a press conference that there was "no juridical connection" between ratification and a Berlin settlement. He conceded, however, that "the time factor" in the ratification process might in itself result in the Berlin agreement coming before parliament could vote on approving the Polish Treaty.[31]

What was doubly disturbing to Washington about *Ahlers'* remarks is that they appeared to be at variance with the position taken by Foreign Minister *Scheel* in private talks with the Western powers at the NATO ministerial meeting held the week before in Brussels. At that time, *Scheel* was reported to have told the American, British and French Foreign Ministers that his government would not submit the Warsaw accord to parliament until there had been a satisfactory agreement on Berlin. In this respect, *Scheel* informed the Western Three, the West German position regarding the Polish Treaty was no different than that pertaining to the pact with Moscow, signed the previous August.[32]

Referring to *Scheel's* remarks in Brussels, *Ahlers* maintained that they had been "interpreted falsely." What "the Chancellor says is almost always right," the Federal spokesman said. But "what the Vice Chancellor *(Scheel)* says is almost, almost always right." Later sources in Bonn amplified *Ahlers'* remarks to say that *Brandt* considered the question of linkage between Berlin and the

31 The Washington Post, December 7, 1970.
32 The Washington Post, December 7, 1970.

Polish Treaty as moot since he expected a satisfactory agreement on the divided city no later than February, 1971.[33]

The linkage issue was not the only matter that served at this time to irritate American-German relations. The six-week recess of the quadripartite talks during the wake of a critical impasse in mid-December touched off a minor crisis in Bonn-Washington relations. Chancellor *Brandt* had been pressing all fall to turn the desultory negotiations into a continuous conference. His conversations with Soviet Communist Party Secretary *Brezhnev* and Premier *Kosygin* five months earlier, plus other indications he received since then, convinced him that the Kremlin wanted a Berlin settlement before its party congress in March.

To urge Washington and its allies into a faster tempo, *Willy Brandt* sent numerous emissaries to Washington in late 1970 and wrote personal letters to President *Nixon* and *Georges Pompidou* of France and to British Prime Minister *Edward Heath*. In his letters, the Chancellor suggested "institutionalizing" the Four-Power talks. According to his plan, the four Ambassadors would designate technical-level deputies to keep the talks going continuously on a five-day-a-week basis. The envoys would then intervene at regularly scheduled intervals, such as once every week or two, to review the work of their deputies and carry on direct discussions themselves. Before broaching this idea to the Western powers, *Brandt* reportedly discussed it with the Soviet Ambassador in Bonn, *Semyon Tsarapkin,* and received assurances that Moscow had no objections.[34]

Brandt's ambitious scheme was subsequently pushed in Washington by State Secretary *Horst Ehmke*. Minister without portfolio in the West German cabinet, *Ehmke* was Head of the Chancellery and served as chief adviser to the Chancellor. Dispatched to the United States in late December, *Ehmke* met in the White House with *Dr. Kissinger,* Assistant Secretary of State *Martin Hillenbrand* and *Helmut Sonnenfeldt,* a member of *Kissinger's* National Security Council staff. *Ehmke* expressed to these sceptical officials the conviction of his boss that the Western Three were not moving fast enough in getting a Berlin settlement.[35]

33 Ibid.
34 The Washington Post, December 23, 1970.
35 The Washington Post, December 23, 1970.

At the same time, the West German is said to have informed them that Bonn no longer considered itself bound to wait for a formal directive from the Four Powers before beginning discussions with East Germany on such aspects of the Berlin situation as access. This last point made by the State Secretary was particularly upsetting to Washington because until now the FRG and the Allies had been agreed upon resolving the Berlin problem through a coordinated, step-by-step approach. This strategy, to which West Germany had previously acquiesced, first called for quadripartite agreement on the principles of a settlement and then direct talks between representatives of the GDR and the FRG to work out specific details of implementation.[36]

The American response to *Brandt's* proposal for permanent Berlin negotiations was cool but not entirely unsympathetic. *Kissinger* and other officials in the Washington establishment promised to study it "with an open mind." They added, however, that any so-called "institutionalizing" of Allied talks with the Soviet Union should depend on sufficient progress being made under the current format for such a change to appear promising.[37]

At the same time, the Americans were reported to have told *Ehmke* that the United States was concerned about the apparent backing away by Bonn from solidarity with the Western powers over Berlin. They pointed out that any independent approach to the question by the Federal Republic could very well jeopardize the Allied claim that only the Four Powers have jurisdiction over the divided city. Although these officials did not say so, they clearly suspected that *Brandt* was so anxious for a Berlin settlement he would settle for less than the Western Three deemed acceptable.

As far as the Chancellor's Ostpolitik was concerned, Washington expressed its uneasiness with the growing tendency of Bonn to deal bilaterally with the Soviet Union and other East European states. In particular, the Americans criticized *Brandt* for proceeding too rapidly and without adequate consultation with his Allies. Left unmentioned again was the official belief that the West German government had given a great deal more than it had received in its treaties with Moscow and Warsaw.

36 Ibid., December 24, 1970.
37 The Washington Post, December 24, 1970.

Following *Ehmke's* visit to the United States, *Nixon* administration officials tried to play down the growing rift with Bonn over its approach to the Berlin talks and dealings with East Europe. Thus, State Department spokesman *Robert J. McClosky* told newsmen on December 21: "We have said time and time again at virtually every official level in this government that this government does support and has encouraged the Federal Republic, under Chancellor *Brandt,* and his efforts to improve relations with the Eastern neighbors . . ."[38] But official denials like this failed to discourage continuing reports that Bonn and Washington were close to a crisis of confidence.

In large part, reports about the apprehensive attitude of the *Nixon* administration regarding *Brandt's* efforts at rapprochement arose from the sudden decision of the President in December to invite to the White House for private talks leading members of the American foreign policy establishment who opposed the Eastern policy initiatives of the Federal Republic. These men included such distinguished "hard-line" figures as *Dean Acheson,* Secretary of State under *Truman, John J. McCloy,* former U.S. High Commissioner in Germany, General *Lucius D. Clay,* who was the American representative on the Allied Control Council during the Berlin Blockade, and former Governor of New York *Thomas E. Dewey.* Upon emerging from their conversations with Nixon, they publicly admonished *Brandt.* Speaking through *Acheson,* who held a press conference the following day (December 9), they expressed misgivings that the Chancellor was willing to "settle for too little" in the negotiations over West Berlin. Moreover, they declared the situation was such that "West Germany rather than the United States, Britain or France was in a position to call the tune on Berlin." One member of the group was reported to have told *Nixon* that *Willy Brandt* "is writing the (World War II) peace treaty while the Allies are on the sidelines." Apparently reflecting not only the position of his "cold-war" colleague but that of the White House as well, *Acheson* ended his press conference by calling on *Brandt* to "cool off" his "mad race to Moscow."[39]

38 The Washington Post, December 22, 1970.

39 The Washington Post, December 10, 1970. Probably, American-German relations were adversely affected at this time by poor personal relations between Nixon and Brandt. In his recently published memoirs, the former Chancellor provides some insight into his real feelings towards the American

No doubt upset with the emphasis in the Western press during December about a "crisis of confidence" between Bonn and its Allies, particularly the United States, *Brandt* was understood to have subsequently changed his mind on the Berlin discussions. For one thing, he was reported no longer to be convinced that there was a chance for a quick solution to the Berlin problem. Thus, he was said to have stopped pressuring the Western powers for a speed up in the secret talks. For another, the Chancellor was believed now to feel that his fragile coalition government, whose majority of twelve in parliament had been cut in half due to defections over his controversial Ostpolitik, was stronger than previously thought and was not in immediate need of showing results on Berlin.[40]

This alteration in *Brandt's* attitude led him to authorize Deputy Press Secretary *Rüdiger von Wechmar* to issue a "clarification" of Bonn's view of the Berlin negotiations at a press conference on January 5, 1971. According to this statement, the Federal government reiterated its support of the Allied position and hastened to add that it agreed with the Western Three on the criteria of a satisfactory Berlin settlement. Most importantly, *Wechmar's* declaration pointed out that Bonn now recognized the linkage between a solution of the Berlin question and ratification by Parliament of the Warsaw Treaty. Up to this time, West German officials, while admitting the connection between a favorable outcome of the quadripartite discussions and submission of the treaty with Moscow to the Bundestag, had denied a similar link with reference to the Polish accord.[41]

Later in the month, following the thirteenth round of ambassadorial talks (January 19), *Brandt* reaffirmed the new position of his government in his annual "Report on the State of the Nation" speech to parliament.[42] In this address, which was delivered on

President. "There was," writes Brandt, "a shadow of insecurity about him as if he could not come to terms with his humble beginnings." As far as European-American relations were concerned, Brandt adds: "Nixon did not receive on the same wave length I was at pains to broadcast on." Quoted from Newsweek May 31, 1976.

40 The Washington Post, January 20, 1971.

41 For the text of Wechmar's statement see Relay from Bonn, January 6, 1971.

42 For the text see Relay from Bonn, January 29, 1971.

January 28, the Chancellor made a firm new pledge not to submit the West German treaties with the Soviet Union and Poland to the Bundestag for ratification until there was a Berlin settlement satisfactory to Bonn and its Allies. At the same time, he made clear that he had no intention of abandoning the Eastern policy or backing away from the increasingly assertive role that Bonn had played in European affairs ever since he became Chancellor.

In this major policy speech, *Brandt* also focused on allegations that his government was attempting to make a Berlin deal over the heads of its Allies. He conceded that Staatssekretär *Egon Bahr* in his talks with East Berlin's *Michael Kohl* had discussed the question of access to the isolated city. But he said: "Both sides must accept," that the "Four Powers have, and will retain, competence for Germany as a whole and for Berlin."

The sudden closing of ranks by Bonn behind the Allies in January served to greatly encourage them when the Soviets and East Germans unexpectedly chose twice that month to interfere with access to Berlin. On the 11th and 12th of January Russian checkpoint officials informed American, British and French military personnel using the Autobahn that their "movement papers" should have an official stamp by their own commanders on the back. Allied authorities rejected this demand and after delays up to ten hours their vehicles were allowed to pass. Soviet harassment of Allied military traffic was regarded by the Western powers as particularly serious for it represented the first such interference in several years. And it raised doubts as to how strongly the USSR really objected to East German interference with civilian access.[43]

The second communist interference with access took place at the end of January. This time only civilian transit was affected. And harassing measures were carried out exclusively by East German control point officials. They instituted a five-day slow-down of traffic that left some vehicles stalled on the Autobahnen between the city and West Germany for as long as thirty hours. The East German action was allegedly directed against a meeting of

43 The Allies did note at the time that Warsaw Pact troops were holding maneuvers in East Germany and, by some accounts, their vehicles were using the highways. Hence there was some feeling that the holdup over documents may have been designed to prevent Allied observation of the maneuvers. See The Washington Post, January 12, 1971.

Free Democratic Party members in West Berlin and separate visits to the city by West German President *Gustav Heinemann* and Chancellor *Willy Brandt*. The Soviet Union lent its support by protesting these political demonstrations to the Allies.[44]

The Western powers responded to this assault on the accessways by vigorously supporting the right of the Federal Republic to hold meetings in Berlin and by threatening to adopt retaliatory "countermeasures" if the harassment continued. Thus, on January 27, an American spokesman told journalists that the Western Three had the "sole responsibility" to determine which meetings took place in their Sectors. He pointed out that persistent interference with access could only have a "negative effect" on the quadripartite discussions. When the holdup of civilian traffic continued into February, American, British and French officials cancelled the February 2 session of experts that was supposed to smoothe the way for the fourteenth Four-Power conference scheduled the following week.[45]

Improved Intra-Berlin Telephone Communication

Communist harassment on the transit routes tended to dominate the headlines of the West German press during January. So much so that scant attention was paid to other important inner-German developments such as the partial restoration of inter-city telephone service that month. At the time, reluctant East German authorities were prodded by Bonn into adhering to the terms of a supplementary oral agreement, concluded in the context of a general accord between the two countries the previous April. This quid pro quo had called for the GDR to install 150 telephone lines linking the two parts of Berlin for the annual payment by the Federal government of some 30 million West marks. Apparently, East Berlin only agreed to open ten manually-operated telephone circuits (five in each direction) on January 31 after Federal officials threatened to suspend any more payments.

The opening of these lines meant that residents of the divided city could once again place "local" calls across the dividing line. Since May 27, 1952 (when the GDR severed 3,910 intra-Berlin

44 The Washington Post, January 28, 1971.
45 The New York Times, February 3, 1971.

145

circuits), it had not been possible to dial directly from West Berlin to East Berlin and the GDR. (Telegraphic and telex connections, however, continued to function.) West Berliners, wishing to telephone relatives and friends in the other part of the city, had to place their calls via West German long-distance operators – a circuitous, expensive and not always successful procedure.

Under the new system, all calls crossing the city's dividing line first had to be routed over the East German switchboard in Potsdam. Although this measure represented a considerable improvement over the old situation, telephone conversations were limited to three minutes, and each call had to be "booked" in advance. There was no direct dialing. Whereas West Berliners paid one local call unit for each connection with East Berlin, citizens of East Berlin and the GDR had to pay "international" charges for a call to West Berlin.

During the first month of operations, an average of 750 calls per day were put through to East Berlin (900 on week-ends), totalling some 22,000 telephone conversations. This telephone traffic, of course, represented but a fraction of requested connections. It is estimated that hundreds of thousands of Berliners at this time spent long hours on the phone just to get through to swamped switchboards. And those very few persons who succeeded in scheduling a call often had to wait fourteen hours or more before the booked call could be put through via Potsdam.[46]

The Western Draft Proposal

On February 5, 1971, the Western powers presented their draft proposal for a satisfactory agreement on Berlin.[47] Although this Allied position paper was not made public by the Ambassadors, a copy was later leaked to the West German press. The major importance of this paper was that for the first time it detailed exactly what advantages London, Paris and Washington expected to obtain from a settlement and what concessions they were prepared to make.

46 For details see The Bulletin, April 27, 1971.
47 The unofficial German translation of the Western draft proposal was pub
lished by the West German weekly Quick, No. 32, August 4, 1971.

Sixteen pages long, it was divided into a preamble and three main sections and annexes. The preamble stated the desire of the Four to contribute to practical improvements in the area of "Greater Berlin" without prejudice to their legal positions. Parts one through three outlined the general provisions of a satisfactory agreement. These in turn were spelled out in greater detail in annexes one through three. In addition, the annexes contained two models for Soviet communications to the Western Three on arrangements concerning civilian surface access and communication within the city and its environs; and one written Western statement, explaining the relationship between the Western Sectors of Berlin and the Federal Republic.

The prime importance of the Western plan, from the Allied viewpoint, stemmed from its detailed provisions in the field of access. For the first time, the Soviets were to commit themselves in writing to maintain unimpeded civilian surface traffic to and from Berlin. Realizing that communist harassment on the access lanes in the past occurred for the most part only where processing procedures were not clearly spelled out, the Western Three were determined that any satisfactory accord would have to contain more than just a simple statement calling for identification procedures rather than control. Consequently, they took special pains to list in detail their minimum requirements for simple and expeditious facilitation of transit traffic. Noteworthy here were provisions for Soviet acceptance of the principles of sealed freight shipments, simplified documentation inspection for all goods traffic and the exemption of travellers in private vehicles, buses and through trains from searches of their persons, vehicles and personal luggage. Moreover, under the terms of the draft proposal, travellers would not be asked to pay individual tolls or fees for use of the transit routes; these would be paid annually by the West German government in one lump sum. In short, then, the Western paper was designed to obtain definite guarantees which would prevent East Germany from taking such measures to interfere with access as the implementing of checks against "lists of undesirables," the turning back of individuals or taking them into custody and the searching and confiscating of their property.

Aside from these detailed access procedures, the Western working paper called for numerous practical improvements in the situation in and around Berlin. First, West Berliners were to be able to make regular visits to the Eastern Sector of the city for the first time since the East Germans issued them "holiday passes" in 1966. Second, intersector telephone and telex communication, which had been terminated in 1952, were to be completely restored. Third, the Teltow Canal, which forms the southern boundary of the city for a short distance but whose only lock is in the GDR, was to be opened for use as a through waterway between the Elbe and the Oder. Fourth, additional crossing points between East and West Berlin were to be erected, particularly at U-Bahn (subway) stations, to facilitate inter-sector travel. Finally, a realignment of the boundaries of Berlin was to be implemented through an exchange of territory thereby linking more closely to the mainland the isolated areas of Eiskeller (British Sector) and Steinstücken (American Sector). All these ideas, which if implemented would represent significant practical improvements in the geographic facts of life in the Berlin situation, had been worked out in detail between Allied and West Berlin officials, backed up by the "brainstorming" efforts of individuals in the various Foreign Ministries in Washington, London and Paris.

In order to achieve these improvements in the lives of Berliners, the Allies offered two major "concessions" regarding Bonn's claim that West Berlin is an integral part of the Federal Republic. They stated that the Western Sectors would "continue not to be a constituent part" of the FRG and that there would be a "reduction" in the "demonstrative Federal presence" (i.e. official functions and organs specified in the West German Constitution — Basic Law or Grundgesetz) there. (The word "continues" was the key here — and later to the whole agreement. Importantly, this term kept intact the legality of both Allied sovereignty over Berlin, and the provision of the Basic Law that says Berlin is a Land (state) of the Federal Republic — although that status was temporarily in suspense by virtue of Allied action.) In the case of political demonstrations of West German presence in the city, the Allies declared there would be no further meetings in Berlin of the Bundestag (lower house of parliament) and Bundesrat (upper house). And the Federal President would be barred hereafter from performing official state functions in the city. Nevertheless, despite these proposed changes in West Berlin's political relationship with Bonn, the Federal Republic would continue to represent the city abroad and issue passports to its citizens for foreign travel. Moreover,

148

West Berlin's economic, social and cultural links with West Germany were not to be disturbed.

If the extent of Allied readiness to make concessions at this stage was not great, their proposal nevertheless represented a serious attempt to end the deadlock in the quadripartite talks. It was presented at a preliminary meeting of the "Big Four" experts, which had been postponed earlier by the West in view of communist interference with access. This strategy gave the Russians a full week-end to study the draft before the Ambassadors convened three days later to discuss it at length during their fourteenth round on February 8.

Although Western officials did not expect the Soviets to accept the working paper as presented, they were encouraged by the conciliatory response made by Ambassador *Abrasimov*. He took a much less negative line than he had before. His main objections to the Allied proposal concerned its access provisions and the ties of West Berlin to West Germany. In the first place, he said, the Western Three failed to take into account the rights of the GDR; in the second, the Russian did not feel the Allies had made enough of an effort to cut back on the Federal presence in the city. Thus heartened, Britain, France and the United States anticipated that negotiations could now move from a "sounding out" of the other side to a lively discussion of specific principles to be incorporated in a final settlement.[48]

Negotiations between East and West Berlin

Although this provision did not receive much attention at the time, the Western proposal also suggested that final details of the settlement should be worked out between West and East Berlin under supervision of the Four Powers. Previously, the Allies had strongly resisted all attempts by the GDR to initiate separate negotiations with Bonn and West Berlin. They had adopted this stance in order not to give support to the East German claim that West Berlin is an "independent political entity" and to prevent the GDR from driving a wedge between the Western governments and the Federal Republic. Now apparently, with talks well underway between Bonn and East Berlin, the Allies were prepared to accept

48 Der Spiegel, February 15, 1971.

similar negotiations between East and West Berlin provided they could control the subject matter discussed and provided they took place after the conclusion of a basic agreement with the Soviet Union.

Premier *Stoph* had made a wide-ranging proposal for the beginning of direct talks between East and West Berlin on February 4.[49] In a move interpreted in Allied quarters as an attempt to bypass the Four-Power talks and change the status of Berlin before a quadripartite agreement could be reached, the East German head of government announced that the GDR was prepared to allow West Berlin to retain its technical, economic and cultural links with West Germany if Bonn ended its political presence in the city. He also proposed to negotiate a series of accords permitting West Berliners to visit the GDR and improving access. *Stoph* made this announcement before a delegation of West Berlin SEW (communist) officials in East Berlin and drew maximum propaganda effect from it.

But the West Berlin Senat showed absolutely no interest in the East German offer to the gratification of the Western Three. In fact, the SPD-FDP coalition government rejected *Stoph's* proposal as an attempt to provide indirect support to the small communist party in West Berlin during the upcoming municipal elections in March. This negative reaction by West Berlin city administrators found resonance in the West German capital where the GDR effort was denounced as a ploy to create disunity between the Federal government and the Senat.[50]

Failing to stir any interest in West Berlin by his offer of direct, broad-gauged discussions, Premier *Stoph* switched tactics in late February. In a personal letter to Mayor *Klaus Schütz* on February 24, he proposed negotiations with a more moderate goal. Terming "current efforts for a reduction of tensions in the center of Europe and for normalization of the situation of West Berlin as being of greatest importance," the East German leader suggested that both sides begin deliberations on visits by West Berliners in the GDR "including its capital." He indicated that if negotiations proceeded smoothly it might be possible to arrange for West Berlin citizens

49 For details see Archiv der Gegenwart, February 4, 1971.

50 For the various German reactions see German Press Review (prepared by the Press Office of the Embassy of the Federal Republic of Germany in Washington, D.C.), February 10, 1971.

to travel to East Germany before, during and after Easter even though talks on "all matters involving West Berlin" were not concluded by that time.[51]

The implications of this shift in tactics were not lost on the West Berlin government. But Mayor *Schütz*, with Allied backing, decided to respond positively, if cautiously, to *Stoph's* initiative. Thus, in his answer published two days later,[52] *Schütz* welcomed the interest shown by the GDR in a reduction of tensions and the normalization of the situation. He stated that his government was prepared to join in the proposed discussions on visits by West Berliners across the Wall. But he warned that any conversations between GDR officials and representatives of the Senat would have to be limited in scope and subject to Allied approval.

Subsequently (on March 6), *Ulrich Müller*, Head of the Senatskanzlei, and *Günter Kohrt*, an Undersecretary in the East German Foreign Ministry, met to work out the details of an accord which would allow West Berliners to visit East Berlin and East Germany. But as events were to show *Kohrt* was bent on turning what the West Berlin government regarded as "Easter pass negotiations" into an open forum for the discussion of broader issues such as access. When *Müller* refused to "serve as a tool for disturbing the Four-Power talks or even making them more difficult" (Mayor *Schütz's* words), the East Germans refused to grant the holiday passes.[53]

In retrospect, it was no doubt extremely unrealistic for the GDR régime to assume it could influence the outcome of elections held in West Berlin during mid-March. As past experience clearly showed, it would take more than the incentive of "holiday passes" to boost the communist share of the vote in West Berlin elections. This point was driven home once again as the SEW received but 2.3 percent of the total votes cast in municipal-wide elections on March 14.[54]

Conclusions

If the highly-publicized signing of the Bonn-Moscow Treaty in

51 For the text of Stoph's letter see Frankfurter Allgemeine Zeitung, February 26, 1971.

52 For the text of Mayor Schütz's letter see Der Tagesspiegel, Feb. 27, 1971.

53 Quoted in Relay from Bonn, April 5, 1971.

54 For detailed election results see Der Tagesspiegel, March 16, 1971.

August 1970 led *Willy Brandt* and others in the West to predict an early conclusion of the Berlin negotiations, this optimism soon dissipated. For as the next six months of protracted negotiations clearly revealed, the Berlin agreement the Soviets wanted turned out to be different and more costly than some optimists had anticipated. It was not just that Moscow insisted that the Federal Republic trim its political presence in West Berlin. But it also demanded a greater degree of Western acceptance of the German Democratic Republic. This was their price for making it tougher on themselves to harass civilian surface traffic to Berlin — for giving up some of their political leverage in the center of Europe.

Therefore, with a fine show of appearing to rise above the trivia, Moscow proceeded during the winter months of 1970/71 to increasingly associate itself with the demands of the GDR for Allied recognition of its sovereignty over the question of access. To underscore this point, the USSR apparently lent its support to East German efforts between November and February to interfere with civilian traffic to Berlin — timed to correspond with the deliberate scheduling of conferences in the city by West Germany's three major political parties. And in its conversations with the Western Powers, the Soviets tried to slip the GDR into the "Big Four" talks through the side door; it asked that Bonn fix up details of Berlin access with East Germany and that the West Berlin Senat arrange Wall-crossing matters with East Berlin. London, Paris and Washington naturally frowned on such moves. For the Allies realized they were designed to deprive them of the authority they claimed by virtue of being victors in World War II. Nevertheless, the Russians seemed convinced that the Chancellor was so eager for a Berlin package, which would allow him to submit the Soviet-West German Treaty for parliamentary ratification, that he would accept a lesser one, loosely tied.

The speed of *Brandt's* diplomatic Drang nach Osten, which on December 7, 1970 resulted in the second major breakthrough — this time with Poland — and the eagerness of the West German leader for similar progress in the dilatory Berlin discussions, touched off a major furor in Washington. Convinced that the Kremlin wanted a settlement on the isolated city before its party congress in March, he urged the United States to take the lead in stepping up the tempo of Allied Soviet conferences. But President *Nixon* and his advisers strongly resisted this pressure, putting out not too thinly veiled hints that the former Mayor of West Berlin was ready to bargain away the future of the city for an immediate electoral success and an ultimate place in history.

Apparently behind this difference of views over the pace of the Berlin negotiations was *Nixon's* present unhappiness with the state of Russian-American relations. Back in 1969 the President had been convinced that Moscow's desire for agreement in the projected strategic arms limitations talks would enable him to extract concessions on the Middle East and Vietnam. He added Berlin to that list at the urging of then Chancellor *Kiesinger.* But in 1970 *Nixon* suddenly found himself in a series of confrontations with the Soviet Union over the Middle East. And Soviet help in achieving peace in Vietnam had not been forthcoming. Soviet missile submarines were calling at Cuban ports. And the SALT talks were bogged down. Under these circumstances, the President did not feel it would be wise to make concessions to the Russians on Berlin.

The American President had made his dissatisfaction known to the Kremlin in late 1970, when he invited *Gromyko* to the White House for a private chat. Apparently, the Soviet Foreign Minister had been impressed by his conversations with *Nixon* and conveyed Washington's sense of determination to the leaders of the Soviet Union. For soon thereafter Ambassador *Abrasimov* began to adopt a more flexible line in the Berlin talks, particularly in reference to the crucial issue of access. And it wasn't long before the structure, if not the content, of an agreement was accepted by both sides.

Thus encouraged, the Western Three submitted their draft proposal in early March. On the face of it, the plan appeared to represent major concessions by the Allies. And this impression was strengthened by the fact that Chancellor *Brandt·* gave it his enthusiastic backing. But the major concession — namely, that West Berlin continued not to be a constituent part of the FRG because of Allied suspension, — was more apparent than real. For Britain, France and the United States had never recognized the constitutional claim of Bonn to the city but only the existence of "naturally grown ties" between it and West Germany. Nonetheless, the Russians evinced interest in the proposal, and the Western powers could now sit back and wait for Moscow to come forth with a positive counter-offensive of its own.

Chapter VI

MOVING TOWARD AGREEMENT

The first year of quadripartite negotiation on Berlin resulted in no substantial improvements in the daily lives of West Berliners. And it demonstrated what experienced Allied diplomats had long known. Namely, that the Russians are tough bargainers. If in the beginning, however, the Western side had been sceptical of the seriousness of Soviet intentions regarding a Berlin settlement, as time passed it became clear that the men in power in the Kremlin were prepared to reach agreement on the city. But hardly in the habit of stating immediately all the concessions they were prepared to make, they deliberately bided their time.

The Make-or-Break Stage

If the general mood in the West during early 1971 was one of optimism, events on the Berlin accessways in the first week of March seemed to belie this feeling. Communist harassment of civilian traffic resumed again, causing cars to stall and creating long delays. East German checkpoint authorities turned traffic lights red on the Autobahnen on March 3 as CDU state legislative leaders from the Federal Republic assembled in West Berlin for a three-day meeting. This interference was promptly protested by Western diplomats who crossed the Wall into East Berlin to deliver notes to Soviet Embassy officials.[1]

The Allied notes stressed that this was the fourth case of East German harassment on the access routes in four months. And they warned that such actions could not help but affect the sensitive

1 Frankfurter Allgemeine Zeitung, March 4, 1971.

Berlin talks. To underscore this point, the Western Three postponed the lower-level counselors' meeting with the Soviets that was to prepare the groundwork for the next gathering of the four Ambassadors.

Apparently, the Western response to the East German action was effective. For GDR officials, although they continued to interfere sporadically with civilian traffic through March 5, were careful not to escalate their harassment. Privately, Allied authorities admitted that East German restrictions were relatively milder than in other recent cases and that some action by the communists was to have been expected in view of the Soviet negotiating stance. In its talks with the U.S., Britain and France, the Soviet Union had made clear that appropriate retaliation would follow every assertion of the West German political presence in Berlin.

As things turned out, the delays on the access lanes did not seriously disturb the secret deliberations of the Four Powers. The meeting of the diplomatic specialists, which had been postponed earlier in the week, was held a few days later. And the "Big Four" Ambassadors convened for their sixteenth round on March 9. Speaking before a West German radio audience that same week, *Willy Brandt* said it was "highly unlikely" that the quadripartite talks would now fail.[2]

In fact, they were now entering what Western officials labeled the "make-or-break stage." At the last two plenary sessions, the Russian negotiator had proposed numerous amendments to the draft proposal submitted by the Western Three. As one informed source put it, "One can go through the text once, twice, three times — but after that there is either an agreement or a deadlock."[3]

West Berlin's Ties with West Germany

The main stumbling block in the talks continued to be the question of West Berlin's ties with the Federal Republic and the closely associated issue of Bonn's demonstrative presence in the city. Although the Allies were prepared to make concessions in this area, they insisted that any agreement must recognize the basic rela-

2 Quoted from the Frankfurter Allgemeine Zeitung, March 8, 1971.
3 The Washington Post, March 9, 1971.

tionship between West Berlin and West Germany. In order not to leave any doubt on this point, which was the subject of great controversy in the Federal Republic, Ambassador *Rush* addressed himself to the question in a major speech on March 17 before the American Chamber of Commerce in Hamburg. At that time the American representative emphasized he only would sign an accord that brought substantive improvements in access and left intact the basic special ties between West Berlin and West Germany.[4]

The Soviet response was immediately forthcoming. The following day *Valentin Falin,* Chief of the German Division in the Soviet Foreign Ministry and the Kremlin's Ambassador-delegate to Bonn, stated flatly that an agreement on West Berlin would not be possible as long as the Federal government maintained its presence in the city in its current form. In a talk with *Jürgen Echternach,* Chairman of the Junge Union, the national youth organization of the CDU, *Falin* called the preservation of the West German presence in Berlin demanded by the Christian Democrats a "political fantasy." The senior Soviet diplomat, who had played an important role in the negotiations leading to the Bonn-Moscow Treaty the previous year, said the presence of the Federal Republic in the city was "illegal" because by Allied admission it was not part of the FRG. *Falin* reminded the CDU youth leader of the pledge the Soviet Union gave the German Democratic Republic in a treaty in 1964.[5] At that time the diplomat said Moscow committed itself to regard West Berlin as "an independent political entity." This promise, he warned, should not be underestimated in the Federal Republic.[6]

Two days later (March 19), *Walter Scheel,* commenting on *Falin's* remarks, touched of a heated political exchange between the government and opposition. The West German Foreign Minister stated that the new Soviet Ambassador really had said nothing

4 U.S. Mission (Berlin), Berlin 1971 — An Unofficial Chronology (46) (Berlin: USIS, April 1971), p. 6.

5 This Treaty of Mutual Assistance and Friendship was signed on June 12, 1964 and reiterated Soviet guarantees of GDR sovereignty. However, in an important (but often overlooked) provision the USSR at the same time retained its sovereign prerogatives in Germany by stating in Article 9: "This treaty does not affect the rights and obligations resulting for both parties from other bilateral and international agreements including the Potsdam Agreement."

6 For details see Süddeutsche Zeitung, March 19, 1971.

new. Referring to the demonstration of Federal presence in West Berlin, he described it as "unusual." He pointed out that no Bundestag committee meetings were held in other West German state capitals such as Munich or Stuttgart. *Scheel* added that the FRG only had been able to develop its ties with the isolated city by permission of the United States, Great Britain and France. Originally, he said, such sessions in Berlin were meant to underscore the capital function of the former Reichshauptstadt. But since no one today seriously believed the reunification of Germany could be achieved through free elections or other means, the role of Berlin had changed.[7]

The Foreign Minister's remarks were immediately pounced on by former Chancellor *Kiesinger* and other opposition Christian Democrats. They charged that the flexibility indicated by *Scheel* would imperil the future of West Berlin. Generally, these men felt that the government was prepared to concede too much on the city. If both sides were to recognize existing conditions in Berlin, then the Federal Republic had the same right to be in West Berlin as the GDR had in East Berlin.[8]

The vehemence of the attack from the right led the coalition government in Bonn on March 22 to issue a "clarification" on the critical matter of Federal presence in Berlin. According to this official statement, there would be no Four-Power agreement on the city without simultaneous confirmation of the presence of the Federal government in Berlin. But beyond this, if an accord were to guarantee access and secure the economic and administrative ties between West Berlin and West Germany, then there would be little need to assert Bonn's presence by meetings more frequent than in other major cities in the Federal Republic.[9] The importance of this carefully worded announcement stemmed from the fact that it spelled out government thinking on the subject more clearly than heretofore. At the same time, it was designed to serve as a rebuke to the CDU which *Brandt's* supporters felt were blowing up the presence issue in an attempt to block the Chancellor's larger policy of improving relations with Eastern Europe.

7 Taken from Archiv der Gegenwart, March 19, 1971.
8 Die Welt, March 20, 1971.
9 For the text see Relay from Bonn, March 23, 1971.

The same day that Bonn issued its official declaration on Federal presence in Berlin, *Brandt* made public a hitherto unpublished promise by the Soviet Union. It concerned the intention of the Kremlin to refrain from making use of the so-called "enemy-state clauses" contained in the Charter of the United Nations.[10] According to these two clauses, which can be found in Articles 53 and 107, the USSR had the right to intervene, under certain circumstances, in the Federal Republic. This situation came about because the original essence of the U.N. was the war alliance formed against the Axis powers. Through these clauses, arrangements and measures of the Allies directed against the enemy states of the Second World War were placed outside the competence of the United Nations.

The Chancellor told a caucus of Social Democratic members of parliament he would reveal the text of the Soviet promise when he asked the Bundestag to ratify the treaties with the USSR and Poland. *Brandt* made his announcement under pressure from the opposition Christian Democrats. They claimed that the Russians intended to retain their right of intervention despite agreement to a nonaggression pact.[11]

The controversy arose because of *Falin's* reported statement that the U.N. articles had not been invalidated but "superceded"

10 The text of this pledge was made public during May 1972 when the debate over ratification of Bonn's treaties with Moscow and Warsaw took place. In the memorandum the Federal government submitted to the Bundestag for initiating the process of ratification, mention was made of the following statement of the Soviet Foreign Minister to the Federal Minister for Foreign Affairs:

The second question on principle in which we have come to meet you is the renunciation of force with regard to the UNO Statute. In spite of this we have decided to conclude with you a renunciation of force, i.e., to undertake the obligation and to ratify it. The text we have approved includes the word 'exclusively' (by peaceful means). We have not contemplated any exceptions whatsoever. That is our reply to your domestic political discussion. I stress again the word 'exclusively'. Do you believe that for us that is only a scrap of paper? It is not.

For details see Federal Republic of Germany Member of the United Nations: A Documentation (Bonn: Federal Press and Information Office, 1974), p. 18.

11 The Washington Post, March 24, 1971.

by West Germany's treaty with the Soviet Union. However, as government spokesman *Conrad Ahlers* hastened to point out: "the only way to have the two articles set aside would be through a two-third's vote of the U.N. General Assembly." And this was extremely unlikely. Later *Ahlers'* deputy *Rüdiger von Wechmar* told newsmen that "supercede" meant in fact "to make obsolete."[12]

The Soviet Draft

On March 26 — at the seventeenth meeting of the "Big Four" — Soviets submitted their long-awaited draft of a Berlin settlement. Coming one year to the day after the start of the quadripartite talks, it initially sparked a great deal of enthusiasm that perhaps a breakthrough had been reached. However, a close reading of the text revealed that optimists once again were to be disappointed.

The Soviet draft was received with reserve in official quarters. As one West German source described it, the paper — while comprehensive and detailed — consisted of nothing more than a gathering together in one document of the various proposals that the Russians made in piece-meal fashion during earlier stages of the negotiations. In this view, the "document adds nothing to the bargaining position that Moscow had previously made clear to the Western Allies. Nor does it detract from it. There are no concessions and no retreat to a tougher stance — merely an indication that the Soviets have decided on their maximum bargaining position and are sticking with it for now."[13]

12 In September 1973 the debate over the enemy state clauses was revived. At that time both Germanies were admitted to the United Nations, and the Bonn government took the view that U.N. admission of former "enemy states" logically cancelled the last vestiges of their "enemy" status and thereby rendered Articles 53 and 107 respecting special intervention rights in enemy states inapplicable. This position was adhered to by the Western powers as well as the former enemy states Italy and Japan, which attained U.N. membership in 1955 and 1956 respectively. The Soviet Union, however, challenged this view and took advantage of the anomalous situation that no peace treaty had ever been concluded with Germany to perpetuate the threat of intervention in the affairs of the FRG. See the chapter by Wilhelm Kewenig in Ulrich Scheuner and Beate Lindermann (eds.), Die Vereinten Nationen und die Mitarbeit der Bundesrepublik Deutschland (Munich: R. Oldenbourg Verlag, 1973).

13 The Washington Post, March 30, 1971.

This "maximum bargaining position" was termed a "very tough one" by Allied officials. One that remained leagues apart from the proposals advanced by Washington, London and Paris. As *Kenneth Rush* recalled later: "Some on the Western side felt the Soviet draft evidenced this impossibility of reaching some compromise between the two proposed agreements."[14]

A study comparing the Soviet position paper with the Western draft advanced earlier reveals that the USSR sought in the first place to weaken the status of Berlin and thus, over the long run, the position of the Western powers in the city.[15] For one thing, while the U.S., Britain and France in their paper spoke only of the "Western Sectors" in order to avoid additonal difficulties related to defining the city since they did not want to accept the title "capital of the German Democratic Republic," the Russians were much less precise on this point. They used the words "Berlin (West)" but also talked of the "area whose situation was studied during the negotiations." Another element the Soviets brought in was the "existing situation" without defining it. Through such terminology, the communist side apparently hoped to focus the negotiations on West Berlin alone and thus reinforce their long-term goal of isolating the city.

The demand contained in annex five of the Russian plan seems to point in this direction. It proposed the opening of a Consulate General as well as other steps to assure that "the interests of the Soviet Union in Berlin (West) are properly respected." In an apparent show of great flexibility, *Abrasimov* said this matter could be settled outside the Berlin arrangement now under discussion.

In respect to West Berlin's ties with West Germany, the Soviets took a less flexible stand than they had earlier in the talks. To be sure, the Russian paper acknowledged the existing special relationship asserted by the Allies. And it raised no objections to the economic dimension such as the substantial financial contributions by Bonn to the Senat's budget. But if the USSR was ready to respect the economic ties between West Berlin and the FRG, its

14 Kenneth Rush, "Berlin: The Four-Power Agreement" in Department of State, Current Foreign Policy (Washington, D.C.: U.S. Government Printing Office, 1971), p. 4.

15 See Frankfurter Allgemeine Zeitung, April 29, 1971.

political links with West Germany were an entirely different matter. Here the Soviets were adamant. Whereas the Western draft merely conceded that West Berlin was not a "state" of the Federal Republic, the corresponding passage in the Russian text maintained that the city was not "part" of the FRG. Moreover, while the Allies proposed to restrain the constitutional organs of the Federal Republic from any longer performing official acts in West Berlin, the Soviets also demanded a ban on meetings of parliamentary committees and factions as well as other Federal institutions if they represented an extension of official competence to Berlin. Finally, in this regard, the Soviets proposed the establishment in the Western Sectors of a special contact agency, which would take care of Bonn's interests vis-à-vis the West Berlin government and the three Western powers.

On the question of West Berlin's representation abroad, and the inclusion of the city in treaties negotiated by West Germany, the Soviets were prepared to agree only in part. In the former case, they were willing to permit West German diplomats to represent the city and its residents in third countries provided no claim was made to citizenship of the Federal Republic.[16] In the latter case, the Russians stated their readiness to accept the right of Bonn to include West Berlin in treaties with other states so long as these were not of a military or political character, and both parties to the treaty agreed to its extension to West Berlin.

Soviet-Western differences over the matter of access were also quite pronounced. The Allies wanted this crucial problem settled in the form of a Four-Power agreement. But the Russian paper continued to maintain that like any arrangement for West Berliners to visit the GDR and East Berlin this was a matter involving East German sovereignty. The GDR, it said, was prepared to enter into negotiations on this issue "with interested parties," an obvious reference to the Bonn government and the Berlin Senat. Similarly, the Western Three wanted to make sure that traffic on the transit routes would proceed without hindrance and that identification checks would be done only in cases of individual travellers while

16 This was not a major point as the West German Constitution (Grundgesetz or "Basic Law") recognizes only "German citizenship." This is because the authors of the Grundgesetz designed it to be provisional in nature, serving as a substitute for a formal, permanent constitution which would be drawn up once German reunification was achieved.

long-distance passenger trains and buses would not be checked. But the Soviet paper took up these points only in part. It accepted the principle of sealed vehicles containing "civilian cargo," but provided for East German checks to see whether shipments conformed with statements made on the transit documents. No mention at all was made of sealed trains, earlier Soviet promises notwithstanding.

To an objective observer the Soviet draft, if "tough," was certainly not the "document of surrender" it was subsequently made out to be by the Berlin SPD.[17] In fact, it contained numerous concessions or hints of concessions, though admittedly they fell far short of Allied expectations. If the Western Three were disappointed, they nevertheless resolved not to rule out the chances for compromise. As Ambassador *Rush* pointed out later, although Allied negotiators were discouraged, they "plugged on step by step, first subjecting the Soviet draft to detailed analysis and criticism." Then an attempt was made "to identify common concepts and language in the two drafts." The next step was "to develop a joint text containing common language."[18]

Publication of Position Papers

On April 15, on the eve of the eighteenth Four-Power session, a leading Polish daily (Zycie Warszawy) published a copy of the Soviet working paper submitted to the Allies on March 26. The text was subsequently reprinted in Neues Deutschland and distributed without comment by Tass, the official Soviet news agency. The Polish paper said it had obtained its information from reliable political circles in Brussels. But Allied officials viewed the incident as a deliberate Soviet leak, made in violation of an agreement by the four Ambassadors to keep their negotiations confidential (so that neither side would see itself publicly committed to a position at any one stage in the talks).

17 See U.S. Mission (Berlin), Berlin 1971 — An Unofficial Chronology (47) (Berlin: USIS, July 1971), p. 1.

18 Kenneth Rush, "Berlin: The Four-Power Agreement" in Department of State, Current Foreign Policy (Washington, D.C.: U.S. Government Printing Office, 1971), p. 4.

The publication of the Soviet draft caused quite a stir in the West. To dampen somewhat the propaganda effect, a West German government spokesman declared the next day that the text had been published in an incomplete and rather positively phrased way and therefore put the Soviet position in a highly favorable light. Apparently, the Russian working paper had been leaked in this fashion to provide "proof" of a general willingness by the Soviet Union to compromise without drawing attention to its unyielding position on many specific issues. In any case, an allegedly complete Soviet text and the Western proposal of February 5 were published at the end of April in a number of West German newspapers including Bonn's Generalanzeiger, West Berlin's Der Tagesspiegel and the Hannoversche Allgemeine Zeitung. Details of the two plans were attributed by the SPD-Pressedienst, official daily organ of the Social Democratic Party, to "diplomatic circles in Bonn." This created the impression that their publication represented a kind of Western counter to the Soviet leak.[19]

Soviet Consulate General in West Berlin

Following the publication of Soviet and Western papers, really difficult negotiations got under way. Instead of meeting once every third or fourth week, the "Big Four" proceeded to hold full-dress sessions at intervals of ten to fourteen days. Each of these gatherings was preceded, of course, by extensive preparations of the "experts" — the political advisers of the Ambassadors.

During the fourth week of April, amid a flock of reports about the increasingly gloomy outlook of *Brandt's* Ostpolitik, State Secretary *Bahr* was dispatched to the United States to help break the log-jam in the Berlin talks. The substance of his conversations with American officials was subsequently reported by Welt am Sonntag, a conservative West German weekly sympathetic to the opposition Christian Democratic Party. It published the texts of several secret telegrams the West German Ambassador to the United States *Rolf Pauls* had relayed to Chancellor *Brandt*.[20] Its reports were supplemented by similar disclosures of confidential informa-

19 See Frankfurter Allgemeine Zeitung, April 29, 1971.
20 See Welt am Sonntag, July 18, 1971.

tion by the illustrated weekly Quick, owned by the conservative press magnate *Axel Springer*.[21] Presumably, information was leaked to these sources by West German officials critical of Bonn's policy of seeking détente with the Soviet Union and its East European allies.

These publications revealed that *Bahr* and *Pauls* met in Washington on April 23 with *Henry Kissinger,* his assistant and expert on the Soviet Union *Helmut Sonnenfeld,* and two State Department officials, *John Irwin,* Undersecretary of State, and *James Sutterlin,* Director of the Office of German Affairs. At this gathering, *Bahr* was reported to have urged American officials to accept the establishment of a Soviet Consulate General in West Berlin. Interestingly, and probably significant, this initiative took place just one week after the signing in Moscow of a protocol between the FRG and the Soviet Union providing for the opening of a German Consulate General in Leningrad and a Soviet one in Hamburg.[22]

According to German reports, *Bahr* viewed the proposal of a Soviet Consulate General as an object of barter with which the Western Three could secure communist recognition of West Germany's right to represent the interests of West Berlin abroad, including the touchy matter of its legal affairs. He is reported to have argued that Kremlin approval on this issue would serve to document West Berlin's ties with the Federal Republic. As a consequence, it would then be easier (in the face of West German public opinion) to agree to substantial cutbacks in Bonn's demonstrative presence there.

There were other advantages as well. For instance, the presence of a Soviet Consulate General in West Berlin would demonstrate for everyone to see that Moscow did not possess original rights in the city as it had claimed for some time. Since the Russian facility would be accredited to the Western powers (not the West Berlin Senat), this would signify that the USSR was a foreign country among others having military missions or Consulates in the Western Sectors.[23]

21 Consult Quick, August 4, 1971.

22 For details see Relay from Bonn, April 21, 1971.

23 One of the relics of Four-Power administration in post-war Berlin are the military missions located in the Western Sectors. These continue to represent the different states which in World War II were allied with the victo-

But American officials were not convinced. For one thing, they were afraid that the Soviets would use the presence of a Consulate General as evidence of West Berlin's independent political status. For another, they were concerned that the Kremlin would utilize the facility as a center for conducting espionage activity. *Bahr* apparently did not deny the possibility of this happening. But he justified his proposal with the argument that one had to make compromises in order to reach agreement.[24]

No doubt *Bahr* realized the precariousness of appearing to push acceptance of the Soviet proposal on a reluctant Ally. Therefore, he sought to leave the impression that the idea was his own and had arisen "spontaneously" in his talks with American officials. In fact, however, his initiative earlier had received the endorsement of the Chancellor and his Foreign Minister.[25] In that he completely surprised Ambassador *Pauls*, who had not been let in on the plan and subsequently reported misgivings about *Bahr's* "going it alone" in his cables to the Chancellor, he may well have succeeded in fooling the Americans.

Whether he duped U.S. officials or not, *Bahr's* maneuvering behind the scene created suspicions and problems for friend and

rious powers or were liberated by them. Provision for these installations was made through Article 8 of the London Protocol of November 14, 1944, and they were established originally to represent their governments vis-à-vis the Allied Control Council. Following the walk-out of that body by the Soviets in 1948, and its de facto dissolution a year later, the majority of military missions remained open. Altogether, fifteen countries chose in 1945 to erect such missions. In 1977, only ten were still in existence. These are those of Belgium, Denmark, Greece, Yugoslavia, Canada, Luxembourg (with residence in Köln), Norway, Poland, South Africa (with residence in Köln) and Czechoslovakia. Three states (Brazil, India and The Netherlands) have converted their military missions into Consulates or Consulates General and today form part of a larger group of Consulates, Consulates General and delegations in West Berlin. The heads of mission of those remaining military missions are the respective Ambassadors of these countries in Bonn. This situation prevails in order to counter communist claims that the military missions have an independent diplomatic status in the "independent political entity" of West Berlin. Exceptions to it are the military missions of Yugoslavia, Czechoslovakia and Poland, which are headed by local chiefs of mission with the rank of Minister. For details see Walter Krumholz (ed.) Berlin-ABC, second edition (Berlin: Press and Information Office, 1968), pp. 428-429.

24 See Quick, July 29, 1971.

25 See Der Spiegel, September 20, 1971.

foe alike. British and French authorities felt especially bitter about not being properly informed of the German's attempt to construct what they perceived to be a triangular relationship involving Bonn, Moscow and Washington. Furthermore, London and Paris — like Washington — were sceptical of the proposal which obviously was so favorable to the USSR and annoyed with Bonn for interfering in such a critical area of Allied concern.

When *Bahr's* involvement later became publicly known in the Federal Republic, *Brandt's* domestic critics cried betrayal. To a large extent this discontent was reflected in the West German press. The German weekly Quick published *Paul's* secret telegrams as evidence of *Bahr's* "doubledealing." And the nationalistic National-Zeitung denounced him as "Moscow's Trojan horse." Whereas the arch-conservative Bayernkurier accused the Chancellor's adviser of "selling out Berlin."[26]

In parliament, the CDU/CSU vigorously attacked *Bahr* and the idea of "importing" a Soviet presence into West Berlin. The opposition charged him with exerting undue pressure on the Western Three to approve a totally unacceptable idea. Like the Allies, the Christian Democrats were concerned lest the Soviet facility be used to infiltrate spies and promote Soviet and East German claims regarding West Berlin's independent political status.[27] Although the attempt by the government to defend *Bahr* and refute charges of pressuring the U.S., Britain and France was not very successful, the intensity of the debate showed clearly that the quadripartite discussions had entered a serious stage.

A Breakthrough at Last

In May 1971, there was an important breakthrough in the talks. The Soviet government decided to move towards the Western position and to "re-interpret" some of its earlier demands. As one source close to the negotiations reported subsequently, the Soviets

26 For general press reaction in the Federal Republic to Bahr's initiative see German Press Review, August 4, 1971.

27 See U.S. Mission (Berlin), Berlin — An Unofficial Chronology (48) (Berlin: USIS, October 1971), p. 1.

"have shown a readiness to make commitments in fields of interest which are significant and new."[28]

This dramatic movement in the Berlin discussions during May was not an isolated event. Rather, it should be seen against the backdrop of the 24th Soviet Party Congress, which convened from March 30 to April 9, 1971. The Soviet decision to break the East-West deadlock in the quadripartite talks completed the trilogy of major Kremlin moves in the area of foreign policy, apparently agreed upon at this major convocation. The other two consisted of Soviet agreement to a new formula with Washington in negotiating a first-stage SALT accord. The other took the form of an invitation by Soviet Party leader *Leonid Brezhnev* to discuss with the West a "reduction of arms and armed forces" in central Europe. All three of these initiatives were advertised by Moscow in the "struggle for peace" program, enunciated by *Brezhnev* in his speech on March 30 before the party congress.[29]

Ulbricht Steps Down

The first major casualty of the new Soviet "peace effort" was the GDR's *Walter Ulbricht*. On May 3, in a move which radically changed the outlook of the East German leadership, the ailing 77-year-old leader was replaced by his long-time heir apparent *Erich Honecker* , 58, as First Secretary of the Socialist Unity Party. "Regrettably," *Ulbricht* informed communist party members, "there is no prescription against advancing years."[30] Thus, he tendered his "resignation" to startled participants at the 16th SED conference.[31]

This transition marked the first changeover of the top East German leadership since the creation of the German Democratic Republic in 1949. And it went off so smoothly that many Western observers began to search for hidden meanings. The most generally

28 Keesing's Contemporary Archives, July 10, 1971.

29 See The Washington Post, May 25, 1971.

30 Newsweek, May 17, 1971.

31 Besides his party post, Ulbricht gave up the Chairmanship of the important National Defense Council, remaining only Chairman of the Council of State. He died holding this office two years later in East Berlin; at his death he was eighty years old.

held view was that the aged party leader had become a growing embarrassment to Soviet hopes for reaching an agreement on Berlin and accommodation with West Germany and consequently had been nudged out by the Kremlin.[32]

This feeling was reinforced by subsequent events. Once installed in power *Honecker,* who as *Ulbricht's* chief adviser of defense and security had been personally responsible for directing operations in 1961 leading to the erection of the Berlin Wall, disclosed that he was opposed to many of his predecessor's most cherished domestic and foreign policies. Indeed, he went beyond merely disassociating himself from the *Ulbricht* line and obliquely charged his former boss with "subjectivism, righteousness, painting rosy pictures and abuse of the collective."[33]

Very quickly, the new East German leader indicated his intention of becoming more dependent on the Soviet Union. This major change in the East Berlin-Moscow relationship was made abundantly clear by *Honecker's* stand on Berlin. He made it known immediately that he supported a quick settlement of the problem. Consequently, he proceeded to dilute *Ulbricht's* demands on the West in return for ratification of the accords with the USSR and Poland and agreement on West Berlin. The quid pro quo was no longer the establishment of diplomatic relations with the Federal Republic, plus the acknowledgment of West Berlin's status as an independent political entity on East German soil. It was now toned down to mere recognition of East German sovereign rights and "the reality that West Berlin is a city with a special political status."[34]

About two weeks after assuming power, *Honecker,* accompanied by other key East German officials, paid a much heralded visit to Moscow. As expected, the East German delegation was warmly welcomed by top Soviet authorities including Party leader *Brezhnev* and Premier *Kosygin.* Although details of this important meeting were not published, Western analysts suspected that the Kremlin had called the session to reveal to the GDR leadership its

32 This is the view of a majority of Western scholars today. See Hilary Black, "Honecker's First Year," The World Today, Vol. 28, No. 6 (June, 1972), p. 235.

33 For an excellent analysis of this transition see Peter C. Ludz, "Continuity and Change Since Ulbricht," Problems of Communism, Vol. 2 (March-April, 1972), pp. 56-63.

34 See Neues Deutschland, May 4, 1971.

new international strategy and the terms of the deal it had decided to make with the Allies on Berlin.

In this respect, two points in the joint communiqué, published on May 18,[35] were singled out as especially significant. First, the communiqué said that "in the discussion of international problems, the GDR representative stated that the peace program adopted by the 24th Party Congress was met with general approval in the GDR and was regarded as an expression of the two countries common aims and interests." This statement fell far short of a hearty East German cheer for the Kremlin's intentions as explained to *Honecker,* but it did show the two states were no longer at loggerheads. Second, the communiqué reported that "the participants in the meeting expressed their views on the course of the four-sided negotiations on West Berlin" and that they were "unanimous that an understanding on this question would meet the interests of all parties to the negotiations and would remove the grounds for disputes and conflicts in this region." This language was seen in Allied capitals as meaning that the diverging views of the GDR and the USSR on how to proceed in the Berlin talks had not been completely reconciled, although both sides now seemed to think a settlement with the West would be useful in terms of Moscow's "peace program."

Concrete Phase Begins

Following the East German-Soviet summit, reports circulated in Washington that the Soviet Union soon could be expected to modify its position on Berlin. The first evidence of this came on May 25, at the twentieth round of talks. At that time, the Soviet negotiator indicated the readiness of his government to draft a common text with the Allies. The focus of the draft, it was asserted, would be practical improvements in and around Berlin; all questions dealing with status were to be excluded. The Western Three quickly agreed to proceed in this fashion. With this decision, the negotiations entered what French Ambassador *Sauvagnargues* termed a "concrete stage."[36]

35 See joint communiqué in Pravda, May 19, 1971.
36 See U.S. Mission (Berlin), Berlin 1971 — An Unofficial Chronology (47) (Berlin: USIS, July 1971), p. 3.

Subsequently, in three days of intensive conversations at the experts' level, the first common draft accord was concluded.[37] This text outlined at length those points of common agreement; all issues that remained unresolved were put in footnotes or in brackets. The result of this major effort revealed that substantial progress had been made on the key matters of West German presence in West Berlin, access to the city, its ties with the Federal Republic, representation of West Berlin abroad and communications across the Wall. Ambassador *Rush* viewed the progress on access, a principal stumbling block in the talks, as most significant. As he commented later: "there was finally a move on the Soviet side to undertake a Soviet commitment that access to and from the Western Sectors would be unimpeded. From that time onward, the pace of the negotiations accelerated."[38]

Early in June, the NATO Foreign Ministers gave a deliberate spur to Soviet movement on Berlin. Meeting in Lisbon on the 3rd and 4th of that month for their semi-annual council session, they decided to delay responding to Moscow's call for exploratory talks on mutually balanced force reductions (MBFR) in Central Europe until they had "a clearer idea" where the Berlin negotiations were going.[39] Unlike their reiteration of the highly publicized tie between the conclusion of a satisfactory agreement on the city and multilateral preparations for the European security conference, however, they carefully refrained from formally linking progress on Berlin with talks on force reductions. To a large extent, this distinction was made because NATO, in proposing MBFR discussions back in 1968 and repeating the offer ever since, had never made such a link. But if the formal tie between the two was not officially declared, it was nevertheless there. And every bit of evidence showed that it was clearly understood by the Soviets.

The Ambassadors of the Four Powers held their twenty-first meeting on June 7. And for the first time all parties to the deliberations showed themselves pleased with the results. A Western diplomatic observer optimistically concluded that about half the problems involved in reaching an overall settlement had

37 Before this time the experts had met only seven times. See Archiv der Gegenwart, July 23, 1971.

38 Kenneth Rush, op. cit., p. 4.

39 The Washington Post, June 5, 1971.

already been solved. Ambassador *Rush* was more reserved. He said merely: "We have made progress. I am encouraged."[40]

The most important breakthrough pertained to the troublesome problem of access. Although important details still remained to be worked out, the Soviets appeared to have abandoned their original stand that they would have nothing to do with guaranteeing free transit between West Berlin and West Germany for Germans and citizens of non-Allied nations. (Soviet responsibility for free and unhindered Allied transit was not at issue here.) This question, they had once insisted, was purely an internal affair. If *Abrasimov* later came to acknowledge Soviet responsibility for unhindered passage, he also disconnected linkage of concessions on access with the issue of Federal presence in West Berlin — an Allied responsibility. He now treated them as two separate issues.

The second major issue on which there was important movement concerned Bonn's official profile in West Berlin. Earlier the Soviets had demanded the wholesale withdrawal of Federal offices and personnel from the city. But now the Soviet negotiator hinted Moscow might be willing to let Bonn keep in West Berlin those departments and agencies already established there.[41]

Still to be resolved were the other three pillars of the projected settlement. These were more freedom of movement between West and East Berlin, improved inter-sector communications and confirmation of the ties between Berlin and the FRG. Moreover, the controversy over the Soviet request to open a Consulate General in the Western Sectors had not been successfully handled. While the Allies were showing signs of acceptance of this proposal, they had not yet decided on an adequate trade-off. They definitely did not want to obtain permission for respective Consulates in East Berlin since the East Germans consider it the capital of the GDR and opening such facilities there would be interpreted as a step toward diplomatic recognition.

Eighth SED Party Congress

In the middle of June, with all available indicators pointing to a quickening of the pace on Berlin, *Erich Honecker* opened East

40 The Washington Post, June 8, 1971.
41 Ibid., June 11, 1971.

Germany's Eighth Party Congress of the SED. In his maiden speech, which although low key in tone lasted six hours, *Honecker* gave several signs that the GDR would stop obstructing East-West efforts to ease tensions in Central Europe.[42] The speech drew a distinct line between the more conciliatory stance of the new party leader and the militant hostility displayed in the past by his predecessor.

Notably absent from the party gathering was *Walter Ulbricht,* who failed to show up to deliver his scheduled opening-day remarks. Subsequently, the East German government issued the hasty explanation that the former Party Secretary had been stricken with a "circulatory ailment" and confined to bed. But stories making the rounds in the Federal Republic maintained that, in fact, *Ulbricht* had been so enraged by critical references to him in *Honecker's* speech, that at the last moment he had petulantly refused to attend the congress.[43]

Honecker's address was carefully studied in Allied quarters, particularly as it seemed to articulate a new policy for the GDR regarding the Berlin issue and his country's status in international affairs. Unlike his former boss, who insisted on turning West Berlin into a special political entity, *Honecker* spoke merely of a "city with a special political status." This latter phrase had first been used in an editorial in Neues Deutschland on February 3 and had been picked up at that time by the Allies, who interpreted it as meaning significant moderation on the part of East Berlin.

The new party chief also discussed the "Big Four" negotiations on Berlin in his opening speech. With occasional glowing nods to Soviet Party leader *Brezhnev,* sitting a few feet away, he hailed the talks and wished them "success." Western observers later pointed out that this was something *Ulbricht* had never done.[44]

In his speech, *Honecker* de-emphasized the failure of Western nations to recognize the German Democratic Republic. He did not demand that the West recognize the GDR before conclusion of a Berlin accord. Moreover, he indicated that East Berlin would settle for something less than full diplomatic recognition by Bonn when the time came to exchange representatives. These declarations

42 For the text of Honecker's remarks see Neues Deutschland, June 16, 1971.
43 Newsweek, June 28, 1971.
44 See The New York Times, June 16, 1971.

172

were significant, for full diplomatic recognition by the West, including West Germany, had been one of *Ulbricht's* insistent demands.

The following day, June 16, *Leonid Brezhnev* took the opportunity to speak to the East German communist party congress. His hour-long speech was moderate in tone and had the effect of balancing lavish praise for the *Honecker* régime with some conciliatory-sounding remarks about the atmosphere of détente in Europe. On Berlin, the Soviet leader said that the quadripartite talks were entering the stage of examination of "concrete proposals on the content of a possible agreement." And he indicated that the Soviet Union was now prepared "to make efforts to bring this matter to a successful conclusion."[45]

In the United States, *Willy Brandt,* who was in the midst of concluding several days of talks with American leaders went out of his way to respond promptly to *Brezhnev's* remarks. That same day the Chancellor told a news conference in New York City: "I attach particular importance to the fact that he (*Brezhnev*) chose East Berlin to go beyond his earlier statements and speak of a positive Berlin settlement." *Brandt* also emphasized that *"Brezhnev's* words made clear the importance the Soviet Union attaches" to the treaty on the renunciation of force signed with the Federal Republic the previous August. Both during his press conference and in a speech later in the day before the American Council on Germany, the West German leader exuded confidence that East-West relations had finally entered a relaxation of tensions.[46]

A Rush to Finish

The Four Powers continued their discussions on Berlin through late June and July. During this time there were more and more frequent meetings of the Ambassadors and, in between these, more detailed sessions of the experts. For the first time in the talks the Ambassadors met four times in one month. The twenty-third through twenty-sixth sessions were held on July 8, 16, 22 and 30. It was clear that the negotiations had entered a critical phase.

45 Ibid., June 17, 1971.
46 Quoted from The New York Times, June 17, 1971.

Toward the end of July the four Ambassadors were close enough to the long-sought agreement that they decided the time had come to finish their discussions. In a dispatch, published by the prestigeous Frankfurter Allgemeine Zeitung on August 3, it was reported that the parties agreed to make their next gathering the "final phase" of their deliberations. They were prepared to keep talking, it was said, for four consecutive days in a supreme effort to reach accommodation.

This story, coming in the aftermath of highly publicized leaks in the German press, which included the publication of secret Western and Soviet position papers and cable exchanges, immediately touched off a controversy between Bonn and the Western powers. The Allies, in particular Washington, while acknowledging the general accuracy of the reports, were angered because they feared that failure to reach agreement in the negotiation marathon might be interpreted as a sign of the collapse of the talks. Since the Ambassadors suspected that many of the press leaks originated inside the *Brandt* government, their pique was directed at Bonn. Ambassador *Rush* registered a blistering protest with *Paul Frank,* Undersecretary in the West German Foreign Office. Subsequently, both the Allies and the Federal Republic announced a total blackout on information about the delicate discussions.[47]

As expected, the four-day marathon opened on August 10 with a great deal of publicity. The first session lasted almost nine hours, making it the longest meeting yet in the 17-month-old negotiations. Following this exhausting round of talks, Ambassador *Abrasimov* informed reporters that "two big steps forward" had been taken. Other Soviet sources dropped broad, if non-specific, hints of significant progress. But the Allies were non-committal.[48]

The following day similarly intensive bargaining took place. But progress was slow, and the hope of the Allies that the week would see a breakthrough toward Four-Power agreement began to fade. As usual, the most outspoken of the Ambassadors was the Soviet representative. He smilingly told reporters: "Today it was more difficult. It was warm. But we go ever forward together."[49]

The Ambassadors continued their long, drawn-out conversations through August 12, the third consecutive day of the marathon

47 The Washington Post, August 5, 1971.

48 Ibid., August 11, 1971.

49 Ibid., August 12, 1971.

and, by a twist of fate, the first anniversary of the signing of the Bonn-Moscow Treaty. But it was now evident that the Soviets were still not willing to budge on some issues which the Allies considered essential.

The expected fourth consecutive meeting of the diplomatic envoys was not held. By an ironic coincidence, it fell on the tenth anniversary of the sealing of the East Berlin Sector border. And the Allies realized that this day would be commemorated by an enormous parade in East Berlin and by memorial services and protest demonstrations in West Berlin. Consequently, they felt a session on August 13th would be inappropriate and could even act as a spark for demonstrators, angered by the presence of the Soviet Ambassador in West Berlin.

The second week of August closed then without a settlement and with the lines firmly drawn between the two sides. No further progress was expected unless one or the other substantially changed its present position. To be sure, the Ambassadors for the first time went through the entire range of issues and tried to formulate a comprehensive draft accord that they could refer to their governments. Moreover, the four were understood to have reached tentative agreement on some minor points in dispute. But on the big questions such as access, Federal presence in West Berlin and Soviet rights in the city, there was no breakthrough.

The situation looked something like this. On access, the Soviets were willing to concede, as before, that they had a share in ultimate responsibility. But despite intensive wrestling with the problem no precise formula was established satisfying the Allied demand for guaranteed free and unimpeded passage for civilian surface transit.

In respect to West Berlin's ties with West Germany, the Soviets were prepared to acknowledge various economic and cultural links between the two. But they continued to insist there be no political connection. For their part, the Western Three maintained that Moscow recognize some form of political association.

As far as the Federal presence in West Berlin was concerned, the Soviets continued to argue for substantial cutbacks in West German offices and personnel. Although the Allies were ready to limit Bonn's constitutional presence in the city, they drew the line at any withdrawal of agencies or persons. West German public opinion would not stand for it, they argued.

Regarding the touchy matter of the right of the FRG to represent West Berlin abroad, the USSR was willing to compromise. It agreed to accept some form of representation of the city in consular and foreign commercial affairs. But it still refused to sanction the proposition that West Berliners could carry passports of the Federal Republic.

Lastly, no decision had been reached with respect to Russian commercial representation in West Berlin and the opening of a Consulate General there. This latter issue had become especially irksome in recent discussions because the Western Three viewed it as a major trump card to be surrendered only after Moscow made significant concessions. One participant recounts how this issue was used to best advantage: "We never promised the Russians during the negotiations that we would allow them to open a Consulate General. But we did dangle the possibility before their eyes and then withdrew it to encourage them." This strategy almost backfired, however. For the Soviets threatened not to make any concessions unless they were first promised the consulate.

In general, London, Paris and Washington felt at the week-end that they had gone more or less as far as they could in trying to reach an accommodation with the Soviets. The feeling in these quarters was that further concessions in any but a few minor areas would raise the twin risks of undermining their legal status in Berlin and producing an accord so watered down that it would be unacceptable to West German public opinion. Consequently, the Western Three were content to play a waiting game to see what concessions could be squeezed out of the Soviets, who were obviously in a hurry to wrap things up. As one Western diplomatic observer neatly summarized the situation: "we are waiting now to see whether they will blink and how long it will take for that to happen."[50]

Agreement at Last

This change in Western strategy was made apparent to *Abrasimov* when the talks resumed the following Monday, August 16. At the meeting, which lasted some eight and a half hours, the Allies made it clear that unless agreement on some of the key outstanding issues could be reached soon, the talks would have to be recessed until

50 The Washington Post, August 13, 1971.

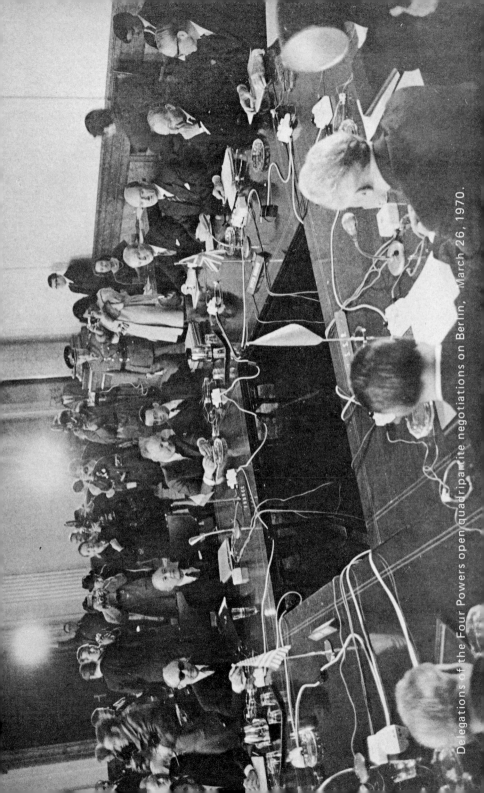

Delegations of the Four Powers open quadripartite negotiations on Berlin, March 26, 1970.

Ambassadors Pyotr Abrasimov (USSR), Kenneth Rush (USA), Sir Roger Jackling (UK),and Jean Sauvagnargues (France) relax after finishing Four-Power talks in the Zehlendorf villa of Ambassador Rush, August 23, 1971

September. The Soviet negotiator was reportedly not happy with this "threat," but he remained optimistic that the discussions could be completed by the end of the week if the Allies would only continue the marathon. After conferring privately among themselves, *Rush* and his British and French colleagues agreed.

Apparently, the Western Three, if a little wary of being rushed into damaging, last-minute compromises, were impressed by Soviet eagerness for quick agreement. Soviet resolve in this regard had been stressed repeatedly during the last days by *Abrasimov*. But more convincing than any oral declarations of good intention by the Soviet representative were "hard" intelligence reports that *Gromyko* secretly had come to East Berlin to take personal charge of his country's negotiating team.[51] Several times during breaks in the marathon bargaining *Abrasimov* or members of the Soviet delegation were seen scurrying off to visit the Eastern Sector, presumably to seek the Foreign Minister's advice in resolving points of disagreement. So favorable, indeed, were the signs that one Western diplomat predicted: "Unless the heavens fall in, we're going to have an agreement."[52]

The four Ambassadors continued their lengthy bargaining through the next couple of days. Finally, on Wednesday, August 18, at the thirty-second meeting, the long-awaited breakthrough in the dialogue was accomplished. Most of the important outstanding issues were resolved in an unprecedented 14-hour session which lasted until after midnight. Upon emerging from this exhausting ordeal, a weary but ebullient *Rush* told reporters that "every subject" at issue "has now been covered fully." It was "a good meeting," he said. "I'm pleased." Ambassador *Abrasimov* seemed to share the American envoy's enthusiasm. For he informed newsmen in his broken German: "Ende gut, alles gut." (If the end is good, all is good.)[53]

If the August 18th session resulted in the resolution of most of

51 Gromyko's unexpected presence in East Berlin was made official by the East German news agency ADN on August 19. It reported that the Soviet Foreign Minister had been in the GDR capital "the past few days" for political talks with SED leader Erich Honecker. The announcement did not say when Gromyko had arrived. See U.S. Mission (Berlin), Berlin 1971 — An Unofficial Chronology (48) (Berlin: USIS, October 1971), p. 3.

52 Newsweek, August 30, 1971.

53 Der Tagesspiegel, August 20, 1971.

the troublesome issues, the Four-Power negotiations were not yet complete. The political advisers of the Ambassadors still had to conclude a formal text before their bosses met again on Monday for final agreement. And several ticklish matters remained to be settled.

The most important of these concerned the hammering out of the details closely proscribing the activities of the Soviet Consulate General in West Berlin. As expected, the Western Three waited until the very end to play this "trump card." At the last minute, they used it to secure Soviet agreement to West German representation of West Berlin abroad. This decision, it was revealed later, had been made personally by President *Nixon*.[54]

The thirty-third and final quadripartite negotiating session was held on Monday, August 23. In view of this special occasion, the four Ambassadors met not in the ACA building, where formal discussions had been held for so long, but at the invitation of the American representative they sat down for talks in the more congenial atmosphere of *Rush's* picturesque residence in the fashionable district of Dahlem. There, with drinks readily available, the "Big Four" concluded their deliberations and initialed the draft text of the Berlin agreement. It was subsequently sealed with handshakes all around.

The following day, the draft accord was submitted to governments for their consideration and approval. In addition, copies were made available to members of the West Berlin Senat and the Federal government in Bonn. Otherwise, the text was kept secret until after it met with the formal approval of all parties concerned.

On August 25, the West German government unanimously approved the draft agreement. The endorsement by Bonn came in the form of a resolution, adopted by Chancellor *Brandt's* Cabinet. It said the accord "preserved the interests of West Germany and Berlin" and that it represented a major "contribution to easing tensions in the center of Europe." The Federal government declared itself ready to initiate talks with East Germany on working out the details as soon as the signature of the Ambassadors was attached. That same day the West Berlin Senat also gave its hearty approval.[55]

54 U.S. Mission (Berlin), Berlin 1971 — An Unofficial Chronology (48) (Berlin: USIS, October 1971), p. 4.

55 The Washington Post, August 26, 1971.

Two days later, President *Nixon* gave his personal stamp of approval to the basic draft. Meeting with Ambassador *Rush* at San Clemente, he called it a "significant step toward the reduction of world tension." It was clear that the President was pleased with *Rush's* work. "There's a feeling," reported one *Nixon* aide, "that he's done a damn good job and that we got a better package than anyone expected."[56]

During the interval between the initialling of the agreement on August 23, 1971 and the actual signing a week later the accord was hotly debated in the German press. For the most part, newspaper reaction was fairly reserved. The independent Stuttgarter Zeitung, which praised the text, said it "lifted the bar which up to now prevented further and more comprehensive East-West negotiations." But the Rheinische Post, a Düsseldorf paper that favored the opposition Christian Democratic Party, declared that measured "in terms of hopes for the German future" the emerging agreement "seems at best an interim solution." The Springer papers were almost unanimous in their opposition to it. While some called the accord a "sellout" of German interests, others charged *Brandt* as being responsible for granting the Soviet Union too many concessions on Berlin without getting enough in return. Only the more respected Die Welt, a Hamburg paper that is right of center, took a wait and see position. It refrained from judging the settlement until the text could be seen and studied. "What we know now," it stated, "is that we must treat all reports of success with a healthy dose of skepticism."[57]

A Problem over Translation

Before the Berlin agreement could be signed formally by the four Ambassadors, following approval by their respective governments, there were some further dramatic moments. Originally, a common text had been scheduled to be signed in an official ceremony on September 2. But this had to be postponed a day because of a last-minute failure of the United States, Britain,

56 Newsweek, September 6, 1971.

57 For a more comprehensive analysis of West German press commentary see German Press Review, September 8, 1971.

France and the Soviet Union to accept a binding, uniform German translation of the pact.

Difficulties arose due to differing translations into German from the official English and Russian versions of the quadripartite accord. The East German version of the text had been translated from Russian; whereas the West German one, from English. The matter was crucial because the two Germanies were scheduled to work out the sticky details implementing the principles agreed to by the "Big Four".

The popular account of the controversy over translation difficulties, as it appeared in many papers in the U.S. and abroad, goes something like this: The demand for an official German text was made by *Egon Bahr*. The West German Staatssekretär foresaw that conflicting German translations could cause a major domestic controversy. The powerful conservative opposition in parliament had never approved of the negotiations, and it was now poised to attack *Brandt* with the hope of toppling his government.[58]

Already on July 19th the Western Three had formally transmitted a proposed German translation of the working draft then taking shape. At that time, they informed their Soviet colleague that it would behoove them all to reach agreement on a joint German text as soon as possible. But nothing ever came of the suggestion as the four Ambassadors became preoccupied with ironing out their still unresolved major differences.

This omission was severely criticized by officials in Bonn. One West German Undersecretary (reputedly *Bahr*) subsequently told reporters of the newsweekly Der Spiegel that this mistake was due to "an occupation mentality" on the part of the negotiators. This attitude he summarized in the following fashion: "We are here among ourselves and the Germans are of little interest to us."[59]

One day before the signing ceremony was to take place two German translations were delivered to the experts. But only at the last minute were the two translations compared by the Allies. This study of the texts revealed more than eighty points of conflict and put the Western Three in a desperate situation.[60]

Subsequently, three working groups were set up to thrash out

58 The New York Times, September 3, 1971.
59 Der Spiegel, September 6, 1971.
60 Ibid.

the differences. In this effort, the Allies received generous editorial assistance from East and West German sources. Several times West German Foreign Ministry officials *Günter van Well* and *Hans-Otto Bräutigam* crossed the Wall into East Berlin to consult with East German officials. Largely as a result of this unprecedented effort, most of the disputed passages were resolved by the time of the scheduled signing ceremony. Nevertheless, in that three particularly difficult albeit important points remained unsettled, the highly publicized Four-Power meeting had to be postponed at the last minute.

One disputed phrase pertained to access to and from Berlin. The East Germans, who had spent more than two decades in an unrequited quest for recognition as a sovereign state, wanted to insert the word "transit" (Transit). This language would allow them to take advantage of the international legal usage of "transit" as a noun, rather than an adjective — implying movement across the territory of a sovereign state. On the other hand, the West Germans, who had clung no less tenaciously to the dream of ultimate German reunification, argued for the use of the phrase "through traffic" (Durchgangsverkehr) which would deny that fateful implication.[61]

Two other phrases that were subject to dispute concerned the German equivalents of "ties" in reference to relations between West Berlin and West Germany and "constituent part" in regard to what West Berlin was not to be considered in terms of the Federal Republic. In the first case, GDR officials insisted on using the "Verbindungen," a weaker word akin to "links," rather than the West German term "Bindungen," a much stronger word.[62] In the

61 During the Four-Power negotiations discussion between the Allies and the Soviet Union centered on the question of defining "access" in international law. Although a survey of international conventions pertaining to the access and egress of states revealed that they used often the term "traffic in transit," the Berlin accord utilized the phrases "transit traffic" and "through traffic" without clearly indicating a preference. This state of affairs bolstered the interpretation that the contracting parties did not mean to use the terms within the context of international law but merely as a factual description of existing traffic movements between the Western Sectors and the Federal Republic. See for example Günther Doeker et al, "Berlin and the Quadripartite Agreement of 1971," American Journal of International Law, Vol. 67, No. 1 (January, 1973), pp. 57-58.

62 In the context of the agreement, the English term "ties," implying social ties as well as ties of communications, differs from the Russian word "svjazy," which has more the sense of "communications" than "ties."

second case, the East Germans, to emphasize that West Berlin was not at all part of the FRG, wanted to substitute "Teil" (part) for "konstitutiver Teil" (constituent part).[63]

In the end, after an exhaustive all-night session, a common German text was produced. This compromise version contained a glittering array of foreign words at points in the translation where there had been controversy. But as a precaution to protect the Allied position, this text was declared not binding and unofficial. With this last obstacle out of the way, the signing by the four Ambassadors followed on September 3, 1971.

If there is some plausibility to this story of last-minute problems over agreement on a German translation, Ambassador *Rush* has the following statement to make which would correct the historical record: "the press accounts as to the actual differences in wording between the F.R.G. and G.D.R. translations into a German text were inaccurate. In that connection I might give you some non-classified information concerning the background of the various translations.

"The fact that there should be a single German text for use by all German parties did not, as you seem to have been informed, suddenly arise on a suggestion of Mr. *Bahr* . . . In fact, from the beginning of the negotiations there were three important items with regard to the various languages used:

1. There would be three official translations, namely, English, French and Russian. To this all parties, of course, agreed.
2. Throughout the negotiations English would be the single text used in the official drafting. After agreement was reached, the official translations into French and Russian from English must be acceptable to all the Four Powers. To this all parties also agreed.

Thus, in Russian, "ministerstvo svjazi" means the Ministry of Post and Telecommunications.

63 It is noteworthy that the experts, in drafting English, French and Russian texts of the agreement — all of which were to be equally valid, — did not successfully resolve the confusion over terminology in this area. In accordance with their view that West Berlin is not part of the FRG, the Soviets used the phrase "sostanoj cast'ju," which has more the meaning of "part" than the English "constituent part" or the French "élément constitutif." For an analysis see Hartmut Schiedermair, Der Völkerrechtliche Status Berlins nach dem Viermächte-Abkommen vom 3. September 1971 (Berlin: Springer Verlag, 1975), p. 90.

3. There was an absolute need for a single German translation, which would be unofficial, in order that all German parties would be operating under the same language and interpretation. The Americans and British in particular were very insistent upon this and were fully supported by the F.R.G. The Soviet Union was strongly opposed, arguing that only the three official translations were needed. The French took a more neutral position.

"The issue as to the single German translation was not resolved until it came to a head after tentative accord on the Quadripartite Agreement had been reached in August 1971. The Russians only capitulated after it became clear that I would not sign the Quadripartite Agreement until acceptance of a single German text had been reached by the two German parties, the F.R.G. and the G.D.R. After some all-night sessions, a single German text was agreed upon precisely in accord with the translation desired by the Allies and the F.R.G. Otherwise, the agreement could very readily have been subverted by interpretations differing from the actual Quadripartite Agreement."[64]

Upon the signing of the long-awaited draft agreement, which was not to go into effect until after the East and West Germans had reached subsidiary arrangements on the details of its implementation, the first phase of the quadripartite talks was formally concluded. Altogether the settlement was the product of thirty-three rounds of extraordinarily tough and hard-fought ambassadorial exchanges, lasting more than 152 conference hours, and many more hours of private exploratory conversations.

Conclusions

If during the fall of 1970, American and West German officials had been at loggerheads over the pace of the Four-Power negotiations, with the Bonn government — anxious to restore its waning popularity — arguing for a faster tempo and the administration in Washington, tied up in other crises and unwilling to make unnecessary concessions, in the spring of 1971 both partners were once again closely aligned. And there was hope that the Western

64 Letter from Ambassador Kenneth Rush to author, dated June 28, 1976.

proposal, which had taken some time to work out, would bring agreement nearer. Both *Brandt* and *Nixon* wanted to achieve a settlement on Berlin in order to take further steps towards détente. Just as the West German government had committed itself not to submit the Soviet and PolishTreaties to the Bundestag for approval without a satisfactory quadripartite accord, it was clear to the United States that an agreement on Berlin was an indication of Soviet goodwill which must be given before any progress could be made in discussing a conference on security in Europe (or later multibalanced force reductions inCentral Europe).

For the most part, Western officials were optimistic despite continuing East German harassment on the transit routes. But the real question, as one American diplomatic official put it, was whether the Western Three would "get firm, detailed Soviet and East German commitments" or whether they would have to "settle for a brief, vague set of promises." His own conclusion was "Probably something in between."[65]

As events showed, the Allies did not have long to wait. For on March 26 — at the seventeenth meeting of the Ambassadors — the Soviets submitted their proposal for a draft agreement. This position paper was subsequently subjected to careful study in Allied quarters, although Western officials were hard put to hide their initial disappointment. For the most part, they were puzzled why *Abrasimov,* who must have known that it was unacceptable to the West, had put on such a show when he unveiled the plan. Some observers speculated that the Kremlin wanted to have on paper a comprehensive set of proposals on Berlin in time for the 24th Soviet Party Congress which was held just four days later. By putting forward the document at this time, these sources thought, Soviet leaders would be able to use it as a basis for public pronouncements on the Berlin question at the all-important congress.

But if this analysis appeared to explain the timing of the Soviet initiative, it did not account for the inflexibility of Moscow's position. The answer to this question was less clear. A number of Western officials believed that the rigidity of the Soviet position was directly attributable to the upheavals which had shaken Poland the previous December. These revolts had resulted that month in the replacement of *Gomulka* by *Edward Gierek* as First

65 The Washington Post, March 10, 1971.

Secretary of the Polish Communist Party.[66] The echo from the Polish riots, they said, apparently strengthened the hand of *Walter Ulbricht,* who was having his own upsurge of trouble with discontented workers.[67] In this view, *Ulbricht's* efforts were having temporary success in persuading the Soviets to brake the movement towards accomodation with the West.

Whatever Soviet motives were, the American, British and French Ambassadors resolved to look at the Russian draft proposal in the most positive light. In adopting this strategy, the Western Three were inadvertently following the advice of *W. Averell Harriman,* one of the United States' most experienced and distinguished negotiators. As the former troubleshooter for American Presidents pointed out in an interview in 1969: "to be successful in any negotiation, you must look at the most constructive proposals the opponent or the enemy offers. You need to find a position offered by one side acceptable to the other and try to build from there." Too often, he said, "Foreign service officers, like the Chiefs of Staff, are trained, or imagine that they are trained, to expose every conceivable obstacle to negotiations. They think they get points in their favor when they show themselves to be tough and hard boiled in protecting U.S. interests. To take the constructive approach to negotiations, we must re-educate both our foreign service and our military."[68]

66 Twice in the post-war history of Poland have workers' revolts set that nation on a new economic and political course. The first time was in 1956, when factory employees in Poznan took to the streets to demand food. This demonstration produced a political convulsion that brought Wladyslaw Gomulka to power as leader of the communist party and ended much of the repression associated with the Stalinist period. Some fourteen years later, in December 1970, port workers in Gdansk (formerly German Danzig), frustrated in their negotiations over a new "incentive" payroll plan — under which bonuses would be based on quality rather than quantity — became enraged over a weekend announcement of a nationwide increase of food prices and marched in protest thus setting in motion a train of events culminating in Gomulka's downfall and his replacement by Gierek.

67 It should be recalled that Ulbricht's decision back in 1953 to raise work norms by at least ten percent had sparked a mass uprising of the East German people in June of that year — a rising which had to be crushed by Soviet tanks.

68 Quoted from an interview with Edward W. Barrett, Director of the Communications Institute of the Academy for Educational Development, and

If the Soviet draft agreement left much to be desired, its submission nevertheless demonstrated that the Russians were taking the Four-Power talks seriously. This interpretation was bolstered by events following the Soviet party congress in March-April. The most important of these occurred in May. During that month the Soviets publicly agreed to negotiate a first-stage SALT pact, formally accepted a NATO proposal to talk about mutually balanced force reductions and purportedly put pressure on *Ulbricht* to hand in his resignation. This last move was decisive in smoothing the way for the conclusion of the quadripartite discussions (but according to confidential intelligence sources was made much before May).

All the circumstances surrounding *Ulbricht's* "retirement" from his all-powerful post as Party Secretary suggest that his relinquishment of East German leadership was less than voluntary. To be sure, his advancing years were a factor — as well as a face-saver — in his acceptance of a much lesser role in the régime. Yet the very fact that for twenty-five years he had guided the destiny of East Germany — first as the Soviet Occupation Zone and then as the German Democratic Republic — imply that his step-down, which was suddenly announced, was not of his own making. While there is no way of telling what went on behind the scenes, the signs surrounding *Ulbricht's* replacement make it seem reasonable to believe that Soviet leaders intervened to force the aged leader out. If so, the transition of power could well have been arranged at the 24th CPSU Congress. Many experts believe that this is when the Kremlin decided to make a deal on Berlin and that the new East German Party chief *Erich Honecker* was informed of this upon his visit to Moscow on May 18.

Ironically, *Ulbricht's* withdrawal from active leadership came at a time when his prestige both at home and in the communist world was at its peak. In particular, he had received a large share of the credit for transforming the GDR into a dynamic, performance-oriented state — the second strongest industrial society after the USSR in Eastern Europe. Moreover, he had become famous for his adeptness at neutralizing political opponents. If for a time

reprinted in "Observations on Negotiating: Informal Views of W. Averell Harriman," Journal of International Affairs, Vol. 29, No. 1 (Spring, 1975), p. 1.

in 1970 it seemed that the East's leading opponent of détente with the West was no longer capable of exercising his old powers of persuasion on his fellow communist leaders, this situation began to change dramatically in December 1970, when worker riots in Poland forced out *Gomulka*. Since that time, the Eastern European countries had sharply braked their impulse towards further accomodation.

Nevertheless, once the surprise was sprung, and *Ulbricht* was ejected from the top position, it was not difficult to see a number of reasons for this development. Not the least important of these was his declared obstinacy over Berlin. It was well known at the time that the increasingly arbitrary and erratic behavior of the aged leader had annoyed the Russians and that his unyielding stance on the isolated city was creating an impediment to progress in the Four-Power talks. Beyond this issue was the renewed Soviet interest in arriving at certain international accords with the United States and its continuing rapprochement with West Germany, where *Brandt* was offering tempting prospects of credit allowances and future industrial collaboration. In addition to these considerations, was the broader question of future relations between Eastern Europe and the Common Market. These were becoming increasingly important in view of the impressive progress of Western Europe towards economic integration. From this view, then, Moscow could not afford to allow *Ulbricht*, who appeared unwilling to adjust to the change in international climate and the shift in Soviet objectives, to spoil the show. Therefore, *Honecker* was almost certainly installed in the expectation that he would conduct a foreign policy better attuned to that of the Soviet Union.

A further, and conclusive, impetus to the Berlin negotiations came in mid-July from a quite unexpected direction. This was the improvement in relations between the United States and mainland China. It may be recalled that on April 19, 1971 the leadership in Peking astonished the world by inviting an American ping-pong team to make a nine-day tour of the country. This announcement represented the first formal invitation to an American group to enter China since *Mao Tse-Tung* had founded the People's Republic twenty-one years earlier. President *Nixon* quickly responded by proclaiming new measures to warm up Sino-American relations. This surprise turn-around of relations between two former staunch enemies culminated in the bombshell announce-

187

ment of July 15, 1971. At that time, the American chief executive went on national television to say that he had received an invitation himself to visit China. He declared his acceptance, explaining that he hoped to visit Peking early in 1972.

If this sudden reversal in relations between China and the United States came as a shock to the Western world and the Soviet Union, it was as Kremlinologist *Adam Ulam* has pointed out "the logical outcome of the two governments' changing the assumptions that governed their policies." In this view, it had been a somewhat naive belief of American foreign policy makers in the late 1960s to consider that the USSR was now a "responsible" power while China stood for militant communism. It was little appreciated, *Ulam* asserts, that "Peking's violent rhetoric was largely the means of pressuring the Soviet Union toward a more anti-American position" and thus "preventing that accommodation between the United States and the Soviets which is the Chinese Communists' worst nightmare."[69]

In any case, by the beginning of the 1970s both countries had good reason to alter their stance. For its part, the leadership in Washington hoped to gain China's help in extricating the U.S. from Vietnam. (The Soviets — contrary to the expectations of the *Johnson* and *Nixon* administrations — had shown little sign of doing this.) Then there was the feeling that the United States could take advantage of the Sino-Soviet split by playing one power off against the other.

For its part, the Chinese leadership began to realize that Washington posed much less of a threat to it. Bogged down in a seemingly unwinnable war in Vietnam and with domestic discontent on the increase, the United States now appeared incapable of achieving its original goals in South-East Asia. If the Chinese once feared joint action by Washington and Moscow, they now feared that détente between the two at the very least would free the USSR to concentrate its military efforts more sharply along its borders with the People's Republic and at worst might lead the Americans in their frustration over Vietnam to offer the Kremlin a free hand in China for help in extricating themselves from the war on less than humiliating conditions. Thus *Adam Ulam* concludes: Peking "realized, if no one else did that the disenchantment of the

69 See Adam Ulam, Expansion and Coexistence: Soviet Foreign Policy 1917-73, second ed. (New York: Praeger Publishers, 1974), pp. 766-767.

United States with the whole course of the foreign policy it (had) pursued since 1947 threatened to remove that unwitting and paradoxical protecting which the mere fact of American power and role in the world afforded China vis-à-vis the Soviet Union."[70]

As events were to show, Moscow viewed this opening of China to the United States with a great deal of uneasiness. Generally, the Kremlin saw it as an attempt to isolate the USSR. Therefore, in order to protect its Western flank and enable it to cope, if need be, with China, Moscow pressed specially hard in the summer of 1971 for a final settlement on Berlin.

But if it appeared that the China opening induced Moscow in July 1971 to be more responsible to Western views on Berlin, so as to bring about an agreement which would prevent a dangerous degree of isolation, decision-makers in Washington likewise redoubled their efforts at this time to reach a settlement on Berlin to counter the accusation that rapprochement with Peking would necessarily disrupt détente with the Soviet Union. No doubt due in part to what has been termed "this fortuitous conjunction in Sino-American relations,"[71] American objections to certain Soviet demands concerning Berlin were dropped. For example, Washington — which was the last of the Allies to agree on the establishment of a Soviet Consulate General in West Berlin — was finally persuaded to do so in August 1971 (although — as one insider points out — "there were many in the bureaucracy who never reconciled themselves on this point.")

The decision to hand Moscow this long-sought plum was later severely criticized in the Federal Republic (and elsewhere). The conservative opposition argued that in its eagerness to persuade West Germany to ratify the nonaggression treaty of the previous year, the Kremlin was so ready to strike a deal on Berlin that it was not necessary to give the Soviets the Consulate. But apparently the Western Three were unwilling to take the risk of bluffing on this point. As one Western diplomat said in retrospect: "We never would have permitted the installation of a Soviet Consulate if it hadn't been part of such a very satisfactory package."[72]

70 Adam Ulam, op. cit., pp. 766-767.

71 Roger Morgan, The United States and West Germany 1945-1973 (London: Oxford University Press, 1974), p. 216.

72 Newsweek, August 30, 1971.

Until now the Western publics have been kept in the dark regarding the background to the marathon sessions which were responsible at the end for winding up most of the substantial points of disagreement between the Allies and the USSR. The idea of holding these "continuous sessions" until an agreement was reached was actually the result of one of Ambassador *Rush's* initiatives. As one insider reveals: *"Rush* wanted to prevent the bureaucracy from interfering. Up to then it had been trying to control every move he made. The Soviets were in a hurry to sign," this source continues, "and *Rush* knew that. The order had come down from Moscow to settle. So *Rush* devised this strategy to take advantage of the opportunity to finish off the talks." The Four Powers "would complete negotiations before the bureaucracy could react." The State Department gave its approval of the marathon, and the British and the French went along.

At the time, the key people in State — *Martin Hillenbrand,* Assistant Secretary of State for European Affairs, and *James Sutterlin,* Director of the Bureau of German Affairs, "didn't think the marathon would make any difference." They were both on vacation. They were "not expecting anything to happen, and we caught them by surprise," this official says. "In rapid fire, we reached agreement with the Soviets on practically all the major outstanding issues. The State Department was in an immediate uproar. *Bill Rogers* (U.S. Secretary of State) was upset and so were all the lawyers." People "said that *Rush* had exceeded his authority. He was even accused of disobeying a NSSM"(National Security Staff Memo). As this person tells it, "they were all afraid the White House would hold them responsible" (for a poor agreement?)

Soon "word of this upheaval filtered back to Germany, and German officials (under attack by a vigorous opposition for allegedly pushing the Allies into a quick agreement) began to get nervous." Eventually, "the Soviets found out," this source adds, and "they became very upset. They began to think the agreement was off." The U.S. envoy "had to rush back to Washington to straighten things out." *Rogers* "immediately called *Hillenbrand* and *Sutterlin* back from vacation, and they sat down and studied the agreement. After talking with them, *Rush* went to see President *Nixon* at San Clemente." *Nixon,* it is said, "quickly approved the agreement, and so that was that."

The last minute squabble over the translation of the Four-Power accord into German provided a fitting end to the long months of intricate talks between the Allies and the Soviets. But if the quibbling over words and phrases in the German text appeared merely semantic, it was not. From all accounts, East German officials sought through translation manipulation to gain for themselves what had been lost by their patrons — the Russians. Textual disputes focused on the most troublesome issues in the negotiations — access and West Berlin's relations with the Federal Republic. And they pointed up the fact that the "Big Four" did not completely resolve these matters; they merely passed them on to the Germans to deal with themselves. Although it was disappointing to see the final signing postponed, it was probably just as well to have the general euphoria by the Western publics punctured in this way and to draw the world's attention to the parties — the Germans — who were going to have to live with the arrangement made by Washington, Moscow, London and Paris in their name.

Chapter VII

THE INNER-GERMAN NEGOTIATIONS

The signing of the quadripartite accord on Berlin — welcome as it was — represented but the first part of a triptych. The four Ambassadors agreed in their initial pact of September 3, 1971 on a declaration of principles and guidelines to bring about improvements in the situation in and around Berlin. But this "umbrella" agreement — as it was called — was not to go into effect until after West and East German representatives had worked out the sticky "technical" details for its implementation. These officials were relegated the delicate task of drawing up separate understandings which, together with the conclusion of a final protocol noting approval, would make up a comprehensive settlement.

The inner-German talks were to take place on two distinct levels. In the one track, the West Berlin Senat was given the responsibility of negotiating with the GDR arrangements, which would allow West Berliners to visit East Berlin and East Germany and provide for the solution of tiny exclaves of the city through an exchange of territory. The aim of the Senat representative was to achieve as generous a settlement on these matters as possible, while parrying attempts by GDR authorities to give weight to their contention that West Berlin is an independent political entity. In the second track, the Federal government in Bonn was charged with the important task of working out the sensitive question of road, rail and water access between West Germany and West Berlin. In making this effort, the West German negotiator was instructed to turn back ploys by the GDR to widen East German control over the access lanes and strive to secure a "watertight" accord, which would make certain that concessions won at the Four-Power level would not be lost at the inner-German level.

Ambassador Abrasimov (USSR) and Rush (USA) and Sauvagnargues (France) and Jackling (UK) comment on Quadripartite Agreement at signing ceremony September 3, 1971.

Senatsdirektor Müller (West Berlin) and Günter Kohrt (GDR) address press after initialing agreements on visits and the exchange of territory, December 11, 1971.

Both sides initially viewed the prospects for a successful outcome as good. Political sources in the GDR maintained that their government was committed to cooperate "fully and speedily" with West Berlin and West German officials in filling out the details of the draft accord.[1] In the Federal Republic, authorities were equally confident. *Egon Bahr,* who was scheduled to meet with his East German counterpart to thrash out the details of a transit agreement, estimated that his conversations would not take very long: "Minimum six weeks; maximum six months," he prophecied. [2]

The Allies, too, were optimistic. Although they were somewhat concerned the Soviet Union would urge the GDR to regain as much political ground as possible in this stage of negotiations, few experts believed the inner-German dialogue would break down. "It's almost inconceivable," remarked one U.S. diplomat, "that after putting so much effort into these negotiations, the Soviets would let the East Germans torpedo them. When the crunch comes, *Gromyko* will make another trip to East Berlin, and that will be that."[3]

Maneuvering for Advantage

The balloon of official euphoria about the prospects for success in the inner-German discussions burst on September 4, just one day after the signing of the quadripartite accord. At that time, the communist paper Neues Deutschland published a German-language text which differed considerably from the one previously agreed to by both East and West Germany. It was clear that the East Germans, in preparing for the tough negotiating ahead, were maneuvering for early strategic advantage. This turn of events was immensely disappointing to Western officials. Ambassador *Rush,* for one, was led to comment sharply that he would not have signed the Four-Power agreement had he known that the East Germans "would immediately start playing tricks with the text."[4]

The tone of the deliberations between the two Germanies was thus set when their representatives met face to face in two separate

1 See The New York Times, August 26, 1971.
2 Der Spiegel, September 6, 1971.
3 Newsweek, September 6, 1971.
4 The Washington Post, September 11, 1971.

encounters on September 6. The first meeting took place in West Berlin between *Ulrich Müller,* Head of the Senat Chancellery, and *Günter Kohrt,* Undersecretary in the GDR Foreign Ministry. These officials had conferred several times since the opening of an earlier dialogue between the Senat and the GDR on March 6, 1971. And they were to begin discussing liberalized rules for West Berliners to visit East Berlin, improved communications between the two halves of the city and the exchange of territory, having been authorized by the Four Powers to undertake these negotiations to implement Annex II of the Quadripartite Agreement. The second — and by far the more important session — was held in Bonn between *Egon Bahr,* Undersecretary in the Federal Chancellery, and *Dr. Michael Kohl,* Undersecretary in the GDR Council of Ministers. And it was to take the form of concrete discussions on the facilitation of civilian transit traffic between West Berlin and West Germany to implement Annex I of the Four-Power accord. Since this latter sitting actually marked the seventeenth time that *Bahr* and *Kohl* had met since November 27, 1970, it was generally supposed that the two men had already done some secret fencing over the Berlin access question in the preparation of a draft general traffic agreement between the two German states.

During these preliminary talks both teams of negotiators came almost immediately into conflict over what Bonn was authorized to negotiate with East Germany and what was the responsibility of the West Berlin government in talks with East Berlin. The argument over translation played a key role in this dispute. The GDR's *Michael Kohl* asserted in the first round of deliberations with *Bahr* that his government no longer regarded the uniform German text, worked out by both sides just before the Berlin agreement was signed, as binding. He proceeded to introduce a new version and declared his willingness to use it as the basis for negotiations. His explanation for this sudden about-face was that the West German news DPA had sent out the joint translation prematurely and in such a way as to make it clear where the GDR had given way. This caused the East German régime to lose face.[5]

One major change initiated by GDR officials concerned West Berlin's relations with West Germany. The communist side transformed the word Bindungen (ties) into the looser Verbindungen

5 The New York Times, September 23, 1971.

(connections or links) to describe these. Using this new language and a similar change, Dr. *Kohl* interpreted the quadripartite accord to mean that East Germany could negotiate separately with authorities in Bonn and West Berlin on details of civilian traffic to and from the isolated city. The discussions between *Bahr* and himself, *Kohl* argued, should be limited to the movement of West Germans (i.e., permanent residents in the Federal Republic) to West Berlin, while those between Senatsdirektor *Müller* and East Berlin's *Günter Kohrt* should focus on the passage of West Berliners (i.e., individuals with a permanent residence in the city). If this demand by *Kohl* was unacceptable to Bonn and its Allies, the GDR's political motivation was readily understood. After all, as one Western observer shrewdly pointed out, from the East German point of view the Western interpretation supporting *Bahr's* "competence to negotiate on all questions of access (did) imply a large dose of 'Federal presence" and a corresponding denial of the independence of West Berlin."[6]

Admittedly, the responsibility of Bonn to negotiate on access was not spelled out precisely in the text signed by the "Big Four". All that was said there was that this matter would be settled by "the competent German authorities." Nevertheless, the Allies maintained that provisions in the accord regarding West Germany's right to represent West Berlin abroad gave Federal officials the competence to negotiate on behalf of the Senat on this question. And, as they did not hesitate to add, the Soviets did not challenge this interpretation.

East German persistence in the demand for separate negotiations on access caused the inner-German dialogue to stall even before it got off the ground. Officials in Bonn and West Berlin were careful to coordinate their bargaining positions so that the East German attempt early in the talks to play off one against the other was made more difficult. The Western side chose to refrain from discussing the larger issues until the impasse on this question was successfully resolved. As things turned out, however, neither side demonstrated a willingness in the first several rounds to back down so *Brandt* was compelled to break off the negotiations in the middle of September.

6 See Dieter Mahncke, "The Berlin Agreement: Balance and Prospects," The World Today, Vol. 27, No. 12 (December, 1971), p. 518.

The Chancellor was more than just a little peeved with this maneuvering for position on the part of the GDR, but he remained confident. For one thing, he was fairly certain the deadlock was only temporary. For another, he had just received a personal invitation from *Leonid Brezhnev* to visit him on the Crimea to exchange views on their mutual relations and other matters of concern to Moscow. And he thought he could take this opportunity to persuade the CPSU Chairman to exert pressure on the GDR to bargain seriously. Thus, to increase his leverage over East Berlin, *Brandt* accepted the Soviet leader's invitation.

The Chancellor flew to the Black Sea on September 16, taking *Bahr* along with him. Together, they spent sixteen hours of the next two days talking, drinking, walking and speedboating with *Brezhnev* around the resort town of Oreanda in the historic region of Yalta, where in February 1945 *Roosevelt* and *Churchill* had sat with *Stalin* to decide the fate of post-war Germany. The visit made a deep impression on the West German leader, who came home aglow with a new feeling about "the first man of the Soviet Union."

Brandt describes the encounter vividly in his memoirs of the period. He says before serious talks started he was required to take a Russian "drinking test." He claims to have passed it with flying colors, holding his vodka better than *Brezhnev*. In the extensive talks that followed, the Chancellor was impressed with the Soviet Party Chairman's new and positive "realism." But *Brandt* was sober in evaluating his own position vis-à-vis that of *Brezhnev*.

The Russian seemed most interested in learning from his guest what was to become of the Bonn-Moscow Treaty. He was very worried that it would not be ratified. "If this happens," *Brezhnev* threatened, "there will be a setback in our relations which can last decades." The Chancellor hastened to reassure him that the fate of his government rested on a favorable outcome, and he stated his opinion that ratification would be accomplished.

Brandt was the one who introduced the subject of the inner-German talks. Here he detected a little annoyance on the part of his host, who it appeared was afraid that this topic would be brought up. The Chancellor expressed concern about the delaying tactics of the East Germans and pressed his host several times for assistance in this matter — but apparently to no avail. First, *Brezhnev* pretended not to know what *Brandt* was talking about. So the West German explained the trouble over translation. The Russian leader said he couldn't understand how such difficulties could arise since the official text, which the four governments had signed, was "clear." In any case, he declared the Soviet Union would not intervene. "We did not ask for" a German translation, he said and "we will not now interfere."[7]

Brandt's description in 1976 of his discussions with *Brezhnev*, however helpful in reconstructing events, contrasts sharply with press reports of these talks circulating in the West at the time. According to these accounts, the Chancellor was said to have received private assurances that the USSR would exert pressure on the GDR to be more forthcoming. However, as a face-saving device, no progress could be expected in the inner-German dialogue until the *Bahr-Kohl* discussions had gone through one or more sessions.[8]

The general accuracy of these latter sources seems to be borne out by subsequent developments. Thus, *Bahr* and *Kohl* met for their third round of talks on September 22, less than a week after *Brandt* and *Bahr* returned from the Crimea. And the two sides parted after only thirty minutes, reporting that the deadlock over translation and competence remained. This impasse, however, was merely temporary, as a "breakthrough" in the negotiations came at the end of the month with the signing in East Berlin of a highly touted postal agreement.[9] This accord provided, among other things, for greater mail service and improved telecommunication between the two German states and thus was in accordance with the Four-Power agreement, calling for increased communication. But most importantly, it signified that the East Germans had retreated from earlier demands that two separate pacts be negotiated on transit travel by conceding that Bonn could speak and act for West Berlin. "For the first time ever," *Bahr* remarked at a news conference the following day, "East Berlin accepted an

7 Der Spiegel, May 31, 1976.
8 See The Washington Post, September 23, 1971.
9 For the text of this agreement see Federal Ministry for Inner-German Relations, Texte zur Deutschlandpolitik, Vol. 9 (Bonn: Deutscher Bundes-Verlag, 1972), pp. 158-167.

agreement in which the Federal Government negotiated also for West Berlin."[10]

In his talk with reporters on October 1 *Bahr* gave a lengthy and intricate explanation of how the three-week impasse had finally been broken. Essentially, he said, the main source of friction — differences over textual language in the German translation of the quadripartite accord — had not been settled but was being bypassed for the time being. The Undersecretary stressed that the important thing was not the actual words such as Verbindungen for Bindungen but the way they were interpreted. He maintained that the version offered by the GDR in the postal agreement was "fully in the spirit of the Four-Power agreement's intent." If the East Germans speak of Verbindungen, *Bahr* observed, "and the result of these Verbindungen is something similar to the postal accord, then as far as I am concerned" they "should do that."[11] On the basis of this understanding, therefore, both sides were now able to proceed to bargain seriously.

Reverse Junktim

During October the inner-German discussions took on a new life as West Berlin and West German representatives hammered out the details of arrangements on access, visits and the exchange of territory. *Bahr* compared this phase in the dialogue to a "mountaineer's climbing the first hill on the way to the summit."[12]

Serious negotiating got underway just as the opposition CDU resolved its internal leadership crisis and took the offensive against *Brandt's* Deutschland- and Ostpolitik. Former Chancellor *Kurt-Georg Kiesinger* was replaced as Party Chairman on October 4 by the younger and more dynamic *Rainer Barzel,* who soon became CDU/CSU candidate for Chancellor. He immediately began to assail Bonn's treaties with Moscow and Warsaw "as not a sound basis for an Eastern policy." *Barzel* called for a new government that would conclude a treaty to "assure true rapprochement,

---

10 Quoted in The New York Times, October 2, 1971.

11 Quoted in Der Spiegel, October 5, 1971.

12 U.S. Mission (Berlin), Berlin 1971 — An Unofficial Chronology (49) (Berlin: USIS, January 1972), p. 1.

198

détente and peace."[13] *Franz-Josef Strauss,* speaking before a convention of his Bavarian CSU, fulminated in a similar vein against *Brandt's* policies. For his part, the Chancellor tried to promote an image of aloofness from the caustic domestic battle that was shaping up. In this respect, he was helped considerably when in the middle of the month he was notified that he was to be awarded the Nobel Peace Prize.

As the two-tract inner-German talks continued under a tight veil of secrecy, another element of uncertainty was thrown into the negotiations by the Soviet Foreign Minister. Reporting from Washington on October 6, the conservative Die Welt indicated that *Gromyko* was turning the time-table around on final settlement of the Berlin problem. The Soviet diplomat informed his West German colleague during their meeting at U.N. headquarters in New York that even if the two Germanies reached agreement the USSR would withhold its endorsement until after the Bundestag ratified the Bonn-Moscow Treaty.

Western analysts assumed this latest Soviet initiative was designed to influence German domestic policy. The West German government was obviously reckoning on a wafer-thin majority of six in the lower house to get the treaties with the Soviet Union and Poland through over the massed negative votes of the powerful opposition. But the Soviet leadership was becoming anxious about the ability of the Chancellor to keep his promise to obtain ratification after a "satisfactory" Berlin settlement. By coupling a final Berlin package to treaty ratification, the Soviets apparently hoped to put the CDU/CSU in the unhappy position of having to vote for or against the Four-Power agreement — something the Kremlin thought the conservative opposition could scarcely afford to do.[14]

Western reaction to this "reverse linkage" was immediately forthcoming. The Frankfurter Allgemeine Zeitung (October 8), reflecting the position of *Brandt,* pointed out that the Federal government had never spoken of a "legal" linkage between the conclusion of a final Berlin protocol and ratification of the two treaties but always emphasized the "factual" linkage of the two. The Allies, while reportedly warning Moscow in private that their

13 Quoted in Peter H. Merkl, German Foreign Policies, West and East: On the Threshold of a New European Era (Santa Barbara, California: ABC — Clio Press, 1974), p. 163.

14 Die Welt, October 7, 1971.

coupling idea might hold up the general movement toward easing of tensions in Central Europe, decided to play down the matter. To do otherwise, they felt, might create a prestige problem for the Kremlin and thereby harden the Soviet stance. The conservatives, at which the Soviet move was primarily directed, chose to respond more forcefully. Stung by *Gromyko's* ploy, they demanded that the Chancellor "immediately take a position" on it. In the meantime, they prepared to launch an embittered campaign against the Russian linkage in parliament.[15]

Brezhnev's Intervention

That Soviet interest in the fall of 1971 continued to be focused to a great degree on its relations with Bonn was demonstrated aptly by the surprise (and unofficial) appearance in East Berlin of *Leonid Brezhnev* on October 30. Arriving in the East German capital on his way home from a six-day visit to France, the Soviet Party leader was reported "disturbed" by some of the wrinkles that had developed in the two-stage inner-German negotiations. Apparently, he feared the two Germanies were holding up Soviet plans for moving ahead in seeking improved relations with the West.

The trouble seemed to stem from East German intransigence in the delicate negotiations with West Berlin and Bonn. Despite the highly-publicized "breakthrough" of the previous month, GDR representatives *Kohrt* and *Kohl* had now hardened their stand and were pursuing what *Bahr* described as a "go-slow policy." In the talks with Senatsdirektor *Müller,* this strategy was manifested in the dispute over the "immediate and nondiscriminatory entry" from West Berlin to the surrounding East German areas. The East German leadership saw in this matter a threat to the "integrity" of its borders with West Berlin, although no opportunities for East Germans to visit the West were involved as yet. To be sure, the GDR had reasons to be concerned. The smaller and in almost every respect the weaker state, it saw its vulnerability to the West as being considerable. Consequently, the GDR negotiator felt he could not permit a "quota-free invasion" by West Berliners who, unlike their fellow citizens in the FRG, had been barred from East

15 The New York Times, October 8, 1971.

Berlin and East Germany since 1961. For his part, *Müller* maintained that there could be no question of talking about a limited number of visits by West Berliners to East Berlin and the GDR, since the Four-Power agreement specified that conditions should be "comparable to those applying to other persons entering those areas."[16]

If differences over the question of visits by West Berliners proved in the long run to be the most difficult to resolve, most public attention was, for the moment at least, focused on the problems being encountered by *Bahr* and *Kohl* over access. In the main, difficulties here had to do with the closing of many hundreds of loopholes for possible renewed GDR obstruction. Both sides attached special importance to these conversations. For they realized that the settling of far-reaching "technical details" on transit could very well determine the whole application of the quadripartite accord.

Of the many complex points, which were still subject to dispute, three of the most critical pertained to the sealing of vehicles, the method of collecting tolls and misuse of the transit routes. In the first case, argument centered on where and by whom vehicles should be sealed. On the one hand, the West German side, which did not want to provide East German control officers with any excuse to hold up traffic, insisted that sealing be done before Western vehicles crossed the frontier. On the other, the East German side, which did not trust the proposed sealing of conveyances by Federal authorities, demanded that GDR representatives be authorized to apply their own seals at the border.[17]

Controversy arose in the second case over defining the exact procedure for fixing annual compensation for fees, tolls and other costs relating to transit traffic. The Federal government wanted to avoid being faced perennially with new and difficult negotiations over higher claims — possibly linked to other demands and offering, in instances of disagreement, a pretext for hindering access. So it had instructed *Bahr* to hold out for agreement on a fixed sum to be payed at the end of each year. But *Kohl* resisted this effort, citing the impossibility of judging adequate compensation over the years.[18]

16 Archiv der Gegenwart, December 11, 1971.
17 Der Spiegel, November 15, 1971.
18 Der Spiegel, November 15, 1971.

No doubt the most serious point of conflict involved the misuse of the access routes by Western travellers. The East German negotiator was particularly adamant on this point. In cases where the GDR suspected any wrongdoing, it wanted to be able to search and arrest travellers. While admitting that East Berlin had legitimate cause for concern here, Bonn was again afraid of giving the East German leadership, which was viewed as being almost paranoid on the issue of escape attempts, any leverage to interfere with the smooth processing of traffic. "We must have absolute clarity" on what constitutes "misuse," declared *Egon Franke,* West German Minister for Inner-German Affairs. And it must not be left up to checkpoint officials to determine what are "sufficient grounds for suspicion." To leave no room for arbitrariness on this vital matter, Bonn sought to lay down a detailed catalogue of precise and binding criteria, covering every conceivable development in transit — from travellers taking a rest break to their smuggling out of refugees.[19]

The significance of this haggling over seeming "technicalities" was not lost on *Brezhnev.* But it was obvious from his special trip to East Berlin that he had more important things on his mind. He had only recently (in October) extended a personal invitation to President *Nixon* to meet with him in the Soviet Union before the President visited China. And the Soviet leader evidently expected to see the closely linked East-West negotiations — on final Berlin arrangements, on opening a European security conference and on starting troop reduction discussions — reach a decisive stage by that time.

To press this sense of urgency home, *Brezhnev* conferred at length with the entire leadership of the GDR, including the former Party chief, *Walter Ulbricht.* According to informed sources, he urged them for the "fastest possible" conclusion of their talks with West Berlin and West German officials. Underscoring the importance of this point, and to remove lingering doubts among the East German leaders over the implications of improved East-West relations for their régime, *Brezhnev* postponed his scheduled departure from East Berlin by one day.[20]

---

19 Der Spiegel, November 15, 1971.
20 The New York Times, November 2, 1971.

This "jaw-boning" on the part of the CPSU leader apparently had the desired effect. For, The New York Times reported on November 2, *Brezhnev* had obtained a "pledge of cooperation" from *Erich Honecker,* who said that if all sides showed good will the talks "could be concluded soon." Three days later, the SED chief reiterated GDR interest in the conclusion of the inner-German dialogue by the end of November and promised to come forward and meet every constructive approach made by the *Brandt* government.[21] *Honecker's* remarks were warmly welcomed by Western officials, who had been led by the delay in progress in the talks to assume that detailed arrangements of the Berlin accord would not be reached by the two sides until early the following year.[22]

Scheel's Visit to Moscow

Toward the end of November, with the inner-German discussions entering what reliable sources termed the "conclusive phase," the West German Foreign Minister at the invitation of the Soviet government paid an official visit to the USSR. During his stay, which lasted from November 25 through November 30, *Walter Scheel* was cordially received by Soviet Party leader *Brezhnev* and Premier *Aleksei Kosygin.* While the German diplomat was reported to have reached a remarkable degree of understanding with his Russian hosts over the questions of a European security conference and MBFR,[23] he failed to break a procedural impasse over the completion of a final Berlin protocol and ratification of the Bonn-Moscow Treaty.

Earlier in the year the Soviets had startled the West by reversing the linkage between the two. Whereas the Federal Republic had previously indicated that ratification of its treaty with Moscow

21 See Neues Deutschland, November 5, 1971.

22 U.S. Mission (Berlin), Berlin 1971 — An Unofficial Chronology (49) (Berlin: USIS, January 1972), p. 2.

23 For the text of a statement issued by the German Foreign Office in Bonn upon the return of Scheel from the Soviet Union, see Relay from Bonn, December 1, 1971.

would only take place after the conclusion of a "satisfactory" Berlin settlement, the Russians proceeded to reverse this time-table by tying a final package on the city to ratification. As a way out of this deadlock, *Scheel* proposed a compromise solution whereby both events would occur simultaneously, provided the "Big Four" issued a declaration that the Berlin agreement was "complete" and would "not be amended." Such a statement, the Chairman of the Free Democrats pointed out, would allow *Brandt* to initiate the long and cumbersome process of ratification even before the U.S., Britain, France and the Soviet Union signed the final protocol on Berlin.[24]

Scheel supported his "compromise" with two telling arguments. The first stressed the West German interest in a solution to this impasse; the second emphasized the Soviet stake. To begin with, he said, a delay in implementation of the Berlin agreement would greatly complicate his government's fight to win ratification. And it might even be enough to bring it down. Russian officials seemed impressed by this cataclysmic description of events, thus encourag-ing *Scheel* to stress next Soviet enthusiasm for détente in Central Europe. Given the nature of the joint NATO position on proposed talks on a security conference and mutually balanced force reductions, he stated that he did not think multilateral prepara-tions for them would be approved until after the troublesome Ber-lin issue had been cleared up. Although Soviet leaders agreed to study *Scheel's* proposal, they declined to commit themselves to agree to any concessions on Berlin so long as their bilateral treaty with Bonn had not been validated by the FRG.[25]

Conclusion of the Bahr-Kohl Talks

If *Scheel* was unsuccessful in winning Moscow's acceptance of his compromise plan, he and colleagues in the FDP wielded decisive influence over the inner-German negotiations, particularly as the two sides began to quicken their pace in the last days of November.

24 The Washington Post, November 30, 1971.
25 For details see the interview with Walter Scheel, published shortly before his trip to the USSR in Die Zeit, November 19, 1971 and the article printed upon his return in that same paper, December 3, 1971.

By the middle of that month, a great many difficult points had been settled in the conversations between *Bahr* and *Kohl* over access — what was generally regarded as the heart of the Four-Power accord. So much progress had been made, in fact, that Under-secretary *Bahr* was led to remark soon thereafter: "I can see the summit now."[26] But if the Chancellor's aide was optimistic about the results of discussions with his East German counterpart, the Foreign Minister and other members of his party were upset with what they perceived to be *Bahr's* eagerness to make concessions in order merely to bring deliberations to a speedy conclusion.

One matter in particular is reported to have caused them special irritation. This was the East German intention to arrest one-time refugees in transit through the GDR. The East German leadership considered Republikflucht (fleeing the GDR) a grave offense and in the past had dealt harshly with any offenders it was successful in apprehending. When *Bahr* asked for advice on how to proceed on this delicate matter, he was told to move cautiously. Of all *Brandt's* advisers, it was Interior Minister *Hans-Dietrich Genscher,* who apparently reacted most strongly to the domestic political danger of making concessions too readily here. He instructed *Bahr* to hold the line until the bitter end while attempting to find some kind of a trade-off.[27]

Subsequently, *Bahr* and *Kohl* went round and round over the problem of how to treat the great number of Germans who earlier had resided in the GDR but later fled to the West. In the process, however, the Chancellor's representative appeared to make headway. First, he extracted from his counterpart a guarantee that all persons who had left East Germany "illegally" prior to the construction of the Wall would be permitted to use the accessways without having to face arrest. Later this promise was extended to include all those who had "voted with their feet" up to the time of implementation of the agreement.

But if *Kohl* seemed overly generous on this issue, this illusion was quickly shattered. In the attempt to recover some lost ground, he introduced the following condition: unhindered passage would not apply to one-time escapees who, in the process of engineering their flight, had committed "serious crimes" (schwere Straftaten).

26 Quoted in Relay from Bonn, November 30, 1971.
27 Der Spiegel, December 6, 1971.

Moreover, the whole question of so-called schwere Straftaten would be interpreted from the viewpoint of East German laws and ordinances. According to reports, *Bahr,* although he was unhappy with this turn of events, was ready to give in at this point.[28]

However, in *Walter Scheel,* the Undersecretary found himself up against a formidable adversary. The Chairman of the Free Democratic Party, who did not try to hide his distrust of Bonn's negotiator, was firmly opposed to such a concession. And he is said to have encouraged the Western powers to lodge a protest.

One day before departing for Moscow the Foreign Minister summoned *Bahr* to his office. There he reportedly had it out with the Undersecretary. Flanked by his aides Undersecretary *Paul Frank* and *Bernt von Staden,* his Departmental Chief for Political Affairs, *Scheel* demanded to know what had transpired in private between *Bahr* and *Kohl.* Evidently, the Foreign Minister had been tipped off to suspicious doings by his representative in *Bahr's* delegation, *Hans-Otto Bräutigam.* This individual warned *Scheel* that "the private talks between *Kohl* and *Bahr* were getting longer and the written reports on them shorter." By having it out with the Chancellor's aide, the FDP leader wanted to prevent learning about details of the inner-German dialogue from the Soviets in Moscow when he should have been informed of them by *Bahr.*[29]

In this heated discussion with the Undersecretary, *Scheel* ordered him to formulate Bonn's approval in such a way that only "really serious lawbreakers" would be barred from travelling freely to and from Berlin — and not those who just had committed so-called "political crimes." *Bahr,* who was obviously upset at what he viewed was an interrogation, is reported to have responded: "If I demand that, then Kohl will depart and break off negotiations." In face of the Foreign Minister's insistence, *Bahr* threatened to resign his commission.

Later other FDP members intervened with the Chancellor. Travelling from Berlin, Free Democratic emissaries *Wolfgang Lüder* and *Hermann Oxfort* told *Brandt* that the compromise arranged between *Bahr* and *Kohl* regarding the "misuse clause" was unacceptable. In their view, it would merely open the door for the GDR to make more irresponsible claims.[30]

28 Der Spiegel, December 6, 1971.
29 Der Spiegel, December 6, 1971.
30 Der Spiegel, December 6, 1971.

Upon returning to the negotiating table, *Bahr* did what he was instructed and achieved what before had appeared to him impossible. Namely, he secured *Kohl's* agreement to spell out definitively what constituted "serious crimes." The formula, to which both sides concurred, defined these as "crimes against life, premeditated offenses against bodily health or serious offenses against property." Political crimes, for instance the mere act of fleeing the GDR, were not to be considered a schwere Straftat. But even in cases where it could be proven that transit travellers had committed a serious offense, as outlined above, East German authorities were limited in the action they could take. Former refugees could not be arrested; control officers only had the right to turn them back. (Such was the magnitude of this last concession on the part of the GDR that *Kohl* later did not want to admit publicly that his government had surrendered the right to apply its laws pertaining to Republikflucht on the transit routes — its own territory.) Thus, with this exception, East Berlin promised to treat one-time refugees in all respects as normal transit travellers, so that no disadvantages would result from their having left "the worker's paradise."[31]

With this most important hurdle overcome, the way was now clear for a speedy wind-up of the East-West German talks on access. And these were tentatively concluded in what was thought to be a final bargaining session on December 3. In announcing this momentous event to his government, *Bahr* declared: "What the cabinet wanted is positively settled." Praising the efforts of his aide, *Brandt* remarked: "I am surprised; I did not believe that such a positive and reasonable agreement could be reached."[32]

But although both sides appeared to have finished their negotiations on access, Undersecretary *Bahr* refused to initial his accord

31 See Article 16 of the "Agreement between the Government of the Federal Republic of Germany and the Government of the German Democratic Republic on Transit Traffic of Civilian Persons and Goods between the Federal Republic of Germany and Berlin (West)," signed on December 17 by Undersecretary Egon Bahr (Federal Chancellery) and Undersecretary Michael Kohl (GDR Council of Ministers) in Bonn. For a complete English text see The Bulletin, Vol. 19, No. 45 (December 20, 1971), published by the Federal Press and Information Office. For a German text see Dokumentation Berlin: Die Vereinbarungen und das Abkommen (December, 1971), published by the West Berlin government.

32 Der Spiegel, December 6, 1971.

with *Kohl* on the following day as expected. By way of explanation he pointed to last-minute difficulties encountered in the discussions between representatives of the GDR régime and the West Berlin Senat. The West German said he would only attach his initials after a parallel agreement had been completed by *Günter Kohrt* and *Ulrich Müller*. After making this announcement, *Bahr* and *Kohl* sat down to play chess for five hours to pass the time waiting for "the other Germans" to finish their discussions. However, *Kohrt* and *Müller* did not settle their differences. And so the acts of initialing had to be postponed indefinitely.[33]

In taking the position that the process of initialing had to be "simultaneous," *Bahr* was acting not on his own initiative but on the firm instructions of his government. And here again the influence of the SPD's coalition partner evidently was decisive. *Brandt's* advisers were fully aware that the communist side was counting heavily on concluding the inner-German dialogue in time for the upcoming meeting of the North Atlantic Treaty Organization in Brussels on December 9. For NATO members had made it clear earlier that they would evaluate at this gathering their willingness to consider a European security conference based on developments in the Berlin talks. Consequently, FDP leaders — recognizing that the East German leadership was under pressure from the Russians, who were in a hurry to open talks on their pet project, — argued successfully for the postponement of the initialing ceremony. They hoped that by taking such a countermeasure on one level of the dialogue to be able to exert leverage on the other.[34]

As things turned out, the *Bahr-Kohl* accord, which had been prepared earlier for the initialing of both parties but could not be initialed because of the deadlock in conversations between *Kohrt* and *Müller*, was not to be left undisturbed by last-minute attempts to change it. Not satisfied that the text was as clear on the point of "serious offenses" as it could be, the FDP once again intervened. Taking advantage of the delay in the conclusion of the visiting negotiations, *Hermann Oxfort*, Chairman of the Free Democrats in Berlin, and his compatriot *Wolfgang Lüder* sought to bring political pressure to bear on *Willy Brandt*. They were suc-

33 The New York Times, December 5, 1971.
34 See Relay from Bonn, November 30, 1971.

208

cessful, and *Bahr* — by now thoroughly peeved — was ordered to resume his talks with *Kohl.*

These discussions took place in a late-night session on December 4. At first, the East German negotiator tried publicly to pass off this secret negotiating session as "a round of chess." But this effort to cover up the final bargaining proved a failure, and reporters eventually learned the truth. Whereas the language in the passage spelling out schwere Straftaten originally had appeared somewhat fuzzy to FDP members (allowing, for instance, GDR officials to brand as "serious offenders" deserters of the national people's army, who escaped to the West with their uniforms and weapons), it was for the second time made more precise. With the insertion of eight new words, several major loop-holes were closed.[35]

Difficulties over the Visiting Accord

In general, the dispute in the second level of deliberations centered on the troublesome issue of visits by West Berliners to the GDR and East Berlin. Specifically, the two sides were bogged down over the phrasing of a passage regulating East German issuance of one-day visas to West Berliners on demand.

Previously, the East German side had argued for stringent limitations on entry, maintaining that there was nothing in the quadripartite accord which gave inhabitants the right to visit the GDR and East Berlin by car 365 days a year. For the most part, the insistence of *Kohrt* on this matter reflected the concern of his government for "uncontrolled situations" that might arise with a large number of West Berliners suddenly flooding the East. In the beginning, the Western side had vigorously rejected this attempt to limit entry, referring to the provision in the Four-Power agreement which said that entry by West Berliners to East Berlin and the GDR was to be governed by procedures comparable to those applying to other persons entering these areas. But eventually the Senat came to recognize GDR security concerns as legitimate and agreed on a compromise thirty-day visiting period a year, with the days upon which visits were to take place being spread over any length of time within this total.

35 For details see Der Spiegel, December 20, 1971.

However, if the general question of the duration of visits had been resolved, this was not true of matters concerning the issuance of one-day visas to West Berliners to visit GDR areas on demand and the mode of transportation to be used. Although the SED leadership was willing to say in the text that entry permits could be (actual words: "can be") issued on request, it attached several telling stipulations. First, these visas were to be distributed by GDR authorities in West Berlin. Five special application offices would be opened for this purpose. Second, these offices would maintain normal "business hours," that is, they would close four p.m. daily and remain shut on weekends and holidays (thus precluding many spot visits in the afternoons and evenings, on Saturdays and Sundays and on other non-working days). Lastly, the issuance of these permits was to be made dependent on official confirmation by telegram from officials in East Germany. As far as the movement of visitors was concerned, they were obliged to make use of public means of transportation.[36]

For the most part, these conditions were unacceptable to Senat officials, who were only too well aware of the domestic political implications. Specifically, they rejected as "too vague" *Kohrt's* language that West Berliners could (but did not have to) be granted visas for immediate entry. But they also took issue with some of the obstacles he tried to put in the way of visitors. The most important of these was the provision, making the issuance of permits dependent on offices which were closed during the most desirable times for trips of short notice. The city administration demanded in this case that West Berlin residents, after giving a maximum of thirty-days' notice, be issued immediate entry visas for visits on any day or time of their choice. Although Senat authorities were ready to concede limited auto entry, they argued that at least families with many children or invalids should be allowed to enter East Berlin and East Germany by car. In summary, then, the Western side maintained that the imposition of such restrictions created a situation which could not be considered "comparable" but only "discriminatory."[37]

This was the situation when *Bahr* and *Kohl* tentatively finished their conversations on December 3. Several attempts were made

36 Archiv der Gegenwart, December 11, 1971.
37 See Relay from Bonn, December 8, 1971.

subsequently to break this impasse. But the determination of each side to "hang tough" in the talks, which were now receiving a great deal of attention in the international press, led to little progress. Finally, the exchanges were broken off on December 4, giving both parties time to re-evaluate their bargaining position.

During the break in the dialogue, which lasted two days, both sides traded recriminations and tried in other ways to force the other to make concessions. For its part, the East German government accused Mayor *Schütz* of relapsing into the "cold war" and raising illusionary demands. GDR commentaries stressed the sovereignty of the East Berlin régime and the right of its leadership to decide on its own arrangements. In defense of the Western position, West Berlin leaders and the mass media criticized the inadequacy of the communist offer.[38]

The East German side attempted to put propaganda pressure on the Senat by declaring unilaterally that the final texts of the two German accords had been "agreed upon and were ready for initialing." It also offered to open crossing points in the Wall for thirty days, including the Christmas holidays, to West Berliners — provided the Western side accepted the GDR version of the agreement. This proposal, if agreed to, would have permitted residents to visit relatives in East Berlin for the first time in five and one-half years. When the Senat was not forthcoming, however, the plan was cancelled.[39]

Following the resumption of negotiations on December 7, the two sides were able through compromise to breach their differences. Evidently, in a demonstration of its earnestness to conclude discussions in one final round of intense bargaining, the East German leadership appointed a new negotiator. (According to ADN, the official East Berlin news agency, *Günter Kohrt* had "fallen ill.") *Peter Florin,* a Deputy Foreign Minister, was formally charged by his government with rapidly completing the talks "to prepare the initialing of agreements with the West Berlin Senat." And he proceeded to do just that, reaching agreement with *Müller* on all outstanding issues at four in the morning of December 8.[40]

38 U.S. Mission (Berlin), Berlin 1971 — An Unofficial Chronology (49) (Berlin: USIS, January 1972), p. 4.

39 See Neues Deutschland, December 5 and 7, 1971.

40 The New York Times, December 9, 1971.

This tentative accord foresaw three major concessions on the part of the GDR. First, *Florin* rescinded the so-called "can be" condition on visits. Whereas his predecessor earlier had argued for language saying that visas could (but did not have to) be issued immediately on demand, the Deputy Foreign Minister now stipulated that they "would be" issued on demand. Second, he said West Berliners would not only be able to pick up entry permits for immediate entry to East Berlin and East Germany every weekday but also for several hours on Saturday and Sunday and holidays. Lastly, he relented somewhat on the bar to entry by automobile. Although all other individuals would have to use the elevated railway, subway, buses and taxis or come on foot, disabled persons, families with small children and residents travelling a considerable distance into the GDR would be allowed to make visits in private cars.[41]

But as attractive as this "compromise" was, it was almost not to be. For six hours later, when West Berlin spokesman *Günter Struve* appeared at the House of Ministers in East Berlin with Senat approval of the agreement in his pocket, a dispute took place with GDR officials that put the completion of the accord in danger a second time. Later, *Struve* maintained that he had sought only to fix a date for the initialing ceremony and add "several cosmetic corrections" to the text.[42] But the East German press denounced this maneuver the next day in an especially virulent propaganda barrage, claiming that he had attempted to sabotage the pact by introducing further unacceptable demands after all provisions had already been settled.[43]

After consulting with *Struve,* the Governing Mayor of West Berlin fired off a personal letter to the GDR premier. In his message to *Willi Stoph, Schütz* defended *Struve* and asserted that "no additional demands were raised by our side." Claiming that this representative had merely sought "clarification" on two points in the accord, the Regierender Bürgermeister suggested that "possible misunderstandings have arisen on your side as to the position of the Senat." Whatever the case, the Mayor declared the readiness of his delegation — despite misgivings — to sit down with the GDR

41 For details see Die Welt, December 9, 1971.
42 Der Spiegel, December 13, 1971.
43 Neues Deutschland, December 9, 1971.

212

negotiator and put the finishing touches on the tentative agreement reached on December 8.[44]

In his response, which was transmitted by TELEX to the Senat the same day (December 9), *Stoph* welcomed *Schütz's* offer to conclude the visiting pact. But he took the Mayor to task for trying to alter it at the last minute and then claiming the opposite. Towards the end of his letter, the East German Premier proposed that *Florin* and *Müller* meet the next day to wrap up details. *Stoph* expressed hope that the two would at this time accept the terms previously negotiated and would make no additional changes in the text.[45]

As the GDR Premier desired, the two sides met again on December 10 to complete the visiting agreement and prepare it and the other accord, dealing with the exchange of territory, for initialing. But no initials were attached that day because of the Western wish for initialing ceremonies in the two-tract negotiations to take place simultaneously. These gatherings, which were to take place in Schöneberg Townhall and the House of Ministers respectively, had to be delayed one day to permit *Egon Bahr* to return from Oslo, where he attended the presentation of the Nobel Peace Prize to *Willy Brandt*.[46] The official initialing process went off smoothly on December 11. And after government consultation with the Allies, the three accords (on access, visiting arrangements and the disenclavement of territory) were formally signed with a great deal of fanfare in separate meetings in Bonn and East Berlin on December 17 and 20.

Immediately after signing was completed, the West German government informed the Western Three that the agreements were ready for endorsement by the "Big Four". The Allies replied that they considered the inner-German arrangements in accordance with Four-Power instructions. As expected, however, the Russians — although they expressed their "satisfaction" over the conclusion of the three accords — chose to withhold formal approval until after West German ratification of the Bonn-Moscow Treaty.[47]

44 For the text of Schütz's letter see Archiv der Gegenwart, December 11, 1971.

45 For the text of Stoph's letter see Archiv der Gegenwart, December 11, 1971.

46 The New York Times, December 12, 1971.

47 See Relay from Bonn, December 21, 1971.

Unable to budge Soviet leaders in their steadfastness on this matter, Federal officials initiated the ratification process by submitting both the Warsaw and Moscow pacts to the Bundesrat, the upper house of parliament. Then they sat back to await the response of the opposition to these developments.

Conclusions

With the completion of the relatively short, but extremely tedious, inner-German negotiations, the two Germanies made — in *Bahr's* words — "their first joint contribution to the relaxation of tensions in Europe." Not only did they "fill in the blanks" left in the Quadripartite Agreement. But they also set the stage for the taking of further steps along the road towards normalizing their relations. These, it was now demonstrated, were to be organized on the basis of complete equality, non-discrimination and respect for mutual autonomy and independence.

It is possible to evaluate East German actions and declarations during the three-month inner-German dialogue in terms of three major policy objectives. First, the GDR sought to demonstrate and assert its role as an independent (or at least semi-autonomous) actor; second, the régime strove to limit the impact of the apparently unavoidable opening to the West inherent in the quadripartite accord; and three, it aimed to exploit the momentum created by that agreement to obtain further improvements in its own international standing. All of these goals were extremely important to the SED leadership, but because they were responsible at times for bringing it into conflict with the expressed wishes of the USSR they had to be advanced selectively and with no inconsiderable amount of skill.[48]

Seemingly, the intransigence displayed by *Kohl* and *Kohrt* on various occasions in the "technical discussions" was designed to promote the first of these objectives. Consequently, Soviet intervention could hardly have been gratifying to GDR officials. For developments between September and December 1971 appear to

---

48 For an excellent analysis of East German objectives during the inner-German negotiations see Karl E. Birnbaum, East and West Germany: A Modus Vivendi (Farnborough, England: Saxon House, 1973), pp. 61-62.

confirm the impression that Moscow's influence on East Germany's foreign policy had increased, and that East Berlin was compelled to trade an improvement in international status against a further limitation of its scope for independent action.

This point was aptly demonstrated by *Leonid Brezhnev's* unofficial visit to the GDR capital October 30-31. Prior to this date, the East German side had hardened its stand in the negotiations, leaving Western officials to speculate that no settlement was likely before the first part of 1972. However, shortly after the Soviet leader's departure, *Honecker* suddenly expressed an interest in concluding discussions before the end of November. This surprise turn-around on the part of the SED leadership, although enthusiastically greeted in the West, tended to jeopardize rather than advance the image of the German Democratic Republic as a self-assertive actor in the international arena.

In regard to the other two goals pursued by the GDR, East German authorities could take greater satisfaction in what was achieved by their negotiators. From the beginning, the communist side had expressed concern about the effects on "political stability" of allowing into the GDR a sudden and uncontrolled influx of West Berliners. But the Senat, intent on adhering to the letter of the Four-Power agreement, especially the provision requiring equal treatment of West Berlin visitors, was at first unmoved. Only later, when the talks threatened to break down, did the West Berlin government give ground on this crucial matter and agree to limitations on entry, particularly regarding the length of visits and the mode of transportation to be used by West Berliners.

Lastly, with respect to the international standing of the GDR, the SED leadership seems to have operated on the assumption that time was on its side. True, the East German demand for diplomatic recognition was not met. But the signing of three arrangements represented a breakthrough in this direction. As *Erich Honecker* stated in Neues Deutschland on December 18, 1971, these "agreements were the first international obligations incurred between the Federal Republic and the GDR, and they involved once more a recognition of the borders of the GDR."

From the point of view of Bonn, the two-track negotiations signified first and foremost increased safety for West Berlin. Of special importance here were the suggestions for improved access. Fitted into the broader spectrum of the Federal government's

215

Deutschlandpolitik, however, the talks were useful in opening up prospects for a substantive normalization at the very place where the abnormal situation created by the division of Germany was most evident. At the same time, the dialogue — slotted into the framework of Bonn's relations with Moscow — was handy for utilizing the Soviet interest in the formalization of the status quo to elicit consent of the USSR to some improvements in inner-German relations.

This latter point was demonstrated most vividly by *Brandt's* controversial trip to the Crimea in mid-September. One of the tasks he set for himself in his meeting with *Brezhnev* was the speeding up of the Berlin dialogue. The communiqué from the encounter in Oreanda and its timing suggest that the inter-dependence of preparations for the European security conference and the pace of the inner-German discussions was recognized by both sides even if the CPSU Chairman in his personal remarks to the Chancellor said he would not press the GDR to make concessions.

On his return from the Soviet Union, the West German leader explained that the Federal Republic was now playing "an equal role" in East-West negotiations. It was "forming its own opinion on the most important Western issues and then making its own contributions in talks with GDR and East European leaders. To be sure, *Brandt* made these declarations primarily for home consumption. But the fact that he accepted *Brezhnev's* invitation without consulting Bonn's American, British and French Allies was further evidence of his intention not to rely so heavily on others, to make his own assessments of prospects for easier, safer relationships with Moscow and its Allies and to take his own initiatives — on occasion his own risks — to bring these about.

During the fall of 1971 the Kremlin seemed primarily interested in its bilateral arrangement with the FRG. In this regard, the main incentive for the USSR to intervene in the all-German conversations was its desire to speed up ratification of the Bonn-Moscow Treaty. Indeed, the limitations of West Germany's leverage on Soviet leaders regarding multilateral preparations for the convening of a European security conference were made clear during *Walter Scheel's* visit to Moscow in late November. At that time, the West German Foreign Minister dangled prospects of quick NATO approval of the Kremlin's pet project before the eyes of both *Brezhnev* and *Kosygin* but was unable to persuade them to agree to the signing of a final Berlin package as soon as the inner-German talks had cleared the way. The Russians, who had instituted in October 1971 a sort of "reverse linkage" to the attempt by Bonn to tie ratification of its treaty with the Soviet Union to a satisfactory Berlin settlement, refused to commit themselves to signature of a final protocol until after the West German parliament had endorsed the pact. And there the situation stood, at least for the moment.

Chapter VIII

THE RATIFICATION DEBATE

The first half of 1972 in West Germany was dominated by the ratification debate. During this period arguments for European détente were weighed against the demand that binding commitments not be preceded by genuine freedom of movement and opinion across the "iron curtain."[1] As we have seen, a great deal depended on parliamentary approval of the treaties with Moscow and Warsaw. On the one hand, the success of *Willy Brandt's* policy of improving relations with communist Europe hinged on the event. On the other, a major part of the policy of his Western Allies to ease tensions hung in the balance, since neither the Quadripartite Agreement nor the supplementary inner-German arrangements (nor for that matter the final conclusion of a SALT I accord, expected to occur when *Nixon* visited Moscow at the end of May) could be counted on coming into effect unless the two pacts were formally endorsed by Bonn's parliament. And ratification was extremely uncertain what with the government's slim majority in the Bundestag in the process of being eroded virtually to nothing by defections to the opposition, and the CDU/CSU hoping — in what was deemed a plausible gambit — to defeat the Chancellor's coalition by way of defeating his Ostpolitik.

Confrontation in the Bundesrat

With the submission of the Eastern treaties to the West German parliament in mid-December 1971, the Federal government started the complex ratification process and drew international attention there and on the rules of the parliamentary game. As expected, the

1 See the speech by Rainer Barzel, CDU opposition leader, to this effect, as reported in Frankfurter Allgemeine Zeitung, January 5, 1972.

ruling coalition immediately clashed head on with the opposition. Since the CDU/CSU fraction had declared it would leave not a single point in the two treaties unchallenged, it came as little surprise that its first point of dispute focused on matters of procedure.

The first confrontation over the treaties took place in the Bundesrat or upper house of parliament which represents West Germany's eleven Federal states. There the conservatives enjoyed a majority of 21 to 20. In submitting the treaty legislation to the Bundesrat, government officials announced a time schedule for the three required "readings," proposing that the first one be completed within the customary six-week period. But the conservatives in the upper house, under the forceful leadership of *Gerhard Stoltenberg,* Governor of Schleswig-Holstein, rejected this six-week request, saying that extra time should be allowed because of the upcoming Christmas holidays. CDU leaders also sought to delay official acknowledgment of the arrival of the legislation by declining to put the Bundesrat's official purple-ink stamp on the paper. They charged that the drafts had not been properly stamped by the Federal Chancellery.[2] In the end, the conservatives had their way; a new time-table was announced, calling for the first reading to take place in late February and the second and third in early May, 1972.

In January, when the treaties came up before the legal committee of the upper house, they were put to the test of constitutionality. Of the eleven West German Länder, represented on this committee, five were governed by the CDU or CSU at this time. Their delegations, after meeting to work out a common strategy to defeat the pacts, presented a list of formal charges condemning them. Among other things, conservative representatives charged that the treaties violated the mandate for reunification as expressed in the preamble to the Basic Law (Grundgesetz).[3] But the conservative effort was defeated, as the legal committee decided by a vote of seven to four that the accords were constitutional and eight to three that they were not subject to the absolute veto the Bundesrat enjoys on certain types of legislation.

2 See The New York Times, December 14, 1971.

3 For the text of the government statement listing charges by the opposition to the German-Soviet and German-Polish Treaties and answers given by the government, see Relay from Bonn, January 17, 1972.

Early in February, the Eastern treaties came up for a "first reading" vote before the plenary session of the upper house. At that time, the Bundesrat voted twenty-one to twenty to accept a resolution sponsored by the CDU/CSU listing twelve "reservations" against the pacts. For the most part, these conditions represented a reiteration of previous opposition arguments. Most importantly, they included charges that the Moscow pact might serve as an instrument of Soviet interference in the domestic affairs of the FRG, that it might jeopardize German reunification and self-determination, that European integration might be handicapped and that the USSR did not formally renounce any rights to intervene in West Germany under Articles 53 and 107 of the U.N. Charter. The Berlin accords were termed "unsatisfactory."[4]

Under the rules of the German parliamentary system, the adoption of the CDU/CSU sponsored reservations was not conclusive. Rather this vote merely represented at this preliminary stage in the ratification struggle the "official opinion" of the upper house. As such, it was not binding but had to be transmitted to the Bundestag, or lower house, for its consideration. Nevertheless, if not decisive, this "first reading" vote now made it necessary for the government to obtain an absolute majority in the Bundestag to win ratification. The Chancellor had lost the first major battle in the debate.

Defections

While the two treaties were studied and debated in committee in the lower house during March in preparation for the inevitable test of strength in plenary session, the West German capital was swept with rumors that *Brandt* no longer had the votes in parliament necessary for ratification. Up to this time, the Chancellor had been counting on mustering an absolute majority of 249 votes in the 496-member Bundestag (exclusive of the twenty-two West Berlin delegates who may not vote on substantive matters); his coalition officially numbered 251, and *Brandt* claimed that 250 of them could be counted on to support the treaties. (Since all 245 members of the opposition were expected to cast negative votes,

4 For details see The Washington Post, February 10, 1972.

the Chancellor was compelled to rely on the solidarity of the government benches — a coalition of his own Social Democrats and the tiny Free Democratic Party.) But in early March this claim started to come unstuck.

First one Social Democratic deputy, *Herbert Hupka,* announced he was quitting the party and going over to the Christian Democrats. *Hupka* was Chairman of the Silesian Regional Association and a Vice President of the Union of Expellees. His defection cut the government's slender majority in the lower house from six to four. However, damage was minimal. Since *Hupka* was a well-known opponent of the treaties, *Brandt's* coalition had long ago written off his vote.[5]

Much more ominous were revelations that FDP deputy *Knut von Kühlmann-Stumm* was having misgivings about the pacts. The views of this deputy were cause for concern because the loss of his vote would remove the government's last margin of safety in terms of its ability to muster an absolute majority. One more defection from government ranks — or even the failure of a deputy to be present at the crucial vote — would put the coalition below the requisite figure and prevent ratification. (A tie meant failure.) Moreover, the attitude of *Kühlmann-Stumm,* an influential individual among Free Democrat conservatives, touched of fears that other back benchers with reservations about the treaties might now be emboldened to follow his lead. For their part, the Christian Democrats did what they could to influence these waverers by reportedly engaging them in secret conversations about the rewards of switching.[6]

Rumblings and Gestures from Moscow

The sudden and unexpected deterioration of *Brandt's* position in the Bundestag caught the Soviet Union by surprise. Though Moscow never appeared to take ratification of the treaties for granted, up to recently it had shown no signs of seriously fearing their rejection. Whatever the case, communist spokesmen began in March to utter threatening noises about Soviet wrath should passage fail.

5 See The Washington Post, March 8, 1972.
6 For details consult Der Spiegel, March 5, 1972.

To convey its concern, the Soviet leadership in the beginning relied primarily on the communist press. An authoritative article in Pravda of March 8 signed "Observer" stated the case most clearly. According to this source, either the treaties would be approved and further progress toward détente would be made, or they would be defeated and West Germany would return "to the policy of the 'cold war.'" The article ruled out any middle ground. And it described the argument advanced by the opposition that good relations could be achieved with Moscow without the treaty as either "a conscious deception of the Bundestag ... or an actual display of losing touch with reality." Irregardless, any return to past West German policies "would damage the Federal Republic of Germany seriously," Pravda concluded.

If the article in Pravda and other articles appearing in the Soviet press tended (as many experienced diplomats in the West believed) to understate the strength of Moscow's real feelings, a middle-ranking Soviet official speaking in West Berlin was more frank. When he was asked by reporters what would happen if *Brandt* lost his fight for ratification and an anti-treaty opposition took power in Bonn, he responded: "Then everything would be destroyed, everything we have accomplished so far. Then a new cold war would break out, and a hot war might be possible."[7]

To strengthen *Brandt's* hand in the ratification debate, the Russians followed up their propaganda barrage by allowing him to announce some significant new Soviet concessions. Appearing before the Bundestag's Foreign Affairs Committee, the Chancellor revealed in late March a Soviet offer to pay at least lip service to the notion of eventual reunification. The leaders in the Kremlin, he stated, had promised to ask their legislature (in effect a rubber stamp of Soviet policy) to take note of a letter from the Bonn government declaring that the treaties in no way affect the possibility of eventual German reunification. In addition, *Brandt* disclosed, the Soviet leadership was now ready to sign a new trade agreement with West Germany which, for the first time, would recognize the right of the FRG to represent West Berlin in trade matters.[8]

The most dramatic attempt by the Soviet Union and its Allies to

7 Quoted in The Washington Post, March 10, 1972.
8 See Newsweek, March 27, 1972.

influence the mood in the Federal Republic occurred at the end of the month. On March 29, GDR authorities temporarily put into effect parts of the Berlin deal which were only supposed to enter into force after the conclusion of a final protocol. Consequently, they simplified the transit procedures for trips between West Berlin and West Germany and opened East Berlin and East Germany to West Berlin visitors. More than 450,000 West Berliners crossed the Wall during the holiday week and some 620,000 persons took advantage of liberalized access procedures.[9] Thus, the SED leadership conceded in one fell swoop what it had so tenaciously sought to avoid in previous negotiations with the West; namely, it accepted a mass assault of visitors instead of introducing the Besuchersystem gradually, with care, in small doses.

The general verdict on this "gesture of good will" was mixed. On the one hand, proponents of a relaxation of tensions acclaimed it a workable experiment which promised a great change in the siege-like conditions under which West Berlin had so long existed. To sceptics, however, the "trial run" of the improvements brought about by the Berlin accords was seen merely for what it was: a propaganda exercise to rally West German public opinion behind the treaties. Apparently, it had the desired effect, for public reaction was so favorable that the visiting arrangement was repeated seven weeks later over Pentecost.[10]

State Elections and Another Defection

During April, with the ground around *Brandt's* feet crumpling, the ruling coalition pushed relentlessly toward final ratification of the Moscow and Warsaw Treaties. For their part, the Christian Democrats continued to demand renegotiation and a "German preamble" as their price for going along. *Strauss* even came up with an opposition draft of the Moscow Treaty, stressing a formal renunciation by the Kremlin of any rights of intervention under the U.N. Charter. But the most the Chancellor would agree to was

9 U.S. Mission (Berlin), Berlin 1972 — An Unofficial Chronology (51) (Berlin: USIS, June 1972), p. 2.

10 For a summary of German press reaction to East German measures, see German Press Review, March 29, 1972.

an all-party resolution of the lower house to accompany ratification.[11]

If the situation were not so critical in the Bundestag, *Brandt* should have taken heart from the results of two public opinion polls, published in the early and late spring of 1972. The first survey was conducted by the Institute for Applied Social Sciences (Infas) before the debate in the Bundestag got underway. It showed that more than half the people in the FRG (56 percent) were of the opinion that the Chancellor's Ostpolitik was in the best interests of their country. Whereas 60 percent said Berlin would benefit, only 17 percent thought the divided city would suffer; 23 percent gave no opinion.[12] The second representative national sample, which was taken by the distinguished Institut für Demoskopie in the middle of the parliamentary debate, revealed great popular support for the treaties. It demonstrated that 52 percent were for speedy enactment of the pacts, while only 26 percent opposed them; 22 percent had no opinion.[13] All in all, these results should have caused the opposition to ponder the wiseness of pursuing its present collision course with the government. But they apparently had little effect on the CDU/CSU, which had already committed considerable prestige to holding the line.

Matters in the Bundestag were brought to a head on April 23 with the holding of state elections in Baden-Württemberg. With a decisive ratification vote expected for early May, a positive outcome here was critically important to the Social Democrats for two reasons. First, as *Hans Filbinger,* Ministerpräsident of Baden-Württemberg, suggested, the outcome there might be considered a sort of rump plebiscite on *Brandt's* Ostpolitik. Approximately, one-seventh of the national electorate resided in the Land; and both sides had campaigned vigorously there. Second, a SPD victory in Baden-Württemberg would have resulted in radical

11 For an analysis of Ostpolitik as a divisive factor among the Christian Democrats, see Geoffrey Pridham, "The Ostpolitik and the Opposition in West Germany," in Roger Tilford (ed.), The Ostpolitik and Political Change in Germany (England: Saxon House, 1975), pp. 45-58.

12 For a more detailed analysis of the findings of the survey data, see Lübekker Nachrichten, January 22, 1972.

13 Quoted in Peter H. Merkl, German Foreign Policies, East and West (Santa Barbara, California: ABC — Clio Press, 1974), p. 171.

alteration in the composition of the Bundesrat in favor of the Chancellor's forces. As things turned out, however, although the SPD did its best in the state since the war (winning 27,5 percent of the vote), the CDU won by a convincing margin (with 53 percent of the total vote). Consequently, the conservatives retained control of the Bundesrat, and the *Brandt* government was dealt another crushing blow.[14]

Hardly were election results in, when the ruling coalition in Bonn was ravaged by still another critical defection. This time a member of the FDP abandoned the Free Democrats to become an independent deputy. The defector was *Wilhelm Helms,* an obscure middle-aged deputy from Lower Saxony, who had gone into debt on his family farm. Reportedly turned down by the FDP agricultural minister in his quest for financial assistance, *Helms* turned on election night to the opposition for backing.[15] His defection reduced the coalition's majority in the Bundestag to one vote. (If *Helms* had gone all the way and joined the opposition, the Christian Democrats would have achieved their goal of breaking the Chancellor's majority.)

A Move to Unseat Brandt

The decision by *Helms* to "jump ship" at this crucial point in time almost proved fatal to the government. For it gave CSU leader *Franz Josef Strauss* and other ambitious pols in the Christian Democratic Party the opening they needed to press *Rainer Barzel* into a showdown with *Brandt.* Their plan called for dumping the Chancellor in a so-called "constructive vote of no-confidence."[16]

14 For a breakdown and analysis of the vote, see Frankfurter Allgemeine Zeitung, April 24 and 25, 1972.

15 See David Binder, The Other German: Willy Brandt's Life and Times (Washington, D.C.: The New Republic Book Co., 1975), p. 291.

16 Under the West German Constitution, a Chancellor cannot simply be voted out of office by a parliamentary (i.e., Bundestag) majority, as is the case in Great Britain. Rather, the opposition can remove him only through the election of a successor by a majority in a secret ballot and then requesting the Bundespräsident to dismiss the incumbent. (In these circumstances, the President must comply with the request.) This provision, which represents considerable improvement upon the British parliamentary system, was inserted in Article 67 of the Grundgesetz because of the experience of

225

The plan to overthrow *Brandt* represented a monumental gamble on the part of *Barzel.* Not only had the process never been tried before, but lurking in the ranks were the CDU floor leader's own enemies. He had considered the possibility of attempting a no-confidence vote a month earlier (in mid-March), but he subsequently changed his mind and decided to wait out the Chancellor. Now he was equally nervous about seizing power, but this time he apparently was unable to resist immense political pressures brought to bear on him within his own party and from outside. As one of *Barzel's* aides later described it, the floor leader's rivals were "shoving (him) against a rusty knife."[17]

The showdown was set to take place on April 27, shortly before the final decision on the two treaties was rendered. Proclaiming that the Stunde der Abrechnung (hour of reckoning) was near, the CDU Chancellor candidate confidently announced the composition of his prospective cabinet and began work on his "government declaration" — the first address he would give as Kanzler. His party colleagues made equally optimistic plans.

Brandt was widely reported at the time as being very unsure of his chances in the upcoming showdown with *Barzel.*[18] Two years later, *Willy Brandt* made public his own recollection of events. "At the time," he said, "I awaited the vote count not at all with sureness of success but in greater calm than many suspected."[19]

Although *Brandt* survived a critical test of strength, he was not in the clear yet. For their part, *Barzel* and his colleagues showed no signs of giving up the fight over ratification, and they had their revenge the next day: a vote over the budget for the Chancellor's Office, resulted in a 247-247 tie. And as subsequent votes showed, neither side could now muster a majority.

For *Brandt,* the implications were ominous. He could no longer count on pushing through in early May his non-aggression treaties. Beyond that, the crisis called into question his ability to govern

the Weimar period. During that time, it was always easier to establish a negative majority rather than a constructive one, thus causing great political instability. — For more detailed analysis see Guido Goldman, The German Political System (New York: Random House, 1974), p. 80.

17 The New York Times, April 26, 1972.

18 Newsweek, May 8, 1972.

19 Willy Brandt, Über den Tag Hinaus — Eine Zwischenbilanz (Hamburg: Hoffmann & Campe, 1974), p. 46.

properly and led him to think seriously of ordering new general elections. Earlier, the Chancellor's strategists had contemplated turning the vote on the treaties into a confidence vote. At that time it was thought that were the coalition to be defeated, requiring new elections, then *Brandt* would be sure to win. But the SPD leader vetoed this proposal, partly out of deference to the FDP, which was afraid of premature elections, and partly because he did not share the optimism of some of his colleagues in the party.[20]

He preferred first trying to break out of the standoff in the Bundestag by reaching an understanding with the opposition leadership over ratification. Since there was no majority for any side, the Chancellor argued in a four-hour meeting with *Barzel* and *Strauss* on April 28 the Bundestag might as well proceed with the task at hand. In the end a compromise was reached. For its part, the ruling coalition agreed to delay the ratification procedure a few days and supplement the treaties with a bipartisan declaration on German unity, which would be "acknowledged" by the USSR. In exchange, *Barzel* promised to free a sufficient number of his CDU deputies from party discipline to assure safe passage of the accords. With the conclusion of this agreement a cloud seemed to lift from above *Brandt.*

What followed proved anticlimatic, but absorbing drama. Joint commissions proceeded to draft a foreign policy declaration on European integration, intra-German freedom of movement and the right of self-determination and German re-unification. But then the opposition refused to adopt it formally until the Soviet Union first acknowledged its binding nature. The SPD/FDP leadership saw in such a move an attempt to amend the Bonn-Moscow Treaty and was infuriated. Eventually, however, the Soviet Ambassador, *Valentin Falin,* was called in, and in his presence the two sides hammered out an agreement. The result was a "joint resolution," which was subsequently passed on to Soviet leaders in Moscow for their acceptance.[21]

About this time, the Russians and their Allies tried to influence the proceedings and public opinion by several demonstrations of "good will." First, the Kremlin announced that a group of ethnic Germans would be permitted to emigrate to the Federal Republic.

20 Willy Brandt, op. cit. p. 39.

21 For the text of this resolution see The Bulletin, May 23, 1972.

227

Second, East Germany's *Michael Kohl,* after balking earlier, proceeded to initial with *Egon Bahr* a general transportation treaty, which included some notable improvements for visits to the GDR and broadened the opportunities for East German citizens to visit the FRG. In the end, all these efforts paid off.

On May 17, 1972, the Bundestag approved the Moscow Treaty. There were 248 ayes, 10 nays and 238 abstentions. The Warsaw Pact was accepted that same day. This time there were 248 votes in the affirmative, 17 negative votes and 231 abstentions. The government showed its party cohesion in this final vote. Not so the CDU/CSU: the only basis of intra-party unity displayed was on the Joint Resolution, which passed with 491 votes and 5 abstentions. When the two treaties came up for their final reading in the Bundesrat, they were approved 20 to zero, with 21 opposition delegates abstaining.[22] This massive abstention allowed the CDU/CSU to "save face" by not having to vote in favor of the pacts. At the same time, it spared the ruling coalition the embarrassment of having to try to override a negative Bundesrat veto with an absolute majority of 249 in the Bundestag. With the ratification issue now settled, the way was clear for the signing of the Final Berlin Protocol.

Conclusions

As a result of parliamentary ratification of the Moscow and Warsaw accords, the "die had finally been cast in the direction of revolutionizing the status quo in Europe."[23] The threat that the intricate Berlin settlement, which only had been reached after considerable pain and anguish, might come unglued suddenly disappeared. And the heavy shadow thrown over the prospects of convening a European security conference, opening formal discussions of reductions in armed forces and concluding a SALT I agreement was at last dispelled. *Brandt's* efforts, within a thicket of Junktims making one series of accords dependent on the ratification of another, to reach conciliation in Central Europe had managed to bridge the gulf between the East and West.

22 See U.S. Mission (Berlin), Berlin 1972 — An Unofficial Chronology (51) (Berlin: USIS, June 1972), p. 2.

23 Peter H. Merkl, op. cit., p. 165.

It had been apparent from the beginning that the vote on the treaties would be close. The Social Democratic Chancellor had been ruling with only a six-vote majority in the Bundestag. Over the years, the German tradition of strict party discipline had enabled governments to achieve stability and assurance with even narrower margins. But in the crucible of parliamentary debate over a major foreign policy departure the SPD/FDP coalition's slim edge slipped away through a series of unprecedented defections. Caught by surprise, *Brandt* was almost unseated in his country's first "constructive vote of no-confidence."

Brandt's plight in the Bundestag put the United States, Britain, France and the Soviet Union in a difficult position. The Four Powers, who wanted a final Berlin protocol signed so they could move farther down the road towards a reduction of tensions in Central Europe, had a vested interest in the outcome of the ratification debate. But they were forced to exercise great caution and discretion in helping the Chancellor secure passage of the treaties for fear that any outside interference would backfire. This was particularly true of the United States.

If Washington officially remained neutral during the Bundestag crisis, Moscow played an active role in public as well as behind the scenes. The Soviet leadership even went so far as to permit its representative in Bonn to sit down with German parliamentarians in *Brandt's* villa on Venusberg to "referee" the drafting of a "Joint Declaration" on the Bonn-Moscow Treaty. This strategy paid off, for Soviet acceptance of this key foreign-policy guideline was critical in mollifying the opposition just before the decisive vote was taken.

As things turned out, the treaties were saved only by an unexpected change of heart by the opposition. After years of adamant obstruction, the CDU/CSU finally came around to the realization that it too could not afford to allow the treaties to fail. This surprise reversal of opinion was largely due to the "face-saving" efforts of *Rainer Barzel,* the CDU floor leader. He foresaw that rejection of the treaties could well isolate the opposition not only from Germany's friends and allies alike but also from the majority of domestic opinion. In fact, if national elections were held at this time, he feared the undoing of the Christian Democrats.

Barzel attempted to bring his party around to voting in favor of the treaties after working out an agreed formula with the government for a declaration on the aims of West German foreign policy. He did not succeed because he switched positions too suddenly and failed to "educate" his party to take a more positive stand. At the last moment, *Barzel* was forced by pressures from within the joint Fraktion to back down in public in favor of an abstention vote. (As later events were to show, this turnaround, coming as it did after *Barzel's* failure to replace *Brandt* in the "constructive vote of no-confidence," had harmful consequences for his leadership; he never succeeded in getting off the hook on Ostpolitik, and in May 1973 chose to resign his position rather than oppose the entry of the two Germanies in the United Nations.)

Barzel's dilemma during the ratification crisis was above all due to the obstinacy of *Franz-Josef Strauss,* the leader of the CSU sister party. He set in motion the pressures operating against *Barzel's* wish to create bipartisanship on the treaties. The decision by the opposition to abstain facilitated passage of the controversial pacts. But it also intensified ill feelings between the two sister parties and between fundamentalist and moderate elements within the Christian Democratic Party. This conflict erupted in a more violent way during the fall of 1972, when *Strauss* threatened to withdraw his party from the combined Fraktion of the CDU and CSU.

Two days after the ratification test, the erosion of the government's slender majority in the Bundestag led *Barzel* to demand *Brandt's* immediate resignation. The Chancellor, realizing that the deadlock in parliament represented the de facto loss of his electoral mandate, requested assurances of cooperation from the opposition. Since the West German constitution provides for the dissolution of the Bundestag following the resignation of the Chancellor, *Brandt* did not want the Christian Democrats to exercise their right to try to form a government in the meantime if they could muster a majority.

After consulting the Free Democrats and discussing strategy with them, *Brandt* announced in June that his government coalition would seek new national elections in November. His plan was unprecedented. Basically, it called for his own party to initiate in the Bundestag a motion of no-confidence against him.[24] The idea

24 One of the peculiarities of West German constitutional law provides this alternative to starting the election process when the Bundestag, normally elected for four years, has not completed its full term. — According to

was that the Chancellor's own Cabinet would topple him by with-holding its votes, and then *Brandt* would ask the Bundespräsident — a member of his own party — to dissolve the chamber.

Brandt thought his coalition would have the best chance of winning elections in November 1972; by that time the Berlin settlement would have been implemented, bringing significant new improvements in the lives of West Berliners and West Germans alike, the Ostpolitik harvest would have begun, resulting in the Westward movement of thousands of ethnic Germans, and considerable progress would have been made on a "Basic Treaty"between the GDR and the FRG, opening further the door between East and West. This meant a parliamentary decision in September, since the Grundgesetz prescribed elections sixty days after dissolution of the Bundestag.

The Chancellor was under the impression that the opposition would not take advantage of its right to move to unseat him during the vote-of-no-confidence process. But just at the time when *Herbert Wehner,* the SPD Floor Leader, agreed to seek and lose a confidence vote, thereby initiating new elections, the Christian Democrats launched a last-minute maneuver to undercut *Brandt's* strategy. Their idea was to try once again for a constructive vote of no-confidence, which would have lifted *Barzel* immediately into the Chancellorship, by "buying" a deputy from the Social Democrats. This attempt was thwarted only because the man selected for defection turned down the lucrative offer and reported back to *Wehner* on September 21.[25] The next day *Brandt* succeeded in carrying off the no-confidence vote.

When the voters had their say on November 19, 1972, the result was a ringing endorsement of *Brandt's* Ost- and Deutschlandpolitik. A record 91 percent of the forty million electorate turned out at the polls. They gave the SPD an edge over the CDU/CSU for the first time since the creation of the Federal Republic. The SPD won

Article 68, the Chancellor is compelled to place his motion forty-eight hours before a vote is taken. In case of dissolution, new elections must be held within sixty days. However, the right to dissolve lapses as soon as the Bundestag elects another candidate for Chancellor by a majority vote. Thus, it was very risky for Brandt to take this step except with prior agreement of the opposition, since he could have found himself suddenly displaced rather than able to compel new elections.

25 The New York Times, September 26, 1972.

45.8 percent (42.7 percent in 1969), the CDU/CSU 44.9 percent (46.1 percent in 1969), and the FDP made an unexpected comeback to 8.4 percent (5.4 percent in 1969). In terms of strength in the Bundestag, the election gave the coalition 271 seats — a safe majority of 23. *Brandt* had weathered the storm, and his government now had the mandate needed to move rapidly ahead.[26]

---

26 For an analysis of the 1972 Federal elections on the basis of opinion polls and statistical research see Werner Kaltefleiter et al, Zwischen Consensus und Krise — Eine Analyse der Bundestagswahl (Cologne, 1973). For a summary view see R.E.M. Irving et al., "The West German Parliamentary Election of November 1972," Parliamentary Affairs (Spring, 1973), pp. 218-239.

A horse has four legs and yet it stumbles.

Pushkin

Chapter IX
THE BERLIN SETTLEMENT

With the ratification of the Moscow and Warsaw Treaties on May 17, 1972, the way was at last clear for the signing of the Final Protocol on Berlin. This step was taken one month later, when the Foreign Ministers of the United States, the Soviet Union, the United Kingdom and France gathered in the Western half of the city on June 3. Together they put into force the final East-West package. Simultaneously, the Federal government and Soviet and Polish representatives exchanged in Bonn ratification documents of their treaties. For all appearances, the Berlin problem was treated as resolved, ending the city's twenty-seven-year history as a center of "cold war" confrontation.

The Compromises

In general, the Berlin settlement can be analyzed in respect to its general structure and ten major problem areas:
(a) the status of Berlin;
(b) recognition of the GDR;
(c) relations between West Berlin and the Federal Republic;
(d) FRG representation of West Berlin abroad;
(e) visits by West Berliners to East Berlin and East Germany;
(f) access to Berlin;
(g) the question of exclaves;
(h) improvements in external communication;
(i) increased Soviet presence in West Berlin; and
(j) the consultation mechanism.
All of these substantive provisions will now be examined in detail in the attempt to make clear the kinds of compromises that were reached by the Four Powers.

233

General Structure

The Berlin settlement consists of three key elements. The first — and most important — part of the package is the Quadripartite Agreement of September 3, 1971. It sets forth the principles and guidelines agreed upon by the "Big Four" to bring about improvements in the situation in and around Berlin. The second element is composed of three understandings, reached by German authorities to supplement and implement the umbrella agreement. Lastly, there is the Final Protocol, which was signed on June 3, 1972. It put the whole complex of accords into effect.

For the most part, the Quadripartite Agreement is an elaborate and highly technical piece of writing. The style is laborious and convoluted. In many places, the text is not even grammatically correct — or more importantly, clear in meaning. This is because the "spirit of compromise" developed by the negotiators called in many cases for the "pasting together" of critical words and phrases favored by all the parties and their governments. As one U.S. official, familiar with the track-record of the negotiations, points out: "Every word counts."

The agreement, of course, is significant for what it says as well as for what it does not say. The words spoken by Staatssekretär *Bahr* at the conclusion of his talks with *Dr. Kohl* are apropos: "Beim Ausklammern waren wir Meister." (We were experts at excluding.)

One of the popular misconceptions about the Quadripartite Agreement is that it is responsible for resolving most of the important problems surrounding the Berlin issue. Throughout, the Ambassadors were concerned primarily with working out mutually acceptable practical improvements for the Berlin population. Indeed, the Four Powers — afraid of becoming bogged down in unnecessary detail and thus losing sight of agreement altogether — were very wary about tackling problems that had defied all efforts at resolution for the past twenty years or so.

Even in dealing with that narrow range of questions impinging directly on so-called "practical improvements," the negotiators did not resolve satisfactorily all disputed points. True, much elaborate planning had gone into the preparations of both sides. But the four Ambassadors, constantly fearful that their efforts would either be upstaged or undermined by the swiftness with which international events unfolded, worked under the terrible pressure of time — particularly towards the end, when the breakthrough came. Consequently, they struck bargains and skipped across especially thorny matters in the attempt to bring negotiations to a speedy conclusion.

Formally, the Quadripartite Agreement consists of a preamble and three parts. But also attached to the text are four annexes, two agreed minutes, a letter to the Federal Chancellor and an exchange of notes — all of which give further detailed and binding instructions for interpretation. From a Western Allied legal viewpoint, no part of the accord is more important than any other; all are of equal validity.* Not formally part of the Four-Power accord — but of great importance in understanding the agreement — are the classified diplomatic reporting cables of the Allies, which represent the negotiating history of the basic document, and the two "gentleman's agreements" which supplement the text.

The decision of the "Big Four" to construct the Berlin settlement in this seemingly complicated way was not made haphazardly. Rather, it was the product of very meticulous planning and was consistent with the pragmatic philosophy which prevailed through much of the discussions. Basically, the parties were concerned first and foremost with obtaining agreement on general principles before moving on to tackle the drafting of detailed provisions. Thus, the basic document (parts one through three) is very short — representing approximately one-sixth of the total text and containing only general principles. The complex details are to be found in the accompanying documentation.

The preamble reaffirms the rights and responsibilities of the "Big Four" under the war-time and post-war agreements and decisions. It specifies that existing legal positions are not to be affected by the accord.

Part I contains some general provisions concerning future policies and confirms the legal position defined in the preamble. In this

---

* This viewpoint is questioned by some internationel legal scholars who distinguish between "constituent parts" of the Quadripartite Agreement and so-called "accompanying instruments." For a detailed discussion see Ernst R. Zivier, Der Rechtsstatus des Landes Berlin: Eine Untersuchung nach dem Viermächte-Abkommen vom 3. September 1971, 3. erw. Aufl. (Berlin: Berlin Verlag, 1977) pp. 173-194.

section, the four governments commit themselves to "strive to promote the elimination of tension and the prevention of complications" in the area in question. Here the U.N. Charter is cited as a guideline in that the signatories "agree that there shall be no use or threat of force in the area and that disputes shall be settled solely by peaceful means." It has been pointed out that the enunciation of these principles might be interpreted as legally ruling out any future Berlin crisis through a blockade or major intervention in transit traffic.[1] And this view would seem to be substantiated by a declaration in the same part, saying that "the situation which has developed in the area . . . shall not be changed unilaterally."

Part II represents the cornerstone of the quadripartite accord. For it includes the basic quid pro quo worked out by the Four Powers. It outlines a set of rough principles leading to significant practical improvements in the situation in and around Berlin in exchange for a reduced demonstrative Federal presence and increased Soviet presence in West Berlin. It should be noted, however, that the parties merely "declare" that these agreed principles (which will be discussed in detail subsequently) will be carried out. No legal obligation is undertaken that they have to be carried out. Moreover, they have to be read in conjunction with the four annexes appended to the agreement and the miscellaneous accompanying documents. Lastly, the Final Protocol has to be taken into account together with the three understandings concluded by German authorities.

Part III of the Quadripartite Agreement provides for the entering into force of the accord. This section of the agreement was implemented on June 3, 1972 through the signing of a final protocol.

Annex I takes the form of a communication from the government of the USSR to the governments of France, the United Kingdom and the United States. In it, guidelines are established for facilitating civilian transit traffic by road, rail and waterways through the territory of the GDR. — This annex confers upon the competent German authorities the power to negotiate the necessary arrangements implementing and supplementing the umbrella agreement. A letter by the three Ambassadors to the Federal Republic requests that the proposed negotiations take place between

1 See for instance Günther Doeker et al, "Berlin and the Quadripartite Agreement of 1971," American Journal of International Law, Vol. 67 (January, 1973), p. 56.

the authorities of the FRG, also acting on behalf of the West Berlin Senat, and the authorities of the GDR. These negotiations took place subsequently, and the accord between the two German states on Transit Traffic of Civilian Persons and Goods between the FRG and Berlin (West) was signed on December 17, 1971.

Annex II consists of a communication from the governments of France, the United Kingdom and the United States to the government of the Soviet Union. It spells out the new relationship between the Western Sectors of Berlin and West Germany and provides for the establishment in West Berlin of a permanent liaison agency. Since the problems of defining "ties" arises here, this part of the agreement must be read in conjunction with the attached letter to the Federal Chancellor presenting the understanding of the Allies of this annex.

Annex III takes the form of a communication from the government of the USSR to the governments of France, the United Kingdom and the United States. It provides for the improvement of external relations, the entry of West Berliners to East Berlin and East Germany and the solution of the problems of the small exclaves around Berlin. Like Annex I, this part of the accord authorizes the appropriate German authorities to hammer out detailed provisions implementing and supplementing the agreement. These negotiations took place subsequently and resulted in the signing of two arrangements on December 20, 1971.

Annex IV consists of a communication from the governments of France, the United Kingdom and the United States to the government of the USSR. It outlines the framework by which the FRG may represent abroad the interests of the Western Sectors. And it provides for the opening of a Soviet Consulate General in West Berlin. These provisions have to be read in accordance with the agreed minutes on Federal passports to West Berliners (I) and on Soviet activities in West Berlin (II).

Agreed Minute I concerns the issuance of Federal passports to West Berliners with respect to their being able to travel on them to the USSR.

Agreed Minute II carefully circumscribes the activities of the Soviet Union in the Western Sectors.

The note from the three Ambassadors to the Soviet Ambassador calls the latter's attention to the intention of the Western Three to send to the Chancellor immediately following signature of the

Quadripartite Agreement a letter containing clarifications and interpretations representing the understanding of the Allies of the statements contained in Annex II. A copy of the letter to the Chancellor is attached to this note.

The letter of interpretation, addressed by the Allies to the Federal Chancellor, spells out their view of the provisions of Annex II, dealing with West Berlin's relations with the FRG.

The Soviet note of reply by the Ambassador of the USSR in Bonn to the Allies acknowledges receipt of the note of the Western Three.

The Final Protocol declares that the original agreement and all the inner-German accords shall enter into force together, that they constitute a resolution of negotiated issues and that they shall remain in force together. This last stipulation makes clear that the inter-se arrangements between the two Germanies are solely derivative from and accessory to the Agreement of September 3, 1971 and other Four-Power agreements even though questions are involved over which the GDR claims unlimited sovereignty.

Secret Protocols

Not formally part of the Four-Power accord — but of great importance in interpreting the agreement — are the highly secret "protocols" (minutes) of the negotiations. For the most part, the general public is unaware of the existence of these documents and the role they have played in helping to settle conflicts which have arisen in the application of the Four-Power Agreement.*

To begin with, one must distinguish between the informal protocol notes taken by the parties during the negotiations and the

---

* One high-level Allied official takes issue with this interpretation. He has this to say: "You refer to the importance of so-called 'protocols' in interpreting the QA. You may well know more than I do about this, but I believe you may be over-emphasizing their importance. There are of course a multitude of reporting cables covering the day-to-day negotiations, but these are U.S. unilateral documents, with no Four-Power or even Allied status, they depict a dynamic situation, and could hardly be of much use in interpreting the final agreement. The best indication of this is that no one I know of ever bothered to root through all that material when we had a true interpretation problem, as for instance the one stemming from the setting up here of the Federal Environmental Office."

highly sensitive "gentleman's agreements" or "understandings" reached by the Four Powers. The former represent cabled summaries of conversations held at the ambassadorial and expert levels.[2] And they are useful in clarifying the background behind the insertion of particular provisions in the agreement. Moreover, they make clear the nature of the "horse trades" carried out by the participants. The latter consist of two oral pledges by the Ambassadors. Although their binding nature is questionable,[3] these "understandings" represent part of a secret quid pro quo worked out by Soviet and Allied diplomats in the context of the overall written accord.

Contrary to the view of some outsiders, the secret protocol notes (not the two "gentleman's agreements") do not take the form of easily read documents which officials merely have to look up in a neat, accessible binder. Rather they consist (as far as the Western Three are concerned anyway) of thousands of pages of telegrams transcribed and dispatched from Germany during the seventeen months of tortured negotiations. In the case of the United States, the protocols are tucked away in the Department of State in Washington, D.C. in a huge wall-length filing cabinet marked "top secret" in the file room of the Office of German Affairs. Thus, from a practical point of view, their number and bulk seriously impede their frequent use by officials. As one former Berlin Desk officer readily concedes: "It would be a hell of a job to consult them."

2 In the case of the United States, the key participants (i.e. Rush and Dean) have recorded for posterity their impressions of the Four-Power talks. Unfortunately, however, these documents are unavailable to researchers at present, being kept under strict security wraps by the State Department. In addition, the Historical Office of the Department of State has compiled a "top secret" study of the negotiations.

3 Legislation passed by the U.S. Congress in 1972 requires that all executive agreements be reported to it or in special cases only to the House and Senate foreign affairs committees. According to constitutional experts, this legislation serves "as an implicit warning to foreign countries that they cannot count on any secret understanding being considered as legally binding by a future administration unless it had been embodied in an executive agreement and communicated to the relevant committees of Congress." For details see Francis O. Wilcox et al, The Constitution and the Conduct of Foreign Policy (New York: Praeger Publishers, 1976), p. 26.

It should be inserted here that there are actually "four negotiating histories" of the Quadripartite Agreement, for each power kept its own report of the substance of discussions. But as one insider points out, the American record of the talks "is the most detailed because 'Jock' Dean had a penchant for detail."

The official position of the United States government is that these protocol notes are not necessary to the application of the Quadripartite Agreement. "The agreement must stand on its own," says one high State Department official. But this view clearly does not take into account the importance of these documents to the understanding — and interpretation — of the Four-Power accord in conflict situations.

As to the oral so-called "gentleman's agreements," these are of course part of the record even though in one case their provisions are a closely kept secret. According to one official, "they do not take the form of agreed, written-down documents signed by the powers — but exist in the form of highly classified diplomatic reporting cables from the field."* The "Big Four" could have signed a minute on the two "understandings" — and the Russians would have preferred it that way, — but the American side decided to leave it to the Soviets to abide by their word (and they have!)

One of the two oral assurances, which represents a concession by the Allies, restricts the public activities in West Berlin of West Germany's National Democratic Party, sometimes called "neo-Nazi." This commitment was a closely held secret until now. It was made to accommodate the Soviet Union, which previously had made the ultra right-wing NPD a focus of allegations that Nazism was returning to the Federal Republic.

The National Democratic Party, which has been described as a successor to *Hitler's* Nazi Party, was founded in 1964. It is a relatively small organization, consisting of fewer than 23,000 paying members — most of them elderly men with Nazi pasts. Today the party is on the wane, but in the late 1960s it was seen in some quarters as a major domestic threat and was the focus of world attention.

At that time, West Germany was emerging from its first major recession and was plagued by student unrest at the universities

---

* As far as the U.S. government is concerned, the only physical evidence of this second "gentleman's agreement" consists of a reporting cable (telegram) to this effect by Ambassador Rush to the State Department and it is kept there.

Old (above) and new (below)
access roads to Steinstücken.

Soviet Foreign Minister Andrei Gromyko and U.S. Secretary of State William P. Rogers exchange pleasantries

which sometimes spilled out into the streets. Fears were acutely aroused when the NPD succeeded in gaining more than 5 % of the vote in eight of West Germany's eleven state legislatures. Neo-Nazi leaders were confidently predicting that the party would enter the Bundestag in the 1969 Federal elections.[4]

As might be expected, the pressure on the Bonn government to outlaw the NPD then was intense "if only because the Federal Republic's image abroad was suffering."[5] The precedents were already well established. Twice before, in 1952 and 1956, the Federal Constitution (Grundgesetz), which declares in Article 21 that antidemocratic parties can be banned by the Federal Constitutional Court, had been invoked to outlaw first an extremist right-wing party and then a left-wing political group.

It was in this context that the Soviets and East Germans protested Allied tolerance of the party's presence in the Western Sectors. They claimed that the city was more and more being converted into a "theater of neo-Nazi, revanchist and militarist activities."[6] Then, in March 1968, the GDR took steps to ban NPD members and West Germans and West Berliners engaged in neo-Nazi activities from passing through its territory. Subsequently, in the effort to ease tensions over Berlin, West Berlin's Governing Mayor *Klaus Schütz* tried to persuade the Allies "to examine the possibility of banning the National Democratic Party in Berlin." But he was unsuccessful.[*]

In Bonn, West German politicians were persuaded to let voters repudiate the NPD. Although many had their doubts, this strategy worked well. The National Democratic Party failed to obtain the necessary five percent of the total vote or win three electoral districts and thus was shut out of the lower house of parliament.

Following the implementation of the Four-Power Agreement in 1972, the Soviet-Allied "understanding" on the NPD was given practical effect. This was done through a series of Allied decrees or

4 See the New York Times, July 20, 1969.

5 Until persuaded otherwise, this was the view held by then Foreign Minister Willy Brandt among others.

6 Quoted in U.S. Mission (Berlin), Berlin 1968 — An Unofficial Chronology (37) (Berlin: USIS, July 1968), p. 2.

* However, in response to a request from Mayor Klaus Schütz, the Allied Kommandatura did ban in October 1969 a party congress of the NPD which was scheduled to be held in West Berlin that month.

Berlin Kommandatura (BK) orders. Thus, the NPD was effectively banned from participating in West Berlin elections in 1974 and prohibited from staging a national party congress there more than a year later. Most recently, in a BK order, which was publicly disclosed in April 1977, the Allies prohibited the public distribution of books pamphlets, posters, badges and other printed material as well as all publications promoting the goals of the party.

One of the reasons for originally deciding to keep the NPD commitment a closely kept secret had "to do with the unstable domestic situation in West Germany in 1971." Chancellor *Brandt* was in the process of losing his 12-vote SPD/FDP majority in the Bundestag. And Ambassador *Rush* did not want the NPD issue to "become a political football" – in the words of one official.

The NPD[7] pledge was but one of two oral "understandings" reached by the Four Powers. The second verbal pledge, which represented a "counter Soviet concession," is a more technical arrangement. It provides essentially that committees of the Bundestag and Bundesrat may "meet in West Berlin not just 'singly' as specified in the written agreement but also 'jointly' or 'simultaneously' when the matter under consideration makes this appropriate."* Under the terms of the written, published accord, the bicameral Federal parliament may no longer meet in plenary session in the divided city.

Unlike the NPD commitment, this second "gentleman's agreement" was conveyed to the West German government and is reflected in the publication it issued on the day of signature of the comprehensive settlement. As things turned out, however, very few individuals outside government actually comprehended the nature and form of the committee interpretation – certainly not its political background. "They were just too dazzled by the complexity and ambiguity of the whole settlement," one official recalls.

---

7 Originally, the Soviets wanted the NPD banned altogether, but the Allies replied that this was impossible given the political situation in the FRG. Moreover, they argued, an outright ban would just cause this party to change its name as the KPD did and resurface. In the end, the Russians accepted an Allied understanding restricting the public activities of the NPD in Berlin.
* See statement by the British negotiator Sir Roger Jackling in an interview with Süddeutsche Zeitung on November 10, 1971.

The Status of Berlin

As may be recalled, the question of legal status was one of the key points of dispute in the quadripartite negotiations. In the twenty years since the end of the Berlin blockade, both sides had developed precise but highly contradictory interpretations of the city's legal status. For its part, the Soviet Union argued that it had long ago transferred full control over the Eastern part of the city to the German Democratic Republic, which had made it the "capital of the GDR".[8] Consequently, the USSR maintained there was only a West Berlin problem, and it insisted that discussions should focus only on the status of West Berlin.[9] For their part, the Western Three refused to accept this limitation of their jurisdiction. They held tenaciously to their position that the Four-Power status continued to be valid for all of Berlin while insisting that the issue under negotiation was the whole of Berlin, i.e. "Greater Berlin."[10] For almost nine months, both sides went round and round on this matter, with neither side showing any willingness to back down from its respective position.

In the end, this controversy only was laid to rest through the personal intervention of President *Nixon.* He met at length with Soviet Foreign Minister *Gromyko* at the White House in October 1970, and the two of them agreed to a tacit understanding. The substance of this "compromise" was later summed up rather poignantly by Ambassador *Rush:* "We decided . . . to forego legal

8 For an analysis of the city's legal status from the Soviet viewpoint see Gerhard Wettig, "Die Rechtslage Berlins nach dem Viermächteabkommen aus sowjetischer Sicht," Deutschland Archiv, Vol. 7, No. 4 (April, 1974), pp. 378-388.

9 As one insider recalls: "Originally, the Soviets wanted us to accept the term 'West Berlin' in the agreement. We couldn't accept that wording because of Four-Power responsibility for all of Berlin. Getting them to accept 'Western Sectors of Berlin' was a major victory for our side. For it implied that there is also an Eastern Sector and thus undermined their argument that there is only a Four-Power status for West Berlin."

10 For an analysis of Berlin's legal status after the Four-Power Agreement see Hartmut Schiedermair, Der völkerrechtliche Status Berlins nach dem Viermächte-Abkommen vom 3. September 1971 (Berlin: Springer Verlag, 1975) and Ernst R. Zivier, Der Rechtsstatus des Landes Berlin: Eine Untersuchung nach dem Viermächte-Abkommen vom 3. September 1971, 3. erw. Aufl. (Berlin: Berlin Verlag, 1977).

arguments in favor of practical improvements."[11] As both sides were fully aware, the probable alternative was: no agreement at all.

The result of this practical decision was that no agreement was reached in the quadripartite agreement on the legal status of East and West Berlin. The preamble and the first part of the accord merely refer to the situation "in the relevant area" or "in the area," with these phrases equally applicable to the whole of Berlin or only to West Berlin. At differing times immediately after the agreement was signed, both sides tried to claim (and still continue to do so) that the accord applies only to West Berlin (the Soviet[12] and East German position)[13] or all of Berlin (the position of the Western Allies[14] and the Senat)[15] as the case may be. However, an objective reading of the agreement does not confirm either point of view (although it is obvious that the various practical improvements agreed upon were designed primarily for the benefit of West Berliners); the accord merely points up the imprecise formula-

11 Kenneth Rush, "Berlin: The Four-Power Agreement," Current Foreign Policy (Washington, D.C.: Department of State, 1971), p. 2.

12 See Pravda, September 4, 1971.

13 In an interview, given on the day of the signing of the Four-Power Agreement, SED Party leader Erich Honecker stressed that the accord deals only with Berlin's Western Sectors and not with East Berlin, the capital of the GDR. See Neues Deutschland, September 4, 1971.

14 In an address before the Berlin Chamber of Commerce on September 22, 1971, Ambassador Rush exclaimed: "It is clear without qualification that the agreement pertains to all of Berlin, and not, as some have said, to the Western Sectors alone." See Kenneth Rush, "The Berlin Agreement: An Assessment," The Atlantic Community Quarterly, Vol. 10, No. 1 (1972), p. 53. Contrast this statement with the final communique issued on May 29, 1977 at the end of President Nixon's visit to Moscow.

15 In a speech before the Royal Institute for International Relations in Brussels on October 26, 1971, Governing Mayor Klaus Schütz declared: "I would like to clear up a misunderstanding one hears . . . that East Berlin was not the subject of the Quadripartite Agreement. The Four Powers declared that they concluded their Agreements acting on the basis of their quadripartite rights and responsibilities, and of the corresponding wartime and postwar agreements and decisions of the Four Powers. And these are rights and responsibilities and agreements and decisions concerning Berlin as a whole. The relevant area mentioned in the Agreement is therefore not restricted to the Western Sectors, it is all Berlin." See Klaus Schütz, "The Four-Power Agreement," Chronique de Politique Etrangère, Vol. 24, No. 4 (1971), p. 547.

tions, which were chosen deliberately to bypass the differing legal positions of East and West. Perhaps the most important wording in the Four-Power agreement on this point is the phrase in the preamble, which expressly states that the parties concluded the accord "without prejudice to the legal positions."[16]

Legal considerations aside, the four Ambassadors decided as a practical matter to focus on West Berlin during the negotiations. According to one Allied official familiar with the proceedings, "The Soviet Sector was written off because Western negotiators realized they could not influence developments there." In this view, the major concern of the Allies was to obtain "adequate safeguards" for the Western legal position "so that the Soviets couldn't come back later and say we had agreed to a Four-Power status for West Berlin."

Recognition of the GDR

Closely linked to the status question was the delicate issue of East German recognition and the nature of the future East German-Allied relationship. Ever since the creation of the German Democratic Republic in 1949, the Western powers had strongly resisted granting the communist régime diplomatic recognition and establishing formal relations with it. For the most part, the GDR was considered a puppet of the Soviet Union and was treated accordingly.

There were many ideological reasons against recognition, including the belief that it would only perpetuate the division of Germany and contribute to instability in Europe.[17] But of great practical concern to the Western Three was the question of its impact on the Allied legal position in Berlin. Generally, it was feared that full diplomatic recognition of the GDR would make untenable (or seriously undermine) the gradually eroding Western legal viewpoint. In particular, Allied officials were afraid the

16 On problems of interpretation see for instance Dennis L. Bark, Agreement on Berlin: A Study of the 1970-72 Quadripartite Negotiations (Washington, D.C.: AEI, 1974), pp. 101-106.

17 See undated (1961?) position paper "Why the United States does not recognize the so-called 'German Democratic Republic'?," put out by the Bureau of Public Affairs, U.S. Department of State.

granting of recognition might seriously call into question the absolute rights (including military presence) which the Western powers claimed to have in Berlin, stemming from the right of conquest and the assumption of supreme authority in Germany in 1945.[18]

One of the many important breakthroughs in the Berlin negotiations was the decision to consider seriously the reversal of this decades-old policy and to think through the effects of eventual recognition and the establishment of diplomatic relations. This step was taken by the United States only very reluctantly and under pressure from its British and French Allies, who argued for a more realistic policy. This change is believed to have come directly from *Henry Kissinger* in the White House. The result of this policy review, which came in the middle of the talks, was the Allied decision to accept in principle the establishment of diplomatic relations with the GDR sometime after the conclusion of the Four-Power accord. This decision was subsequently communicated to the Soviets and helped create a more flexible and realistic atmosphere in which further concessions and counter-concessions on practical improvements could be made.[19]

The practical effect of this major policy reversal found expression in a compromise on status in the Quadripartite Agreement. Not only was the official name of the East German state expressly included in the text of the accord (seven times to be exact), but the "Big Four" also authorized the communist régime to negotiate follow-up accords, which constitute an integral part of the overall settlement. These moves were generally regarded by diplomats as de facto recognition of the GDR even if the Allies did not agree

18 For an illuminating analysis of the recognition question and its implications for West Germany see Wilhelm A. Kewenig, "recognition — an end in itself or a means of German policy," German Tribune, No. 10 (July 16, 1970), pp. 11-13.

19 According to one insider "the decision to recognize the GDR was no sudden one. It was implicit throughout the negotiations; indeed one impetus for the negotiations was the fact recognition seemed so inevitable and the US wanted Berlin pinned down first. Besides, since the Soviets wanted recognition badly, it could be used as leverage. The decision came from the White House (not necessarily Henry Kissinger) after the pros and cons had long been debated. That request for a policy review was made when the negotiations were far enough along to make an updating of the many earlier reviews prudent."

with the East German interpretation that the Four-Power Agreement confirmed "for the first time the sovereignty of the GDR's relations with the other state (FRG) and West Berlin."[20]

To be sure, the Soviets were compelled in the compromise worked out with the West to sacrifice the use of the phrase "capital of the GDR." The term "areas bordering on the Western Sectors" was inserted as an acceptable euphemism for East Berlin (the Soviet Sector). But this word play did not alter the basic fact that the existence of the GDR for the first time was officially acknowledged by the Western powers, and the way was now open for widespread recognition of the German Democratic Republic.

Relations between West Berlin and the FRG

One of the most controversial aspects of the Quadripartite Agreement deals with the nature of West Berlin's "ties" with the Federal Republic. This question is dealt with — albeit not satisfactorily — in Part II (Section B), relating to the Western Sectors of Berlin (as well as in Annex II and the Allied "Letter of Interpretation"). Here the Allies — not the Soviet Union — "declare"[21]

> that the ties between the Western Sectors of Berlin and the Federal Republic of Germany will be maintained and developed, taking into account that these Sectors continue not to be a

20 See communication from Erich Honecker to Leonid Brezhnev, September 8, 1971, published in Second Session of the Central Committee of the Socialist Unity Party of Germany, Berlin 16 and 17 September 1971, Vol. 1 (1971), p. 72.

21 The form of Four-Power agreement on "ties" is not unimportant here. Nowhere in the text does the Soviet Union expressly commit itself to the provision that the ties between West Berlin and West Germany will be maintained and developed. The quadripartite accord merely contains a communication by the Western Three, in which they alone "declare" this. This procedure was agreed upon, partly out of deference to Soviet wishes — they did not want to be directly linked with guaranteeing or encouraging these ties, — and partly because the Allies viewed this as a matter within their exclusive jurisdiction. None the less, if the Soviets do not expressly agree in the text that the ties between West Berlin and the FRG may be maintained and developed, they are bound to accept this in the view of many Western international lawyers and seem to do so in practice as far as non-political and non-legal ties are concerned.

constituent part of the Federal Republic of Germany and not to be governed by it.

The major difficulty here centers on what is meant by "ties". It may be recalled that this problem became critical in the dispute over translation of the Four-Power Agreement into German and was not resolved in the inner-German negotiations; it was merely bypassed. In the context of the quadripartite accord, the English term "ties" would seem to imply social ties as well as ties of communication. Thus, the word differs considerably from the Russian word "svjazy," which would seem to refer mainly (only?) to technical links such as traffic communications.

The problem of interpreting the Russian word for ties was discussed during the Four-Power negotiations, but no consensus was achieved. The question first became acute on March 26, 1971, when *Abrasimov* submitted the Soviet draft proposal for Allied consideration. At that time, the Soviets proposed that

Links and contacts between Berlin (West) and abroad (including the FRG) in economic, technical, cultural and other peaceful matters will be maintained in accordance with the fact that Berlin (West) is not part of the FRG and cannot be governed by it.

The Soviet delegation was careful to point out then that the Russian word for "ties" clearly possessed no political connotations.[22]

This problem of interpretation was subsequently discussed by the Western Three, and the following general "game plan" was adopted.[23] The Western negotiators would insist on a "re-wording" of the critical passage in the Soviet draft so as to secure a Russian commitment "safeguarding" West Berlin's political and legal ties with West Germany. This aim was not fully realized, but the two sides did agree to a remarkable compromise, which resulted in a more positive description (from the Western view) of the relationship. On the one hand, the Soviet Union — in an apparent retreat

---

22 See Gerhard Wettig, op. cit., p. 383.

23 When a U.S. participant in the Berlin talks was asked how "ties" are to be interpreted, he responded: "We didn't want to spell that out. Like the Fourteenth Amendment and the Commerce Clause in the Constitution we wanted provisions general enough to allow for change over time. We were also afraid that if we made things too specific we would lose something. This was in contrast to our position on access. There we wanted as much detail as possible."

from earlier demands for "an independent political entity" of West Berlin — agreed to tolerate links with the Federal Republic of an economic, financial, cultural — and in a more limited sense — legal and political nature.[24] On the other, the Allies conceded what the Soviets had long desired; namely, they granted confirmation that the Western Sectors "continue" not to form part of the constitutional framework of the FRG[25] and accepted the elimination of demonstrable traces of any such de facto connection. (The compromise reached here should be seen as part of a larger series of "trade-offs".) Later Ambassador *Rush* attempted to explain the rationale behind Allied agreement to reduce the demonstrative Federal presence:[26]

Over the years, the Allies allowed the Federal Republic to

24 The Soviet Union does not subscribe to the view expressed by Mayor Schütz (and shared by the Allies) shortly after the signing of the Four Power Agreement, namely, that Moscow in the Berlin accord recognized the integration of West Berlin in the economic, financial and legal system of the Federal Republic, and that this relationship "would no longer be disputed." See G.M. Akopov, Zapadnyi Berlin: Problemy i reshenija (West Berlin: Problems and Decisions) (Moscow: International Relations Press, 1974), p. 238. This book, which is one of the first Russian monographs to appear on Berlin after the conclusion of the Four-Power Agreement, is read by officials in the West as representing the view of the Soviet government. The author worked in responsible positions in the Soviet Control Commission for Germany, the Soviet High Commission and the Soviet Embassy in East Berlin.

25 The exact wording is "that these Sectors continue not to be a constituent part of the Federal Republic of Germany and not to be governed by it." This passage represents a classic example of the kind of careful writing that went into the drafting of the text. Here every word counts. For instance, the phrase favored by the West "continue not to be a constituent part" was chosen over the Soviet wording "are not" in the attempt, as one U.S. official recalls, "to maintain our options." According to this source, if the Allies had accepted the phrase "are not a constituent part" this would have precluded the possibility of the Western Sectors ever becoming part of the constitutional order of the FRG — a concession the Western Three were not prepared to make. In addition, the word "continue" kept intact the legality of both Allied sovereignty over Berlin and of the Basic Law provision that Berlin was a Land of the FRG, although this status was temporarily in suspense by virtue of Allied action. (The Soviets, it is said, have been trying ever since to negate the "continue not to be" language and did so officially in the GDR-USSR Treaty of October 1975.)

26 Kenneth Rush, "Berlin: The Four-Power Agreement," Current Foreign Policy (Washington, D.C.: Department of State publication, 1971), p. 6.

develop this demonstrative presence as a means of countering Soviet claims that there were no legal ties between Berlin and the FRG. Now that these ties have been officially recognized, this demonstrative presence becomes less important.

As far as the interpretation of "ties" was concerned, part of the compromise called for the Allies to present their understanding of the word (and all of Annex II for that matter) in a letter, which would be delivered to the Federal Chancellor shortly after the Quadripartite Agreement was signed and then sent to the Soviet Union for acknowledgement. This communication now forms an integral part of the overall Berlin settlement. In this way, the Western Three achieved greater precision, without entailing too obvious a loss of face on the part of the USSR.

According to the Four-Power Agreement, the links between the FRG and West Berlin may not only be maintained but also developed. But what exactly is meant by "developed"? A comparison of the final agreement with the Soviet draft shows that inclusion of the term was not pushed by the Soviet side. Actually, the word contradicts the major Soviet goal throughout — namely, the promotion of the "independent political entity" of West Berlin. Thus, the word is clearly there due to Western insistence, and this interpretation is confirmed by U.S. officials.

Because of Allied disagreement with the USSR here there is no clarification or interpretation of this wording in the Quadripartite Agreement. The view of the Western Three — under pressure from certain quarters in Bonn — is that the word today should be interpreted very broadly. From their standpoint, the term is seen as permitting — at least in theory — the expansion of all Federal ties unless specifically restricted in the accord.

The Soviets take exception to this "broad-gauge" interpretation. But it is not clear how they define the term. One theory among scholars in the West is that the Kremlin understands "developed" to mean the possible expansion of those previously existing ties — but not the establishment of entirely new links. While this view seems plausible at first glance, it does not appear to describe the Soviet position accurately. As one Allied official in Berlin points out: "The Russians would not at all like to see the sudden ballooning of presently existing Federal offices in the city. There are already more Federal officials here than in Bonn without adding new links."

Soviet sources take pretty much the following view on this matter. In their eyes the Four-Power Agreement confirmed that West Berlin is a "special political entity" or a "third state political entity" situated on German territory. This representation is allegedly drawn from the passage in Annex II of the text which states that "these Sectors continue not to be a constituent part of the Federal Republic of Germany and not to be governed by it."[27] Arguing from the separate state existence of West Berlin, these sources see as axiomatic that relations between the city and the FRG (as well as between West Berlin and the GDR and between the FRG and the GDR) "may develop as is usual between two sovereign states." Thus, all three are left to develop their relations "on an international legal basis and exchange appropriate representatives.[28]

By way of re-enforcing this interpretation of the Quadripartite Agreement, Soviet sources point to that section of the accord which provides for the establishment of a permanent FRG liaison agency (Bundesbevollmächtigter) in West Berlin. According to Annex II, this body is accredited to the three occupying powers and the Senat and is responsible for representing the Federal Republic vis-à-vis the Allies and the West Berlin government.[29]

From interviews with Allied officials in Berlin, it appears that neither side is sure what the other means by the term "developed." One thing is certain, however. Moscow clearly takes a more restrictive interpretation than the West, possibly allowing only for the expansion of non-political and non-legal ties.[30]

The Quadripartite Agreement confirms that the Western Sectors "continue not to be a constituent part of the Federal Republic of Germany and not be governed by it." The central passage here is

27 See for instance the article by the Soviet writer Viktor Boldyrew, "Das Vierseitige Abkommen über Westberlin — ein Schritt zu Frieden, Sicherheit und Zusammenarbeit in Europa," Deutsche Aussenpolitik, Vol. 5 (September-October, 1972), p. 879.

28 Consult G.M. Akopov, op. cit., p. 227.

29 The provision in the Quadripartite Agreement for the creation of a permanent West German liaison agency in Berlin did not bring into being an entirely new situation. Rather it merely confirmed — with minor changes — what had been the practice between the Allies and the FRG since November 30, 1953, when the West Berlin office of the first West German plenipotentiary was opened.

30 See Gerhard Wettig, op. cit., pp. 383-384.

contained in the previously cited Part II, Section B of the accord (as well as Annex II which goes into more detail on restrictions). This position is in accordance with that taken by the Western Three at the time the FRG was established and reflects the political reality that the Allies retain final governing authority over the Western Sectors.[31]

Within this framework, the Four-Power accord provides for significant limitations of Federal presence. (In the Western view, these restrictions concern only organs and functions specified in the West German Constitution as organs and functions of the central government.) For the most part, these restrictions pertain to matters which before 1971 had increasingly been criticized from the Allied side because of the perennial crises with the Soviets arising from them. Importantly, there will be no further plenary meetings in Berlin of the Bundestag (which last convened in the divided city in 1965) and Bundesrat (which last met in Berlin in 1969). Moreover, the Bundesversammlung will no longer meet in the city to elect the Federal President. However, single committees of the parliament may continue to conduct business in Berlin in connection with maintaining and developing ties between West Berlin and the FRG. Otherwise, the Fraktionen (caucuses) of the Bundestag may convene in Berlin — but not simultaneously. Finally, the Federal President, the Chancellor and other high government officials are prohibited from performing over the Western Sectors "constitutional or official acts" (for instance, the signing of laws or issuing of executive orders). This ban also extends to members of parliament, Federal ministries and their branches and all Federal courts.

At first glance, these restrictions on the Federal demonstrative presence seem quite encompassing. But it should be recalled that early in the talks the Soviet Union presented to the Allies a rather detailed and complete list of those institutions and groups it wanted banned from "performing official acts or other activities." This included a ban on all meetings in Berlin of parliamentary committees and Fraktionen, among other groups. Thus, the end product represents somewhat of a compromise. And if it is a

31 See Department of State, United States Foreign Policy 1971: A Report of the Secretary of State (Washington, D.C.: U.S. Government Printing Office, 1972), p. 46.

little lopsided, this is because Western concessions here made possible Soviet counter-concessions in other areas.

In their letter to the Chancellor, the Western Three spelled out their interpretation of what constituted "constitutional or official acts." The key passage is that which reads:

The phrase in Paragraph 2 of Annex II of the Quadripartite Agreement which ' . . . will not perform in the Western Sectors of Berlin constitutional or official acts which contradict the provisions of Paragraph 1' shall be interpreted to mean acts in exercise of direct state authority over the Western Sectors of Berlin.

This provision makes plain that the Federal Republic will be forbidden to exercise direct state authority over the Western Sectors. But it does not say that organs of the FRG may not function in those sectors. In other words, the Four-Power Agreement protects those Federal employees now living and working in the city, the Federal agencies which have their headquarters there and the branch offices of Federal ministries — so long as they do not attempt to exercise direct state authority over West Berlin. Through this important clause the administrative presence of the FRG in the city is secured.

There is one last major question to consider in interpreting the relevant passages of the Quadripartite Agreement on "ties" or "Federal presence." Namely, is everything that is not forbidden, permitted? Or put another way: is everything not permitted, forbidden?

This problem arose in the negotiations and was the cause of great concern to the Western side. In the main, the nature of East-West differences here was very basic — if not philosophical. For its part, the Soviet delegation was of the opinion that everything which was not expressly sanctioned in the text was not to be considered permissible. This view was consistent with the Soviet concept of the role of law in society, but — as might be expected — it clashed sharply with the outlook of the Allied delegations, which saw the function of law in the context of a more liberal, democratic tradition. The Western Three took the position in principle that everything which was not specifically forbidden in the accord would be allowed.

In the end, this ideological deadlock was only resolved through a far-reaching compromise. As far as this modus vivendi touched on the relationship between West Berlin and West Germany, it provided that both sides would spell out precisely in the text those mutually acceptable restrictions on Federal presence. This decision meant, from the Western viewpoint, the elimination of political ties which would not seriously undermine the substantive relations that have developed between West Berlin and the FRG; from the Soviet point of view, the eradication of highly visible — and thus particularly objectionable — Federal demonstrations. One part of this tacit understanding involved the insertion of the phrase *"will be maintained and developed"* (author's italics) in the text with regard to West Berlin's ties with West Germany.[32] Another part took the form of a Soviet promise to refrain from asserting its opinion in the Quadripartite Agreement that all demonstrations of Federal presence in Berlin not expressly provided for by the agreement are forbidden. This compromise was not made public at Soviet insistence but was incorporated in the classified reporting cables of the talks.

Representation of West Berlin Abroad

Just as the matter of West Berlin's ties with the Federal Republic is treated in detail by the Quadripartite Agreement so did the issue of the city's representation abroad receive particular attention. The relevant passages here are to be found in Part II, Annex IV and Agreed Minute I. For the first time, the Soviets — after strenuously objecting for years to the foreign representation of West Berlin by the FRG — agreed to "raise no objection" to certain practices which had been uniformly accepted in non-communist countries. As recounted earlier, Moscow consented to this major concession as part of a quid pro quo involving the establishment in the Western Sectors of a Soviet Consulate General.

According to the terms of the agreement the Federal government may perform "consular services" for permanent residents so long as Allied responsibilities regarding the security and status of Berlin are not affected. The substitution of the more normal phrase "consular functions" by "consular services" provides

---

32 According to one source close to Rush in the negotiations: "We got more than we expected here."

another example of the importance attached by all sides to precise — if not convoluted — writing. Apparently, the Four Powers inserted the unique phrase "consular services" to describe usual consular duties with the exception of passport matters, for which special provisions were made.[33]

The use of the term "permanent residents" in the same provision is noteworthy also, for it suggests the way in which the question of FRG consular representation of West Berlin was finally settled. The "Big Four" were meticulous in their choice of words here, avoiding resolving the matter in the usual way — on the basis of citizenship. Instead, they chose to settle the issue on the highly irregular basis of place of residence. This meant that the FRG could represent abroad foreigners who were permanent residents of West Berlin as well as Germans who resided there. The Ambassadors agreed upon this strange procedure in order to bypass irreconcilable differences over the question of the citizenship of West Berliners. (In the main, these differences stemmed from Soviet refusal to recognize the West German practice of treating these persons as German citizens.)

Under the terms of the agreement, the Federal Republic is entitled to represent the "interests" of West Berlin in international organizations and conferences — excluding matters of status and security. At the same time, the USSR recognizes the right of "permanent residents" of the Western Sectors to form part of West German delegations and team competitions and agrees not to object to the holding of international meetings in West Berlin, sponsored either by the Senat or jointly by the West Berlin government and that of the FRG.

In their selection of words in describing how the city is to be represented in international organizations and conferences, the negotiators once again exercised extreme caution. The major concern here on the part of the Western Three was to draft the provision in such a way so as to preclude giving support to the Soviet view that West Germany would be representing an "independent legal entity." Thus, the term "interests" was carefully inserted — at Allied insistence — before the phrase "Western Sectors of Berlin."[34]

33 For details, see Frankfurter Allgemeine Zeitung, September 25, 1973.
34 Consult Hartmut Schiedermair, op. cit., p. 131.

Where appropriate, the city is to be included in international agreements concluded by the Federal Republic through a special "Berlin clause." The exact wording here is the product of a hard-fought compromise. Originally, the Soviets wanted to introduce terminology that would have given them a clear veto over the extension of such arrangements to Berlin. But the Western powers would not have this. Consequently, both sides settled as a face saver on the mutually acceptable qualifier: "provided that the extension of such agreements and arrangements is specified in each case." If this phrase was not completely satisfactory to the Western side, it was also less than the Russians wanted.[35]

One of the more difficult problems the Western Allies faced in the negotiations was to obtain Soviet acceptance of the Western practice of allowing West Berliners to travel abroad on Federal passports. Here again the dispute over citizenship played a major role. In the end, differences of opinion were only surmounted through the construction of an elaborate compromise formula. (See Agreed Minute I.) This modus vivendi provided that the "permanent residents" of West Berlin could travel abroad (to the Soviet Union) on a West German passport if it contained a special stamp reading "issued in accordance with the Quadripartite Agreement of September 3, 1971". To be issued a visa to the USSR, local residents must submit a passport with the appropriate stamp and an identity card (Ausweis) or other similar documentation as proof of domicile. While in the Soviet Union, inhabitants are free to travel with either or both documents. In other words, instead of being compelled to use only the Berlin ID card for travel to the USSR, as the Soviets wanted, or merely Federal passports, as the Western Three wished, residents would be permitted the use of both by the carefully engineered "trade-off".

By obtaining Soviet agreement to these practices, the Allies hoped to secure for West Berliners the right to travel to all parts of the world with the same rights and protection as residents of the

---

35 It should be noted that the Quadripartite Agreement does not represent the only word on the extension to Berlin of international agreements concluded by the Federal Republic. According to Allied reservations made at the time that sovereignty was granted to West Germany (1955), the Western Three retained the right, among other things, to nullify legislation in conflict with Allied rights and to review international agreements concluded by Bonn that are also to apply to the Western Sectors.

Federal Republic. (It was expected that the East European countries would follow the Russian lead in this matter.) At the same time, the Western Three hoped that these provisions would improve the ability of the city to take part in the full breadth of international life in the East as it could in the West. If all went well, there would no longer be any trouble or difficulties when West Berliners and West Germans appeared together in sports, cultural or other events wherever these took place. The city's attractiveness as a center for international exchange would be enhanced, and its role as a meeting place between East and West would be strengthened.[36] This was the hope, but as it will be shown later (in the second volume) the practice has not completely borne out these expectations.

Visits by West Berliners to East Berlin and the GDR

One of the most important questions treated in the quadripartite and inner-German negotiations was the re-opening of visits by West Berliners to East Berlin and East Germany. This difficult matter is taken up somewhat generally in Part II (Section C) and Annex III of the Four-Power Agreement and in great detail in the so-called *Müller-Kohrt* accord.[37]

The Soviets in the former agreement "declare" that communications between the Western Sectors of Berlin and "areas bordering on these Sectors and those areas of the German Democratic Republic which do not border on these Sectors will be improved." In particular, the "permanent inhabitants" of West Berlin are to enjoy access to East Berlin and East Germany for "compassionate, family, religious, cultural or commercial reasons, or as tourists." While visiting these areas, West Berliners are to be treated "under conditions comparable" to "those other persons (i.e. West Germans)

36 See Kenneth Rush, "The Berlin Agreement: An Assessment," The Atlantic Community Quarterly, Vol. 10. No. 1 (1972), p. 60.

37 For an English-language text see Foreign Affairs Bulletin, Vol. 11, No. 35 (December 23, 1971), published by the Press and Information Department of the Ministry of Foreign Affairs of the German Democratic Republic. For a German text see Dokumentation Berlin: Die Vereinbarungen und das Abkommen (December, 1971), published by the West Berlin Senat.

entering these areas." To facilitate this travel, the Soviets promised the opening of additional crossing points.

The details of these visiting arrangements are incorporated in an agreement signed on December 20, 1971 in East Berlin by *Ulrich Müller* of the West Berlin Senat and *Günter Kohrt* of the GDR government. This inner-German accord about "easing and improving travelling and visiting" contains nine articles, an oral declaration by the GDR Staatssekretär, a reference concerning the record of negotiations (minutes), a statement of information to Senatsdirektor *Müller* by *Kohrt* about border crossing points, a confirmation by *Müller* of having received this statement and a reference in the minutes of the proceedings about an agreement on an improvement in communications.

The nine articles of this inner-German accord provide that permanent residents will be able to visit East Berlin and the GDR for a total of thirty days annually. These may take the form of one-day visits or visits of longer duration. Additional visits beyond the thirty-day quota will be possible in cases of urgent family and humanitarian matters or in connection with social, scientific, economic, commercial and cultural affairs. To facilitate this travel, additional crossing points will be opened as will offices where West Berliners can obtain authorization from East German representatives for the visits. Upon entering East Berlin or East Germany, every visitor is obliged to carry an "entry permit," issued by East German authorities.

This last point is especially significant. During the difficult inner-German negotiations the East German side — in accordance with Article I of the GDR constitution, which provides that East Berlin is part of the German Democratic Republic, — insisted that visitors must carry a visa issued by it when entering the GDR. But the Western side refused to accept this condition because of the implication of recognition contained in the issuance of visas. Thus, the term "entry permit" represents a major retreat for East Germany.[38]

Under the terms of the *Kohrt-Müller* accord, both sides have the responsibility of naming representatives who are charged with clearing up misunderstandings and difficulties that arise from the agreement's application. These mediators may be requested to

38 For details see Günther Doeker et al, op. cit., p. 60.

258

convene at the request of one side or the other. Problems that they cannot resolve will be referred to the GDR government and the West Berlin Senat. They will settle matters by negotiation.

Certain categories of persons are denied entry altogether to East Berlin and the GDR. According to the oral declaration made by State Secretary *Kohrt* to Director *Müller,* these include individuals who, under East German law, have committed crimes and former citizens of the GDR, who unlawfully fled to the West after the passing of security regulations in the GDR during August 1961.

The note in the minutes of the proceedings confirms the details on the lengths of times and categories of persons laid down in the accord. It affirms that the use of motor vehicles may be permitted in special circumstances: that is, when passengers are physically handicapped, when the visit otherwise could not be made within the available time, when the visit includes children up to three years of age, when the intended destination of the visit is difficult to reach or farther than one hundred kilometers (about sixty miles) from West Berlin.

For the most part, the details of the visiting arrangement negotiated by *Müller* and *Kohrt* are in accord with the principles outlined in the Four-Power Agreement. One major departure, however, concerns the controversial provision of a thirty-day quota. Such a limitation, giving West Berliners only one-twelfth the visiting rights held by West Germans, was not foreseen by the Ambassadors. They had taken pains to specify that area residents would be able to travel to the Eastern Sector of Berlin and to East Germany under the same conditions applying to other persons. What brought the Western Three finally around to accept this significant modification of their agreement with the Soviets was pressure from officials in Bonn and West Berlin and the realization that most of their wishes had been fulfilled.

Access to Berlin

In the Western view, the issue of access was the most important question resolved by the quadripartite negotiations. This is evidenced by the preeminent place of transit provisions in the text. A general statement on access introduces Part II, which summarizes practical improvements, and Annex I is exclusively devoted to fill-

259

ing in many of the details. Previously, the sketchiness of arrangements on surface communications between Berlin and the FRG had provided East Germany, sometimes acting alone, more often with explicit Soviet approval, with considerable margin for obstructing and disrupting traffic on the transit routes. However, with the conclusion of the September 3, 1971 accord, the legally unclarified status of civilian surface traffic was settled within the framework of "Big Four" agreement for the first time since the end of World War II.

First, the USSR is to share responsibility for ensuring that "transit traffic by road, rail, and waterways through the territory of the German Democratic Republic of civilian persons and goods . . . will be facilitated and unimpeded." This provision is highly significant in that Moscow limits the sovereign rights of the GDR over the accessways which it had unilaterally granted the GDR in September 1955. Nothing is said about military transit or air transportation across East Germany because they have been regulated since 1945 exclusively by France, Britain, the United States and the Soviet Union.

Second, after consultation and in agreement with the GDR, the Soviet Union "declares" that civilian surface traffic "will receive the most simple, expeditious and preferential treatment provided by international practice." It is important to note here that the Soviet Union does not grant a right of access to the Allies. (They always had this right.) The USSR merely extends certain assurances regarding transit for non-allied civilian traffic.

Third, the USSR provides for the replacement of time-consuming East German customs controls with an inspection of shipment seals and accompanying documents. Freight conveyances which are sealed before leaving the Federal Republic or West Berlin will not be subject to inspection or delay by GDR authorities. Goods vehicles that cannot be sealed will, in general, be subject only to an inspection of cargo papers.

Fourth, there is provision for the smooth processing of persons travelling by rail, bus or private car. In the case of through trains and buses, formalities are limited to identification checks. Travellers in private vehicles will — except in certain special instances involving misuse of the transit routes — be exempt from search of their persons, vehicles and baggage and detention or exclusion from the use of the accessways. Procedures pertaining to travellers will not involve delay. And individual visa fees and road tolls are no longer to be charged. Instead, lump-sum payments are to be made on an annual basis. These include visa fees for German nationals and non-Germans having permanent residence in the FRG or West Berlin.

The access provisions represent the most detailed part of the Quadripartite Agreement. This is because the Western Three — at the urging of *Egon Bahr* — sought to "cram as many details as possible into their accord with the Soviets." The Allies were determined that "nothing was to be left to chance" in the inner-German negotiations. The "dark chapter of searches and waiting times, of impediments and chicanery, of rejections and arrests, this dark chapter which started in the late forties and continued until 1971" was to come to an end with the signing of the September 3 accord.[39]

More specific arrangements, providing for the supplementation and implementations of access benefits agreed upon by the Ambassadors, are contained in the transit agreement signed on December 17, 1971 in Bonn by Staatssekretär *Michael Kohl* (GDR Ministerial Council) and Staatssekretär *Egon Bahr* (Federal Chancellory). This inner-German accord consists of twenty-one articles, an annex, protocol notes and a declaration on the conditions for the transportation of certain goods and livestock.

In the main, the German transit arrangement sets forth the control procedures governing the movement of persons across East German territory. Its most important provisions are outlined below:

Facilitation of transit traffic. Article two re-affirms that surface access will be facilitated and unimpeded. "It will receive the most simple, expeditious and preferential treatment provided by international practice."

Transit traffic of civilian persons. According to Article four, transit travellers are to be issued visas at GDR border crossing points. And in the interest of expeditious processing, their issue is for the most part to take place at the vehicle or, in the case of buses and trains, inside them.

As far as travellers in motor vehicles are concerned, Article nine provides that these persons, their conveyances and personal bagage

39 Quotes from Klaus Schütz, op. cit., pp. 549-550.

will not be subject to search, detention or exclusion. The only exception is where sufficient grounds exist for suspicion of misuse of the transit routes.

For travellers in buses and trains, inspection procedures may not include any formalities other than the identification of persons. While in transit through the GDR, these individuals are not to leave their compartments or trains. The only exceptions are when special circumstances occur, such as accidents, breakdowns or natural catastrophies, or when East German personnel make a specific request or give their permission. Resting places for train passengers on long journeys are to be provided by GDR officials. (Articles eleven and twelve.)

Transit traffic of civilian goods. Article six deals with the transportation of civilian goods in transit and prescribes the use of conveyances fitted with seals before departure. According to it, the West German side promises to ensure that vehicles are equipped to the greatest possible extent with seals. The seals affixed by appropriate officials will be inspected along with accompanying documents by competent East German authorities.

Article seven foresees that, in special cases where there is sufficient reason to suspect that conveyances contain materials which are "intended for dissemination along the designated routes, or persons or material put on board along these routes," the content of unsealed vehicles may be inspected by East German officials.

Inland navigation. Matters covered in this section (Article thirteen) include the provision of berths as resting places, the rendering of assistance by GDR authorities in the event of an accident or breakdown and the supplying of information by East German personnel on such matters as water levels and operating times of locks as well as on any obstructions or impediments.

Misuse of the agreement. One of the key elements of the accord (Article 16) concerns the so-called "misuse clause." Misuse is deemed to be present if a transit traveller (a) disseminates or receives material; (b) picks up persons; (c) leaves the designated transit routes (unless so caused by special circumstances such as accident or illness); (d) commits other criminal offenses; or (e) is guilty of an infringement by contravening road traffic regulations. Misuse is also present if a person, incites, aids or abets a transit traveller in an act of misuse.

In cases where "sufficient reason" for suspecting misuse is present or where "certain facts or concrete evidence indicate a certain degree of probability that misuse . . . is intended," GDR authorities are authorized to search travellers, their means of transportation and their baggage or turn them back. Should suspicions be confirmed, East German officials "will, commensurate with the gravity of the act of misuse," (a) reprimand or impose a disciplinary penalty on, or issue a caution with fine to the person concerned, or impound articles; (b) seize or confiscate articles; (c) turn persons back or temporarily exclude them from the use of the transit routes; or (d) detain persons. In the last two instances, GDR officials are obliged to notify West German authorities and give the reasons.

Article seventeen foresees that the Federal Republic will "to the extent possible" take the necessary steps to prevent misuse of the transit routes.

Payment of transit fees. Article eighteen covers those tolls, fees and other costs relating to transit traffic "including the maintenance of adequate routes, facilities and installations used for such traffic." These shall be paid by the West German government in the form of an annual lump sum. For the years 1972-1975 this figure is set at 234.9 million marks (representing the total estimated fees for East German visas and road tolls paid in 1971 by individual travellers).

Establishment of grievance commission. An important provision of the transit agreement is Article nineteen. It provides for the creation of a joint East-West German commission to settle "any difficulties or differences of opinion" regarding its "application or interpretation." Delegations to this body will be headed by a plenipotentiary of the Federal Minister of Transport and of the Minister of Transport of the German Democratic Republic respectively. The commission shall meet at the request of either of the two Germanies. Should it be unable to resolve a difference of opinion, the point at issue "shall be submitted by the two sides to their respective governments, which will then resolve the matter by negotiation."

Like the inner-German visiting arrangement, the provisions of the German transit accord follow pretty much the guidelines outlined by the Four Powers.[40] In many instances, the same

40 See Dieter Mahncke, Berlin im geteilten Deutschland (Munich: R. Oldenbourg Verlag, 1973), p. 207.

phrases are repeated in whole or part in the German text. One of the major discrepancies between the Quadripartite Agreement and the *Bahr-Kohl* understanding, however, pertains to the controversial "misuse" arrangement. In the former accord, the Allies were successful in obtaining Soviet acceptance of the principle of non-interference in transit traffic "except where there is sufficient reason (author's italics) to suspect that misuse of the transit routes is intended for purposes not related to direct travel to and from the Western Sectors of Berlin and contrary to generally applicable regulations concerning public order." But the German version, which attempts in Article sixteen to define misuse precisely, contains watered-down language which is still the subject of hot debate. GDR authorities are authorized to carry out searches of travellers and their property, detain people or turn them back not only where "sufficient reason" for suspecting misuse exists but where "certain facts or concrete evidence indicate a certain degree of probability that misuse . . . is intended." This wording, according to some sources in the CDU opposition, would seem to give the East Germans a "blank check" to interfere with access on the slightest pretext.[41]

At the same time, the way "misuse" as defined by *Bahr* and *Kohl* leaves a lot to be desired. In this respect, clause(d) of Paragraph 1, Article 16 is singled out for special criticism. There misuse is said to occur if a traveler "commits other criminal offenses." Critics would have liked to see this rather vague language eliminated or at least replaced with the spelling out of specific offenses for which the misuse clause can be applied.

The Question of Exclaves

No detail was too small for consideration by the Ambassadors as the provisions regarding Berlin's "exclaves" or "enclaves" — depending on one's point of view — demonstrate. When Western officials began casting around for likely areas of improvement that could be easily brought into the Four-Power talks, a suggestion

41 For a detailed analysis of the transit agreement and its weaknesses see Lutz Gusseck, Die internationale Praxis der Transitgewährung und der Berlin-Verkehr (Frankfurt/Main: Athenäum-Verlag, 1973).

was made by this writer to include the "exclaves" of West Berlin.[42] The idea, as it was originally conceived, was to propose to the Soviets a trade of some of those uninhabited discontiguous areas situated on the perimeter of the old German capital for a Western-owned land corridor to Steinstücken, the only permanently inhabited one.[43] This would make it possible for some 190 Steinstücken residents to commute to their jobs in the city without having to pass through East German controls at each coming and going. The suggestion was accepted by the U.S. State Department, according to one high official, as "another card in the deck to test Soviet sincerety."[44]

It was against this background that the "Big Four" provided for a solution of the "problems of the small enclaves, including Steinstücken, and of the other small areas" by "an exchange of territory." A comprehensive agreement on this territorial swap was subsequently hammered out by Senatsdirektor *Müller* and State Secretary *Kohrt* and signed in East Berlin on December 20, 1971. In the main, it provided that:[45]

42 Technically, an exclave is a portion of one state completely surrounded by another and is seen from the viewpoint of the state to which it belongs. An enclave, on the other hand, is the same territory, only it is viewed from the point of view of the surrounding state. See Honoré M. Catudal, Jr., "The Exclave Problem in International Law," Revue de Droit International, Vol. 50, No. 1 (January-March, 1972), p. 21. G.W.S. Robinson calls Steinstücken and the other territorial fragments of Berlin "temporary exclaves" because they were created as a result of the division of what was one state "by an avowedly temporary or provisional line." See his article entitled "Exclaves," Annals of the Association of American Geographers, Vol. 49 (September, 1959), pp. 283-295.

43 The idea to trade some of the uninhabited exclaves for a corridor to Steinstücken had been proposed many times during the "cold war" by insecure Steinstückeners. But each time the suggestion was not taken seriously by Allied officials. See Honoré M. Catudal, Jr., Steinstücken: A Study in Cold War Politics (New York: Vantage Press, Inc., 1971), pp. 59-60.

44 Atlantic Standard, August 31, 1971. See also The Washington Post, January 2, 1972.

45 For the complete English text of the exclave agreement see Foreign Affairs Bulletin, Vol. 11, No. 35 (December 23, 1971), published by the Press and Information Department of the GDR. For a German text see Dokumentation Berlin: Die Vereinbarungen und das Abkommen (December, 1971), published by the West Berlin Senat.

(1) Six exclaves and one adjacent border territory — totalling about 15.5 hectares (about 39 acres) — were to be given by West Berlin to the GDR in exchange for two exclaves and two adjacent border areas — consisting altogether of about 17.1 hectares (approximately 42 acres), — the latter including a strip of territory one kilometer long and twenty meters wide (about 0.6 miles by 22 yards) with additional border areas, which was to serve as a land corridor to Steinstücken. (Article one.)

(2) Since complete equality in area and value of the territory to be exchanged was lacking, the Senat agreed to pay the government of the GDR monetary compensation in the amount of four million marks within two weeks of the exchange of territory. (Article two.)

(3) Property rights of natural persons or private juridical persons to land, buildings and installations in the areas exchanged would not be affected by the agreement; indemnity claims would be settled by the side on whose territory the land, buildings and installations were recorded prior to the exchange of territory. Other land, buildings and installations would be considered as having been transferred to the other side free from any encumbrances and with legally final effect. Any compensation claims between both sides arising therefrom would be considered settled by the payment under article two. (Article four.)

(4) Existing registers, deeds and other documents relating to the territories in question would be exchanged within three months of the signing of a final protocol. (This protocol was to be drawn up after the completion of a survey of the areas and was to form an integral part of the agreement.) (Article five.)

(5) Finally, further discussions with regard to the exclaves and other small areas not included in the agreement would take place at an appropriate time, and corresponding accords would be reached; in the meantime, the existing situation concerning the remaining exclaves and other territories would remain unchanged. (Article six.)

No doubt the little community of Steinstücken gained the most from the swap of territory. For it is no longer completely isolated in the GDR, and it now has utilities administered by West Berlin. But the trade also represents a considerable improvement in the daily lives of the twelve permanent inhabitants of Eiskeller, a border territory belonging to the District of Spandau (British Sector) but which was previously almost entirely cut off from the rest of Berlin. Access to it has been broadened considerably by the cession of a strip of East German territory. Lastly, the agreement brings to the city that part of Frohnau Cemetery which previously lay in the GDR — an important improvement for those West Berliners who have relatives buried there.[46]

These arrangements are primarily of local interest. Nevertheless, they also have political and legal importance. For instance, geographical charts defining the boundaries established by the exchange of territories distinguish between borderlines of Berlin vis-a-vis the GDR and borderlines of West Berlin vis-à-vis East Berlin. This practice would seem to imply that there are areas (i.e. East Berlin) which are not part of the GDR.[47]

Improvements in External Communication

Part II (Section C) and Annex III of the Quadripartite Agreement provide for the expansion of external communications between West Berlin and the surrounding East German region. Specifically, they call for improvements in "telephonic, telegraphic, transport and other external communications." Again detailed arrangements implementing and supplementing this provision were left to be settled by "competent German authorities."

Subsequently, the heads of delegations from East and West German Postal and Telecommunications Ministries signed in East Berlin on September 30, 1971 a protocol on postal services and telecommunications and an agreement on the setting up of a color television relay system between the two states. Among other things, these accords provide that:[48]

46 For an analysis see Honoré M. Catudal, Jr., "Berlin's New Boundaries," Cahiers de Géographie de Québec, Vol. 18, No. 43 (April, 1974), pp. 213-226.

47 In addition, representatives of the Senat and the GDR signed on July 21, 1972 another arrangement concerning the territory surrounding the former Potsdam railway station; this constitutes part of the agreement concluded on December 20, 1971.

48 For the text of these agreements see The Bulletin (October 2, 1971), published by the Federal Press and Information Office.

(1) An agreement concluded on April 29, 1970, whereby the West German government consented to pay East German authorities an annual lump sum, totalling thirty million marks as compensation for the cost of inner-German postal communications, would be extended to 1976. For the period prior to that covered by the 1970 agreement, a lump sum of two hundred and fifty million marks would be paid as compensation, this sum fully covering East German indemnity claims against the West Berlin Senat.

(2) The number of telephone lines between East and West Germany was to be increased by thirty lines in each direction by the end of December 1971 and by an additional sixteen lines by March 31, 1972; in the case of telephone lines to and from West Berlin, sixty more lines in each direction were to be brought into operation by December 15, 1971, in addition to the existing fifteen in each direction. By December 31, 1974 subscriber trunk dialing would be gradually installed between East and West Germany, and a partial introduction of the system was also foreseen for telephone links with West Berlin.

(3) Communications by telex and telegram would be improved and a more rapid delivery of letters and parcels would be made by East German officials.

(4) Finally, arrangements would be made for the transmission of television programs between East and West Germany, the relay system in question being also available for the exchange of programs between the radio and television organizations affiliated with Eurovision and Intervision.

The conclusion of these postal accords represented a significant improvement and expansion of telephone, telegraph and television communications between the FRG and the GDR and West Berlin and East Germany. They also represented the first settlement between respective German authorities as provided for by the Four-Power Agreement.

Increased Soviet Presence in West Berlin

One of the most controversial elements of the quadripartite accord has to do with those passages authorizing the establishment of a Soviet Consulate General in West Berlin. (See Part II,

Section D, Annex IV, Paragraph 3 and Agreed Minutes II.) From the very beginning, the Allies — in particular, the United States — were loathe to grant his concession to the Soviet Union. For one thing, there was the general apprehension about Soviet missions in the West, which are often viewed as centers of espionage. For another, there was concern that the creation of a Russian diplomatic presence in the Western Sectors would give added impetus to the communist contention concerning the "independent political entity" of West Berlin. However, in the end, the Western Three consented to the opening of the Consulate General as part of a quid pro quo, whereby the Kremlin agreed to tolerate the representation abroad of West Berlin by the FRG. According to Ambassador *Rush,* this step was taken because in seeking "a normalization of the situation in Berlin, we could not properly exclude the USSR from the Western Sectors."[49] In other words, a final settlement with the Soviets was contingent on redressing the imbalanced nature of the agreement, which involved substantial Soviet concessions but with fewer corresponding counter-concessions by the West.

The Allies were very careful in the Quadripartite Agreement to circumscribe the number of personnel, facilities and functions of the Soviet diplomatic agency. Moscow originally suggested that it should have a staff of some thirty people — roughly the number of applications made each day by West Berliners for visas to travel to the Soviet Union. But "in the interests of security," the total number of Soviet nationals was limited to twenty. In this connection, the USSR was permitted to take possession of certain property belonging to it in the Western Sectors either for utilization, sale or exchange.

The Western Three took great pains to make clear that the establishment of this office in no way alters the status of Berlin. Thus, they limited its activities purely to consular matters; at no time would it be allowed to involve itself in political affairs. The Allies informed the Soviets that they would continue their contact with the Embassy of the USSR in East Berlin on all political matters and on any question concerning the Allied administration of

49 Kenneth Rush, "Berlin: The Four-Power Agreement," in Department of State, Current Foreign Policy (Washington, D.C.: U.S. Government Printing Office, 1971), p. 7.

Berlin. It was understood that applicable Allied and German legislation and regulations would apply to the Consulate General. To underscore the point that it would be responsible to the Allies, the Western powers insisted that the Soviet Consulate General be accredited to the British, French and American Commandants — and not the West Berlin Senat.

By way of deflecting criticism of the Allied decision to allow the Soviets to open a Consulate General in West Berlin, Ambassador *Rush* attempted to explain things in the following way: "There is ... nothing unique about one of the Allies having a Consulate General in Berlin or, in fact, having one outside of its own Sector," he said. The "French Consulate General is located in the British Sector," for example. And the "British and French have had Consulates General in Berlin almost from the beginning of the occupation period. We now have a Consulate and are giving consideration to raising its status to equate with the other two."[50]

Besides permitting Moscow to establish a diplomatic presence in the Western Sectors, the Allies also authorized it to expand its unofficial commercial representation there. This included the setting up of an office of the Soviet Foreign Trade Association, the opening of bonded warehouses to provide storage and display for goods, the expansion of the activities of Intourist (the Soviet travel office) and the establishment of an office of the Soviet airline Aeroflot. As in the case of the Soviet Consulate General, regulations regarding personnel, facilities and functions of these commercial organizations in West Berlin are precisely defined.

Consultation Mechanism

One of the major concerns of the Western Three throughout the Four-Power negotiations was the workability of the agreement that was then taking shape. They realized that they could not resolve all the problems to everyone's satisfaction — thus the vague language in some parts of the text; but they wanted to provide a framework within which inevitable differences of opinion and

50 Kenneth Rush, "Berlin: The Four-Power Agreement," in Department of State, Current Foreign Policy (Washington, D.C.: U.S. Government Printing Office, 1971), p. 7.

questions of interpretation could be settled peacefully. In lieu of anything better, they held out for the insertion of a so-called "consultation clause."[51]

This mechanism is contained in paragraph four of the Final Protocol. It consists of unusually cumbersome language but in the main it gives any one of the "Big Four" the right, in case of difficulties in application or cases of nonimplementation of either the Quadripartite Agreement or the inner-German accords, to conduct consultations with the other three governments "in order to ensure the observance of the commitments undertaken and to bring the situation into conformity with the Quadripartite Agreement and this Protocol." According to *Kenneth Rush*, the Allies felt it necessary to provide such a mechanism to make as clear as possible "the linkage between the Quadripartite Agreement and the inner-German implementation arrangements" and to "leave no doubt that it is the Four Powers who are responsible for seeing that the entire package will be implemented correctly."[52]

Striking a Balance

Official response to the signing of the Final Protocol, like the diplomatic ovation following the initialing of the original document in 1971, was extremely favorable if not euphoric. As might be expected, opposition to it came mainly from the combined parliamentary factions of the Christian Democratic Union and Bavarian Social Union. But after years on the front many West Berliners were also highly sceptical. In this section, an attempt will be made to examine principle arguments against the Quadripartite Agreement raised by opponents and to evaluate the total East-West package.

51 Tomislav Mitrović, a Yugoslav international lawyer, argues that the existence of this provision points up the limited sovereignty of the FRG and the GDR. See his article "Das Berlin Abkommen, die Entspannung und die deutsche Einheit," Deutschland Archiv, Vol. 5 (1972).
52 Kenneth Rush, "Berlin: The Four-Power Agreement" in Department of State, Current Foreign Policy (Washington, D.C.: U.S. Government Printing Office, 1971), p. 6.

In the first place, critics allege that the legal and political status of Berlin has been undermined. By recognizing that West Berlin is not part of the Federal Republic and is not to be governed by it, the Four Powers have made it what the Soviets insisted all along — an "autonomous political entity." This is how West Berlin is officially referred to on the entry forms that visitors to East Berlin are now required to fill out.

Secondly, the reduction of the political presence of the Bonn government called for in the basic document further contributes to the erosion of the city's legal and political status. The agreement specifically forbids the further holding of plenary sessions of the Bundestag and Bundesrat in the Western Sectors. At the same time, the President of the FRG is forbidden to be elected again in what was once the capital of the German Reich. Moreover, the agreement declares unambiguously that the "provisions of the Basic Law of the Federal Republic of Germany and of the Constitution operative in the Western Sectors of Berlin which contradict the above have been suspended . . ." While East Berlin is to retain its unchallenged status as the capital of the GDR, West Berlin is no longer even in a symbolic sense to be part of the Federal Republic.

Thirdly, it is pointed out that the provisions pertaining to access contain "dangerous gaps." Specifically, the clauses governing exceptions and "misuse" give the other side pretexts for arbitrarily intervening in traffic and sabotaging the accord. In addition, regulations regarding surface transit depend on the continued bona fide cooperation of the USSR and the GDR. And past experience makes this improbable for any length of time.

Fourthly, even though West Berliners are able to cross the border, under the terms of the inner-German arrangements they are to be discriminated against. For they can only visit East Berlin and East Germany for thirty days in any year. This represents one-twelfth of the visiting rights enjoyed by West Germans and others and is a clear violation of the basic document of September 3, 1971, which specifically provides for "comparable" treatment.

Fifthly, East Germany is expressly included under its formal name in the Berlin agreement. References to it in the text as "the German Democratic Republic" represent de facto recognition of that régime. What was once regarded as provisional and abnormal is now to be viewed as permanent and normal.

Sixthly, nothing is said about the inhuman conditions along the boundaries of Berlin. The barded wire, fortifications, watchtowers and "death strip" remain. Furthermore, East German border guards can still shoot to kill all refugees trying to escape.

Lastly, but importantly, the Allies are accused of making a major concession to the USSR by granting it an unprecedented diplomatic presence in the Western Sectors. The establishment of the Soviet Consulate General represents a potential danger and may even lead to the quasi-quadripartite control over West Berlin.[53]

An Evaluation

As the intricate talks and the long, drawnout signing of the Berlin settlement make clear, negotiation is the continuation of confrontation by other means. Neither side was ready to abandon its long-range goals. For the West, this meant the hope of reconciling a divided Europe. For the Soviet Union, this meant the consolidation of the gains in empire and security it sought to reap from World War II. However, instead of trying to advance their respective aims by the force of arms, the great powers were satisfied in an atmosphere of détente with promoting their conceptions by diplomacy.

Seen in this context, it is obvious that any kind of agreement over Berlin would represent a quid pro quo, i.e. the granting of concessions by one side for counter-concessions. To the West, a major concern was maintaining the existing position, gaining acceptance of it by Moscow and obtaining practical improvements. For the USSR, which had long ago folded its Sector of East Berlin into its client state — the GDR, the immediate problem was to get the West to recognize East Germany and to agree to negotiate on just the Western Sectors. Both sides were pretty much successful in

53 These arguments against the quadripartite settlement have been compiled from the official statement by the CDU/CSU opposition, published in The German Tribune, September 23, 1971, and the article by Curtis Cate, "Is Berlin Our European Taiwan," National Review, April 14, 1972, pp. 400-403.

realizing their limited aims but only after being forced to cede something in return.

On the whole, the settlement is better than many in the West dared hope. Importantly, it recognizes the rights and responsibilities of the Four Powers for Berlin. Thus, it acknowledges the continued right of the Allies to stay in West Berlin. The old Soviet argument that the Western powers had forfeited their right to remain in the city has been effectively discarded.

No doubt the most important gain for the West deals with free transit through East Germany. On the one hand, access is of decisive psychological and practical importance. On the other, it is here that the isolated city is most vulnerable. Now for the first time there is quadripartite agreement governing civilian transit between West Germany and Berlin. Border controls, often tedious and irritating, have been greatly simplified — if all but eliminated.

The clauses relating to presumptive misuse of the access routes are somewhat flexible and would seem to be susceptible to manipulation by GDR officials. However, in case of infringement on the document, any one of the signatory governments has the right to call for the requisite quadripartite consultations to rectify the situation.

The opportunity afforded West Berliners to travel to East Berlin and the GDR after years of separation is significant. Although provisions of the inner-German arrangements are more restrictive than anticipated by the "Big Four," they nevertheless help to overcome some of the sinister effects of the Berlin Wall. Moreover, other technical improvements respecting communications, travel and exchanges of territory remove many irritations and lower tensions between the two parts of the city.

These gains made by the West, of course, had to be purchased with certain concessions to the East. Among the latter, probably most significant is the expanded presence of the Soviet Union in the Western Sectors. The establishment of a Soviet ConsulateGeneral was much feared by West Berliners, even though the Allies argue there is nothing unique about one of the Four Powers having a Consulate General in Berlin, or for that matter, having one outside its own Sector.

Another major Western concession entails the implied de facto recognition of the German Democratic Republic. However, this is not considered as serious a concession as would have been the case

274

a few years earlier. Ever since Chancellor *Brandt* stated on October 28, 1969 that the Federal government accepted the existence of the GDR as a second state within Germany, the two German states have been moving at a fast clip toward defining a new realitonship. This, in turn, has opened the way for widespread recognition of East Germany by the West.

The provisions describing West Berlin's relationship with the Federal Republic are the result of a key compromise. The Soviets agreed to accept the right of the FRG to represent West Berlin in international organizations and agreements and to provide consular services for local residents (rights long contested by the communists). Furthermore, they consented to the city's de facto economic, financial and social ties with West Germany — indeed these links may even be developed — but not some of its political and legal bonds. For their part, the Allies — while maintaining the right of Federal authorities to travel to Berlin and hold meetings there — agreed to cut back the West German demonstrative presence. From the Allied point of view, the acknowledgment that the Western Sectors "continue not to be a constituent part of the Federal Republic of Germany and not to be governed by it" marks no actual change from past practice. It should be noted, however, that as subsequent events have shown the limitations put on the Federal presence in Berlin are not free from ambiguities.

CONCLUSION

Since the implementation of the Quadripartite Agreement in June 1972, Berlin has entered a new phase in East-West relations. Once a city of perpetual crisis, it is taking on significance as a symbol of a new form of balanced interests in Europe. To be sure, the insolated city remains as vulnerable as ever to sudden changes in East-West relations — as recent events have demonstrated once again. Nevertheless, times have changed, and inhabitents, formerly on the front of the "cold war," have become accustomed in the last five years and more to the pleasant effects of détente.

To some extent, recent media reports about a major clash between East and West over the interpretation of specific provisions of the accord have obscured the many practical improvements which have made the life of Berliners much easier and defused the city of much of its explosive potential. In some quarters, one even hears charges of a "breach of faith" by one side or the other. Actually, the dispute over interpretation is not new. Rather, as this writer has tried to show, it has its roots in the nature of the "trade-offs" surrounding the conclusion of the final settlement.

One high-level Allied official, looking back on the experiences of the last five years, puts the conflict in the context of "general as opposed to local concessions" that had to be made to bring about the Quadripartite Agreement: "To get détente really moving, the Soviets realized they had to agree to a QA which would have solid benefits in it to the West. They obviously bit the bullet on this." The chief benefit to the West was "the liberalized and guaranteed access rights." But once "the basic extra-QA concession was made, the localized horse-trading began, with each side intent on securing language as unprejudicial (sic.) as possible to its own deeply-held (and still maintained) positions on Berlin." This accounts "for the fact that despite what the QA itself says about ties, foreign representation, invitations, etc., the Soviets continue to argue the case about the same way they always did when there are specific manifestations they don't like." With few exceptions, the Soviets "have not interfered with or permitted the GDR to interfere with access arrangements. But they have been pretty consistent in following what one could call a pre-QA pattern with respect to the various other things covered by the agreement. There is nothing surprising in this, just as there is nothing surprising in our continuing to argue our own point of view."

This analysis, which puts the agreement in the proper political perspective, also points up what may be one of the most important elements in any evaluation of the accord. Namely, that in the last analysis, an assessment must rise above the local context and take into account the impact of the agreement on European politics. In this respect, it is largely responsible for allowing the FRG to continue to pursue its *Ostpolitik* and the normalization of relations between the two Germanies. At the same time, it has cleared the way for negotiations about the control and limitation of forces and armaments in Central Europe and laid the foundation for closer cooperation between East and West.

But if the Berlin Agreement was largely responsible for getting détente moving, it is now taking on a new role as the barometer of détente. And it is this new role which ultimately will demonstrate its worth in this new era of East-West politics.

276

APPENDIX I

"Western and Soviet Draft Proposals of Quadripartite Agreement"

Western Draft
February 5, 1971

Soviet Draft
March 26, 1971

Preamble:

. . . practical improvements consistent with the wishes of the inhabitants . . .

Part I:
General Provisions

Part II:
Provisions relating to

the Western Sectors of Berlin (WSB)
A. Civilian Access on Surface Routes
1. Surface traffic by road, rail and waterways between the WSB and the FRG for all persons and goods shall be unhindered and on a preferential basis.
2. . . .
3. . . .
4. In order to deal quickly and effectively with any hindrances, complications, or delays in such movement, arrangements shall be maintained for consultation in Berlin between representatives of the Four Powers.
5. Detailed arrangements . . . are set forth in Annex I. Measures to implement them will be agreed between the appropriate German authorities.
B. Communications within the City and its Environs
. . . .

Berlin (West)
1. Berlin (West) is not a part of the FRG and is not governed by it . . .
The relations between Berlin (West) and the FRG must not contradict this.
2. The maintenance and development of vital links and contacts between Berlin (West) and the outside world in the economic, scientific, technical, cultural, and other peaceful fields shall be facilitated. This presupposes in particular, that agreements concerning civilian transit will be concluded between the authorities, so that this transit will be carried out on the basis of customary international norms and without interruption.
3. (Visits in the GDR)
. . . .

277

(Written Soviet communication to the three Western ambassadors on arrangements concerning civilian access on surface routes)

(Letter from the three powers to the USSR)

1. . . . the three powers state that the Federal President, the Federal Government, the Bundestag and the Bundesrat as well as their committees and Fraktionen, the Bundesversammlung or other Federal or Länder governmental institutions of the FRG are not to perform in Berlin (West) any official acts or activities which would signify extension of their competence to Berlin (West)

. . . .

2. Links between Berlin (West) and the FRG, including those of nongovernmental nature, will be maintained in accordance with the fact that Berlin (West) is not part of the FRG and cannot be governed by it.

Annex II:

(Soviet communication to the three Western ambassadors on detailed arrangements concerning communication within the city and its environs)

(Communication from the government of the USSR to the governments of the three powers concerning civilian transit)

Annex III:

(Written Western communication to the Soviet ambassador concerning the relationship between the WSB and the FRG)

1. In exerci   of their supreme authority, the three governments determine the nature and the extent of the relationship between the WSB and the FRG. They approve special ties between the WSB and the FRG.

2. They state that the WSB are not to be regarded a Land of the FRG and are not governed by it . . .

(Communication from the government of the USSR to the governments of the three powers concerning visits in the GDR)

3. Constitutional organs of the FRG, ..., will not perform official constitutional acts in the WSB. The Bundesversammlung will not be held in the WSB.

4. In exercise of and without prejudice to their supreme authority the three governments have authorized the FRG to ensure the representation abroad of the WSB and their inhabitants. Such representation includes, inter alia, a) consular matters and the issue ... of Federal German passports ... stamped in appropriate manner; b) inclusion of the WSB in international agreements and obligations of the FRG as authorized by the three governments.

....

Annex IV:

(Representation of the interests of Berlin (West) abroad)

A. The governments of France, the UK and the US ... inform the Soviet government ... that, in accordance with the rights and responsibilities in Berlin (West), they will continue to exercise their competence in matters concerning relations between Berlin (West) and other states ... Without prejudice to their competence and to quadripartite agreements, they consider it possible:

1. for the FRG to assume consular services for permanent residents of Berlin (West)

2. to extend to Berlin (West) subject to established procedures, the application of treaties ... concluded between FRG and other countries ...

B. (Soviet reply)

Annex V:

(Soviet interests in Berlin (West))

Final

Quadripartite Protocol	Act
. . . .	1. This act brings into force the agreement.
	2. The Four Powers proceed from the premise that the agreements and settlements concluded between the German authorities will enter into force simultaneously with the agreement between the USSR, France, the UK and the US.

APPENDIX II

"Quadripartite Agreement on Berlin of September 3, 1971"[1]

The Governments of the United States of America, the French Republic, the Union of Soviet Socialist Republics and the United Kingdom of Great Britain and Nothern Ireland,

Represented by their Ambassadors, who held a series of meetings in the building formerly occupied by the Allied Control Council in the American Sector of Berlin,

Acting on the basis of their quadripartite rights and responsibilities, and of the corresponding wartime and postwar agreements and decisions of the Four Powers, which are not affected,

Taking into account the existing situation in the relevant area,

Guided by the desire to contribute to practical improvements of the situation,

Without prejudice to their legal positions,

Have agreed on the following:

1   U.S. Department of State, "Berlin: The Four-Power Agreement," Current Foreign Policy (Washington, D.C.: U.S. Government Printing Office, 1971), pp. 13-14. Letter from FRG Chancellor to three Ambassadors supplied by Federal Press and Information Office.

Part I
General Provisions

1.   The four Governments will strive to promote the elimination of tension and the prevention of complications in the relevant area.

2.   The four Governments, taking into account their obligations under the Charter of the United Nations, agree that there shall be no use or threat of force in the area and that disputes shall be settled solely by peaceful means.

3.   The four Governments will mutually respect their individual and joint rights and responsibilities, which remain unchanged.

4.   The four Governments agree that, irrespective of the differences in legal views, the situation which has developed in the area, and as it is defined in this Agreement as well as in the other agreements referred to in this Agreement, shall not be changed unilaterally.

Part II
Provisions Relating to the Western Sectors
of Berlin

A.   The Government of the Union of Soviet Socialist Republics declares that transit traffic by road, rail and waterways through the territory of the German Democratic Republic of civilian persons and goods between the Western Sectors of Berlin and the Federal Republic of Germany will be unimpeded; that such traffic will be facilitated so as to take place in the most simple and expeditious manner; and that it will receive preferential treatment.

Detailed arrangements concerning this civilian traffic, as set forth in Annex I, will be agreed by the competent German authorities.

B.   The Governments of the French Republic, the United Kingdom and the United States of America declare that the ties between the Western Sectors of Berlin and the Federal Republic of Germany will be maintained and developed, taking into account that these Sectors continue not to be a constituent part of the Federal Republic of Germany and not to be governed by it.

Detailed arrangements concerning the relationship between the Western Sectors of Berlin and the Federal Republic of Germany are set forth in Annex II.

C. The Government of the Union of Soviet Socialist Republics declares that communications between the Western Sectors of Berlin and areas bordering on these Sectors and those areas of the German Democratic Republic which do not border on these Sectors will be improved. Permanent residents of the Western Sectors of Berlin will be able to travel to and visit such areas for compassionate, family, religious, cultural or commercial reasons, or as tourists, under conditions comparable to those applying to other persons entering these areas.

The problems of the small enclaves, including Steinstücken, and of other small areas may be solved by exchange of territory.

Detailed arrangements concerning travel, communications and the exchange of territory, as set forth in Annex III, will be agreed by the competent German authorities.

D. Representation abroad of the interests of the Western Sectors of Berlin and consular activities of the Union of Soviet Socialist Republics in the Western Sectors of Berlin can be exercised as set forth in Annex IV.

Part III
Final Provisions

This Quadripartite Agreement will enter into force on the date specified in a Final Quadripartite Protocol to be concluded when the measures envisaged in Part II of this Quadripartite Agreement and in its Annexes have been agreed.

DONE at the building formerly occupied by the Allied Control Council in the American Sector of Berlin this 3rd day of September 1971, in four originals, each in the English, French and Russian languages, all texts being equally authentic.

Annex I
Communication from the Government
of the Union of Soviet Socialist Republics to the
Governments of the French Republic,
the United Kingdom and the United States of America

The Government of the Union of Soviet Socialist Republics, with reference to Part II (A) of the Quadripartite Agreement of

282

this date and after consultation and agreement with the Government of the German Democratic Republic, has the honor to inform the Governments of the French Republic, the United Kingdom and the United States of America that:

1. Transit traffic by road, rail and waterways through the territory of the German Democratic Republic of civilian persons and goods between the Western Sectors of Berlin and the Federal Republic of Germany will be facilitated and unimpeded. It will receive the most simple, expeditious and preferential treatment provided by international practice.

2. Accordingly,

(a) Conveyances sealed before departure may be used for the transport of civilian goods by road, rail and waterways between the Western Sectors of Berlin and the Federal Republic of Germany. Inspection procedures will be limited to the inspection of seals and accompanying documents.

(b) With regard to conveyances which cannot be sealed, such as open trucks, inspection procedures will be limited to the inspection of accompanying documents. In special cases where there is sufficient reason to suspect that unsealed conveyances contain either material intended for dissemination along the designated routes or persons or material put on board along these routes, the content of unsealed conveyances may be inspected. Procedures for dealing with such cases will be agreed by the competent German authorities.

(c) Through trains and buses may be used for travel between the Western Sectors of Berlin and the Federal Republic of Germany. Inspection procedures will not include any formalities other than identification of persons.

(d) Persons identified as through travellers using individual vehicles between the Western Sectors of Berlin and the Federal Republic of Germany on routes designated for through traffic will be able to proceed to their destinations without paying individual tolls and fees for the use of the transit routes. Procedures applied for such travellers shall not involve delay. The travellers, their vehicles and personal baggage will not be subject to search, detention or exclusion from use of the designated routes, except in special cases, as may be agreed by the competent German authorities, where there is sufficient reason to suspect that misuse of the transit routes is intended for purposes not related to direct travel to and from the Western Sectors of Berlin and contrary to generally applicable regulations concerning public order.

(e) Appropriate compensation for fees and tolls and for other costs related to traffic on the communication routes between the Western Sectors of Berlin and the Federal Republic of Germany, including the maintenance of adequate routes, facilities and installations used for such traffic, may be made in the form of an annual lump sum paid to the German Democratic Republic by the Federal Republic of Germany.

3.   Arrangements implementing and supplementing the provisions of paragraphs 1 and 2 above will be agreed by the competent German authorities.

Annex II
Communication from the Governments of the French Republic, the United Kingdom and the United States of America to the Government of the Union of Soviet Socialist Republics

The Governments of the French Republic, the United Kingdom and the United States of America, with reference to Part II (B) of the Quadripartite Agreement of this date and after consultation with the Government of the Federal Republic of Germany, have the honor to inform the Government of the Union of Soviet Socialist Republics that:

1.   They declare, in the exercise of their rights and responsibilities, that the ties between the Western Sectors of Berlin and the Federal Republic of Germany will be maintained and developed, taking into account that these Sectors continue not to be a constituent part of the Federal Republic of Germany and not to be governed by it. The provisions of the Basic Law of the Federal Republic of Germany and of the Constitution operative in the Western Sectors of Berlin which contradict the above have been suspended and continue not to be in effect.

2.   The Federal President, the Federal Government, the Bundesversammlung, the Bundesrat and the Bundestag, including their Committees and Fraktionen, as well as other state bodies of the Federal Republic of Germany will not perform in the Western Sectors of Berlin constitutional or official acts which contradict the provisions of paragraph 1.

3.   The Government of the Federal Republic of Germany will be represented in the Western Sectors of Berlin to the authorities of the three Governments and to the Senat by a permanent liaison agency.

Annex III
Communication from the Government of the Union
of Soviet Socialist Republics to the Governments
of the French Republic, the United Kingdom
and the United States of America

The Government of the Union of Soviet Socialist Republics, with reference to Part II (C) of the Quadripartite Agreement of this date and after consultation and agreement with the Government of the German Democratic Republic, has the honor to inform the Governments of the French Republic, the United Kingdom and the United States of America that:

1. Communications between the Western Sectors of Berlin and areas bordering on these Sectors and those areas of the German Democratic Republic which do not border on these Sectors will be improved.

2. Permanent residents of the Western Sectors of Berlin will be able to travel to and visit such areas for compassionate, family, religious, cultural or commercial reasons, or as tourists, under conditions comparable to those applying to other persons entering these areas. In order to facilitate visits and travel, as described above, by permanent residents of the Western Sectors of Berlin, additional crossing points will be opened.

3. The problems of the small enclaves, including Steinstücken, and of other small areas may be solved by exchange of territory.

4. Telephonic, telegraphic, transport and other external communications of the Western Sectors of Berlin will be expanded.

5. Arrangements implementing and supplementing the provisions of paragraphs 1 to 4 above will be agreed by the competent German authorities.

Annex IV
A
Communication from the Governments
of the French Republic, the United Kingdom
and the United States of America to the
Government of the Union of Soviet Socialist Republics

The Governments of the French Republic, the United Kingdom and the United States of America, with reference to Part II (D) of the Quadripartite Agreement of this date and after consultation with the Government of the Federal Republic of Germany, have the honor to inform the Government of the Union of Soviet Socialist Republics that:

1. The Governments of the French Republic, the United Kingdom and the United States of America maintain their rights and responsibilities relating to the representation abroad of the interests of the Western Sectors of Berlin and their permanent residents, including those rights and responsibilities concerning matters of security and status, both in international organizations and in relations with other countries.

2. Without prejudice to the above and provided that matters of security and status are not affected, they have agreed that:

(a) The Federal Republic of Germany may perform consular services for permanent residents of the Western Sectors of Berlin.

(b) In accordance with established procedures, international agreements and arrangements entered into by the Federal Republic of Germany may be extended to the Western Sectors of Berlin provided that the extension of such agreements and arrangements is specified in each case.

(c) The Federal Republic of Germany may represent the interests of the Western Sectors of Berlin in international organizations and international conferences.

(d) Permanent residents of the Western Sectors of Berlin may participate jointly with participants from the Federal Republic of Germany in international exchanges and exhibitions. Meetings of international organizations and international conferences as well as exhibitions with international participation may be held in the Western Sectors of Berlin. Invitations will be issued by the Senat or jointly by the Federal Republic of Germany and the Senat.

3. The three Governments authorize the establishment of a Consulate General of the USSR in the Western Sectors of Berlin accredited to the appropriate authorities of the three Governments in accordance with the usual procedures applied in those Sectors, for the purpose of performing consular services, subject to provisions set forth in a separate document of this date.

B

Communication from the Government of the Union
of Soviet Socialist Republics to the Governments of the
French Republic, the United Kingdom
and the United States of America

The Government of the Union of Soviet Socialist Republics, with reference to Part II (D) of the Quadripartite Agreement of this date and to the communication of the Governments of the French Republic, the United Kingdom and the United States of America with regard to the representation abroad of the interests of the Western Sectors of Berlin and their permanent residents, has the honor to inform the Governments of the French Republic, the United Kingdom and the United States of America that:

1. The Government of the Union of Soviet Socialist Republics takes note of the fact that the three Governments maintain their rights and responsibilities relating to the representation abroad of the interests of the Western Sectors of Berlin and their permanent residents, including those rights and responsibilities concerning matters of security and status, both in international organizations and in relations with other countries.

2. Provided that matters of security and status are not affected, for its part it will raise no objection to:

(a) the performance by the Federal Republic of Germany of consular services for permanent residents of the Western Sectors of Berlin;

(b) in accordance with established procedures, the extension to the Western Sectors of Berlin of international agreements and arrangements entered into by the Federal Republic of Germany provided that the extension of such agreements and arrangements is specified in each case;

(c) the representation of the interests of the Western Sectors of Berlin by the Federal Republic of Germany in international organizations and international conferences;

(d) the participation jointly with participants from the Federal Republic of Germany of permanent residents of the Western Sectors of Berlin in international exchanges and exhibitions, or the holding in those Sectors of meetings of international organizations and international conferences as well as exhibitions with international participation, taking into account that invitations will be issued by the Senat or jointly by the Federal Republic of Germany and the Senat.

3. The Government of the Union of Soviet Socialist Republics takes note of the fact that the three Governments have given their consent to the establishment of a Consulate General of the USSR in the Western Sectors of Berlin. It will be accredited to the appropriate authorities of the three Governments, for purposes and subject to provisions described in their communication and as set forth in a separate document of this date.

Agreed Minute I[2]

It is understood that permanent residents of the Western Sectors of Berlin shall, in order to receive at appropriate Soviet offices visas for entry into the Union of Soviet Socialist Republics, present:

(a) a passport stamped "Issued in accordance with the Quadripartite Agreement of September, 1971";

(b) an identiy card or other appropriately drawn up document confirming that the person requesting the visa is a permanent resident of the Western Sectors of Berlin and containing the bearer's full address and a personal photograph.

During his stay in the Union of Soviet Socialist Republics, a permanent resident of the Western Sectors of Berlin who has received a visa in this way may carry both documents or either of them, as he chooses. The visa issued by a Soviet office will serve as the basis for entry into the Union of Soviet Socialist Republics, and the passport or identity card will serve as the basis for consular services in accordance with the Quadripartite Agreement during the stay of that person in the territory of the Union of Soviet Socialist Republics.

The above-mentioned stamp will appear in all passports used by permanent residents of the Western Sectors of Berlin for journeys to such countries as may require it.

September 3, 1971

Protocole n⁰ I

Il est entendu que les résidents permanents des secteurs occidentaux de Berlin, pour obtenir dans les services soviétiques compétents des visas d'entrée en Union des Républiques Socialistes Soviétiques, présenteront:

a) un passeport muni du cachet: "Délivré en conformité de l'Accord Quadripartite du 3 Septembre 1971".

b) une carte d'identité ou un autre document dûment établi, confirmant que la personne sollicitant le visa est un résident permanent des secteurs occidentaux de Berlin et contenant l'adresse complète du porteur et sa photographie personnelle.

2 Initialed by the four Ambassadors on September 3, 1971.

288

Pendant leur séjour en Union des Républiques Socialistes Soviétiques les résidents permanents des secteurs occidentaux de Berlin qui ont obtenu un visa selon ces procédures peuvent disposer à leur convenance des deux documents ou de l'un d'entre eux. Le visa délivré par un service soviétique servira de titre pour l'entrée en Union des Républiques Socialistes Soviétiques, tandis que le passeport ou la carte d'identité servira de titre pour les services consulaires, conformément à l'Accord Quadripartite, pendant le séjour de ces personnes sur le territoire de l'Union des Républiques Socialistes Soviétiques.

Le cachet ci-dessus mentionné figurera sur tous les passeports utilisés par les résidents permanents des secteurs occidentaux de Berlin pour voyager dans les pays qui l'exigeraient.

le 3 septembre 1971

Agreed Minute II[3]

Provision is hereby made for the establishment of a Consulate General of the USSR in the Western Sectors of Berlin. It is understood that the details concerning this Consulate General will include the following. The Consulate General will be accredited to the appropriate authorities of the three Governments in accordance with the usual procedures applying in those Sectors. Applicable Allied and German legislation and regulations will apply to the Consulate General. The activities of the Consulate General will be of a consular character and will not include political functions or any matters related to quadripartite rights or responsibilities.

The three Governments are willing to authorize an increase in Soviet commercial activities in the Western Sectors of Berlin as described below. It is understood that pertinent Allied and German legislation and regulations will apply to these activities. This authorization will be extended indefinitely, subject to compliance with the provisions outlined herein. Adequate provision for consultation will be made. This increase will include establishment of an "Office of Soviet Foreign Trade Associations in the Western Sectors of Berlin", with commercial status, authorized to buy and sell on behalf of foreign trade associations of the Union of Soviet

3 Initialed by the four Ambassadors on September 3, 1971.

Socialist Republics. Soyuzpushnina, Prodintorg and Novoexport may each establish a bonded warehouse in the Western Sectors of Berlin to provide storage and display for their goods. The activities of the Intourist office in the British Sector of Berlin may be expanded to include the sale of tickets and vouchers for travel and tours in the Union of Soviet Socialist Republics and other countries. An office of Aeroflot may be established for the sale of passenger tickets and air freight services.

The assignment of personnel to the Consulate General and to permitted Soviet commercial organizations will be subject to agreement with the appropriate authorities of the three Governments. The number of such personnel will not exceed twenty Soviet nationals in the Consulate General; twenty in the office of the Soviet Foreign Trade Associations; one each in the bonded warehouses; six in the Intourist office; and five in the Aeroflot office. The personnel of the Consulate General and of permitted Soviet commercial organizations and their dependents may reside in the Western Sectors of Berlin upon individual authorization.

The property of the Union of Soviet Socialist Republics at Lietzenburgerstrasse 11 and at Am Sandwerder 1 may be used for purposes to be agreed between appropriate representatives of the three Governments and of the Government of the Union of Soviet Socialist Republics.

Details of implementation of the measures above and a time schedule for carrying them out will be agreed between the four Ambassadors in the period between the signature of the Quadripartite Agreement and the signature of the Final Quadripartite Protocol envisaged in that Agreement.

September 3, 1971

Final Quadripartite Protocol

The Governments of the United States of America, the French Republic, the Union of Soviet Socialist Republics and the United Kingdom of Great Britain and Northern Ireland,

Having in mind Part III of the Quadripartite Agreement of September 3, 1971, and taking note with satisfaction of the fact the agreements and arrangements mentioned below have been concluded,

Have agreed on the following:

1. The four Governments, by virtue of this Protocol, bring into force the Quadripartite Agreement, which, like this Protocol, does not affect quadripartite agreements or decisions previously concluded or reached.

2. The four Governments proceed on the basis that the agreements and arrangements concluded between the competent German authorities (list of agreements and arrangements) shall enter into force simultaneously with the Quadripartite Agreement.

3. The Quadripartite Agreement and the consequent agreements and arrangements of the competent German authorities referred to in this Protocol settle important issues examined in the course of the negotiations and shall remain in force together.

4. In the event of a difficulty in the application of the Quadripartite Agreement or any of the above-mentioned agreements or arrangements which any of the four Governments considers serious, or in the event of non-implementation of any part thereof, that Government will have the right to draw the attention of the other three Governments to the provisions of the Quadripartite Agreement and this Protocol and to conduct the requisite quadripartite consultations in order to ensure the observance of the commitments undertaken and to bring the situation into conformity with the Quadripartite Agreement and this Protocol.

5. This Protocol enters into force on the date of signature.

DONE at the building formerly occupied by the Allied Control Council in the American Sector of Berlin this day of 1971, in four originals, each in the English, French and Russian languages, all texts being equally authentic.

For the Government of the United States of America: (K. R.)

For the Government of the French Republic: (J. S.)

For the Government of the Union of Soviet Socialist Republics: (P. A.)

For the Government of the United Kingdom of Great Britain and Nothern Ireland: (R. J.)

September 3, 1971

Exchange of Notes

Note from the three Ambassadors to the Ambassador of the U.S.S.R.[4]

The Ambassadors of the French Republic, the United Kingdom of Great Britain and Northern Ireland and the United States of America have the honor, with reference to the statements contained in Annex II of the Quadripartite Agreement to be signed on this date concerning the relationship between the Federal Republic of Germany and the Western Sectors of Berlin, to inform the Ambassador of the Union of Soviet Socialist Republics of their intention to send to the Chancellor of the Federal Republic of Germany immediately following signature of the Quadripartite Agreement a letter containing clarifications and interpretations which represent the understanding of their Governments of the statements contained in Annex II of the Quadripartite Agreement. A copy of the letter to be sent to the Chancellor of the Federal Republic of Germany is attached to this Note.

The Ambassadors avail themselves of this opportunity to renew to the Ambassador of the Union of Soviet Socialist Republics the assurances of their highest consideration.

September 3, 1971

Jean Sauvagnargues

Roger Jackling

Kenneth Rush

4 Handed to the Ambassador of the U.S.S.R. prior to the signing of the agreement.

His Excellency
The Chancellor of the
Federal Republic of Germany,
Bonn.

Your Excellency:

With reference to the Quadripartite Agreement signed on September 3, 1971, our Governments wish by this letter to inform the Government of the Federal Republic of Germany of the following clarifications and interpretations of the statements contained in Annex II, which was the subject of consultation with the Government of the Federal Republic of Germany during the quadripartite negotiations.

These clarifications and interpretations represent the understanding of our Governments of this part of the Quadripartite Agreement, as follows:

a. The phrase in Paragraph 2 of Annex II of the Quadripratite Agreement which reads: " . . . will not perform in the Western Sectors of Berlin constitutional or official acts which contradict the provisions of Paragraph 1" shall be interpreted to mean acts in exercise of direct state authority over the Western Sectors of Berlin.

b. Meetings of the Bundesversammlung will not take place and plenary sessions of the Bundesrat and the Bundestag will continue not to take place in the Western Sectors of Berlin. Single committees of the Bundesrat and the Bundestag may meet in the Western Sectors of Berlin in connection with maintaining and developing the ties between those Sectors and the Federal Republic of Germany. In the case of Fraktionen, meetings will not be held simultaneously.

c. The liaison agency of the Federal Government in the Western Sectors of Berlin includes departments charged with liaison functions in their respective fields.

d. Established procedures concerning the applicability to the Western Sectors of Berlin of legislation of the Federal Republic of Germany shall remain unchanged.

e. The term "state bodies" in Paragraph 2 of Annex II shall be interpreted to mean: the Federal President, the Federal Chancellor,

5 The letter was delivered to the Chancellor of the Federal Republic of Germany on Sept. 3.

293

the Federal Cabinet, the Federal Ministers and Ministries, and the branch offices of those Ministries, the Bundesrat and the Bundestag, and all Federal courts.

Accept, Excellency, the renewed assurance of our highest esteem.

For the Government of the French Republic: (J. S.)
For the Government of the United Kingdom of Great Britain and Nothern Ireland: (R. J.)
For the Government of the United States of America: (K. R.)

Reply from the Ambassador of the U.S.S.R.[6]

Translation

The Ambassador of the Union of Soviet Socialist Republics has the honor to acknowledge receipt of the note of the Ambassadors of the French Republic, the United Kingdom of Great Britain and Northern Ireland, and the United States of America, dated September 3, 1971, and takes cognizance of the communication of the three Ambassadors.

The Ambassador avails himself of this opportunity to renew to the Ambassadors of the French Republic, the United Kingdom, and the United States of America the assurance of his very high consideration.

September 3, 1971.   *Pyotr A. Abrasimov.*

France — U.S. — U.K. Letter to the Chancellor of the Federal Republic of Germany
September 3, 1971.

His Excellency
The Chancellor of the
Federal Republic of Germany,
Bonn.

Your Excellency: We have the honor by means of this letter to convey to the Government of the Federal Republic of Germany the text of the Quadripartite Agreement signed this day in Berlin.

6 Handed by the Ambassador of the U.S.S.R. to the three Ambassadors prior to the signing of the agreement.

The Quadripartite Agreement was concluded by the Four Powers in the exercise of their rights and responsibilities with respect to Berlin.

We note that, pursuant to the terms of the Agreement and of the Final Quadripartite Protocol which ultimately will bring it into force, the text of which has been agreed, these rights and responsibilities are not affected and remain unchanged. Our Governments will continue, as heretofore, to exercise supreme authority in the Western Sectors of Berlin, within the framework of the Four Power responsibility which we share for Berlin as a whole.

In accordance with Part II (A) of the Quadripartite Agreement, arrangements implementing and supplementing the provisions relating to civilian traffic will be agreed by the competent German authorities. Part III of the Quadripartite Agreement provides that the Agreement will enter into force on a date to be specified in a Final Quadripartite Protocol which will be concluded when the arrangements envisaged between the competent German authorities have been agreed. It is the request of our Governments that the envisaged negotiations now take place between authorities of the Federal Republic of Germany, also acting on behalf of the Senat, and authorities of the German Democratic Republic.

Part II (B) and (D) and Annexes II and IV of the Quadripartite Agreement relate to the relationship between the Western Sectors of Berlin and the Federal Republic. In this connection, the following are recalled inter alia:

the communications of the three Western Military Governors to the Parliamentary Council of 2 March, 22 April and 12 May, 1949,

the letter of the three High Commissioners to the Federal Chancellor concerning the exercise of the reserved Allied rights relating to Berlin of 26 May 1952 in the version of the letter X of 23 October 1954,

the Aide Memoire of the three Governments of 18 April 1967 concerning the decision of the Federal Constitutional Court of 20 January 1966 in the Niekisch case.

Our Governments take this occasion to state, in exercise of the rights and responsibilities relating to Berlin, which they retained in Article 2 of the Convention on Relations between the Three Powers and the Federal Republic of Germany of 26 May 1952 as amended October 23, 1954, that Part II (B) and (D) and Annexes II and IV of the Quadripartite Agreement concerning the relationship between the Federal Republic of Germany and the Western Sectors of Berlin accord with the position in the above mentioned documents, which remains unchanged.

With regard to the existing ties between the Federal Republic and the Western Sectors of Berlin, it is the firm intention of our Governments that, as stated in Part II (B) (1) of the Quadripartite Agreement, these ties will be maintained and developed in accordance with the letter from the three High Commissioners to the Federal Chancellor on the exercise of the reserved rights relating to Berlin of 26 May 1952, in the version of letter X of October 23, 1954, and with pertinent decisions of the Allied Kommandatura of Berlin.

Accept, Excellency, the renewed assurance of our highest esteem.

For the Government of the French Republic:

Jean Sauvagnargues.

For the Government of the United Kingdom of Great Britain and Nothern Ireland:

Roger Jackling.

For the Government of the United States of America:

Kenneth Rush.

Communication From Allied Kommandatura to the Governing Mayor of Berlin

BKC/L(71)1 dated September 3

The Allied Kommandatura refers to the Quadripartite Agreement signed on September 3 in Berlin.

Part II (C) and Annex III, Paragraph 5 of the Quadripartite Agreement provide that arrangements implementing and supplementing the provisions relating to travel, communications and the exchange of territory will be agreed by the competent German authorities. Part IV of the Quadripartite Agreement provides that the Agreement will enter into force on a date to be specified in a Final Quadripartite Protocol which will be concluded when the arrangements envisaged between the competent German authorities have been agreed.

The Senat of Berlin is hereby authorized and requested to conduct appropriate negotiations on the subjects covered in Paragraphs 1, 2 and 3 in Annex III.

Letter of the Federal Chancellor in Reply
to the Three Ambassadors

Your Excellency:

I have the honour to confirm receipt of the letter of the Ambassadors of France, the United Kingdom and the United States of America of September 3 together with which the text of the Quadripartite Agreement signed on September 3, 1971, in Berlin was communicated to the Government of the Federal Republic of Germany.

I also have the honour to confirm receipt of the letter of the Three Ambassadors of the same date containing clarifications and interpretations which reflect what their Governments understand by the declarations contained in Annex II to the Quadripartite Agreement with regard to the relationship between the Federal Republic of Germany and the Western Sectors of Berlin.

The Government of the Federal Republic of Germany intends taking steps immediately in order to arrive at agreements on concrete arrangements relating to civilian traffic as envisaged in Part II A of the Quadripartite Agreement.

The Government of the Federal Republic of Germany has taken note of the contents of Your Excellency's letter which were communicated to it in exercising the rights and responsibilities which were retained in pursuance of Article 2 of the Convention on Relations between the Federal Republic of Germany and the Three Powers of May 26, 1952, as amended on October 23, 1954, and which will continue to be respected by the Government of the Federal Republic of Germany.

The Government of the Federal Republic of Germany shares the view and the determination that the ties between the Federal Republic of Germany and Berlin shall be maintained and developed. (Formal close)

APPENDIX III:

"Oral Statement on FRG Parliamentary Committee Meetings in West Berlin"[1]

"Gentleman's Agreement"

In an interview with the Süddeutsche Zeitung (Munich) on November 10, 1971, the British negotiator, Sir *Roger Jackling* (Ambassador of the United Kingdom in Bonn) interpreted parts of the agreement and discussed other points.

On "Federal presence" in Berlin, for example, the holding of Bundestag committee meetings in the city, Sir Roger said:

"This is specifically mentioned in the letter of three Ambassadors to the Federal Chancellor, which was communicated to the Soviet Ambassador at the time of signature. This speaks of "single committees" meeting in Berlin in connection with maintaining and developing the ties between the Western Sectors (of Berlin) and the Federal Republic of Germany. The meaning of the term "single" was discussed between the four Ambassadors during the negotiations. The Western Ambassadors stated — and the Soviet Ambassador agreed — that while committees would normally meet singly, they could also meet jointly or simultaneously when the subject matter under consideration made this appropriate. This solution was accepted by the Federal government, and is reflected in the publication they issued on the day of signature of the Quadripartite Agreement."

---

1 The Bulletin (Bonn), November 16, 1971. The oral statement by the British Ambassador with regard to the so-called "gentleman's agreement" on FRG parliamentary committees in West Berlin is, of course, of a different documentary nature than the other appendices included in this book. The statement should not necessarily be interpreted as reflecting the exact language of the original "understanding" if it does represent the essence of the agreement. See Gerhard Wettig, "Fünf Jahre Berlin-Abkommen — Eine Bilanz," Aus Politik und Zeigeschichte, Vol. 42 (October, 1976), pp. 3-46.

BIBLIOGRAPHY

This two-volume study has, for the most part, relied on primary sources. In the preparation of "The Diplomacy of the Quadripartite Agreement on Berlin: A New Era in East-West Politics" and "Five Years of the Quadripartite Agreement on Berlin: Has it worked?" the author has interviewed numerous Allied and German officials in Berlin and Bonn as well as in the capitals of the Western powers. Since much of the information provided him was on a "not for attribution" basis, the footnote citations and bibliography are not intended as sources but rather as references where the general reader and scholar alike can corroborate independently much of the material presented by this writer.

Official Publications

Berlin publications

Bericht über Durchführung des Viermächte-Abkommens und der ergänzenden Vereinbarungen zwischen dem 3. Juni 1972 und dem 31. Mai 1973. Berlin: Abgeordnetenhaus, 1973.

Bericht über Durchführung des Viermächte-Abkommens und der ergänzenden Vereinbarungen zwischen dem 1. Juni 1973 und dem 31. Mai 1974. Berlin: Abgeordnetenhaus, 1974.

Bericht über Durchführung des Viermächte-Abkommens und der ergänzenden Vereinbarungen zwischen dem 1. Juni 1974 und dem 31. Mai 1975. Berlin: Abgeordnetenhaus, 1975.

Bericht über Durchführung des Viermächte-Abkommens und der ergänzenden Vereinbarungen zwischen dem 1. Juni 1975 und dem 31. Mai 1976. Berlin: Abgeordnetenhaus, 1976.

Bericht über Durchführung des Viermächte-Abkommens und der ergänzenden Vereinbarungen zwischen dem 1. Juni 1976 und dem 31. Mai 1977. Berlin: Abgeordnetenhaus, 1977.

Berlin: Anspruch und Leistung. Berlin: Press and Information Office, 1965.

Dokumentation Berlin: zur Anordnung der Regierung der DDR über die Durchführung eines verbindlichen Mindestumtausches vom 5. November 1973. Berlin: Press and Information Office, 1974.

Dokumentation Berlin: Die Vereinbarungen und das Abkommen. Berlin: Press and Information Office, 1971.

British publications

Berlin and the Problem of German Reunification. London: Central Office of Information, 1970.

FRG publications

Bericht zur Lage der Nation 1974. Bonn: Federal Ministry for Inner-German Relations, 1974.

The Basic Settlement: The Quadripartite Agreement on Berlin and the Supplementary Arrangements. Bonn: Federal Press and Information Office, 1972.

Berlin: Crisis and Challenge. Bonn: German Information Center (N.Y.), 1963.

Die Berlin-Regelung: Das Viermächte-Abkommen über Berlin und die ergänzenden Vereinbarungen. Bonn: Federal Press and Information Office, 1971.

Chronik 1961-1962: Der andere Teil Deutschlands in den Jahren 1961 bis 1962. Bonn: Federal Press and Information Office, 1969.

Documentation Relating to the Federal Government's Policy of Détente. Bonn: Federal Press and Information Office, 1973.

Die Entwicklung der Beziehungen zwischen der Bundesrepublik Deutschland und der Deutschen Demokratischen Republik: Bericht und Dokumentation. Melsungen: Verlagsbuchdruckerei A. Bernecker, 1973.

Erfurt March 19, 1970: A Documentation. Bonn: Federal Press and Information Office, 1973.

Kommentarübersicht. Bonn: Federal Press and Information Office, 1970.

SBZ von 1945-1960. 4 vols. Bonn: Federal Ministry of All-German Affairs, 1956-1964.

The State of the Nation, 1971. Bonn: Federal Ministry for Inner-German Relations, 1971.

Texte zur Deutschlandpolitik. Volume 9. Bonn: Federal Ministry for Inner-German Relations, 1972.

Treaty on the Basis of Relations between the Federal Republic of Germany and the German Democratic Republic. Bonn: Federal Press and Information Office, 1973.

The Treaty between the Federal Republic of Germany and the People's Republic of Poland. Bonn: Federal Press and Information Office, 1971.

The Treaty of August 12, 1970 between the Federal Republic of Germany and the Union of Soviet Socialist Republics. Bonn: Federal Press and Information Office, 1970.

Der Verkehrsvertrag zwischen der Bundesrepublik Deutschland und der Deutschen Demokratischen Republik vom 26. Mai 1972. Bonn: Federal Press and Information Office, 1972.

Verträge, Abkommen und Vereinbarungen zwischen der Bundesrepublik Deutschland und der Deutschen Demokratischen Republik. Bonn: Federal Press and Information Office, 1973.

Das Viermächte-Àbkommen über Berlin vom 3. September 1971. Bonn: Federal Press and Information Office, 1971.

U.S. Congressional publications

U.S. Senate, Documents on Germany, 1944-1970. Washington, D.C.: U.S. Government Printing Office, 1971.

U.S. Department of State publications

Berlin – 1961. Washington, D.C.: U.S. Government Printing Office, 1961.

Bulletin. Washington, D.C.: U.S. Government Printing Office, 1961-1976.

Conference on Security and Cooperation in Europe. Current Foreign Policy Series. Washington, D.C.: U.S. Government Printing Office, 1972.

The Soviet Note on Berlin: An Analysis. Washington, D.C.: U.S. Government Printing Office, 1958.

United States Foreign Policy: A Report of the Secretary of State. Washington, D.C.: U.S. Government Printing Office, 1972.

U.S. Mission (Berlin) publications

Berlin Accessways, Transportation, Communications and Utilities. 1st ed. Berlin: Economic Section, 1966.

Berlin Accessways, Transportation, Communications and Utilities. 2nd ed. Berlin: Economic Section, 1970.

Berlin Accessways, Transportation, Communications and Utilities, 1949-1976. 3rd ed. Berlin: Economic/Commercial Sections, 1976.

Post-War Berlin – An Unofficial Chronology. Berlin: USIA, 1961-1977.

Review of United States Aid to Berlin. Berlin: Economic Section, 1963.

Books

Adenauer, Konrad. Erinnerungen, 1959-1963. Stuttgart: Deutsche Verlags-Anstalt, 1968.

Akopov, G.M. Zapadnyi Berlin: Problemy i reshenija.. Moscow: International Relations Press, 1974.

Allardt, Helmut. Moskauer Tagebuch: Beobachtungen, Notizen, Erlebnisse. Düsseldorf: Econ Verlag, 1973.

An, Tai Sung. The Sino-Soviet Territorial Dispute. Philadelphia: Westminster Press, 1973.

Armstrong, Anne. Berliners: Both Sides of the Wall. New Brunswick: Rutgers University Press, 1973.

Arzinger, Rudolf et al. Westberlin – selbständige politische Einheit. East Berlin: 1965.

Bark, Dennis. Agreement on Berlin: A Study of the 1970-72 Quadripartite Negotiations, Washington, D.C.: American Enterprise Institute, 1974.
– : Die Berlin-Frage 1949-1955. Berlin: Walter de Gruyter Verlag, 1972.

Baumeister, Dieter, (ed.). Berlin Fibel: Berichte zur Lage der Stadt. Berlin: Berlin Verlag, 1975.

Baumeister, Dieter and *Zivier, Ernst R.* Die Status-Bestimmungen des Viermächte-Abkommens und die Zukunft Berlins. Berlin: Kuratorium Unteilbares Deutschland, 1973.

Bender, Peter. Offensive Entspannung: Möglichkeit für Deutschland. Cologne: Kiepenheuer & Witsch, 1964.

— : Die Ostpolitik Willy Brandts oder die Kunst des Selbstverständlichen. Reinbek: 1972.

Berger, Alfred. Berlin von 1945 bis 1963. Munich: 1963.

Binder, David. The Other German: Willy Brandt's Life and Times. Washington, D.C.: The New Republic Co., 1975.

Bird, Eugene K. Prisoner No. 7: Rudolf Hess. New York: The Viking Press, 1974.

Birnbaum, Karl E. East and West Germany: A Modus Vivendi. Farnborough, England: Saxon House, 1973.

Brandt, Willy. Begegnungen und Einsichten: Die Jahre 1960-1975. Hamburg: Hoffmann & Campe, 1976.

— : Denke ich an Deutschland. Berlin: Press and Information Office, 1963.

— : The Ordeal of Coexistence. Cambridge, Mass.: Harvard University Press, 1963.

— : Über den Tag Hinaus — Eine Zwischenbilanz. Hamburg: Hoffmann & Campe, 1974.

Catudal, Honoré M., Jr. Steinstücken: A Study in Cold War Politics. New York: Vantage Press, Inc., 1971.

Collier, David S. et al. Berlin and the Future of Eastern Europe. Chicago: Regnery 1963.

Dalma, Alfons. Hintergründe der Berlin-Krise. Karlsruhe: Condor Verlag, 1962.

Dasbach-Mallinckrodt, Anita. Propaganda hinter der Mauer. Stuttgart: 1971.

Davidson, W. Phillips. The Berlin Blockade: A Study in Cold War Politics. Princeton: Princeton University Press, 1958.

Deuerlein, Ernst. Deutschland, 1963-1970. Hannover: Fackelträger-Verlag, 1971.

Deutsch, Karl W. et. al. Germany Rejoins the Powers. Stanford: Stanford University Press, 1959.

Doehring, Karl et al. Staats- und völkerrechtliche Aspekte der Berlin-Regelung. Frankfurt/M.: Athenäum Verlag, 1972.

Dornberg, John. The Other Germany. Garden City: Doubleday, 1968.

Dulles, Eleanor L. Berlin: The Wall is not Forever. Chapel Hill: University of North Carolina Press, 1967.

— : One Germany or Two: The Struggle at the Heart of Europe. Stanford: Hoover Institution Press, 1970.

— : The Wall: A Tragedy in Three Acts. Columbia, S.C.: University of South Carolina Press, 1972.

Eberlein, Ludwig. Experiment Berlin: Plädoyer für eine deutsche Konföderation. Cologne: 1967.

End, Heinrich. Zweimal deutsche Außenpolitik: Internationale Dimensionen des innerdeutschen Konflikts 1949 und 1972. Cologne: Wissenschaft und Politik, 1973.

Fijalkowsky, Jürgen et al. Berlin — Hauptstadtanspruch und Westintegration. Cologne: Westdeutscher Verlag, 1967.

Franke, Egon. Bundestags-Reden. Bonn: Pfattheicher & Reichardt, 1975.

Gablentz, Otto M. von der. Die Berlin-Frage in ihrer weltpolitischen Verflechtung 1944 bis 1963. Munich: 1963.

Galante, Pierre. The Berlin Wall. Garden City, N.Y.: Doubleday, 1965.

Gasteyger, Curt. Die beiden deutschen Staaten in der Weltpolitik. Munich: Verlag Piper & Co., 1976.

Goldman, Guido. The German Political System. New York: Random House, 1974.

Grosser, Alfred. Germany in our Time. New York: Praeger Publishers, 1971.
— : French Foreign Policy under De Gaulle. New York: Praeger Publishers, 1967.

Gusseck, Lutz. Die internationale Praxis der Transitgewährung und der Berlin-Verkehr. Frankfurt/M.: Athenäum-Verlag, 1973.

Hacker, Jens. Die Rechtslage Berlins: Die Wandlungen in der sowjetischen Rechtsauffassung. Bonn: Federal Ministry for All-German Affairs, 1964.
— : Der Rechtsstatus Deutschlands aus der Sicht der DDR. Cologne: Verlag Wissenschaft und Politik, 1974.

Hahn, Walter F. Between Westpolitik and Ostpolitik: Changing West German Security Views. Beverly Hills: Sage Publications, 1975.

Hanhardt, Arthur M., Jr. The German Democratic Republic. Baltimore: The Johns Hopkins Press, 1968.

Hanrieder, W.F. The Stable Crisis: Two Decades of German Foreign Policy. New York: Harper and Row, 1970.
— : West German Foreign Policy, 1949-1963: International Pressure and Domestic Response. Stanford: Stanford University Press, 1967.

Hartmann, Frederich H. Germany Between East and West. Englewood Cliffs, N.J.: Prentice-Hall, 1965.

Heidelmeyer, Wolfgang (ed.). Documents on Berlin, 1943-1963. Munich: R. Oldenbourg Verlag, 1963.
— : Dokumente zur Berlin-Frage, 1944-1966. Munich: R. Oldenbourg Verlag, 1967.
— : Erläuterungen zum Status des Landes Berlin. Berlin: 1970.

Henkin, Louis. The Berlin Crisis and the United Nations. New York: Carnegie Endowment for International Peace, 1959.

Hennig, Ottfried. Die Bundespräsenz in West-Berlin. Cologne: Verlag Wissenschaft und Politik, 1976.

Herzfeld, Hans. Berlin in der Weltpolitik 1945-1970. Berlin: Walter de Gruyter Verlag, 1973.

Hess, Frederick W. (ed.). German Unity: Documentation and Commentaries on the Basic Treaty. Parkville, Missouri: Park College Press, 1974.

Heyen, R. (ed.). Die Entkrampfung Berlins oder eine Stadt geht zur Tagesordnung über. Reinbek: 1972.

Hofmeister, Burkhard. Bundesrepublik Deutschland und Berlin. Darmstadt: Wissenschaftliche Buchgesellschaft, 1975.

Kaack, Heino. Geschichte und Struktur des deutschen Parteisystems. Cologne: Westdeutscher Verlag, 1971.

Kaiser, Karl. German Foreign Policy in Transition: Bonn Between East and West. London: Oxford University Press, 1968.

Kaltefleiter, Werner und *Heymann, Carl.* Zwischen Konsens und Krise: Eine Analyse der Bundestagswahl 1972. Cologne: Carl Heymanns Verlag, 1973.

Keiderling, Gerhard et al. Berlin 1945-1968: Zur Geschichte der Hauptstadt der DDR und der selbständigen politischen Einheit West-Berlin. East Berlin: 1970.

Khrushchev, Nikita. The Soviet Stand on Germany. New York: Crosscurrents Press, 1961.

Korbel, Josef. Détente in Europe: Real or Imaginery? Princeton: Princeton University Press, 1972.

Krisch, Henry. German Politics under Soviet Occupation. New York: Columbia University Press, 1974.

Kroll, Hans. Lebenserinnerungen eines Botschafters. Cologne: Verlag Kiepenheuer & Witsch, 1967.

Krumholz, Walter. Berlin-ABC. 2nd ed. Berlin: Press and Information Office, 1968.

Legien, Roman. Der rechtliche Status des Sowjetsektors. Bonn: Federal Ministry for All-German Affairs, 1965.

— : Die Viermächte-Vereinbarungen über Berlin: Ersatzlösungen für den Status quo?, 2nd ed. Berlin: 1961.

Lippmann, Heinz. Honecker: Portrait eines Nachfolgers. Cologne: 1971.

Ludz, Peter C. The Changing Party Elite in East Germany. Cambridge, Mass.: The MIT Press, 1972.

— : Deutschlands Doppelte Zukunft: Bundesrepublik und die DDR in der Welt von Morgen. Munich: R. Oldenbourg Verlag, 1974.

Männing, Peter. KSZE Gipfelkonferenz — Helsinki: Triumph oder Bankrott der Entspannung? Berlin: Landeszentrale für politische Bildungsarbeit, 1976.

Mahncke, Dieter. Berlin im geteilten Deutschland. Munich: R. Oldenbourg Verlag, 1973.

Mampel, Siegfried. Der Sowjetsektor von Berlin. Berlin: Alfred Metzner Verlag, 1963.

Mander, John. Berlin: Hostage for the West. London: Penguin Books, Inc., 1962.

McDermott, Geoffrey. Berlin: Success of a Mission? New York: Harper & Row, 1963.

Merkl, Peter H. German Foreign Policies, West and East: On the Threshold of a New European Era. Santa Barbara: ABC-Clio Press, Inc., 1974.

Morgan, Roger. The United States and West Germany 1945-1973. London: Oxford University Press, 1974.

Nawrocki, Joachim. Brennpunkt Berlin: Politische und wirtschaftliche Realitäten. Cologne: Verlag Wissenschaft und Politik, 1971.

Nelson, Daniel J. Wartime Origins of the Berlin Dilemma. University, Alabama: University of Alabama Press, 1977.

Nolte, Ernst. Deutschland und der Kalte Krieg. Munich: Piper Verlag, 1974.

Penkovskiy, Oleg. The Penkovskiy Papers. New York: Avon Books, 1966.

Planck, Charles R. The Changing Status of German Reunification in Western Diplomacy, 1955-1966. Baltimore: The Johns Hopkins Press, 1967.

Prittie, Terence. Willy Brandt: Portrait of a Statesman. New York: Schocken Books, 1974.

Prowe, Diethelm. Weltstadt in Krisen: Berlin 1949-1958. Berlin: 1973.

Riklin, Alois. Das Berlin-Problem: Historisch-politische und völkerrechtliche Darstellung des Viermächtestatus. Cologne: Verlag Wissenschaft und Politik, 1964.

Rottman, Joachim. Der Viermächte-Status von Berlin, 2nd ed. Bonn: 1959.

Ruge, Hans-Georg. Das Zugangsrecht der Westmächte auf dem Luftweg nach Berlin. Berlin: 1968.

Salisbury, Harrison E. War Between Russia and China. New York: W.W. Norton, 1969.

Scheuner, Ulrich et al. Die Vereinten Nationen und die Mitarbeit der Bundesrepublik Deutschland. Munich: R. Oldenbourg Verlag, 1973.

Schick, Jack M. The Berlin Crisis 1958-1962. Philadelphia: University of Pennsylvania Press, 1971.

Schiedermair, Hartmut. Der völkerrechtliche Status Berlins nach dem Viermächte-Abkommen vom 3. September 1971. Berlin: Springer Verlag, 1975.

Schild, Helmut et al. Berlin in der Europäischen Gemeinschaft. Berlin: Press and Information Office, 1973.

Schlesinger, Arthur M., Jr. A Thousand Days. Greenwich, Conn.: Fawcett Publications, Inc. 1967.

Schmacke, Ernst. Berlin auf dem Weg in das Jahr 2000. Düsseldorf: Droste Verlag, 1974.

Schroeder, Dieter. Die Rechtslage der Verkehrswege von und nach Berlin. Berlin: 1969.

Schweigler, Gebhard L. National Consciousness in Divided Germany. Beverly Hills: Sage Publications, 1975.

Schwoebel, Jean. Les Deux K, Berlin et la Paix. Paris: René Julliard, 1963.

Shell, Kurt L. Bedrohung und Bewährung: Führung und Bevölkerung in der Berlin-Krise. Cologne/Opladen: Westdeutscher Verlag, 1965.

Sidey, Hugh. John F. Kennedy, President. New York: Crest Books, 1964.

Skriver, Ansgor (ed.). Berlin und keine Illusion. Hamburg: Rütten und Loening Verlag, 1962.

Slusser, Robert M. The Berlin Crisis of 1961: Soviet-American Relations and the Struggle for Power in the Kremlin. Baltimore: The Johns Hopkins University Press, 1973.

Smith, Jean E. The Defense of Berlin. Baltimore: The Johns Hopkins Press, 1963.

Sorenson, Theodore C. Decision-Making in the White House. New York: Columbia University Press, 1963.

— : Kennedy. New York: Bantam Books, Inc., 1966.

Speier, Hans. Divided Berlin: The Anatomy of Soviet Political Blackmail. New York: Praeger Publishers, 1961.

Stanger, R. (ed.). West Berlin: The Legal Context. Columbus: Ohio State University Press, 1966.

Stern, Carola. Ulbricht: Eine politische Biographie. Cologne: Kiepenheuer & Witsch, 1963.

Storbeck, Dietrich. Berlin: Bestand und Möglichkeiten. Cologne: 1964.

Tilford, Roger (ed.). The Ostpolitik and Political Change in Germany. Farnborough, England: Saxon House, 1975.

Triska, Jan et al. Soviet Foreign Policy. New York: The MacMillan Co., 1968.

Tully, Andrew. The Super Spies. New York: Pocket Books, 1970.

Ulam, Adam B. Expansion and Coexistence: Soviet Foreign Policy, 1917-1973. 2nd ed. New York: Praeger Publishers, 1973.

Vali, Ferenc A. The Quest for a United Germany. Baltimore: Johns Hopkins Press, 1967.

Vysockij, V.N. Zapadnyj Berlin: ego mesto v sisteme sovremennych mezdunarodnych otnošenij. Moscow: 1971.

Waldman, Eric. SEW und die sowjetische Berlinpolitik. Boppard: 1972.

Wettig, G. Community and Conflict in the Socialist Camp: The Soviet Union, East Germany and the German Problem 1965-1972. London: 1975.

Whetten, Lawrence L. Germany's Ostpolitik. New York: Oxford University Press, 1971.

Wilcox, Francis O. et al. The Constitution and the Conduct of Foreign Policy. New York: Praeger Publishers, 1976.

Windsor, Philip. City on Leave: A History of Berlin 1945-1962. New York: Praeger Publishers, 1963.

— : German Reunification. London: 1969.

Wyssozki, V. Westberlin. Moscow: 1974.

Zivier, Ernst R. Der Rechtsstatus des Landes Berlin: Eine Untersuchung nach dem Viermächte-Abkommen vom 3. September 1971. 3rd. ed. Berlin: Berlin Verlag, 1977.

Zolling, Hermann and *Bahnsen, Uwe.* Kalter Winter im August. Oldenburg : Gerhard Stalling Verlag, 1967.

Articles

Albrecht, Weber. "Diplomatische Beziehungen zwischen der Bundesrepublik Deutschland und der DDR?," Politische Studien, Vol. 216 (July-August, 1974), pp. 337-51.

Allemann, Fritz René. "Berlin in Search of a Purpose," Survey, Vol. 61 (October, 1966), pp. 129-38.

Anthon, Carl G. "Germany's Westpolitik," Current History, Vol. 62, No. 396 (May, 1972), pp. 234-38.

Ausland, John C. et al. "Crisis Management: Berlin, Cyprus, Laos," Foreign Affairs, Vol. 44 (January, 1966), pp. 291-303.

Bahr, Egon. "Nach dem abgesagten Redneraustausch SPD-SED," Außenpolitik, Vol. 17, No. 8 (1966), pp. 475-79.

Barker, Elisabeth. "The Berlin Crisis 1958-1962," International Affairs, London, Vol. 39 (January, 1963), pp. 59-73.

Bechtholdt, Heinrich. "Der Bilateralismus deutscher Ostpolitik," Außenpolitik, Vol. 21, No. 1 (January, 1970), pp. 5-8.

— : "Die deutsch-deutsche Gipfeldiplomatie," Außenpolitik, Vol. 21, No. 4 (April, 1970), pp. 197-200.

— : "Die zweite Etappe der deutschen Ostpolitik," Außenpolitik, Vol. 21, No. 12 (December, 1970), pp. 209-12.

— : "Moskaus Interesse an der Berlin-Regelung," Außenpolitik, Vol. 22, No. 10 (October, 1971), pp. 577-80.

— : "Zur Ostpolitik der neuen Bundesregierung," Außenpolitik, Vol. 20, No. 11 (November, 1969), pp. 614-44.

Bender, Peter. "The Special Relationship of the Two German States," The World Today, Vol. 29, No. 9 (September, 1973), pp. 389-97.

Bentzien, Joachim. "Die Luftkorridore von und nach Berlin," Außenpolitik, Vol. 12 (1961), pp. 685-90.

Beyme, Klaus von. "The Ostpolitik in the West German Elections," Government and Opposition, Vol. 5, No. 2 (Spring, 1970), pp. 193-217.

Birnbaum, Karl E. "Gesamteuropäische Perspektiven nach dem Berlin-Abkommen," Europa-Archiv, Vol. 27, No. 1 (January, 1972), pp. 1-10.

Black, Hilary. "The East-West German Treaty," The World Today, Vol. 28, No. 12 (December, 1972), pp. 512-15.

— : "Honecker's First Year," The World Today, Vol. 28, No. 6 (June, 1972), pp. 235-39.

Bleimann, Robert. "Détente and the GDR: the Internal Implications," The World Today, Vol. 29, No. 6 (June, 1973), pp. 257-65.

— : "Ostpolitik and the GDR," Survey, Vol. 18, No. 3 (Summer, 1972), pp. 36-54.

Blumenwitz, Dieter. "Der Grundvertrag zwischen der Bundesrepublik Deutschland und der DDR," Politische Studien, Vol. 24 (January-February, 1973), pp. 3-10.

Boldyrew, Viktor. "Das vierseitige Abkommen über Westberlin — ein Schritt zu Frieden, Sicherheit und Zusammenarbeit in Europa," Deutsche Außenpolitik, Vol. 5 (September-October, 1972), pp. 873-99.

Brandt, Willy. "The Berlin Agreement," The Atlantic Community Quarterly, Vol. 9, No. 4 (Winter, 1972), pp. 493-95.

— : "German Policy Toward the East," Foreign Affairs, Vol. 46, No. 3 (April, 1968), pp. 476-86.

Braunthal, Gerard. "West Germany's Foreign Policy," Current History, Vol. 64, No. 380 (April, 1973), pp. 150-53, 181-82.

Bredthauer, Karl D. "Das Westberlin-Problem und die Politik der Entspannung in Europa," Blätter für deutsche und internationale Politik, No. 4 (1971), pp. 332-44.

Carstens, Karl. "Zur Interpretation der Berlin-Regelung von 1971" in Festschrift für Ulrich Scheuner zum 70. Geburtstag. Berlin: 1973.

Cate, Curtis. "Is Berlin Our European Taiwan?," National Review (April 14, 1972), pp. 400-03.

Catudal, Honoré M., Jr. "The Berlin Agreement of 1971: Has it Worked?," The International and Comparative Law Quarterly, Vol. 25 (October, 1976), pp. 766-800.

— : "The Berlin Agreements: An Exchange of Exclaves and Enclaves." Geoforum, No. 11 (September, 1972), pp. 78-80.

— : "The Berlin Exclaves and the Quadripartite Agreement," International Behavioural Scientist, Vol. 5, No. 1 (March, 1973), pp. 64-75.

— : "Berlin's New Boundaries," Cahiers de Géographie de Québec, Vol. 18, No. 43 (April, 1974), pp. 213-26.

— : "Exclaves," Cahiers de Géographie de Québec, Vol. 18, No. 43 (April, 1974), pp. 108-36.

— : "Kiesinger Recalls his Coalition's Successes, Failures," St. John's Magazine (Summer, 1974), pp. 9-11.

— : "Steinstücken: The Politics of a Berlin Exclave," World Affairs, Vol. 134, No. 1 (Summer, 1971), pp. 51-62.

— : "University Reform in the Federal Republic: the Experiment in Democratization at the Free University of Berlin," Comparative Education, Vol. 12, No. 3 (October, 1976), pp. 231-41.

Chopra, H.S. "Willy Brandt's 'Ostpolitik' and its Impact on Franco-German Relations," India Quarterly, Vol. 28 (July-September, 1972), pp. 227-35.

Clay, Lucius D. "Berlin," Foreign Affairs, Vol. 41, No. 1 (October, 1962), pp. 47-58.

Cramer, Dettmar. "Berliner Lehren," Deutschland-Archiv, Vol. 7, No. 9 (September, 1974), pp. 897-99.

— : "Bonn und Moskau: distanzierter," Deutschland-Archiv, Vol. 8, No. 4 (April, 1975), pp. 358-61.

— : "Bonn und Ost-Berlin: Kleine Schritte auf dem Weg zur Normalisierung," Deutschland-Archiv, Vol. 8, No. 3 (March, 1975), pp. 225-26.

— : "Im Interesse Berlins," Deutschland-Archiv, No. 8 (1971), pp. 792-95.

— : "Zwischen Kollision und Kooperation," Deutschland-Archiv, Vol. 7, No. 2 (February, 1974), pp. 113-18.

Croan, Melvin. "East Germany: The Soviet Connection," The Washington Papers, Vol. 4, No. 36 (1976), pp. 1-71.

— : "Party Politics and the Wall," Survey, Vol. 61 (October, 1966), pp. 38-46.

Delbrück, Jost. "Deutschland in den Vereinten Nationen," Europa-Archiv, Vol. 16 (1973), pp. 564-71.

Deuerlein, Ernst. "Die Entstehung der Luftkorridore nach Berlin," Deutschland-Archiv, No. 7 (1969), pp. 735-64.

Dittmer, Lowell. "The German NPD: A Psycho-Sociological Analysis of Neo-Nazism," Comparative Politics, Vol. 2, No. 2 (October, 1969), pp. 79-110.

Doehring, Karl et al. "Die parlamentarische Zustimmungsbedürftigkeit von Verträgen der BRD und der DDR," Völkerrecht und Außenpolitik, Vol. 10. Frankfurt/M.: 1972.

— : "Rechtsfragen der Einbeziehung West-Berlins in den Internationalen Sportverkehr der Bundesrepublik Deutschland und ihrer Sportorganisationen," Deutschland-Archiv, Vol. 7, No. 11 (November, 1974), pp. 1169-87.

Doeker, Günther et al. "Berlin and the Quadripartite Agreement of 1971," American Journal of International Law, Vol. 67 (January, 1973), pp. 44-62.

Duckwitz, Georg F. "The Turning Point in the East," Außenpolitik, English ed., Vol. 21 (April, 1970), pp. 363-78.

Dulles, Eleanor L. "A New Berlin," The Atlantic Community Quarterly, Vol. 11 (1973), pp. 65-78.

Edinger, Lewis J. "Political Change in Germany: The Federal Republic after the 1969 Election," Comparative Politics, Vol. 2, No. 4 (July 1970), pp. 549-78.

Eisenhower, Dwight D. "My views on Berlin," Saturday Evening Post, December 9, 1961, pp. 19-28.

Erler, Fritz. "Les Aspects politiques de l'action soviétique à Berlin," Politique étrangère, Vol. 27 (1963), pp. 5-14.

Frank, Paul. "German Ostpolitik in a Changing World," Außenpolitik, English ed., Vol. 23 (January, 1972), pp. 14-25.

Franke, Egon. "Acht Verhandlungspunkte — Bonns Angebote an Ost-Berlin," Deutsche Korrespondenz Vol. 20 (January, 1970), pp. 2-4.

Franklin, William M. "Zonal Boundaries and Access to Berlin," World Politics, Vol. 16 (October, 1963), pp. 1-31.

Genscher, Hans-Dietrich. "Dimensions of German Foreign Policy," Außenpolitik, English ed., No. 4 (1974), pp. 1-12.

Gloss, Johannes. "Die Entwicklung der deutschen Ostpolitik," Tutzinger Studien, Vol. 1 (1971), pp. 2-16.

Graebner, Norman A. "Germany Between East and West," Current History, Vol. 62, No. 396 (May, 1972), pp. 225-28.

Grawert, Rolf. "Die Staatsangehörigkeit der Berliner," Der Staat, Vol. 12, No. 3 (1973), pp. 289-310.

Guttenberg, Freiherr von und zu, Karl T. "Befriedigende Regelung für Berlin?," Zeitschrift für Politik, No. 1 (January, 1972), pp. 20-31.

Hacker, Jens. "Die Bindungen Berlins (West) zum Bund als Problem der Ostvertragspolitik der Bundesrepublik Deutschland," Osteuropa-Recht, No. 3-4 (1974), pp. 205-34.

— : "Der neue Rechtsstatus für West-Berlin: Die Ostverträge und das Berlin-Abkommen," Die politische Meinung, Vol. 142 (May-June, 1972), pp. 78-94.

Haffner, Sebastian. "The Berlin Crisis," Survey, Vols. 44-45 (October, 1962), pp. 37-44.

Haftendorn, Helga. "Ostpolitik Revisited 1976," The World Today, Vol. 32, No. 6 (June, 1976), pp. 222-29.

Hahn, Walter F. "West Germany's Ostpolitik: The Grand Design of Egon Bahr," Orbis, Vol. 16, No. 4 (Winter, 1973), pp. 859-80.

— : "Whither Germany? " Orbis, Vol. 16 (Spring, 1972), pp. 289-93.

Hailbronner, Kay. "Verfassungsrechtliche Möglichkeiten einer Regelung des Besuchsverkehrs Bundesrepublik - DDR," Deutschland-Archiv, Vol. 7, No. 1 (January, 1974), pp. 12-17.

Hangen, Welles. "New Perspectives Behind the Wall," Foreign Affairs, Vol. 45, No. 1 (October, 1966), pp. 135-47.

Harriman, W. Averell. "Observations on Negotiating: Informal Views," Journal of International Affairs, Vol. 29, No. 1 (Spring, 1975), pp. 1-6.

Hirsch, Felix E. "Ostpolitik in Historial Perspective," Current History, Vol. 62, No. 369 (May, 1972), pp. 229-33.

Irving, R.E.M. et al. "The West German Parliamentary Election of November 1972," Parliamentary Affairs, (Spring, 1973), pp. 218-39.

Jäckel, Hartmut. "Kontakte ohne Anerkennung? Der Briefwechsel Kiesinger-Stoph," Der Monat, Vol. 20, No. 235 (April, 1968), pp. 37-45.

Jansen, Marlies. "Deutschlandpolitik der SED auf Eis," Deutschland-Archiv, Vol. 4, No. 1 (January, 1971), pp. 12-16.

Joffe, Josef. "Westverträge, Ostverträge und die Kontinuität der deutschen Außenpolitik," Europa-Archiv, Vol. 27, No. 3 (February, 1972), pp. 111-24.

Jones, W. Treharne. "East Germany under Honecker," The World Today, Vol. 32, No. 9 (September 1976), pp. 339-47.

Kaiser, Karl. "Prospects for West Germany after the Berlin Agreement," The World Today, Vol. 28, No. 1 (January, 1972), pp. 30-35.

Kanet, Roger E. "The Soviet Union and China: Is War Inevitable?," Current History, Vol. 63 (October, 1973), pp. 145-49.

Kewenig, Wilhelm. "Die Bedeutung des Grundvertrags für das Verhältnis der beiden deutschen Staaten," Europa-Archiv, Vol. 28, No. 2 (January, 1973), pp. 37-46.

Kimminich, Otto. "Die Ostverträge," Internationales Recht und Diplomatie (1971), pp. 15-59.

Kipp, Heinrich. "Einige Aspekte des Viermächte-Abkommens über Berlin vom 3. September 1971" in Recht und Staat, Festschrift für Günther Küchenhoff (Berlin: 1972).

Kohl, Wilfred L. "The Nixon-Kissinger Foreign Policy Systems and U.S. European Relations: Patterns of Policy Making," World Politics, Vol. 28, No. 1 (October, 1975), pp. 1-43.

Korber, Horst. "West-Berlin und die Vereinten Nationen," Vereinte Nationen, No. 5 (1972), pp. 141-42.

Kotov, Y. "West Berlin and its Problems," International Affairs, Moscow, Vol. 43, No. 4 (1966), pp. 47-49.

Kuhn, Helmut. "Germany – Divided Once More" in John H. Hollowell (ed.), Prospects for Constitutional Democracy: Essays in Honor of R. Taylor Cole (Durham: Duke University Press, 1976), pp. 101-17.

Lebedew, Valerian P. "Berlin in der Sowjet Literatur," Kultur, Vol. 1960-61, No. 165, pp. 6-7.

Leicht, Robert. "Von den zwanzig Kasseler Punkten zum Grundvertrag," Frankfurter Hefte, Vol. 28, No. 4 (1973), pp. 241-48.

Loewenstein, Karl. "The Allied Presence in Berlin: Legal Basis," Foreign Policy Bulletin (February 15, 1959), pp. 81-84.

Ludz, Peter C. "Continuity and Change Since Ulbricht," Problems of Communism, Vol. 21, No. 2 (March-April, 1972), pp. 56-64.

– : "Discovery and 'Recognition' of East Germany: Recent Literature on the GDR," Comparative Politics, Vol. 2, No. 4 (1970), pp. 681-95.

– : "The German Democratic Republic from the Sixties to the Seventies," Occasional Papers in International Affairs, No. 26 (November, 1970), pp. 1-100.

– : "Die Neuordnung der Führungsspitze der DDR," Europa-Archiv, Vol. 32, No. 4 (February, 1977), pp. 113-20.

Lummer, Heinrich. "Die Lage Berlins im Ost-West-Verhältnis," Internationale Spectator (May 8, 1967), pp. 696-712.

Lush, C.D. "The Relationship between Berlin and the Federal Republic of Germany," The International and Comparative Law Quarterly, Vol. 14 (1965), pp. 742-87.

Mahncke, Dieter. "The Berlin Agreement: Balance and Prospects," The World Today, Vol. 27, No. 12 (December, 1971), pp. 511-21.

– : "In Search of a modus vivendi for Berlin: Prospects for Four-Power Talks," The World Today, Vol. 26 (April, 1970), pp. 137-46.

Mahnke, Hans H. "Erleichterungen, Vorrechte und Befreiungen für die ständige Vertretung der Deutschen Demokratischen Republik," Recht in Ost und West, Vol. 19, No. 2 (March, 1975), pp. 49-53.

– : "Die Konferenz über Sicherheit und Zusammenarbeit in Europa (KSZE) und die deutsche Frage," Deutschland-Archiv, Vol. 8, No. 9 (September, 1975), pp. 922-33.

— : "Der neue Freundschafts- und Beistandspakt zwischen Sowjetunion und DDR," Deutschland-Archiv, Vol. 8, No. 11 (November, 1975), pp. 1160-75.

— : "Das Recht des zivilen Zugangs nach Berlin," Deutschland-Archiv, Vol. 2 (1969), pp. 148-54.

— : "Zur Rechtslage Berlins: Einige korrigierende Bemerkungen," Deutschland-Archiv, Vol. 4, No. 9 (September, 1971), pp. 901-09.

— : "Rechtsprobleme des Grundlagenvertrages," Deutschland-Archiv, Vol. 7. No. 2 (February, 1974), pp. 130-49.

— : "Zum Status von Berlin," Deutschland-Archiv, Vol. 8, No. 8 (August, 1975), pp. 835-42.

— : "Der Zugang nach Berlin: Die historische Entwicklung," Deutschland-Archiv, Vol. 5, Nos. 2 u. 4 (1972), pp. 140-48 and pp. 364-87.

Mattick, Kurt. "Ein Blick zurück: Die Berlinregelungen und ihre Geschichte," Die neue Gesellschaft, No. 1 (1972), pp. 7-10.

Maxwell, J.A. "West German Ostpolitik," International Behavioural Scientist, Vol. 6, No. 2 (June, 1974), pp. 1-12.

Mehnert, Klaus. "Mit Bundeskanzler Schmidt in der UdSSR," Osteuropa, Vol. 25, No. 1 (January, 1975), pp. 3-10.

Merkl, Peter H. "The German Janus: From Westpolitik to Ostpolitik," Political Science Quarterly, Vol. 89, No. 4 (Winter, 1974-75), pp. 803-24.

Morgenstern, Heinz. "Verhaftungen auf den Transitstrecken und Urteile gegen Fluchthelfer," Deutschland-Archiv, Vol. 7, No. 9 (September, 1974), pp. 1001-04.

Mosely, Philip. "Dismemberment of Germany: The Allied Negotiations from Yalta to Potsdam," Foreign Affairs, Vol. 28 (April, 1950), pp. 487-98.

— : "The Occupation of Germany: New Light on How the Zones were Drawn," Foreign Affairs, Vol. 28 (July, 1950), pp. 580-604.

Muhlen, N. "Bonn and Washington since 1945," Orbis, Vol. 19, No. 4 (Winter, 1976), pp. 1621-26.

— : "Germany's New 'Ost-Politik': An American Dilemma," Interplay, Vol. 3, No. 8 (April, 1970), pp. 4-11.

Nawrocki, Joachim. "Das Berlin-Abkommen nach zweieinhalb Jahren Praxis," Deutschland-Archiv, Vol. 8, No. 1 (January, 1975), pp. 22-32.

— : "Entscheidung in Berlin," Deutschland-Archiv, Vol. 4, No. 7 (July, 1971), pp. 796-800.

— : "The Four Power Agreement on Berlin: An Evaluation of the First Three Years" in Berlin: Report Past and Present. Berlin: Press and Information Office, 1975.

— : "Gibt es in Berlin eine Strukturkrise?," Deutschland-Archiv, Vol. 2, No. 4 (April, 1969), pp. 379-84.

— : "Schwierigkeiten mit den 'drei Z': Die DDR und das Viermächte-Abkommen über Berlin," Deutschland-Archiv, Vol. 7, No. 6 (June, 1974), pp. 582-95.

Nelson, D.N. "The Early Success of Ostpolitik: an Eastern European Perspective," World Affairs, Vol. 138, No. 1 (Summer, 1975), pp. 32-50.

312

Paterson, W.E. "Foreign Policy and Stability in West Germany," International Affairs, Vol. 49, No. 3 (July, 1973), pp. 413-30.

— : "The SPD after Brandt's Fall — Change or Continuity? "Government and Opposition, Vol. 10, No. 2 (Spring, 1975), pp. 167-88.

Pierre, Andrew J. "The Bonn-Moscow Treaty of 1970: Milestone or Mirage?," The Russian Review, Vol. 30, No. 1 (January, 1970), pp. 17-26.

Plischke, Elmer. "Integrating Berlin and the Federal Republic of Germany," The Journal of Politics, Vol. 27 (February, 1965), pp. 35-65.

Probst, Peter. "Neue DDR-Maßnahmen im innerdeutschen Reiseverkehr," Deutschland-Archiv, Vol. 2, No. 4 (April, 1968), pp. 434-440.

Rauschnigg, Dietrich. "Die Berlin-Frage im Neueren Schrifttum," Europa-Archiv, Vol. 16 (November, 1961), pp. 663-74.

Ress, Georg. "La disciplina giuridica del traffico in transito fra la Republica Federale di Germania e Berlino-Ovest," La Communità Internazionale Vol. 28, No. 1 (January, 1973), pp. 41-71.

Rexin, Manfred. "DDR-Politik nach dem Grundvertrag," Liberal, Vol. 15, No. 3 (March, 1973), pp. 170-79.

Robinson, Thomas W. "The Sino-Soviet Border Disputes: Background, Development, and the March 1969 Clashes," American Political Science Review, Vol. 66 (1972), pp. 1175-1202.

Röper, Erich. "Zur Rechtslage Berlins," Deutschland-Archiv, Vol. 4, No. 8 (August, 1971), pp. 801-04.

Rohloff, Adalbert. "Verbesserte Chancen für West-Berlin in einer erweiterten EWG," Die Berliner Wirtschaft, No. 2 (1972), p. 44.

Rush, Kenneth. "The Berlin Agreement: An Assessment," The Atlantic Community Quarterly, Vol. 10, No. 1 (1972), pp. 52-65.

— : "Berlin: The Four-Power Agreement" in Current Foreign Policy. Washington, D.C.: U.S. Government Printing Office, 1971.

Rusk, Dean. "The President," Foreign Affairs, Vol. 38 (Spring, 1960), pp. 353-69.

Rzhevsky, I. "GDR-FRG Treaty: A Major Step on Europe's Path to Peace," International Affairs, Moscow, No. 3 (March, 1973), pp. 78-80.

Sanakoyev, S. "USSR-FRG: A Turn Toward New Relations," International Affairs, Moscow, Vol. 50, No. 8 (August, 1973), pp. 12-17.

Schaefer, Michael. "Die völkerrechtliche Vertretung von Berlin bei einer Aufnahme beider deutscher Staaten in die UNO," Politische Studien, Vol. 24, No. 207 (January-February, 1973), pp. 11-28.

Scharpf, Peter. "Die Bedeutung des innerdeutschen Handels für die Beziehungen der EWG zur DDR," Deutschland-Archiv, Vol. 7, No. 3 (March, 1974), pp. 260-266.

Schiller, Karl. "Berlin, Deutschland und Europa: Die Wirtschaft Berlins und ihre Verflechtung mit dem freien Europa," Europa-Archiv, Vol. 20 (1965), pp. 371-82.

Schmitt, Matthias. "Ökonomische Perspektiven in der Ostpolitik," Außenpolitik, Vol. 22 (April, 1971), pp. 193-208.

Schroeder, Dieter. "Die Bedeutung der Berliner Rechte der Alliierten für den Zugang von Deutschen nach Berlin," Recht und Politik, No. 1 (1969), pp. 11-19.

— : "Berlin — eine Stadt stellt sich vor," Der Journalist, Vol. 3 (1974), pp. 83-6.

Schütz, Klaus. "Berlin in the Age of Détente," The World Today, Vol. 31, No. 1 (January, 1975), pp. 29-35.

— : "Berlin nach den Verträgen," Zeitschrift für Politik," No. 1 (January, 1972), pp. 11-19.

— : "The Four-Power Agreement," Chronique de Politique Etrangère, Vol. 24, No. 4 (1971), pp. 541-52.

Schulz, Eberhard. "Die DDR als Gegenspieler der Bonner Ostpolitik," Europa-Archiv, Vol. 26, No. 8 (1971), pp. 283-92.

Schulz, I. "Zu einigen völkerrechtlichen Aspekten der Lösung der Westberlinfrage," Staat und Recht, No. 7 (1964), pp. 1170-86.

Schweisfurth, Theodor. "BRD und DDR auf internationaler Ebene,·' Außenpolitik, Vol. 21 (May, 1970), pp. 265-82.

— : "Irrtümer über Berlin," Recht und Politik, Vol. 11, No. 1 (March, 1975), pp. 17-19.

Shell, Kurt L.. "Berlin and the German Problem,' World Politics, Vol. 16 (October, 1963), pp. 137-46.

Skubiszewski, Krzysztof. "Poland's Western Frontier and the 1970 Treaties," American Journal of International Law, Vol. 67, No. 1 (January, 1973), pp. 23-42.

Smith, Gordon. "New German Politics," Political Quarterly, Vol. 44, No. 3 (July-September, 1973), pp. 283-93.

Smith, Jean E. "The German Democratic Republic and the West," International Journal (Spring, 1967), pp. 231-52.

Spangenberg, Dietrich. "Berlin nach den Verträgen," Mitteilungen Verein Berliner Kaufleute und Industrielle, Vol. 25, No. 124 (April, 1975), pp. 3-10.

Spittmann, Ilse. "Mit halbem Herzen: DDR-Reaktion auf Helsinki," Deutschland-Archiv, Vol. 8, No. 9 (September, 1975), pp. 897-99.

— : "Von Kassel nach Moskau: Die SED und der deutsch-sowjetische Vertrag," Deutschland-Archiv, Vol. 3, No. 10 (October, 1970), pp. 1103-15.

Uschakow, Alexander. "Germany in Poland's Foreign Policy," Außenpolitik, Vol. 21 (Summer, 1970), pp. 307-20.

Vetter, Gottfried. "Zur Entwicklung der innerdeutschen Beziehungen," Europa-Archiv, Vol. 23, No. 9 (1968), pp. 309-19.

Völkel, Walter. "Zur Reaktion der DDR auf das Karlsruher Urteil zum Grundlagenvertrag," Deutschland-Archiv, Vol. 7, No. 2 (February, 1974), pp. 140-49.

Vysockij, V.N. "Westberlin-Problem ist lösbar," Sowjetunion heute (September 16, 1970), p. 27.

Wagner, Wolfgang. "Aussichten der Ostpolitik nach dem Abschluß der Berlin-Verhandlungen," Europa-Archiv, Vol. 27, No. 3 (February, 1972), pp. 79-86.

— : "Das Berlin-Problem als Angelpunkt eines Ausgleichs zwischen West und Ost in Europa," Europa-Archiv, Vol. 26, No. 11 (1971), pp. 375-82.

— : "Kanzlerwechsel in Bonn," Europa-Archiv, Vol. 29, No. 11 (October, 1974), pp. 345-52.

— : "Ein Modus vivendi in Deutschland: Der Grundvertrag der beiden deutschen Staaten und seine Bedeutung für Europa," Europa-Archiv, Vol. 28, No. 1 (1973), pp. 1-6.

— : "Towards a New Political Order: Ostpolitik and the East-West Realignment," International Journal, Vol. 27, No. 1 (Winter, 1972), pp. 18-31.

Waterkamp, Rainer. "Sind die Verhältnisse in West-Berlin stabil?," Deutschland-Archiv, Vol. 2, No. 6 (June 1969), pp. 588-91.

Weber, Bernd. "Ideologiewandel von Ulbricht zu Honecker," Außenpolitik, Vol. 23 (March 1972), pp. 159-67.

— : "Ulbricht zwischen BRD und UdSSR," Außenpolitik, Vol. 21, No. 2 (February, 1970), pp. 104-09.

Weber, E.F. Albrecht. "Diplomatische Beziehungen zwischen der Bundesrepublik Deutschland und der DDR?," Politische Studien, Vol. 25 (1974), pp. 337-51.

Wettig, Gerhard. "Aktionsmuster der sowjetischen Berlin-Politik," Außenpolitik, Vol. 19, No. 6 (June, 1968), pp. 325-39.

— : "The Berlin Crisis of 1969," Osteuropa, No. 9 (1969), pp. 685-97.

— : "Die Berlin-Politik der UdSSR und der DDR," Außenpolitik (May, 1970), pp. 284-96.

— : "Das Berlin-Problem — Rückblick und Gegenwart," Aus Politik und Zeitgeschichte (March 1, 1969), pp. 3-26.

— : "East Berlin and the Moscow Treaty," Außenpolitik, English ed., Vol. 22 (1971), pp. 256 - 69.

— : "Das Entspannungsproblem Berlin: Die empfindlichste Nahtstelle von Ost und West, Osteuropa, No. 1 (1971), pp. 1-22.

— : "Fünf Jahre Berlin-Abkommen: Eine Bilanz," Aus Politik und Zeitgeschichte, Vol. 42 (October, 1976), pp. 3-46.

— : "Modelle der Berlin-Politik," Deutschland-Archiv, Vol. 2, No. 7 (July, 1969), pp. 711-17.

— : "Der Moskauer Vertrag zwischen UdSSR und DDR," Außenpolitik, Vol. 22, No. 6 (June, 1971), pp. 351-62.

— : "Ost-Berlin im Schatten der Moskauer Deutschland-Politik," Außenpolitik, Vol. 20, No. 5 (May, 1969), pp. 261-72.

— : "Die Rechtslage Berlins nach dem Viermächteabkommen aus sowjetischer Sicht," Deutschland-Archiv, Vol. 7, No. 4 (April, 1974), pp. 378-88.

Wewjura, B. et al. "International Legal Aspects of the West Berlin Problem," International Affairs, Moscow, Vol. 40, No. 4 (1963), pp. 37-42.

Whetten, Lawrence L. "Appraising the Ostpolitik," Orbis, Vol. 15, No. 3 (Fall, 1971), pp. 856-78.

— : "The Role of East Germany in West German-Soviet Relations," The World Today, Vol. 25, No. 12 (December, 1969), pp. 507-20.

Winzer, Otto. "Twenty Years of GDR Foreign Policy," International Affairs, Moscow, Vol. 46, No. 10 (October, 1969), pp. 3-5.

Witte, Barthold. "Die deutsche Nation nach dem Grundvertrag," Europa-Archiv, Vol. 28, No. 7 (1973), pp. 227-34.

Wolfe, James H. "West Germany's Ostpolitik," World Affairs, Vol. 134, No. 3 (Winter, 1971), pp. 210-19.

Wright, Quincy. "Some Legal Aspects of the Berlin Crisis," The American Journal of International Law, Vol. 55 (October, 1961), pp. 959-65.

Zeitler, Franz-Christoph. "Perspektiven der Folgeverträge mit der DDR," Zeitschrift für Politik, Vol. 20, No. 2 (July, 1975), pp. 140-64.

Zorgbibe, Charles. "L'accord Quadripartite sur Berlin du 3. Septembre 1971," Revue belge de droit international, Vol. 8 (1972), pp. 419-30.

Unpublished Material

General

Ausland, John C. Kennedy, Khrushchev and Berlin: The 1961-1964 Berlin Crisis. Unpublished manuscript, 1967.

Theses

Flynn, Gregory A. The Fall of Ulbricht: A Lesson in Soviet Bloc Diplomacy. Unpublished M.A. thesis, Fletcher School of Law and Diplomacy, 1972.

Görlich, Michael. Die staatsrechtliche Stellung des Bevollmächtigten der Bundesrepublik Deutschland in Berlin. Unpublished Ph.D. dissertation, Würzburg, 1971.

Nagel, Willi. Die rechtliche Lage West-Berlins. Unpublished Ph.D. dissertation, Würzburg, 1964.

Bibliographies

Scholz, U. et al. Berlin Bibliographie (1961-1966). Berlin: Berlin Historical Commission, 1973.

Zopf, H. et al. Berlin-Bibliographie (bis 1960). Berlin: Berlin Historical Commission, 1965.

Newspapers and Journals

The most complete local coverage of the quadripartite negotiations on Berlin is given by *Der Tagesspiegel,* West Berlin's most influential morning newspaper, and *Die Welt,* a conservative newspaper which also publishes a Hamburg edition. Also useful is *Der Abend,* the most-read midday newspaper, and *Berliner Morgenpost,* a right-of-center paper with a large number of local subscribers. Outside of Berlin, the best German language accounts appear in *Frankfurter Allgemeine Zeitung* and the *Neue Zürcher Zeitung.* The most important foreign reports are made by *The New York Times* and *The Washington Post.* But also worthwhile are *The Times* (London) and *Le Monde* (Paris). The SED party line is authoritatively reported in *Neues Deutschland* (East Berlin), while the official Soviet party viewpoint is carried in *Pravda.* The most extensive English language coverage of the Soviet press is contained in *Current Digest of Soviet Press.*

In addition to the above media, I have found the following periodicals to be of particular help: *Foreign Affairs, Orbis, The World Today, World Politics, American Journal of International Law, Comparative Politics, The Journal of Politics, Current History, Survey, and the Atlantic Community Quarterly.* Also useful are the news weeklies — *Time* and *Newsweek.* Those German language journals which are important include *Der Spiegel, Die Zeit, Europa-Archiv, Deutschland-Archiv, Außenpolitik, Die politische Meinung* and *Politische Studien.* As far as the Soviet Union is concerned, I have relied, among other journals, on *International Affairs* (Moscow); for the GDR, on *Deutsche Außenpolitik.*

321

152, 155-58, 164, 170, 171, 175,
275
FRG representation of West Berlin, 18, 106, 126, 148, 161, 164,
170, 175-76, 195, 222, 233, 237,
254-57, 269, 275
GDR and East Berlin, 104-05,
107, 109
inter-Sector communications,
106, 109, 145-46, 147, 148, 170,
171
mediation group, 124
Soviet presence in West Berlin,
18, 125, 126, 160, 163-66, 171,
176, 178, 179, 189, 237, 268-70,
273
Steinstücken, 148, 265-66
Teltow Canal, 148
territorial exchange, 148, 233-37,
264-67
ties between West Berlin and FRG,
13, 15, 17-18, 70, 89, 114, 116,
125, 147, 153, 155-58, 160-61,
164, 170, 171, 175, 181, 275
trade, 106
visits to East Berlin and GDR, 69,
89, 107, 148, 161
West Berlin as part of FRG, 14,
17, 148, 153, 155-58, 160-62,
182
meetings of participants,
first meetings, 104-07, 108-09
exchange of "talking papers,"
124, 127
meetings of the "experts," 101-
02, 127, 132, 149, 155, 163, 170,
178, 239
publication of position papers,
162
Western draft proposal, 89, 146-
49, 153, 163
Soviet draft proposal, 89, 159-62,
184, 185, 248-49
"marathon sessions," 19, 20, 174-
76, 190
See also Quadripartite Agree-

ment, Bahr-Kohl and Kohrt-Müller negotiations
Four Powers, 10, 11, 20, 66, 87,
105, 129, 132, 144, 149, 173,
182, 190, 233, 234, 236, 239,
242, 255, 263
See also France, Soviet Union,
United Kingdom and United
States
France, 100n, 260
partner in German occupation,
105
and Wall crisis, 32, 37, 41, 44
role in Four-Power talks, 14, 60,
62, 66, 87, 90, 92, 96-98, 106,
142, 145, 146, 149, 152, 153,
155, 160, 176, 180, 190, 191,
246
and Berlin Agreement, 204, 233,
237
and FRG, 157, 166, 216, 229
and U.S.S.R., 128-29, 200
See also Western powers
Frank, Paul, 174, 206
Franke, Egon, 74, 81, 82, 202
Frankfurt, 46, 128
Frankfurter Allgemeine Zeitung,
174, 199
Free Democratic Party (FDP), 204,
206, 208, 209, 227, 230, 232
and coalition with SPD, 48, 62,
78, 99, 150, 221
and meetings in West Berlin, 145
defections in, 221, 225, 229, 242
See also Genscher, Oxfort, Scheel
Free University (Berlin), 94
French Consulate General, 270
French Foreign Ministry, 97, 98,
148
French Sector (Berlin), 24
FRG. See Federal Republic of Ger-
many
Frohnau Cemetery, 267
Frost, Robert, 23

Gavin, James, 30, 31

324

Gdansk, 185
GDR. See German Democratic Republic
General Traffic Agreement, 228
Genscher, Hans-Dietrich, 205
"Gentleman's agreements," 21-22, 239, 240-42
impact of, discussed, 10-11
George, Scott, 12
German Communist Party (DKP), 111
See also Communist Party of Germany (KPD)
German Democratic Republic (GDR),
border with FRG sealed, 34
efforts to incorporate West Berlin, 14-15, 50
and Wall crisis, 24, 34, 46, 47
and speaker exchange, 77, 80
and 1969 Berlin crisis, 52-55
easing of NATO travel restrictions, 106-08, 109
Eighth Party Congress of SED, 171-73
fall of Ulbricht, 167-69, 185n, 186
negotiations with Senat, 150, 151, 152, 161, 192, 194-96, 200-01, 208-14, 215, 237, 238, 257-59, 265-67, 268
role in Four-Power talks, 75, 87, 97, 106-07, 125, 152, 169, 172, 181-83
and Berlin Agreement, 247
and visits to FRG and West Berlin, 228
and access to Berlin, 13, 14, 16, 109, 133, 144-45, 149, 152, 154-55, 162, 171, 184, 192, 241, 260
Berlin policy of, 13, 49-50
boundaries of, 58, 73
Council of Ministers of, 78
Foreign Ministry of, 151
on FRG presence in West Berlin, 53, 113

recognition of, 62, 66, 70, 72, 73, 82, 107, 115, 120, 121, 134, 168, 172-73, 181, 245-47, 272-73
sovereignty of, 14, 15, 79, 86n, 113, 120, 125, 132, 133, 135, 152, 161, 181, 238
and relations with FRG, 49, 71, 72, 73, 74-75, 76-85, 110-13, 120, 132-33, 192-96, 200-01, 202, 204-09, 213, 217, 228, 231, 237, 238, 261-64, 275
and Poland, 72, 114, 121-22, 134, 136-39, 152
and the Soviet Union, 49, 50, 53, 59, 66, 75, 86n, 90, 100, 109, 128, 133-36, 149, 156, 161-62, 166-69, 186, 193, 200-03, 208, 214-15, 245, 249n, 260, 273-74
and the U.S., 100n, 245-47
See also Honecker, Stoph, Ulbricht
Germany,
division of, 51, 77, 82, 84, 85, 99, 117
Four-Power responsibility for, 61, 74, 144, 156n
reunification of, 71, 82, 116, 157, 219, 220, 227
Gierek, Edward, 184-85
Goerz, Käte, 12
Gomulka, Wladyslaw, 134n, 136, 184, 185n, 187
"Grand Coalition," 48, 58, 63
See also Brandt, Kiesinger
Gray, Major General David, 30
Great Britain. See United Kingdom
"Greater Berlin," 65, 67, 104, 105, 147, 243
See also Berlin, East Berlin, West Berlin
Grechko, Andrei, 135
Gromyko, Andrei, 127, 177, 193
on Berlin, 59, 60, 61, 66, 199, 200
meetings with Bahr, 84, 115

London Prootocols, 15, 104-05,
143n
Lorenz, Peter, 12
Lower Saxony, 225
Lüder, Wolfgang, 206, 208
Luftbrückendank-Stiftung, 11
Lustig, René, 102

Macmillan, Harold, 24, 28
Mannheim, 46
Marienfelde refugee center, 35
Marshall, George, 47
Marshall Plan, 49
Mautner, Karl, 25
Mautner, Martha, 25
Mayor of West Berlin. See Brandt,
Schütz
MBFR talks, 66, 167, 170, 184, 202,
203, 275
McClosky, Robert J., 142
McCloy, John J., 142
McDermott, Geoffrey, 37, 42
McGhee, George, 29
McNamara, Robert S., 29, 45
Middle East, 55, 128, 153
"Misuse clause" in FRG-GDR transit
accord (1971), 262-63, 272
Molotov, Vyacheslav M., 57n
Molotov-Ribbentrop Pact, 56
Moscow. See Soviet Union
Moscow Treaty. See Bonn-Moscow
Treaty (1970)
Müller, Ulrich, 151, 208-14
Müller-Kohrt negotiations. See
Kohrt-Müller negotiations
Munich, 157
Murrow, Edward R., 44, 45

National Democratic Party (NPD),
240-42
National Security Council, 140
role in Four-Power talks, 88, 92,
95
See also under Kissinger, NSSMs
National Security Staff Memoranda
(NSSMs), 89, 190
Nationale Volksarmee. See East Ger-

man People's Army
NATO
and Wall crisis, 28, 30, 32, 33,
44
and meetings of Foreign Ministers, 58-59, 65-66
and quadripartite negotiations,
107, 108
and European Security Conference, 58, 123n, 170, 204, 208,
216
and FRG, 27, 99, 139
and MBFR talks, 170, 186, 204
Nazis, 137
Negotiations. See Four-Power negotiations, Bahr-Kohl and Kohrt-
Müller negotiations
"Neo-Nazis." See National Democratic Party (NPD)
Neues Deutschland, 112, 130, 162,
172, 193, 215
Neumaier, Johanna, 12
New York, 127, 199
New York Times, 27, 203
Nitze, Paul H., 30
Nixon, Richard M., 68, 178, 179,
184
and Rush, 19, 91, 95, 103, 119,
127, 179, 190
and visit to West Berlin, 13, 50-
51, 52, 54, 59
and meeting with Kiesinger, 55
and visit to Rumania, 61
and Brandt, 140, 142-43n, 152,
202
and U.S.S.R., 153, 202, 218
and meeting with Gromyko, 127-
28, 153, 243
and China, 187-88, 202
Normandy, 97
Norway, 108

Occupation (of Berlin), 15
See also London Protocols
Oder-Neiße line, 58, 62, 121
provinces beyond, 117, 137-38

328

recognition of, 115, 136
Oder River, 148
Orwell, George, 118
Ostpolitik, 19, 62, 63, 114, 121, 136, 141, 143, 157, 163, 230, 231, 275
   origin of, 48, 49, 55, 79
   domestic criticism of, 198, 218
   public support of, 72n, 84, 224
   and Four-Power talks, 92, 97, 123
   and Junktim, 119
   and U.S., 141
   See also Brandt, Bonn-Moscow Treaty, Bonn-Warsaw Treaty
Oxfort, Hermann, 206, 208
   See also under Free Democratic Party (FDP)

Pan American Airways. See Air traffic
Pankow, 53
Paris. See France
Parliament (FRG). See Bundesrat and Bundestag
Parliament (West Berlin), 12
Pass agreements. See Wall passes
Pauls, Rolf, 163-66
Peking, 100
Penkovskiy, Oleg, 38
Pentagon. See U.S. Department of Defense
Poland, 100, 114, 124n, 134
   and FRG, 72, 114, 121-22, 134, 136-39, 152
   Volksdeutsche in, 138
   riots of 1970 in, 184-85, 187
   and GDR, 122, 137
   and Four-Power talks, 162-63
   See also Bonn-Warsaw Treaty, Oder Neisse line
Pomerania, 137
Pompidou, Georges, 128-29, 140
Potsdam Agreement, 156n
Potsdam Conference, 137
Potsdam Missions (of Allies), 37
Potsdam Railway Station, 267

Poznan, 185
Prague. See Czechoslovakia
Pravda, 222
President (FRG). See Federal President
President (U.S.). See Kennedy, Nixon
Protocols on Zones of Occupations. See London Protocols
Prussia, 80

Quadripartite Agreement, 8, 9, 10, 11, 13, 21, 139, 178, 192, 194, 214, 215, 218, 233-75
   basic structure of, 234-38
   legal positions of signatories, 15, 235n, 243-45
   provisions of, discussed
   access, 16-17, 18, 19, 181, 195, 233, 236, 259-64, 272
   communications, 18, 69, 145-46, 233, 257, 267-68
   consultation mechanism, 233, 271
   FRG passports for West Berliners, 256-57
   FRG presence in West Berlin, 236, 250-54, 272
   FRG representation of West Berlin, 195, 233, 237, 254-57
   permanent Allied liaison agency, 237
   recognition of GDR, 233, 245-47, 272-73
   resolution of exclave problem, 18, 233, 237, 264-67
   Soviet presence in West Berlin, 18, 233, 236, 237, 268-70, 273
   status of Berlin, 233, 243-45
   Steinstücken, 265-66
   ties between West Berlin and FRG, 17, 181-82, 233, 237, 238, 247-54, 275
   visits to East Berlin and GDR, 201, 209, 233, 237, 257-59, 272
   West Berlin not constituent part of FRG, 17, 181, 233, 249

329

Bonn-Moscow Treaty
Soviet Ultimatum. See Ultimatum
Soviet War Memorial (U.K. Sector), 130-31
Soviet Zone of Germany, 15, 105
   See also German Democratic Republic
SPD. See Social Democratic Party
Spiegel, Der, 180
Springer, Axel, 164, 179
Staden, Bernt von, 206
Stalin, Josef V., 196
Steinstücken,
   and Four-Power talks, 148
   and Berlin Agreement, 265-66
   See also Inner-German Agreements, Exclaves
Stoltenberg, Gerhard, 219
Stoph, Willi, 132
   exchange of letters with Kiesinger, 73n
   exchange of letters with Brandt, 76-77,
   meeting with Brandt, 80-85, 110-113
   exchange of letters with Schütz, 150-51, 212-13
   and Four-Power talks, 150
Strategic Arms Limitations Talks, 53, 55, 65, 153, 166, 186, 218, 228
Strauß, Franz-Josef, 62, 199, 223, 225, 227, 230
   See also under Christian Social Union
Struve, Günter, 212
Stuttgart, 54, 157
Supreme Soviet, 59
Suslov, Mikhail A., 54n
Sutterlin, James, 92, 93, 94, 164, 190

TASS (Soviet News Agency), 28, 162
Taylor, General Maxwell D., 30, 37

Tegel Airport. See Air traffic
Teltow Canal, 148
Tempelhof Airport. See Air traffic
Temporary Travel Documents, 107-08
Territorial exchange, 148, 233, 237, 264-67
   See also Exclaves and Inner-German agreements
Thompson, Llewellyn, 28, 29
Ties between West Berlin and FRG,
   FRG view of, 82, 157, 164, 198
   GDR view of, 90, 130, 133, 150, 181, 194-95
   Soviet view of 90, 120, 125, 126, 130, 133, 149, 160-61, 175, 248-49
   view of Western Allies, 147, 149, 153
   and Berlin Agreement, 13, 15, 17-18, 70, 89, 114, 116, 147, 155-58, 175, 181-82, 233, 237, 238, 247-54, 275
   See also under Four-Power negotiations
"Three essentials," 33
Transit (through GDR). See Access
Transit visas. See Access
Truman, Harry S., 142
Tsarapkin, Semyon K., 54, 140
Tse-Tung, Mao, 187
Tuchman, Barbara, 30
Twain, Mark, 102

U-Bahn, 35, 148
Ulam, Adam, 188
Ulbricht, Walter, 53, 112, 185n
   and Wall crisis, 24, 34, 35, 36
   press conference of (1971), 75-76
   and Four-Power talks, 133, 187
   fall of, 167-69, 186-87
   in retirement, 172
   and FRG, 72, 73, 121, 130
   and Soviet Union, 121, 167-69, 185, 202
"Ulbricht Doctrine," 72-73

335

Other English language titles published by BERLIN VERLAG

Wilhelm Wengler and Josef Tittel, editors
Documents on the Arab-Israel Conflict: THE RESOLUTIONS
OF THE UNITED NATIONS ORGANIZATION
Vol. I 1947-1970, Vol. II 1971-1977 + Annexes, 360 p. $ 14,–

Ernst Fasan
RELATIONS WITH ALIEN INTELLIGENCES –
THE SCIENTIFIC BASIS OF METALAW
Preface: Wernher von Braun. 112 p., carton $ 6,80

Gundolf Fahl, author and editor
INTERNATIONAL LAW OF ARMS CONTROL
Loose-leaf commentary containing 12 basic treaties and the
related protocols, resolutions, and declarations as well as tech-
nical data of weapon systems, nuclear processes, and controls.
The major texts are commented.   Price per page: 12 cts.

Wilhelm Wengler and Josef Tittel, editors
THE UNIVERSITY LEGISLATION OF THE WORLD
Loose-leaf collection of texts in the original languages and
translations into the English language. Price per page: 12 cts.

Two other Berlin titles published by BERLIN VERLAG

Ernst R. Zivier
DER RECHTSSTATUS DES LANDES BERLIN –
Eine Untersuchung nach dem Viermächte-Abkommen.
Third, updated and enlarged edition. 400 p. $ 16,–

BERLIN FIBEL. BERICHTE ZUR LAGE DER STADT.
Theater, music, literature, architecture, painting, sculpture,
museums, sciences, economics, law and politics. Presented by
experts. 384 p. incl. 16 pictures. $ 8,50